LEFT, RIGHT,
HAND AND BRAIN:
THE RIGHT SHIFT THEORY

Left, Right,
Hand and Brain :
The Right Shift Theory

Marian Annett

LAWRENCE ERLBAUM ASSOCIATES, PUBLISHERS
Hillsdale, New Jersey
London

Lawrence Erlbaum Associates Ltd., Publishers
Chancery House
319 City Road
London EC1V 1LJ

British Library Cataloguing in Publication Data

Annett, Marian
Left, right, hand and brain : the right
shift theory.
1. Laterality
I. Title
152.3'35   QP385

ISBN 0-86377-018-5

Typeset by Latimer Trend & Co. Ltd., Plymouth
Printed and bound by A. Wheaton & Co. Ltd., Exeter

To the memory
of my parents

Contents

x   CONTENTS

PREFACE

The purpose of this book is to show that the right shift (RS) theory offers a solution to certain puzzles about human handedness and brainedness. The theory is extremely simple, but it was reached only after some 10 years' work on problems of human laterality. Another 10 years or more has been spent examining the implications of the theory for questions about asymmetries of hands and brains. The process of digging down to discover the "bare bones" of the problem and of reconstructing the surface appearance depended on a series of stages that were experienced as surprises. It is usual to describe theories as if they had been received all at once in some sudden illumination from on high, but this was certainly not true in the present case. The surprises are an important part of the story because they mark the steps or clues leading to the theory. Without them, the theory would seem unconvincing to me, so I could hardly expect to convince the reader. I have no doubt that the theory will lead to further surprises. The book does not claim to tell the "final" story, but it offers an account of the story so far.

One of the most important strengths of the theory is that it can illuminate problems of handedness as posed from several different points of view by neurologists, biologists, geneticists, and teachers, as well as by psychologists. Considered from any one point of view, the solutions offered might look arbitrary, but when it is appreciated that the analysis of the neurological data is also applicable to the genetic data and that the findings for families of two left-handed parents are relevant to those of dyslexics, the theory looks more useful. In journal articles it is not possible to do justice to all these facets of the theory, and it is not surprising that although I have been writing about the RS theory for some years, it seems to be poorly understood.

xi

A possible explanation for this lack of understanding is that the theory requires a paradigm shift, in comparison with the commonly accepted approaches to questions about laterality. Just as it is not possible to see the same object from different points of view simultaneously (without fancy camera tricks), it is not possible to see the problems as usually stated and the RS solution simultaneously. In order to see the advantages of a solution, it is necessary first to understand the problem. The book is organised as a survey of significant questions about handedness and brainedness discussed without reference to the RS theory (Chapters 3 to 8). A close look is then taken at data relevant to the analysis of lateral preference and skill (Chapters 9 to 12). The RS theory is described (Chapter 13), and its implications for the questions reviewed earlier are examined (Chapters 14 to 20). The book starts (Chapters 1 and 2) with an introductory review of assumptions that are basic to later arguments about laterality and that depend on ideas about evolution, genetics, growth, and the structure and function of the central nervous system. It ends (Chapter 21) with a reconstruction analogous to the reconstruction of a crime by a detective or of an extinct creature by a palaeontologist. Readers who prefer to start detective stories knowing the solution can begin with Chapter 21.

Some explanation must be made for the use of the term "brainedness". I agree with the several people who have commented upon its ugliness. However, some word is necessary to refer to the asymmetrical use of the cerebral hemispheres, comparable to the term "handedness" for the asymmetrical use of the hands. Although the term "brainedness" is not in common use, it is not new (see Cunningham, 1902). It is intended in this book to have no implication other than an asymmetrical dependence on one cerebral hemisphere for speech.

My researches on laterality began at the Warneford and Park Hospitals, Oxford, and continued at the Universities of Aberdeen, Hull, The Open University, and Coventry (Lanchester) Polytechnic. I am grateful for the facilities for research offered me by all these institutions. I am indebted to many colleagues for their interest. Particular thanks must be given to J. P. N. Phillips, who drew my attention to the technique of association analysis. John Annett suggested the use of a peg board for the assessment of hand skills in hemiplegic children and later collaborated in a comparison of the skills of preferred and nonpreferred hands of normal subjects.

I am grateful to geneticists who responded to my appeals for help; Dr. C. E. Blank and Dr. Charles Smith must be thanked especially for leading me to think in terms of distributions. Correspondence over several years with the late James Shields was a highly valued source of information and advice. I am grateful to T. P. Hutchinson and J. Wilkin, of the Department of Statistics and Operational Research of Coventry (Lanchester) Polytechnic, for assistance with aspects of the genetic analyses. Any errors in the applications of these techniques are, of course, my own.

For the information gathered on hand and other preferences I am indebted to the teachers who permitted me to examine their pupils, to successive groups of psychology students who tested one another in laboratory classes, and to the families who wrote to me and welcomed me into their homes. The study of children with hemiplegia depended on the collaboration of Dr. R. J. Pugh and on the help of his fellow Consultant Paediatricians, Dr. M. G. Philpott, Dr. J. D. Pickup, Dr. W. Henderson, and Professor R. W. Smithells. Pupils of the Dyslexia Clinic, St. Bartholomew's Hospital, were studied at the kind invitation of Mrs. Beve Hornsby. I am grateful to Dr. Freda Newcombe for the opportunity to use the archives of the British World War II Head Injury series. Information on the handedness of tennis players was given to me by Mr. C. M. Jones, former editor of "Tennis", and by Professor Arthur Benton, who sent me a copy of the Volvo Grand Prix Media Guide (1983). My indebtedness to William Demarest for sending me a copy of his Ph.D. thesis is evident in Chapter 20. I thank Lucy Annett and her teachers for the D.A. sample.

Patrick Hudson, Diana Kilshaw, Andrew Ockwell, and Ann Turner, as research assistants, and John, Lucy, and James Annett as unofficial research assistants are thanked for working well beyond the usual call of duty to accompany me on family visits during evenings and weekends. The association analysis would not have been done without the computer program written for this purpose by Mr. M. J. Norman at the University of Hull. The computer program for the Kolmogorov–Smirnov tests of the distributions predicted by the RS theory was written by James Annett and made operational with the help of Victor Tandy.

Financial support is gratefully acknowledged for several grants from the Medical Research Council and also from the Social Science Research Council, The Spastics Society, and the research fund of Coventry (Lanchester) Polytechnic. The labour of typing most of the manuscript through several versions has been cheerfully performed by Betty Loughridge.

PROLOGUE:
AN INTRODUCTION TO THE
BIOLOGY OF HANDS AND
BRAINS

1 Evolution, Genetics, and Development

This book is about the causes of human hand preference. Why do most people use the right hand for skilled actions, why do a few use the left hand, why are some rare individuals able to write equally well with both hands, and why do considerable numbers of people develop mixed preferences, writing, for example, with one hand but throwing with the other?

Hand preferences show themselves in behaviour and are an example of human behavioural differences. Questions about the origins of human behavioural differences are difficult to answer because of their inherent complexity and also because of the controversies that arise when it is suggested that there might be biological foundations for differences between people. The first two chapters are intended to outline some of the basic principles that must guide an analysis of the origins of behavioural differences. Psychologists and other social scientists have laboured under some weighty misconceptions about the biological analysis of causes of behaviour. While not wishing to claim that all problems are solved, it is possible to suggest more useful ways of looking at some old questions.

Questions about the causes of behaviour can be asked at several levels of analysis. Alcock (1984) distinguished between "why" questions and "how" questions. "Why" questions examine behaviour in the context of evolutionary biology: Why did a particular behaviour pattern give advantages to the individuals who practised it such that it became common in the species? "How" questions ask about the mechanisms by which the behaviour pattern persists in the species: How is the presumed genetic code translated into the anatomy and physiology and behavioural responses of the individual animal? "Why" questions can be further analysed into questions about evolutionary origins and questions about the present advantages conferred on individuals carrying particular traits. "How" questions can be further analysed into questions about the physical and psychosocial pathways of development. In Chapters 3, 4, and 5 questions about human handedness will be grouped broadly under headings of origins, development, and implications.

Chapters 1 and 2 give an introduction to the biological foundations of an analysis of behavioural differences in handedness. Chapter 1 looks at questions of genetics and development and concludes with an introduction to the biology of sex differences. Chapter 2 looks at the mechanisms of behaviour in relation to the structure and function of the brain.

1.1. EVOLUTIONARY ORIGINS
OF THE HUMAN HAND AND BRAIN

Where should questions about the origins of human handedness begin? With the origins of bilateral symmetry in the earliest vertebrates? With locomotion in land animals, in mammals, or in primates? In so far as the human body has features that derive from the earliest vertebrates, it is conceivable that aspects of the control of the human hand depend on mechanisms of similar antiquity. Of course the behaviours we see in living animals, including man, depend on the unique adaptations that each species has made to its environment. These adaptations could be of recent origin and not shared by close "cousin" species. A comparison of resemblances and differences between species indicate the features that were probably present in common ancestors and others that are probably recent acquisitions.

Man was classified as a primate by Linnaeus in the mid-eighteenth century because of the remarkable anatomical resemblances between man and the monkeys and apes. In the mid-nineteenth century, Darwin (1859) showed how structural similarities might depend on common ancestry. A possible scheme of the evolutionary relationships between primates is given in Fig. 1.1. In addition to anatomical comparisons, modern biochemical studies of several body proteins or immunological reactions permit estimates of the resemblance of living species. Humans are astonishingly close to the African apes, the gorilla and the chimpanzee. It has been estimated that more than 98% of the genetic material of humans and chimpanzees is identical. The next closest relatives to man are the Asian apes, the orang-utan, the gibbon, and the siamang. Old-world monkeys are closer to man than new-world monkeys.

The human-like precursors of modern man, hominids, developed from the ape line relatively recently, perhaps 7–8 million years ago (Pilbeam, 1984). The earliest hominids, known as australopithecines, were first recognised and

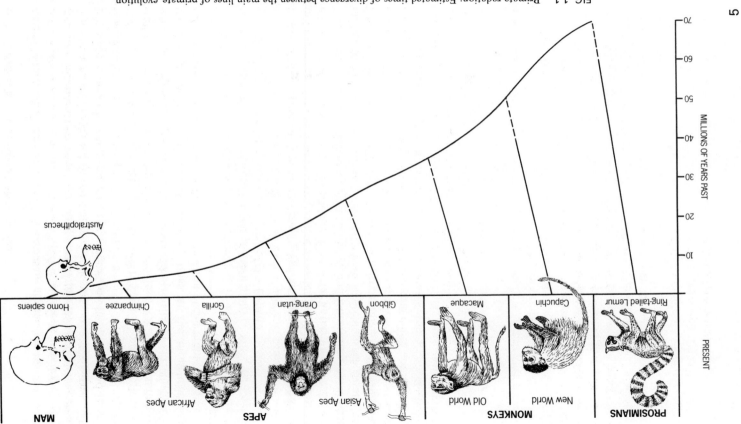

FIG. 1.1. Primate radiation: Estimated times of divergence between the main lines of primate evolution.

named by Raymond Dart in 1925. The most complete and famous specimens have been found in the Afar region of Ethiopa, as exemplified by the remarkable fossil named Lucy by Johanson and Edey (1981), which is about 3 million years old. The australopithecines show a remarkable combination of human and apelike features. The comparative study of these fossils will doubtless be a topic for controversy for some time to come (Cherfas, 1983). What is clear is that the australopithecines were fully adapted for upright walking but had brains about the same size as a modern chimpanzee or gorilla. The footprints discovered by Mary Leakey at Laetoli (Leakey, 1981) dated at about 3.75 million years ago, were made by creatures with fully upright bipedal human gait. Whether or not Lucy and her contemporaries retained some adaptations for living in the trees, it seems that upright walking on an essentially modern foot had evolved in a creature with a small brain; at least, no large-brained specimen contemporary with the Laetoli footprints has yet been found.

Figure 1.2 gives some examples of hands and feet in primates. All are based on the primitive vertebrate five-digit structure, and most show a divergent first digit (thumb), which can be opposed to the other digits for efficient grasping. With four flexible structures that Napier (1980) calls the "hand-foot", primates were well adapted for grasping branches, making life more secure in the trees. Monkeys run along branches and on the ground on all fours; they also use their "hand-foot" to groom and feed. Monkeys, especially of the old-world species, have an efficient pincer grasp for picking up seeds and nuts (Napier, 1971). The ability to make delicate movements using objects held between the tips of the fingers and thumb is present in

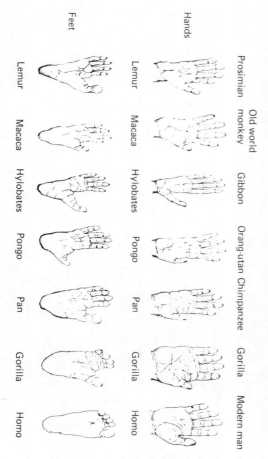

Hands

| Prosimian | Old world | Gibbon | Orang-utan | Chimpanzee | Gorilla | Modern man |
| Lemur | monkey | Hylobates | Pongo | Pan | Gorilla | Homo |

Feet

| Lemur | Macaca | Hylobates | Pongo | Pan | Gorilla | Homo |

FIG. 1.2.   Hands and feet of some primates. After Schultz, 1956.

many primates, but this precision grip is thought to be most highly developed in man.

Apes differ from monkeys in having adaptations for swinging through the trees (brachiation). The apes, like man, have a flatter chest, with rearrangements of the internal organs more suitable for upright posture. All the living apes have very large and powerful arms, with large hands and long fingers that can be used as hooks while hanging from branches. The thumbs of apes have become relatively small in comparison with the fingers and are probably less well adapted than those of monkeys for manipulating small objects (Napier, 1971). The apes best adapted for brachiation, the gibbons and siamangs, are thought to have diverged from the human line earliest; the orang-utans, who are thought to have diverged next, are also very efficient climbers and spend most of their time in the trees, until the older adult males become so heavy as to make it safer to walk on the ground. This they do with a variety of locomotor patterns (Maple, 1980) including bipedal upright walking with a leg-swinging rolling gait (personal observation). Adult chimpanzees and gorillas spend most of their time on the ground, using a characteristic style of movement known as knuckle walking. Infant apes also knuckle walk, whereas human babies put the flat hand to the floor when crawling. The powerful hook-like hands and knuckle-walking posture of apes seem to be characteristics that have evolved in apes *since* their divergence from the human ancestor. When looking for resemblances to human hand use in our primate relations, it is possible that they could be found in apes *or* monkeys, in both, or in neither. Human features that are found in both apes and monkeys can be presumed to be part of the typical primate pattern, while human features that are found in neither are probably unique human adaptations.

The unique feature that is most evident from Fig. 1.2 is the redesign of the human foot for upright walking. Why did man have trouble to stand upright and put strains on his vertebral column, which make the "bad back" one of the most frequent of modern human ills (Medawar, 1957)? The fossil hominid evidence reviewed above suggests that upright walking was one of the earliest distinctively human characteristics to evolve. There have been many suggestions as to why man stood upright, and most have depended on the assumption that the hominid ancestor had a larger brain, which in turn led to the greater use of the hands and the need to free the hands from a support role. Since it is now clear that upright walking evolved *before* the large brain, it can be inferred that the need to free the hands arose before the larger brain made sophisticated technology possible.

Owen Lovejoy (cited in Johanson & Edey, 1981) has drawn attention to another human difference from higher apes—the attempt of the human female to rear several dependent offspring simultaneously. To a psychologist associated with the training of social workers it is clear that this feature of human social organisation is liable to quite as many strains as the human backbone. Both are essentially human adaptations but ones with inherent design weaknesses. Lovejoy's analysis points to a constellation of human characteristics associated with the capacity to rear several children simultaneously, which includes upright walking, transporting food to a home base to share with the family, increased sexual attraction and receptivity in females, and greater male interest in sex. The details of this possible scenario of hominid evolution need not concern us here. Lovejoy makes an important general point, however, when he argues that *several* human characteristics probably evolved more-or-less simultaneously; it is probably fruitless to argue whether heightened sexuality or food sharing, upright walking or having more babies evolved first, since they probably evolved together in mutually reinforcing patterns. Similarly, the evolution of an essentially modern human hand was probably contemporaneous with the evolution of the modern human foot, and both preceded the evolution of a large brain.

Although the brain size of australopithecines as judged from the cranial capacity was about the size of that of a modern chimpanzee, it seems that the early hominid brain was already relatively larger than that of modern apes when considered as a proportion of probable body weight (Passingham, 1982). Modern chimpanzee and human brains are similar in general organisation, but there are differences, in addition to the overall difference in size. In particular, the human brain shows considerable relative expansion in the frontal regions and in the parietal regions. The probable functions of these regions in the planning and execution of hand movements will be considered in Chapter 2. There are also differences between the chimpanzee and human brain in the motor speech area known as Broca's area. It is not possible to be certain whether these characteristics of the human brain were beginning to develop in the brains of australopithecines, but the examination of endocranial casts suggests that expansion in these typically human directions could have originated in early hominids (Holloway, 1974). Later hominids with larger brains show these human features more clearly than the early specimens, but comparative studies suggest that more significant changes occurred between apes and hominids than between early and later hominids (Holloway, 1981). This conclusion has been reinforced by the finding, in early hominid brains, of structural asymmetries like those to be described (Chapter 3) for modern humans (Holloway & La Coste-Lareymondie, 1982—see also Table 9.2).

Do these differences between ape and hominid brains imply that australopithecines were already developing the capacities to speak and to manufacture tools? With regard to speech, the evidence from the fossil record is unlikely to be decisive—speech sounds do not leave natural prints like the human foot. Passingham (1982) considers it would be unwarranted to conclude that australopithecines used language. With their relatively small brains it seems certain that they were unable to use language at a modern human level of complexity. It is important to make a distinction here that will be important in later analyses of the relations between asymmetries of hand and brain—a distinction between speech and language. Attempts to teach the higher apes (gorilla, chimpanzee, and orang-utan) to imitate human speech sounds have all found that the range of sounds that could be produced was extremely limited; since apes are very good imitators of a variety of actions and the animals appeared to be trying to do what their human teachers wished, it seems that the ape vocal apparatus is unsuited to the physical requirements for producing human speech sounds. When alternative methods of symbolic communication were taught to apes, using sign language for the deaf (Gardner & Gardner, 1969), plastic tokens (Premack & Premack, 1972), or specially patterned computer keys (Rumbaugh, 1977), chimpanzees and gorillas have shown rudimentary capacities for language.

However the controversies about ape language may be decided, it seems clear that if australopithecines had begun to develop vocal tracts and the associated areas of the brain capable of producing speech sounds, these sounds could have been used symbolically. It would be as unwarranted to conclude that australopithecines did *not* have rudimentary forms of speech and language as to conclude that they did. Reconstructions of the vocal tracts of fossil hominids have shown important differences from the vocal tract of modern man (Lieberman, 1979). Such differences, if confirmed, might suggest that modern man has an especially efficient vocal tract, but not that other hominids had no speech. (It should be noted that Neanderthal man was a contemporary of modern man and probably not a precursor.)

With regard to the use and manufacture of tools, there are no artefacts that can be definitely associated with australopithecine fossils. Crude stone tools have been linked with hominids with slightly larger brains, and with fossils of increasing brain size there is evidence of increasingly complex technology. Studies of the use of tools in chimpanzees (reviewed by Passingham, 1982) show that sticks, stones, and leaves are used for a variety of purposes and in ways that differ between groups, suggesting cultural transmission of methods of tool use. Chimpanzees can even be said to manufacture tools, in the sense that they trim sticks to make them suitable for poking into termite mounds. Chimpanzees also use branches in dominance displays (Lawick-Goodall, 1971) and to attack potential predators (Kortlandt, 1972, cited by Passingham, 1982). These observations make it reasonable to believe that australopithecines could have used a variety of tools and carried the sticks without which they would have been extremely vulnerable as small primates on the ground.

Dart (1949) reported on a large collection of fossil baboon skulls and endocranial casts, which he believed showed evidence of depressed fractures of the kind that would have been lethal. A variety of cranial bones and some australopithecine skulls were found in the same cave deposits, and Dart argued that the baboons had been hunted by the australopithecines for food. The picture of an aggressive killer man-ape conjured by Dart's analysis and popularised by Ardrey (1976) is regarded as both distasteful and unproven (Johanson & Edey, 1981; Leakey, 1981). The origins of the cave deposits are unclear, and some of the larger australopithecines (*Australopithecus robustus*) show patterns of tooth wear like that of modern chimpanzees, who are predominantly fruit eaters. There is other evidence to suggest, however, that the smaller australopithecines were omnivorous in diet (Johanson & Edey, 1981) and also that chimpanzees do kill baboons in the wild. Lawick-Goodall (1971) described aggressive as well as peaceful encounters between chimpanzees and baboons. From time to time, the chimpanzees seemed to develop a meat-eating craze and would kill and eat baboons and monkeys; one adult male chimpanzee was observed to throw stones at baboons. The brains of the victims seem to be regarded as a special delicacy, and the chimpanzees broke open the skull to extract its contents, in much the same way that Dart deduced that some of the fossilised skulls had been treated. There is also evidence that male chimpanzees sometimes kill chimpanzees from rival groups (Goodall, 1983). It is probably as unjustifiable to portray our hominid ancestors as innocents in the Garden of Eden as it is to portray them as killer apes. It is possible, although no definite evidence has yet been found, that the australopithecines had developed technologies that were already superior to those of their ape contemporaries.

In summary, humans share many features of hand and brain with their primate cousins, and of the many differences between modern humans and apes, it seems certain that upright walking evolved long before the large brain. Along with upright walking came the freedom to use the hands for a variety of tool-carrying, tool-using and tool-making functions, as well as many other changes in human social interactions. These could have included rudimentary capacities to use speech as a means of communication, although there is no certain evidence for this. Controversies about whether modern human brain specialisations originated in requirements for skilled control of the hands or for skilled control of the vocal apparatus are not likely to be productive. Both probably evolved together.

1.2.   GENETICS

The instructions for making a human or ape hand or brain are transmitted from one generation to the next on very long strings of chemically coded information known as DNA (deoxyribonucleic acid). The identifiable units of heredity that code for attributes such as blue eyes or a tendency to baldness are known as genes. The set of genes carried by an individual is known as a genotype. In some respects the genotype is analogous to the sets of instructions that accompany kits for building a model aeroplane or your own home computer. The analogy shows that many factors intervene between the receipt of the instructions and their translation into a complete working model, known as the phenotype. These intervening factors are part of the story of development that will be considered in the next section. The purpose of this section is to outline briefly some of the principles of genetic inheritance that will be used in considering the possible inheritance of handedness. A clear and well-illustrated account of human genetics is to be found in the Bodmer and Cavalli-Sforza (1976) textbook.

All normal humans can be presumed to carry the genetic instructions for making a human hand or foot, as opposed to an ape hand or foot. These well-coded genes are said to be "fixed" or universal to the species. Other genes are variable and differ between members of the species. For example, genes for hammer toes occur in some humans and may be passed on to their children. The rules of transmission of these variable genes were discovered by Mendel in the nineteenth century, but they were not generally understood until this century. The pattern of inheritance depends on the fact that genes are carried in pairs, with one of each pair inherited from each parent. Genes are located at particular places on the chromosomes—structures that become visible when the cell is about to divide. Alternative genes that can occur at a particular locus are known as alleles. There might be 1, 2, or many alleles occurring at a particular locus in all the individuals of the population; some of the alleles may be frequent and others rare. A misconception in some early discussions of handedness was the assumption that if there were a gene for left-handedness and a gene for right-handedness, the two would be of equal frequency.

A particularly useful example of a pair of alleles that illustrates many of the features to be postulated for handedness concerns the forms of human haemoglobin known as A (normal) and S (sickle). The A form is the typical form in most caucasian adults, while the S form occurs in up to 30% of the population in regions of Central Africa. The red blood cells of certain individuals become sickle-shaped and unable to do their normal job of carrying oxygen to the tissues. Individuals with "sickle-cell" anaemia have very poor life chances without modern medical treatment. The parents of children with sickle-cell disease were found to have a mixture of normal and sickled blood cells and were said to carry the sickling trait. The normal and sickle-shaped red blood cells depend on a pair of alleles, A and S, which followed Mendel's laws of inheritance. Figure 1.3 shows how two parents who each carry one A and one S gene produce A- and S-carrying gametes (ova and sperm). These combine at random to give AA, AS, and SS offspring in the classic 1:2:1 Mendelian ratio for heterozygote crosses. In the population as a whole there are nine possible types of mating, with distributions of

| Parental phenotypes | Normal | × | Normal |
| Parental genotypes | AS | × | AS |

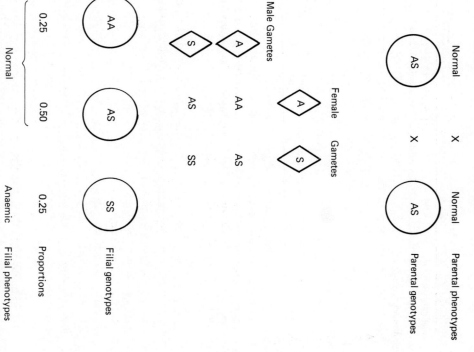

Female Gametes		
Male Gametes	A	S
A	AA	AS
S	AS	SS

Filial genotypes	AA	AS	SS
Proportions	0.25	0.50	0.25
Filial phenotypes	Normal	Normal	Anaemic

FIG. 1.3.   Mating of parents who are both heterozygote for sickle type haemoglobin.

offspring as shown in Table 1.1. In the case of sickle-cell disease, those of SS genotype would not be likely to reproduce (without modern medicines), and their SS genes would be lost from the population. For nonlethal genes, recessive alleles are transmitted to the next generation. It was demonstrated independently by Hardy and by Weinberg that the proportions of genes of each type in the parental generation would be reproduced exactly in the filial (child) generation, provided matings were at random and equally likely to produce viable offspring (the Hardy–Weinberg law). This law probably applies to any genes that may be involved in hand preference.

The A gene could be described as dominant and the S gene as recessive, because the effects of the S gene are evident only in the recessive homozygote (SS), and the heterozygote (AS) is apparently normal. However, it is possible to show by special tests that the AS carry some sickled haemoglobin; that is,

TABLE 1.1

Types of Matings in the Total Population for Normal and Sickle-Type Haemoglobin Genes

Genotypes of Parents	Genotypes of Children*		
Father × Mother	AA	AS	SS
AA × AA	1.00	—	—
AA × AS	0.50	0.50	—
AA × SS	—	1.00	—
AS × AA	0.50	0.50	—
AS × AS	0.25	0.50	0.25
AS × SS	—	0.50	0.50
SS × AA	—	1.00	—
SS × AS	—	0.50	0.50
SS × SS	—	—	1.00

*Proportions expected: 1.00 = all. The proportions are given *within* each mating type. For the population as a whole the proportions must be multiplied by the proportions of each genotype in fathers and in mothers (as in Appendices IV and V).

the S genes are expressed in the heterozygote. The AS-carrying individual may have no symptoms but under special stresses of oxygen deprivation might succumb more quickly than the AA individual. Hence the extent to which a gene can be described as dominant differs from differing viewpoints.

If the SS genes of sickle-cell anaemics are lost from the population, why is the gene found in almost one third of the population in certain parts of the world? The proportion cannot be maintained by the Hardy–Weinberg equilibrium but must depend on other mechanisms. Sickle-cell anaemia is common in those parts of the world in which malaria is endemic. It has now been shown that the AS genotype has an advantage in resisting malaria, because the partially sickled haemoglobin offers a poorer breeding ground for the malaria-transmitting parasites. Hence the AS genotype produces more surviving children than the AA genotype. This heterozygote advantage is sufficient to keep the S gene common in populations exposed to malaria; the frequency of S cannot rise too high, however, or a large proportion of the severely affected SS children would be born. Hence, the population as a whole is said to be in a state of *balanced polymorphism*. Many other examples of balanced polymorphism have now been discovered, and in the majority of cases it is not yet clear what selective advantages and disadvantages keep the genotype frequencies in a stable, balanced state. It is characteristic of balanced polymorphisms that the heterozygote has advantages and each of the homozygotes have disadvantages—but these relative costs and benefits are presumably equalised over the population as a whole.

There is another aspect of the AS story worth noting. The genetic defect giving rise to the S haemoglobin was traced to an error in one letter of one "word" of a part of the genetic code, which is some 146 words long. More than 200 other genetically transmitted errors in the code for human haemoglobin have been discovered (Harris, 1980). Very small changes in the genetically transmitted instructions can lead to significant changes in the efficiency of bodily systems. Some may have serious implications for resistance to disease, others may have no detectable effects. The effects of the S gene differ between people in countries with and without malaria. They probably also differ for people with differing ways of life. An AS carrier may be in good health in everyday life but experience severe problems in training for athletics, when oxygen transport is important. If the S gene had been first identified in failed athletes it might have been described as an "antiathletics" gene.

Dawkins (1982) discusses the possible existence of a gene that impairs the human capacity to learn to read. Such a gene might have been present in our hominid ancestors but have had no detectable effect on behaviour before man invented writing a few thousand years ago. If the gene's main known effect is to hinder learning to read, it might be properly called a gene for "dyslexia", though it might have persisted in the population because of entirely different and advantageous effects. In other words, genes might have become established in the population for many reasons far removed from their present consequences, but it makes sense to label them according to their most salient present effects.

A final and especially important point can be made for social scientists. It is usual to suppose that once a genetic foundation for some defect has been identified, the case becomes hopeless. On the contrary, the identification of certain genes for severe forms of mental deficiency (such as phenylketonuria—PKU) has led to the analysis of how the gene affects biochemical pathways. By modifying the child's diet, it is possible to prevent the poisoning of the brain, which is the immediate cause of mental defect. Similarly, if there were a gene for a specific learning problem such as "dyslexia" and if its mechanism of operation could be identified, it might be possible to devise a teaching method to circumvent the learning block. To discover genetic influences on behaviour is not to condemn us to suffer helplessly, but rather to give hope of eventually discovering ways of alleviating some difficulties.

1.3. DEVELOPMENT

As was said previously, genes are sets of instructions for building organisms. The building materials are provided by the environment. The process of construction starts from the first division of the fertilized egg and continues throughout the life of the individual. Many kinds of environmental influences affect the building process, and even well-coded instructions, such as those for hand or foot, can be mistranslated in certain unfavourable environments—as, for example, when the mother takes thalidomide during a certain period of pregnancy. The effect of environmental influences such as thalidomide or rubella depends critically on their timing; at one period there may be drastic and irremediable consequences, at other periods no noticeable effect. Figure 1.4 depicts an epigenetic landscape (after Waddington, 1957), to explain certain features of the developmental process. Development proceeds along a series of pathways, like a ball rolling down a slope. When the groove is well defined, development proceeds smoothly despite environmental buffetings. At critical choice points, however, a slight nudge could direct the ball into an alternative channel, from which it could not be retrieved.

A detailed understanding of all the influences affecting the developmental process is far from worked out. It is certain that the full story will concern the interacting effects of genetic instructions and the environments in which the genetic messages are being decoded. Genes are mechanisms that use the environment to replicate themselves. The genetic code assumes that the living organism under construction will be part of a "normal" environment, and the code takes for granted that certain features of the environment will be present. Very simple genetic instructions are then sufficient to nudge development into the appropriate pathway. For example, the genetic code does not inform the kitten what it will see when it opens its eyes; it simply gives a message along the lines of "look around". In a normal environment, the

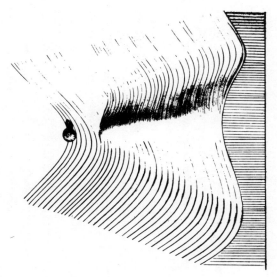

FIG. 1.4.   An epigenetic landscape. After Waddington, 1957.

experience that follows leads to the development of a visual cortex of the brain able to "see" the visual world. Of course, if psychologists rear a kitten in the dark or in opaque diffused light, the developmental path is severely distorted. The genetic codes of chickens and ducklings instruct the newly hatched birds to follow that "largish moving thing", and this is usually sufficient to teach them their own mother. Rhesus monkey genes expect that an instruction to "cling tightly to that warm hairy thing" will lead to all the interactions between monkey mother and infant that lead to normal development and socialisation into monkey society. Human babies prefer to look at roundish face-like shapes and to listen to sounds in the human voice range; from such simple hints about what is worth giving attention to, the infant learns about its parents and through them about what it is to be human. The important point being made here is that apparently complex behaviours may develop from very small beginnings. If it is pleasant to hear the human voice and even more fun to make the noise predictable, the infant is well motivated to "talk" to his mother and to himself. If it is fun to make things happen, the hands are bound to discover how to reach, grasp, shake, pull, push, drop, throw, and many other things. Of course, these developmental pathways depend on the assumption that the child is able to hear and have parents to talk to and is able to see and have objects to play with. But the child with only a few fingers growing from the shoulder will still be trying to make things happen and may do so to very good effect, as many thalidomide children demonstrated.

Psychological theorising has often depended on naïve assumptions about the timing of causal influences. Although some genes may exert their effects very early in the developmental process, others may not show themselves until later life. For example, a tendency to baldness or to peptic ulcer is not likely to become evident until adulthood, and in both these cases the genes involved are more likely to be expressed in males than in females. The predominant view for most of the twentieth century has been that all significant variations in the behaviour of humans are due to experience. Behaviourists and psychoanalysts alike assumed that habits and emotions were attributable to early experiences at the breast, and that the causes of adult behaviours were to be found in their earliest manifestations. The psychological dilemma is posed clearly by Brown (1961). Brown cites Harding's (1953) argument that it would be misleading to say that the grown cat's mousing was "derived from" the kitten's aptness to chase blown leaves and bits of paper that move; it would be equally misleading to say that social desire is "derived from the affection felt by the infant for the mother". Brown responds by saying that without these assumptions psychologists would be driven back to the untenable doctrine of instincts.

Modern approaches to instinctive behaviours (Hinde, 1982; Tinbergen, 1951) are very much more useful than the sort of instinct theory Brown had in mind. It was the work of Lorenz (1970) that demonstrated how the attachment of infant to mother could depend on a very simple innate instruction to behave in a particular way (to keep close or to attend to certain sorts of stimuli), from which a whole train of experiences necessary for normal growth would follow. One of the cleverest tricks the genes devised was to build organisms that could adapt to the environment they found in their own experience—that is, to learn their own mother, own language, and own social mores. Normal growth depends on the innate nudge that makes these aspects of experience interesting and then on the quality of the experiences themselves. Neither "instinct" nor "experience" offer an in-dependent explanation of human behaviour, but they do so in combination.

The essential point being made here is that it may be insufficient to look for *one* cause of handedness. There may be several interacting causes, genetic and environmental, some coded in genes and others depending on de-velopmental pathways. These developmental pathways may begin before or after birth. The question of cause becomes a question of whether the "recipe" can be deciphered, both in the sense of what ingredients go into the making of handedness and in the sense of their timing. Every cook knows that it makes a lot of difference whether the eggs are added before or after beating the cake mixture. Similarly, we need to discover the sequence in which the several "causes" of handedness influence the eventual outcome.

Does the outcome matter? This is a question about the implications of phenotype differences. Left-handers may be indistinguishable from right-handers for all characteristics except hand preference. If there are differences between handedness groups, we can begin to ask why there is a small proportion of left-handers among a majority of right-handers, and whether the proportion is stable or changing. The right shift theory leads to some interesting suggestions about a balanced polymorphism for handedness. But to explain these suggestions requires most of the rest of this book.

1.4. THE GENETICS AND DEVELOPMENT OF SEX DIFFERENCES

Questions about sex differences in lateral asymmetry will be raised in several chapters. Physical sex differences depend on a sequence of developmental processes, first genetic and then hormonal. Humans carry 23 pairs of chromosomes: 22 pairs indistinguishable between the sexes (the autosomes) and 1 pair that differs (the sex chromosomes). Females carry 2 large X-shaped sex chromosomes (XX genotype), and males carry 1 large X- and 1 small Y-shaped chromosome (XY genotype). The Y chromosome seems to carry little genetic information except that required for determining male sex. Early in fetal life the Y chromosome initiates the development of a testis, which produces testosterone, and it is the presence of this hormone that leads to the development of male sex organs. In atypical genotypes such as XXY or XYY male genitalia are formed, but in XXX or XO female genitalia occur. The critical role of hormones is demonstrated by the finding that genetic males who are insensitive to testosterone develop as females, and genetic females who are exposed to testosterone become masculinized.

From birth, psychosocial influences contribute to the direction of behavioural growth along differing sex role pathways. Physical differences in laterality such as in patterns of brain asymmetry could be due to genetic or hormonal influences. Psychological differences in interests or aptitudes such as for reading, mechanical skills, or mathematical thinking might be attributable to physical differences in brain specialisation or to the social definition of sex roles. Of course, there could also be an interaction if some slight difference between the sexes in hemisphere specialisation becomes amplified by cultural expectations.

One possibility that can be eliminated fairly easily is a specific role for the sex chromosomes in determining hand preferences. Recessive genes carried on the X chromosome show a characteristic pattern of inheritance being expressed more often in males than in females and transmitted along the female line (males carry only one X chromosome and it is inherited from the mother). Certain types of colour blindness and types of haemophilia are transmitted in this way. If left-handedness were due to a recessive gene on the X chromosome and it occurred in 10% of males ($p = .1$) then left-handedness would occur in females only when the recessive gene was present on both X chromosomes ($p^2 = .01$), or in 1% of females. This large difference does not occur. On the hypothesis that in females one or other of the sex chromosomes becomes inactivated at random (Lyon, 1962), it would be possible for a genetic influence on handedness to depend on the sex chromosomes, but this hypothesis would not help us to account for the differences observed.

There are many physical differences that are associated with sex but not a direct consequence of the sex chromosomes. Characteristics such as height, strength, tendencies to baldness, or liability to peptic ulcer are influenced by *genes whose expression is sex-modified*. As explained above, the major factors in sexual differentiation after the initial stages are hormonal rather than genetic. Differences between the sexes in the balance of hormones continue to affect the development and expression of many other characteristics. Sex differences in laterality could be the result of differences between the sexes in the expression of genes that occur with equal frequency in males and females.

2

The Brain

2.1. OUTLINE OF THE ORGANISATION OF THE CENTRAL NERVOUS SYSTEM

The role of the nervous system is to control actions in relation to the states of the external and internal worlds. The task of collecting information and acting upon it at speed depends on a variety of sensory inputs and motor outputs whose interrelations are coordinated through central structures, the spinal cord, and the brain. Cells specialised for transmitting information—neurones—have cell bodies in the brain or spinal cord and outgrowths—axons—that extend like an electrical wiring system throughout the body. Impulses travel from cell to cell as an electrochemical discharge, with very rapid transmission along the lengths of the main axons. The excitation or inhibition of the next cell depends on the release of chemical neurotransmitters at the cell junctions (synapses). The speed of travel of impulses depends on fatty material surrounding the axons, known as myelin, which has a whitish appearance. Cell bodies are greyish. At birth, much of the nervous system is unmyelinated, and the process of myelination is not completed for some regions until adolescence, or perhaps later.

There are two main principles of neural organisation relevant to the analysis of asymmetries of hand and brain. First, the nervous system is arranged hierarchically. Second, it is bilaterally symmetrical, except for the special asymmetries to be considered later. These characteristics of the nervous system probably depend on its evolution from a structure that ran along the length of some primitive animal, sending nerves to muscles and sense organs on each side. When such an animal began to move consistently in one direction, it would need symmetrical sensorimotor systems on each side of the body, and it would also tend to become more specialised for detecting interesting smells, sights, and sounds at the front end. The human nervous system continues to make symmetrical neural connections with each side of the body, and it has become enormously complicated at the top or front end as more and more layers of brain were added to make increasingly sophisticated analyses of the world and decisions about how to behave in it. The topmost layer of the brain, the cerebral neocortex, is the most recently evolved and larger in man than all other animals, in proportion to body size (Passingham, 1982).

The bilateral symmetry of the human nervous system extends to the highest levels of the cerebral cortex, the left and right cerebral hemispheres. Each cerebral hemisphere is most directly concerned with the *opposite half of* external space. Although there are many connections between the hemispheres and some links between each hemisphere and both sides of the body, there are also clear divisions of function between the sides, especially for vision and for the control of fine movements of the fingers. Why connections are crossed between the hemispheres and hands and other parts of the body is not known precisely. At some point of evolutionary development the primitive neural plate turned through 180 degrees, and this is repeated in the embryological growth of each individual (Trevarthen, 1974).

When considering how far the left and right sides of the brain control right- and left-sided sensorimotor functions, it is important to take account of the level of complexity of the function. Figure 2.1 illustrates the main stages that have been distinguished in the hierarchy of neural organisation and the types of behaviour associated with each level. As would be expected, lower and more phylogenetically ancient structures serve more basic and automatic functions, whereas newer and higher parts of the system are required for voluntary and controlled movements. The human spinal cord serves reflexes such as those involved in walking and in excretion. Although these activities are normally brought under voluntary control as the child matures, the cortex continues to rely on the spinal cord for the basic mechanisms and cannot compensate for them if the spinal cord is damaged. The postural reflexes required to orient the body in relation to gravity and many automatic aspects of movement depend on subcortical systems. These movement patterns are used in plans executed by the cortex, without our awareness of exactly how they are performed. Elements of walking movements can be elicited at the midbrain level. At the level of the diencephalon (thalamus and hypothalamus), voluntary movements occur in animal subjects but are poorly controlled. The organisation of behaviours that are appropriate for the animal's needs and relevant to the environment depends on the cerebral cortex.

Information about the state of the internal world is transmitted to the

ANATOMY	PREPARATION	BEHAVIOURS
	Normal (cortex)	Performs sequences of voluntary movements in organized patterns; responds to patterns of sensory stimulation
	Decorticate (basal ganglia)	Links voluntary movements and automatic movements sufficiently well for self-maintenance (eating, drinking) in a simple environment
	Diencephalic (hypothalamus thalamus)	Voluntary movements occur spontaneously and excessively but are aimless; shows well-integrated but poorly directed affective behaviour; thermoregulates effectively
	High decerebrate (midbrain)	Responds to simple features of visual and auditory stimulation; performs automatic behaviours such as grooming; performs subsets of voluntary movements (standing, walking, turning, jumping, climbing, etc.) when stimulated
	Low decerebrate (hindbrain)	Performs units of movement (hissing, biting, growling, chewing, lapping, licking, etc.) when stimulated; shows exaggerated standing, postural reflexes, and elements of sleep-waking behaviour
	Spinal (spinal cord)	Shows reflexes (stretching, withdrawal, support, scratching, paw shaking, etc.) to appropriate sensory stimulation

FIG. 2.1.   The hierarchy of neural function. Behaviour that can be supported by different levels of the nervous system. Shading indicates the highest remaining functional area. From Kolb & Whishaw, 1980.

cortex through the hypothalamus, and information about the state of the external world as received by the sense organs is transmitted to the cortex via the thalamus. There are complex sets of neural circuits that link the hypothalamus, thalamus, and frontal lobes of the cortex through several structures known as the limbic system. The limbic system is known to be involved in learning and in emotion. The cortex can be thought of as a computer that can handle a large amount of information. The basic decisions as to what is worth attending to, what is useful to our present needs, and what is worth remembering for future use probably depend on limbic structures.

The gross structure of the human cerebral hemispheres is illustrated from a lateral view in Fig. 2.2A. The cortex consists of a pair of very large sheets of grey matter, folded to fit into the skull in a characteristic pattern; individual variations in the pattern are considered in Section 2.4. Each half brain is

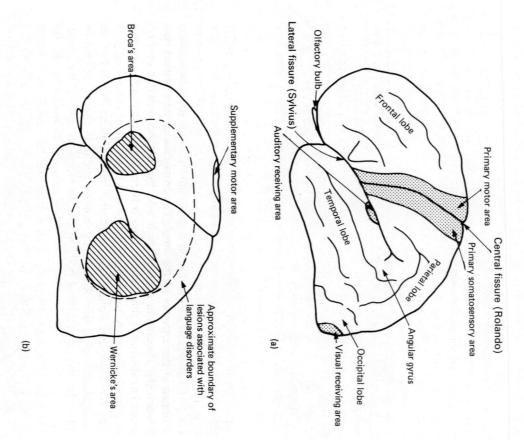

Olfactory bulb

Lateral fissure (Sylvius)

Auditory receiving area

Temporal lobe

Frontal lobe

Primary motor area

Central fissure (Rolando)

Primary somatosensory area

Parietal lobe

Angular gyrus

Occipital lobe

Visual receiving area

(a)

Broca's area

Supplementary motor area

Wernicke's area

Approximate boundary of lesions associated with language disorders

(b)

FIG. 2.2.   (A) Human cerebral cortex, lateral view. (B) Language associated cortex.

divided by two especially deep folds, the central sulcus (or fissure of Rolando) and the lateral sulcus (or fissure of Sylvius). Four lobes are distinguished, the frontal lobe anterior to the central sulcus, the temporal lobe inferior to the lateral sulcus, the occipital lobe forming the posterior brain areas, and the parietal lobe lying between the other lobes. It should be noted that the amount of cortex with direct links to the sense organs and muscles is very small, as revealed by direct stimulation. The motor and somatosensory strips lie on either side of the central sulcus, the auditory receiving area on the superior temporal lobe and the primary visual area on the posterior occipital lobe. There is a broad division of function between the brain anterior and posterior to the central sulcus. Posterior areas receive information from the sense organs, including the skin and postural senses, and the anterior areas plan and execute motor acts (Luria, 1966) but this division is by no means absolute.

Figure 2.2B shows the areas associated with language. Broca identified a region just anterior to the motor cortex for the mouth as necessary for speech. Wernicke suggested that areas adjacent to the auditory receiving cortex are necessary for speech comprehension. Studies of the effects of electrical stimulation (Penfield & Roberts, 1959) and of war wounds (Russell & Espir, 1961) have shown that language functions can be disrupted by insults over a wide area of the lateral surface of the left hemisphere.

One of the chief puzzles about the human brain is why disturbances of language occur very much more often when lesions are on the left side than on the right. There are no obvious anatomical differences between the sides, and until relatively recently no physical asymmetries were recognised as relevant to the difference in language functions (Von Bonin, 1962). Structural asymmetries are considered in section 3.3.2.

The medial view of the brain (Fig. 2.3) shows that a large proportion of cortex lies on the inner surface of the hemispheres. The broad, thick band of white matter known as the corpus callosum consists of the myelinated axons of neurones, which transmit impulses between the cerebral hemispheres. This, and other small commissures (not shown) keep each hemisphere informed of the activities of the other. The cross-flow of information runs between the association areas of each side, but not between the primary areas. The absence of direct connections between the primary motor areas is presumably necessary to maintain independent movement control on each side. When one hemisphere tries to control the ipsilateral (instead of the usual contralateral) side of the body, control could, in theory, depend on either the smaller ipsilateral pathways or on messages sent via the corpus callosum to the other hemisphere. When someone is forced to use the nonpreferred hand for writing, it is not known for certain how this is achieved. For most left-handers, the right hemisphere appears to be the one more actively engaged during writing (Herron, Galin, Johnstone, & Ornstein, 1979).

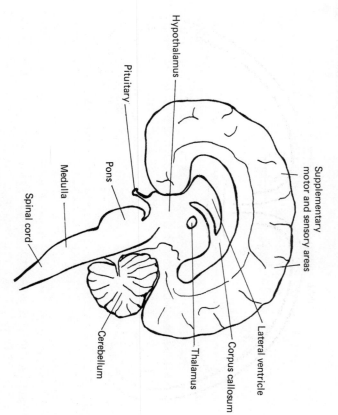

FIG. 2.3.   The human brain: Medial view.

Subcortical structures are also paired. Certain kinds of information can be communicated between the sides at subcortical level, even when the cerebral commissures are cut. Knowledge of the emotional quality of the experiences of one half of the brain seems to be accessible to the other side.

Figure 2.3 shows the cerebellum as a large and distinctively shaped structure. The size of the cerebellum has increased in man, in comparison with other primates, to almost the same extent as the cerebral cortex (Passingham, 1982). The cerebellum plays an essential part in the control of skilled human movements, and this is considered in Section 2.2.

2.2.   MOTOR SYSTEMS

The representation of the body at the motor cortex is illustrated in the left half of Fig. 2.4. The map shows the parts of the body where electrical stimulation of the exposed cortex during surgery elicited responses in the muscles (Penfield & Jasper, 1954). The illustration helps to make the important point that the extent of the cortical areas representing parts of the body is proportional to the complexity of the movements made by that part. Large areas are concerned with movements of the mouth, especially the lips

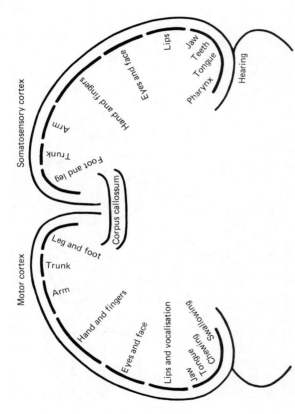

FIG. 2.4.   The representation of the body at the motor and the somatosensory cortex. Based on Penfield & Jasper, 1954.

and tongue, which are required for speech. Large areas are also devoted to the hand, especially the thumb. Notice that the mouth and hand areas are in fairly close proximity. Any special influences on the cortical growth of either area might also affect the other.

There are two other smaller regions of the cortex where stimulation can lead to movement, a secondary and a supplementary motor area. Each has its own schematic map of the body. The supplementary motor area, on the superior border of the frontal lobe (Fig. 2.2), has a special role in planning movements, as activity has been detected there when subjects were asked to imagine movements.

The control of movement, including speech movements, involves subcortical structures, the thalamus, and basal ganglia. There are neural links between the cortex, subcortical structures, and the cerebellum. The cerebellum includes ancient and newly evolved areas. The more recently evolved regions are probably involved in the learning of skilled movements, which can then be brought into use without direct conscious attention (Eccles, in Popper & Eccles, 1977). For example, learning to ride a bicycle, to dance, or to play a musical instrument requires initial slow learning of movements that have to be given careful attention, but with practice these can be performed in rapid sequences. The voluntary aspects of the movements under cortical control probably concern plans about the goals to be achieved, and automatic aspects of execution probably depend on subcortical mechanisms. A review of theories of the neural control of movement is given by Paillard (1982).

The motor tracts that descend from the cortex and subcortical structures through the spinal cord to control movements have been analysed in several papers by Kuypers and his colleagues (Brinkman & Kuypers, 1973; outlined in Kolb & Whishaw, 1980). Three main sets of fibres have been distinguished, each responsible for actions of increasing complexity in the evolution of movement. First, there are cells in the motor cortex that send fibres to both sides of the body to control whole-body movements, as in walking and swimming. Second, there are cells that project to the contralateral limbs, responsible for independent movements of the hands, arms, or legs, as when the limbs are used to reach or kick. Third, there are neurones that travel from the areas of cortex representing the fingers to connect directly in the spinal cord, with the motor neurones serving the digits. These direct projections have been found only in man and other primates, the species capable of independent finger movement. In addition to these corticospinal tracts, there are other motor tracts originating in the basal ganglia and nuclei of the brain stem. These are involved in the control of the limbs but not of the fingers.

After lesions of the cortical motor areas, considerable movement may be recovered in the arms, hands, and legs, but there is no alternative control system for the fingers, and fine movements may remain impaired. The skillful use of instruments such as pens, tweezers, needles, and scalpels requiring the precision grip (Section 1.1) requires an intact neocortex. The earliest movements of the human infant probably depend on subcortical systems that permit reflex stepping and grasping and whole-body activity. Voluntary control increases with the myelination of cortical fibres. The first attempts to grasp at 4 to 5 months of age involve gross movements of the whole hand. The precision grip is not achieved until about the end of the first year (Gesell, 1940).

This analysis of the motor system shows that there are several systems that differ in the skills they serve and in the phylogenetic and ontogenetic levels at which they are expected to appear. Cats, mice, and rats showing paw preferences in reaching for food are using the system for independent limb movements, but not the fine grasp available only to primates. Monkeys and apes showing hand preferences may be using the limb systems available to other mammals, or the primate finger-control system. When humans perform a variety of one-sided actions, they are probably using a variety of control systems. There is no reason to suppose that the same side should be preferred for all of these activities. Similarly, when the actions of infants are examined for the development of asymmetries of preference, it is important to recognise that the motor systems involved in body position, limb movements, and fine finger control differ and develop at different rates.

Although the majority of corticospinal fibres cross in the medulla to serve the opposite side of the body, some do not cross, and there is individual variability in the proportions of crossed and uncrossed fibres. It has been suggested that the paw preferences of monkeys (Glees & Cole, 1952) and the hand preferences of man (Levy & Nagylaki, 1972) might be associated with this anatomical variation. Kertesz and Geschwind (1971) confirmed previous findings (Yakovlev & Rakic, 1966) that most human brains (73%) show a predominant pattern of crossing, but as far as could be judged from the evidence available, atypical patterns of crossing were not related to handedness. An unusual distribution of fibres in one of the corticospinal tracts, noted originally by Barnes, was looked for systematically in 210 adult Japanese brains (Mizuno, Nakamura, & Okamoto, 1968). An ''extra'' ventrolateral tract was found in 20% of cases, either on both sides (7%) or on one side (13%). Mizuno et al. noted that when the extra tract was large, the ventromedial tract on the same side was small. This suggested that the extra tract arose from a group of fibres that crossed earlier to the appropriate side, rather than from misplaced fibres from the other side. The ventromedial tracts control whole-body movements, so it seems unlikely they would be responsible for asymmetries of skilled hand control. Other fibres that fail to cross at the medulla may well cross lower in the spinal cord. The significance of this variability is unknown (Kolb & Whishaw, 1980).

2.3. SENSORY SYSTEMS

If each side of the brain controls the movements of the opposite side of the body, as explained in the previous section, each half-brain needs to be most directly informed about the opposite half of space. This is achieved for the visual system as shown in Fig. 2.5. The arrangements look complicated, but the outcome is simple. The left hemisphere receives stimuli from the right visual field (RVF) and the right hemisphere from the left visual field (LVF). The small central area of vision that is in focus for both eyes is linked with both hemispheres, but all stimuli to either side of fixation are received by one hemisphere only, at the striate or visual cortex. This anatomical arrangement permits stimuli to be presented to each hemisphere independently in split-brain patients (Section 6.1.2). It also offers a rationale for theories linking asymmetries of perception in the visual fields of normal subjects with asymmetries of the hemispheres (Section 6.1.3).

Figure 2.5 shows that information from the visual fields is crossed at the lens. The nasal or inner half of each eye receives input from the corresponding visual field (right nasal from RVF and left nasal from LVF), while the outer or temporal half of each retina receives inputs from the opposite visual field. On reaching the optic chiasma, the nasal fibres cross, and the temporal fibres are transmitted uncrossed to the thalamus (lateral geniculate nucleus). In the LGN the information from the two eyes is brought into a common

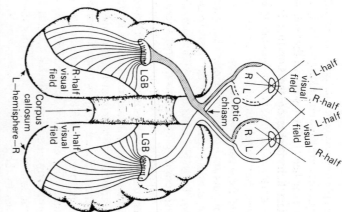

FIG. 2.5.   Representation of the left and right visual fields: The right halves of the visual fields of both eyes go to the left hemisphere and the left halves to the right hemisphere. From Popper & Eccles, 1977.

register (unless there is a squint in one eye) before being sent on to the striate cortex.

At the visual cortex, recordings from single cells in the brains of cats show that cells may respond to stimuli from the left or the right eye only, or more often from both eyes; in binocular cells, responses may be stronger to inputs from one eye (Hubel & Wiesel, 1979). Whether these inequalities of single-cell response are related to eye preference at the behavioural level is unknown. There are no obvious reasons, from the anatomy of the visual system, why one eye should be preferred to the other for tasks such as sighting through a telescope. It is important to be clear that both eyes transmit to both cerebral hemispheres, so that a preference for one eye cannot be directly attributed to hemisphere dominance. The basis for the preference could depend on sensory factors, or it could depend on motor factors related to the control of eye movements through the frontal eye fields, anterior to the motor strip.

As is the case for the hierarchy of motor systems, there are also hierarchies of sensory systems. A second and more primitive visual system transmits information from the eyes to the cortex via a brainstem and thalamic route (the tecto-pulvinar system). This system is concerned with the rapid detection of stimuli and their location in space. Humans who are blind due to lesions of the visual cortex are able to guess, at better than chance levels, the location of light flashes, although they are unaware of any capacity to see (Weiskrantz, 1980; Zihl, 1980). Trevarthen (1970) has shown that split-brain patients have some ability to detect light flashes on the side that is blind to patterned stimuli. The striate cortex is necessary for human awareness of colours, shapes, and patterns, but rapid response to novel and moving stimuli probably depends on the second visual system.

Both ears send inputs to both hemispheres, but there is evidence that messages from the contralateral ear dominate those from the ipsilateral ear when there is conflict. The slight superiority of the contralateral ear has been used to study hemisphere asymmetries in normal subjects by the dichotic listening technique (Section 6.1.3). The anatomical arrangements ensure that, as for vision, each hemisphere is in most direct touch with its own half space. The location of sounds in space depends on extremely fine discriminations of the time of arrival of sounds at the two ears.

Sensations from the skin and joints include information about touch, temperature, pain, and pressure, which are referred to collectively as the somatosensory system. The diagram on the right side of Fig. 2.4 shows that, as for the motor strip, the proportion of cortical space devoted to a body area reflects the sensitivity of that area rather than its absolute size. Large areas are given to the reception of sensations from the mouth and from the hands. A secondary sensory receiving area, within the folds of the lower parietal lobe, has inputs from both sides of the body, but these do not include the hands and fingers, whose fine control is a recent evolutionary acquisition.

The effects of injuries to the somatosensory system include reduced awareness of skin sensations, inability to recognise objects by touch, and loss of awareness of the position of the limbs in space. Comparisons of tactile sensitivity on the two sides in normal subjects have been made with the aim of studying hemisphere asymmetries (Section 6.1.3).

Recordings from single cells in the somatosensory and visual cortices have revealed a principle of neural organization that is believed to be true for all cortical areas. Cortical cells appear to be arranged in columns, perpendicular to the surface, which act as functional units (Eccles, in Popper & Eccles, 1977). Each unit responds to a characteristic pattern of stimulation. The control of language functions may also depend on such units, as will be shown in the next section.

2.4. ASSOCIATION SYSTEMS

The very large areas of cortex that are silent on electrical stimulation (Figs. 2.2 and 2.3) are traditionally described as association areas. Associations, first of ideas and later of stimuli and responses, were assumed to be the foundation of intelligence. In a modern form of this model it must be asked how the information transmitted through the primary sensory and motor areas is analysed and integrated by the rest of the cortex. Investigation of the functions of association cortex depends on research in neurology, neurophysiology, and neuropsychology. The problem is to show how the activities on which intelligence depends, such as learning, memory, recognition of people and objects, language, and decision making are related to cortical functions (Broadbent & Weiskrantz, 1982). Present understanding of these relationships is fragmentary, but there are some important points to be made with regard to the symmetry and asymmetry of functions.

Certain aspects of organisation are common to both hemispheres. Adjacent to the primary sensory and motor areas are strips of cortex involved in the processing of information relevant to each primary area. From adjacent regions, connections are made to other areas of the cortex on the same side and on the opposite side via the corpus callosum. Series of connections are made involving several stages in the frontal and the posterior cortex. These circuits presumably make it possible to coordinate the sensory and motor systems in decoding stimuli and planning appropriate responses. They also make it possible to coordinate information received from several sensory systems about the same stimuli (how objects sound and look or smell and feel).

The parietal association areas (Fig. 2.2A) are especially important for coordinating information from the several senses, as would be expected from their position between the somatosensory, visual, and auditory areas. The parietal cortex immediately posterior to the somatosensory strip is concerned with keeping track of where the limbs are located in space, an essential basis for the planning of new movements. Next to this area is a region that is especially responsive to visual stimuli that are within reach for grasping. These findings by Mountcastle and his colleagues (Mountcastle, Lynch, Georgopolous, Sakata, & Acuna, 1975; outlined in Kolb & Whishaw, 1980) confirm that parietal cortex is involved in the coordination of behaviours of hand and eye. The enlargement of parietal areas in the human brain was presumably a prerequisite for the development of human technological skills. The angular gyrus (Fig. 2.2A) seems to be necessary for connections to be made between visual and auditory inputs (Geschwind, 1979). This area is especially large in man and is one of the last to be myelinated during individual growth. In learning to read and write, the coordination of information about how words look with how they sound is presumed to depend on this region.

In the temporal lobe, areas adjacent to the primary auditory receiving cortex are involved in the decoding of auditory inputs. One of these areas, located on the superior inner margin of the temporal lobe, is known as the planum temporale. This region has been found to be asymmetrical in the majority of human brains (Section 3.3.2). In the lower temporal lobe are areas necessary for the recognition of visual stimuli. The anterior tip of the temporal lobe is without any clearly identified function, except that stimulation has been associated with the recall of specific memories. The temporal poles seem to be especially susceptible to injuries in the neonatal period, which lead to intractable epilepsy. Surgical removal of the anterior part of the temporal lobe may give relief from fits and is followed by few persisting psychological deficits in most cases. There may be defects of auditory perception and memory, however, and the nature of the impairments that follow operations on the two sides is part of the story of lateral asymmetry (Section 6.1.1).

The frontal lobes are concerned with the planning of action and its moderation, inhibition, and appropriateness for current social situations. There are differences between the effects of frontal lesions on the right and the left sides which are related to cerebral asymmetries of function (Milner, 1982; see also Section 6.1.1). As mentioned previously, it was a region of the frontal lobe, just anterior to the motor areas serving the mouth (Fig. 2.2B), which Broca associated with speech.

Some important discoveries about the representation of language functions in the left cerebral hemisphere have been made by electrically stimulating the surface of the cortex when it is exposed prior to brain surgery. When surgical removal of part of the cerebral cortex is planned for the treatment of epilepsy, it is necessary for the surgeon to explore the brain surface with a gently stimulating electrode, to map the location of cortical functions, since there are individual differences in the details of localisation. This is done under local anaesthesia, so that the conscious patient can report on the feelings of tingling or numbness produced in the limbs by the electrical stimulation. No complete movements or illusions of objects are produced by direct brain stimulation, suggesting that the integrated action of several brain areas may be required for meaningful experience. Cortical stimulation does not lead to speech, in the sense of meaningful words, but stimulation over a wide area (Fig. 2.2B) may stop the patient's ongoing speech.

Recent studies by electrical mapping during surgical exploration (Ojemann, 1983a, 1983b; Ojemann & Mateer, 1979) required patients to perform a standard series of tasks that had been practised before the operation. A series of slides was shown, and the patient was asked to name the object represented, to read an 8- to 10-word incomplete sentence and supply an appropriate ending, and then to recall the object previously named. Slides were also shown of mouth movements, such as protrusion of the tongue or pursing the lips, which were to be imitated either alone or in sequences. An audiotape presented elements of speech sounds (phonemes such as /p/, /b/, /d/) for identification. The electrical stimulation was applied at several stages of testing, and the person scoring the patient's response was unaware of the time and location of stimulation.

One of the striking findings of electrical mapping is the individual variability of the location of language functions, within the broad area associated with language. A second striking finding is the discreteness of localisation. Very small shifts in the placing of the electrode may lead to abrupt changes in the function affected. As for the visual and somatosensory cortex, the organisation of the language cortex seems to be in discrete units.

Figure 2.6 illustrates the findings for one patient, a 30-year-old woman whose first language was English, but whose second language was Greek. Stimulation at the site marked "N" disturbed her ability to name objects in English but not in Greek; stimulation at the several sites marked "G" affected her ability to name objects in Greek, but not in English. One of the sites for Greek naming is adjacent to the site for English naming. At A, there was inhibition of all types of speech output and also inhibition of imitation of mouth movements. In all patients studied, a site with this property was found

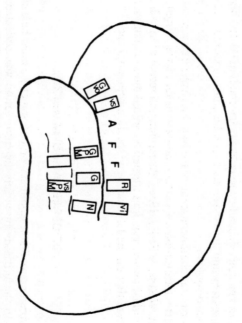

FIG. 2.6.   Stimulation mapping of six language-related functions at nine sites in lateral peri-sylvian cortex of a 30-year-old female, bilingual in English and Greek. Functions measured were: naming in English and Greek; reading of simple sentences; short-term verbal memory; mimicry of single and sequential orofacial movements; and phoneme identification. Each site stimulated is represented by a rectangle. Symbols within the rectangle indicate significant evoked errors at that site: N = naming in English; G = naming in Greek; R = reading; VI = memory with stimulation at the time of input to memory; VS = memory with stimulation during the time the memory must be stored; VO = memory with stimulation at the time of retrieval; P = phoneme identification; M = mimicry of sequences of orofacial movements; A = a site of speech arrest; F = sites of evoked face movement and sensation. Stimulation at 3 mA between pulse peaks. Control error rates 0, except for single errors on 28 control trials of naming in Greek, 27 control trials of phoneme identification, and 26 control trials of mimicry of sequences of orofacial movements. Ojemann, 1983a.

just anterior to the face area of the motor strip (except in one case, where there was a longstanding tumour of this region and motor speech was disrupted from a site in the anterior temporal lobe). Site A is a relatively small part of Broca's area. At R, the ability to read was impaired, while at the several sites marked M the patient was unable to memorise a word that was required for later recall.

The sites marked P and M are especially interesting, since they usually occurred together in all patients. P required the identification of phonemes; M required the mimicry of sequences of mouth movements. This finding suggests that the recognition of speech sounds depends on the same cortical units that are required for the control of mouth movements. There have been several theories that hypothesise close links between the processes of speech perception and production (reviewed by Mateer, 1983). The finding that phoneme identification and the control of mouth movements both depend on the same brain areas implies that the traditional distinction between anterior and posterior language areas, as concerned with speech production and understanding, respectively, must be qualified. It seems that word finding, reading, and memory depend on several adjacent sites in the left hemisphere, and that sensory and motor aspects of production and storage are linked in an interactive system.

Electrical stimulation mapping of the right hemisphere has found evidence for discrete localisation of certain nonverbal functions (Fried, Mateer, Ojemann, Wohns, & Fedio, 1982). Perception and recognition of lines, faces, and emotional expressions was affected by stimulation in areas corresponding to those that on the left side are associated with language.

2.5. METHODS OF STUDY OF CEREBRAL ASYMMETRIES

The information available about cerebral asymmetries must be evaluated in relation to the methods by which the information was collected, and the limitations of certain methodologies should be recognised. There is a general limitation on studies of cerebral asymmetries in that there is no simple, safe, and reliable procedure available at present for establishing which hemisphere serves speech in normal people. The reliable procedures are not without some clinical risk, and the procedures used for normal subjects are not reliably diagnostic for individuals. Hence, all the evidence to be reviewed in later chapters has imperfections, and some of these imperfections have increased rather than decreased the confusion about cerebral laterality.

The main source of evidence concerning human brain functions is found in the study of clinical effects of naturally occurring lesions, such as head wounds, strokes, and tumours. The disadvantages of this source include the fact that what the clinician sees is the capacity of the remaining brain tissue to function when the damaged part is out of action. This is analogous to trying to diagnose how a car engine works by observing the effects of removing a spark plug or battery. The clinician must infer which functions have been lost from an assessment of what the patient cannot now perform. The patient's capacities before injury have to be inferred, and his former skills, including hand preference, must be established from the report of the patient and his relatives. In naturally occurring lesions the precise location and extent of damage are often unknown. There may have been damage to the opposite side of the brain as a result of contre-coup effects of a blow. Verification of lesions depended until recently on direct observation of the brain at operation or post mortem. Recent techniques of brain scanning (computer-ized axial tomography or CAT scan) make it possible to locate lesions more readily, but this technique was not available for the main series that have been analysed in relation to handedness.

A second main source of evidence has come from the exploration of the exposed cortex, as a prelude to brain operations for the relief of surgery, as mentioned in Section 2.4. It must be noted that these brains were abnormal in that they had been subject to epileptic attacks for many years. Further, the surgical exploration of the brain is used to minimise the risk of dysphasia. Surgery tends to be more cautious on the left than the right side in order to reduce the chances of speech loss. Hence in the series of patients described for lesion side, aphasia, and handedness by Penfield and Roberts (1959), lesions of the two hemispheres cannot be assumed to be equivalent.

Since the early 1950s, the laterality of cerebral speech has been assessed prior to surgery, at the Montreal Neurological Institute, using the technique introduced by Wada (cited by Branch, Milner & Rasmussen, 1964). Sodium amytal is injected into the carotid arteries, which supply blood to the central areas of the cerebral hemispheres. A small quantity of the drug is introduced to the artery on one side, each side being tested on different days. The injection impairs cerebral function for a few minutes. While the drug is effective, the opposite arm and leg are paralysed, although the arm and leg on the same side can be moved. Speech is normally affected by injection on one side only. This is the only reliable technique that has been available to date for assessing which hemisphere serves speech. As there is a small but finite risk associated with all surgical procedures, the test is made only in cases where the speech hemisphere is doubtful. That is, the test is given to left-handers and to right-handers suspected of abnormal speech laterality. Hence, the incidences of cerebral speech laterality reported are for a selected sample within a selected sample. Incidences cannot be taken to be representative of the general population.

A major source of evidence as to hemisphere function has been offered by studies of patients treated for intractable epilepsies by dividing the cerebral commissures. Disadvantages of the split-brain material are that relatively few patients have been treated in this way, and that all have brains that have been functioning abnormally for some years. The separation of the cerebral hemispheres is highly abnormal in itself, although some natural cases of agenesis of the corpus callosum occur. In cases of agenesis, the brains have developed abnormally. Nevertheless, the study of split-brain and acallosal patients offers unique opportunities to study the behaviour of the independent hemispheres.

Recordings of the spontaneous electrical activity of the brain were first made by Berger in the 1930s and found to serve useful diagnostic purposes, so that the electroencephalograph (EEG) has become a well-established part of neurological assessment. Recordings are usually made through electrodes placed on the intact skull, but they can also be made when the brain surface is exposed for surgery. The brain's spontaneous electrical activity is continuous throughout life. It shows characteristic patterns of electrical discharge that vary with state of arousal, whether relaxed, sleeping, or actively engaged in solving a problem. The predominant rhythm recorded from the posterior areas of the brain in the relaxed subject with eyes closed is the alpha rhythm (Fig. 2.7). When the eyes are opened and the subject engages in intellectual activity, the regular wave form becomes desynchronised to give beta rhythms. Techniques have been developed for measuring the suppression of the alpha rhythm when the subject is engaged in particular tasks, such as solving problems in arithmetic or writing, in order to compare the relative suppressions of alpha rhythms in the two hemispheres (Butler & Glass, 1974; Galin, Johnstone, & Herron, 1978). Other techniques of EEG analysis have been developed by programming computers to average the EEG responses to specific signals. Over a series of trials timed from signal onset, the random elements in the EEG signal are removed and the systematic elements enhanced by the averaging process (averaged evoked response or AER). Measures have been developed of the synchrony or coherence of EEG activity between regions on the same side of the opposite sides of the brain (Shaw, O'Connor, & Ongley, 1978). For a review of EEG measures used for

(a)

(b)

FIG. 2.7.   EEG rhythms: a = alpha (relaxed with eyes closed) and b = beta (aroused with eyes open).

studying differential hemisphere activity, see Donchin, Kutas and McCarthy (1977).

CAT scans map slices of the brain at specified levels, through computerized analysis of X-rays. This technique has been used to examine structural asymmetries of the hemispheres (Section 3.3.2). Measurements of regional cerebral blood flow (rCBF) permit assessments of levels of activity in cortical areas during resting, speaking, or performing a variety of activities (Lassen, Ingvar, & Skinhoj, 1978). As would be expected from clinical and electrical mapping studies, speaking involves the primary motor and sensory areas of the mouth, tongue and larynx and the auditory association cortex. In addition, Lassen and his colleagues found that the supplementary motor area was active during all voluntary movements, including speech. Further, they were surprised to find that these areas are active in the *right* hemisphere, as well as in the left, during speech. Comparison of the rCBF of the hemispheres suggests that the difference between the hemispheres during speaking is quantitative rather than absolute. Since these techniques involve an element of risk, they can be used only when neurological problems make brain investigations necessary.

A new and noninvasive technique for visualising the interior of the body, including the brain, involves recording extremely small magnetic changes of atomic nuclei (nuclear magnetic recording, NMR, Pykett, 1982). Once some safe, simple, and reliable method of establishing which hemisphere serves speech is available for investigating a large sample of people drawn from the general population, it will be possible to test the theory developed in this book. Until then, the best use possible must be made of the imperfect evidence available.

There is a very large literature concerned with attempts to study cerebral asymmetries in normal subjects. The techniques used compare the performance of the two sides, tested either separately or in competition. The latter depends on presenting auditory stimuli to both ears simultaneously, or visual stimuli to either visual field when the subject fixates a central point, or tactile stimuli to either or both hands. Subjects may be asked to perform simultaneously two tasks that are presumed to depend on the same or different hemispheres, to see whether there is evidence of competition for limited resources. (For recent reviews of methods see Beaumont, 1983; Hellige, 1983.) Some might argue that these studies offer tests of the RS theory. While none of the findings for normal subjects seriously conflict with expectations of the theory, as will be shown below (Sections 6.1.3, 7.2, and 14.5.2), I do not regard the evidence as strong enough to constitute a definitive test.

QUESTIONS ABOUT HUMAN HANDEDNESS

3

Questions about the Origins of Human Handedness

3.1. HOW LONG HAS MAN INCLUDED
A MAJORITY OF RIGHT HANDERS
AND A MINORITY OF LEFT HANDERS?

Speculations about the origins of the human distribution of hand preference have reached back to the earliest hominids recognised to be on the human rather than ape line of evolution, the australopithecines. Dart (1949) reported that of 58 baboon skulls found associated with australopithecine remains, about 80% showed evidence of having been subjected to "purposeful violence, that could only have been inflicted by implements held in hands, or by the crushing hands themselves". Most of the skulls of the australopithecines also showed depressed fractures. It is problematic to deduce, of course, just how the skulls came to be damaged in this way, but Dart was of the opinion that "the depressed areas are so specific that the direction from which the blow was delivered can be reasonably inferred and the type of weapon responsible for the fracture diagnosed". Dart's analysis led him to suggest that most of the blows were inflicted by implements of wood, bone, or stone. As more of the baboon skulls showed evidence of left-sided than right-sided fracture and an attacker would be likely to be facing the animal, Dart inferred that the australopithecines had a preference for the right hand. These conclusions were based on very small numbers of skulls with clearly localisable fractures and must be regarded as highly tentative, pending further evidence.

The stone-age tools and works of art of prehistoric peoples have been examined for clues as to the handedness of their makers. Wilson (1891) tells

39

us that when flakes are struck from a flint or obsidian, the grooves all turn in one direction when the core is held in the left hand and is struck by the right, whereas the grooves run in the opposite direction when the core is held in the right hand and struck by the left. He concluded that right-handedness was the rule and left-handedness exceptional in primitive workmen. Although other analysts did not always concur (Harris, 1980a), recent microscopic examination of the worked surfaces of stone tools led Keeley (1977) to conclude that workers at the Clacton site some 200,000 years ago were consistently right-handed.

Wilson inferred that the majority of stone-age artists were right-handed as most profiles were drawn facing to the left. Were the few that faced right drawn by left-handed artists, as Wilson suggested, or is it that skilled artists can draw in either direction? Studies of spontaneous drawing in children (Blau, 1977; Connolly & Elliott, 1972) confirm that right- and left-handers tend to draw lines from opposite directions, and that right-handers are more likely to draw circles counterclockwise (which would seem the natural direction for drawing a profile to a right-hander) and left-handers to draw circles clockwise. Among the prehistoric cave paintings are outlines of human hands—usually of the left hand as if drawn by a right-hander, but some of right hands. The human figures represented in cave art are usually in the form of stick men and it is not possible to be certain which hand is holding the spear or bow and arrow.

The more sophisticated representations of the human figure found in Egyptian paintings were examined by Dennis (1958) for the hand used in the activities depicted. In the 225 instances where one hand was used, it was the right hand in 211 cases (94%). Coren and Porac (1977) reported on an examination of more than 12,000 works of art representing figures displaying clear hand preference, dating from before 3000 B.C. to the present and grouped in 16 periods. Incidences of dextral hand use were consistent over this time span (mean 92.6%, range 86–98%). Analyses for seven geographical areas, including Europe, Asia, Africa, and America, found a similar consistency. If these representations reflect instances of actual hand use as observed by the artist, then about 7% of mankind has been sinistral for as long as man has drawn the human form.

The earliest written references to handedness in western culture are to be found in the Old Testament. The Good News Bible (1976) version of Judges, Chapter 20, includes the following passage:

From all the cities of Benjamin they came to Gibeah to fight against the other people of Israel. They called out twenty-six thousand soldiers from their cities that day. Besides these, the citizens of Gibeah gathered seven hundred especially chosen men who were left-handed. Every one of them could sling a stone at a strand of hair and never miss.

The 2.6% left-handed slingers do not necessarily include all the left-handers in the army, nor does it imply that there were no right-handed slingers. The passage is interesting for showing that there was a small but substantial proportion of left-handers, and that these men were selected for their skill in a task that must demand high powers of hand–eye co-ordination. We see many left-handers among outstanding performers in tennis and other sports today. Whether left-handers are indeed more likely to be highly skilled or alternatively more clumsy than the rest of the population is a question to be considered later (Sections 5.2.1, 17.1.2, and 19.3).

This early evidence of the distribution of human hand preference in the use of tools, weapons, and art cannot be regarded as conclusive, but as far as it goes, it suggests a majority of right-handers and a minority of left-handers for as long as the data stretch back in time. There are certainly no grounds for suggesting that there was ever a time when *all* humans were right-handed, or alternatively a time when a major portion were left-handed. In other words, there is no reason to doubt that the modern distribution is of very long standing.

3.2. DOES HANDEDNESS DEPEND ON ASYMMETRIES OF THE VISCERA OR THE FERTILISED OVUM?

Some of the oldest and most frequently resurrected theories about handedness concern asymmetries of the internal organs (early theories reviewed by Harris, 1980a). In man and other vertebrates, the viscera are normally arranged in a typical asymmetrical pattern, with the heart and the stomach slightly to the left of the midline and the liver and appendix to the right. The right lung is usually slightly larger than the left. Several nineteenth-century theorists proposed that right-handedness was a result of asymmetries of the body; perhaps the weight of the liver displaces the body's centre of gravity to the right, or perhaps there are differences in the circulation of blood to the arms or to the brain. The difficulty with all these theories is that none can account for left-handedness without supposing that the viscera are also reversed, a condition known as *situs inversus*. It was pointed out over 300 years ago by Sir Thomas Browne, a Norfolk country physician, in his "Enquiries into common and vulgar errors" that, "As for the seate of the heart and liver in one side whereby men become left handed, it happeneth too rarely to countenance an effect so common; for the seat of the liver on the left side is monstrous and rarely to be met with in the observations of physitians" (Browne, 1646/1981, p. 305).

A mass X-ray survey of partial and complete *situs inversus* in Norway estimated the incidence to be .011% of the population (Torgerson, 1950). As

Sir Thomas said, this is far too little to account for the 7–10% who are left-handed. Torgerson clearly showed the independence of visceral and manual asymmetries by his finding that of 160 individuals with *situs inversus* whose handedness was known, 6.9% were left handed—the proportion expected by chance in the population at large.

In the rare and exceptional cases of twins who are joined together at birth (Siamese), one twin may be the mirror image of the other and have transposed viscera, but there seems to be little systematic study of this phenomenon in man. When *situs inversus* has been found in human twins, it may occur in *both* twins and not only one, showing that the mirror image explanation is far too simple (Oppenheimer, 1974). In the Norwegian survey *situs inversus* was found to be independent of twinning, as the proportion of cases of twins was no greater than that expected by chance. Further, in several families having several members with partial or complete *situs inversus*, there was no greater likelihood of twin birth than in the general population.

Morgan (1977) has proposed a new version of the theory that human right-handedness depends on more primitive and universal asymmetries of the body, common not only to mankind but also to the vertebrate kingdom. Noting several examples where the left side of the body or brain seems to develop more quickly or more strongly than the right side, Morgan suggested that there is a left–right maturational gradient determined from the earliest phase of growth of the fertilised egg. Human right-handedness would then be a consequence of the earlier and better development of the left hemisphere of the brain (which controls the right hand). Morgan coined the striking phrase that genes may be "left–right agnosic", to clarify his belief that the maturational gradient is a universal characteristic, determined by some primitive, basic asymmetry of development that does not depend on genes.

The further exposition of the theory by Corballis and Morgan (1978) and Morgan and Corballis (1978), together with commentaries by other biologists, neurologists, and psychologists, brings out some of the difficulties in this theory. The main problem from the present viewpoint is the assumption that handedness depends on a mechanism universal throughout the vertebrates, which governs *all* the main asymmetries including those of the viscera, brain, and hands. If this is so, why is right-pawedness not found in any other vertebrate than man? Why do exceptions occur in man, and why are the exceptions for the viscera independent of those for the hand and also the brain? Any "universal" explanation has to have additional postulates for the exceptions, and it is the exceptions that are interesting about human handedness and brainedness. No other *species* of mammal shows the bias to the right hand typical of humans; and, among humans, why do left-handers differ in this respect? It is clear that a *universal* maturational gradient hypothesis could not account for the main phenomena of interest here.

There is a multitude of left–right asymmetries in nature (Chapter 9); the causal factors are unknown in most cases. Corballis (1983) suggests, "There may be a common thread linking human laterality, other morphological asymmetries in plants and animals, the molecular asymmetries in living tissue and the nonconservation of parity in the fundamental laws of physics." When a full understanding of all these phenomena is reached, common mechanisms may be found to be involved. For the present, the key problem is to find an appropriate level of analysis for research. Maturational gradients can be inferred for many growth processes (Mittwoch, 1973), and their possible relevance to human asymmetries will be considered in Chapter 21. The focus will be on how they might differ between humans and between humans and other species, rather than on their universality.

3.3.   DOES HANDEDNESS DEPEND ON ASYMMETRIES OF THE BRAIN?

3.3.1.   The Effects of Unilateral Brain lesions on speech

Following earlier unrecognised work by Dax, Paul Broca convinced neurologists in the 1860s that the human cerebral hemispheres differ in function, loss of speech being associated with lesions of the left hemisphere (Critchley, 1970a; Harris, 1980a). There is now a great wealth of evidence to support this conclusion from several courses. In examining the association between the asymmetry of the brain for speech (brainedness) and handedness, it is important to bear in mind the advantages and limitations of particular sources of evidence, as discussed in Section 2.5.

To investigate the relationship between handedness and brainedness in the general population, it is necessary to consider studies where patients have been included without bias as to their hand or brain laterality (and not because they were suspected of atypical laterality, as in the Montreal carotid amytal series). The series must be large if the true proportions of atypical cases, left-handers and right-hemisphere speakers, are to be estimated. Zangwill (1967) identified five such series in the world literature, for which information was presented in sufficient detail for inclusion in the analysis summarised in Table 3.1. The highest risk of dysphasia was found in right-handers with left-sided lesion (60%), but the risk to left-handers with left-sided lesions was not much less (55%). The main difference between right- and left-handers was in the risk of dysphasia following right-sided brain lesions, about 2% in right-handers and 29% in left-handers. This comparison

TABLE 3.1

Combined Data From Five Series of Cases of Unilateral Brain Lesion Studied for Presence of Dysphasia and for Handedness

Side of unilateral brain lesion	Left handers		Right handers	
	Left	Right	Left	Right
Total cases	102	89	1047	895
Percent with dysphasia	54.9	29.2	59.7	1.8

Note: Based on Zangwill (1967)

shows that there is a statistically significant difference between the two handedness groups for brain laterality, but the nature of the association between handedness and brainedness is far from clear.

Right-handedness cannot be caused by left-brainedness, nor can left-handedness be caused by right-brainedness. Nor, for those who might wish to suggest that the causal factors operate in the reverse direction, is it possible to suggest that brainedness is caused by handedness. For those who believe that an opposite (contralateral) relationship between hand and brain *ought to* hold (and in popular writing it is often maintained that this opposite rule does hold), there are more exceptions than instances of this pattern in left-handers. Some have suggested, from evidence such as that of Table 3.1, that as left-hemisphere speech is more frequent than right-hemisphere speech in both right- and left-handers, left-brained speech can be taken to be a universal rule, and that handedness is independent of brainedness (Goodglass & Quadfasel, 1954; Penfield & Roberts, 1959). This is not true either, as shown by the significant correlation between handedness and brainedness. It has also been said that since speech functions are on the left in nearly all right-handers and in the majority of left-handers, right-hemisphere speech is so rare as to be of little importance. This evaluation of the evidence has probably led to a general underestimation of the likelihood of right-brainedness (Section 14.4.1).

A hypothesis that has been widely accepted in recent literature is that speech is represented bilaterally in left-handers (Conrad, 1949). In Table 3.1 there are more left-handers (43%) than right-handers (33%) who suffered dysphasia. The difference is one that would occur by chance in less than 1 in 100 observations (beyond the 1% level of significance). Goodglass and Quadfasel (1954) collected all the reports available in the literature on left-handers with unilateral lesions of the language areas and found that more than 50% suffered dysphasias regardless of the side that had suffered the lesion. This last observation could be due to more frequent publication of positive than negative cases for dysphasia, as pointed out by Bingley (1958). Hécaen and Piercy (1956) analysed the records of all cases who were recorded as experiencing an epileptic aura (warning of attack) at a neurological clinic over several years. In several cases the aura involved a loss of ability to speak or to understand speech. Such temporary dysphasias occurred in 37% of 97 right-handers and in 90% of 29 left-handers or ambidexters. In right-handers the paroxysmal dysphasia was usually associated with a left-sided lesion, but in non-right-handers the paroxysmal disturbance of language occurred whether the right or the left side had the lesion. These findings taken at face value (but see Section 14.3) suggest that left-handers have a higher risk of speech disturbances than right-handers, whether the damage is to the right or left hemisphere. Thus, it was suggested that *both* hemispheres must be involved in the language functions of left-handers and ambidexters.

The specific hypothesis that brainedness for speech is typically bilateral in non-right-handers can be tested against the findings for speech and handedness in the Montreal patients tested by the Wada technique. The objection that the latter are epileptic does not apply because Hécaen and Piercy's patients were also epileptic, and the objection that the patients were selected for left-handedness does not apply as the hypothesis is specifically about left-handers. Rasmussen and Milner (1975) reported on 262 patients who had been examined for speech laterality by injection of the carotid arteries, excluding all patients with evidence of early damage to the left hemisphere. Table 3.2 confirms that in the great majority of right-handers speech is on the left side, although these right-handers were selected for testing because there was doubt as to their speech laterality. The findings for left-handers in Table 3.2, as in Table 3.1, show that the left hemisphere serves speech in the majority of left-handers. Bilateral speech, which could not be detected directly from the clinical material in Table 3.1, was found by the Wada test to occur in a small proportion (15%) of left- and mixed-handers. Although no right-handers with bilateral speech are recorded in Table 3.2, later reports have described such cases (Ratcliff, Dila, Taylor, & Milner, 1980). Thus, all three types of speech laterality occur in right- and left-handers, but the

TABLE 3.2

Speech Lateralisation as Related to Handedness in 262 Patients Without Clinical Evidence of Early Damage to the Left Cerebral Hemisphere

Handedness	No. Cases	Speech Representation (%)		
		Left	Bilateral	Right
Right	140	96	0	4
Left or mixed	122	70	15	15

Note: Based on Rasmussen and Milner (1975).

proportions of each type differ between the handedness groups. Bilateral speech cannot be said to be typical of left-handers. In the majority of right- and left-handers the left hemisphere alone is responsible for speech.

3.3.2. Structural Differences
Between the Hemispheres

A structural basis for the functional asymmetry of the cerebral hemispheres was sought by Broca and others in the nineteenth and early twentieth centuries. Von Bonin (1962) reviewed the evidence assembled during the preceding 100 years and found numerous small differences but none that seemed sufficient to account for the astonishing difference in function. One of the chief studies cited by Von Bonin was of measurements made by Hoadley and Pearson (1929) of the internal lengths of the right and left halves of 729 male Egyptian skulls of the 26–30th dynasty, found by Sir Flinders Petrie. The differences between the sides were distributed according to an approximately normal distribution (Fig. 3.1), with the mean displaced to the right from the point of equality by about .58 standard deviations. There was a negative skew, significant at beyond the 1% level—that is, although the mean difference was in favour of a longer right brain and about 70% of the skulls conformed to this pattern, there were more skulls with a difference in favour of the left side than expected for a truly normal distribution.

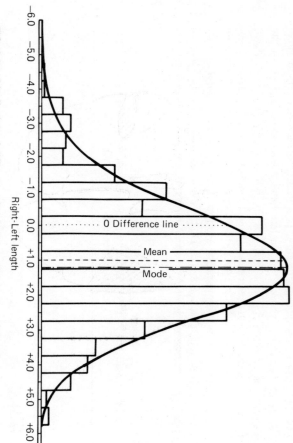

FIG. 3.1.   Distribution of difference of right-side and left-side lengths (internal or cerebral hemisphere lengths) of 729 Egyptian male crania. From Hoadley & Pearson, 1929.

Right–Left length

McRae, Branch and Milner (1968) compared the lengths of the occipital horns of the lateral ventricles, as seen on pneumoencephalograms and ventriculograms, in 100 consecutive patients under neurological investigation. In 87 right-handers, the left horn was longer in 60%, the right longer in 10%, and in 30% the horns did not differ. In 13 left-handed and ambidextrous patients, numbers of each type were about equal.

Geschwind and Levitsky (1968) reported a post-mortem study of 100 brains that found the planum temporale larger on the left in 65 cases, on the right in 11, and not clearly different in 24. The planum temporale lies on the upper surface of the temporal lobe, within the sylvian fissure and close to Wernicke's area (Fig. 3.2). Its location suggests that the larger left-sided planum might be relevant to the role of the left hemisphere in speech, but since the measurements were made at post mortem, no direct test of this relationship could be made. Witelson (1983) has begun to collect data suggesting that the link between this physical and functional asymmetry will be substantiated; it seems that a link with right-handedness will also be demonstrated. Planum temporale asymmetries have been confirmed in several further studies of adult brains (reviewed by Witelson, 1983). They have also been found in the brains of neonates (Witelson & Pallie, 1973) and in fetal brains during the final quarter of normal gestation (Chi, Dooling & Gilles, 1977; Wada, Clarke, & Hamm, 1975). These observations imply that a physical basis for speech and hand asymmetries might be present in utero.

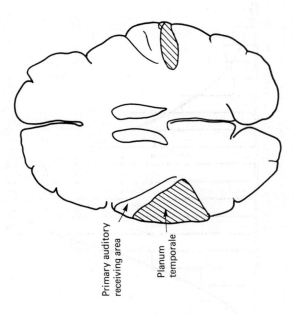

FIG. 3.2.   Asymmetry of the Planum Temporale. Horizontal section of the brain at the level of the sylvian fissure. Based on Witelson, 1980.

Primary auditory receiving area

Planum temporale

The lateral or sylvian fissure was noted by Cunningham (1902) to be often longer on the left than on the right; the greater length on the left is now thought to be correlated with the greater extent of the left planum. Rubens (1977) traced the line of the lateral fissure on standard photographs of the right and left sides of preserved brains, superimposing the reversed transparency of the right side on the normal view of the left, as shown in Fig. 3.3. The fissure of the right turned upward and terminated considerably anterior to that on the left in 69% of 36 brains. The remainder were regarded as roughly symmetric. The course of the sylvian fissures can sometimes be seen in endocranial casts of fossil skulls, and the higher right than left pattern characteristic of modern man has been noted in some fossils of *Homo erectus* and Neanderthal man (LeMay, 1976). Lateral fissure asymmetries have also been examined in the brains of higher apes and monkeys, as will be considered in Section 9.3.

Several physical asymmetries of human brains have now been identified in radiographic studies of patients whose handedness can be investigated. LeMay and Culebras (1972) noted that the angles formed by the posterior branches of the middle cerebral arteries as they leave the sylvian fissure were wider on the right than the left in a majority of right-handed patients but not in a majority of left-handed patients. Hochberg and LeMay (1975) confirmed this observation with new data shown in Table 3.3. Of the right-handers, 67% showed the wider angle on the right, but only 21% of left-handers. The majority of left-handers were symmetrical. Further evidence from arteriographic studies will be considered in Section 14.5.1.

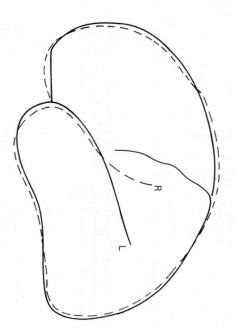

FIG. 3.3.   Asymmetry of the height of the Sylvian fissure. Example of a composite tracing of the hemispheric outlines, central and sylvian fissures. Dashed line indicates features of the right hemisphere; solid line indicates those of the left. Note shorter and higher sylvian fissure on the right side. Based on Rubens, 1977.

TABLE 3.3

Sylvian Point Asymmetries in Carotid Arteriograms

	N	Right angle Larger Than Left (%)	R = L (Within 10°) (%)	Left angle Larger Than Right (%)
Right-handers	106	67	25	8
Left-handers	28	21	72	7

Note: Based on Hochberg and LeMay (1975).

Asymmetries of the skull that have been noted for some time (Clark, 1934) have become more amenable to study with the advent of CAT scans (Section 2.5). Figure 3.4 gives an example of a skull showing the typical pattern of slightly greater protrusion of the left occipital and the right frontal regions. (The skull is said to show torque or petalia.) This pattern has also been found in fossil hominid crania (Table 9.2). Table 3.4 gives LeMay's (1977) findings for a large number of right-handers and left-handers whose scans had been taken for a variety of neurological problems, but omitting any with lesions that might have distorted the hemispheres. The distributions of right-handers resemble those found for planum temporale and carotid artery assymetries. The left-handers clearly differ from the right-handers. Left-handers are not the *opposite* of right-handers, but rather they are about evenly divided for biases to each side.

In summary, it may be said that the findings for structural asymmetries in left-handers resemble those for functional asymmetries of hemisphere speech. Left-handers do *not* show asymmetries opposite to those of right-handers. They show the same kinds of asymmetries as right-handers but to a reduced extent, or no bias to either side. One of the surprising features of the findings for structural asymmetry is that rather *fewer* right-handers show the

TABLE 3.4

Asymmetries of the Skull: Percentages of Right-Handers and of Left-Handers Showing Protrusions of the Frontal and of the Occipital Bones on Each Side

	Frontal			Occipital		
	↑L	=	↑R	↓L	=	↓R
Right-handers	14	20	66	77	11	12
Left-handers	36	27	37	36	29	35

Note:
N = 120 or more per group.
Based on LeMay (1977).

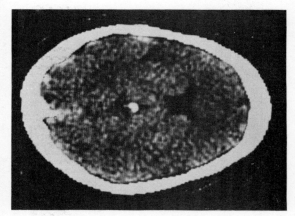

FIG. 3.4.   Example of CAT scan showing left occipital and right frontal petalia. From LeMay, 1976.

typical biases than expected if the structural asymmetries are directly linked with brainedness for speech.

3.4.   IS HUMAN HANDEDNESS DETERMINED BY GENES?

3.4.1. Is there a recessive gene for left-handedness?

Sir George Humphry wrote in 1861, "I am driven, therefore, to the rather nice distinction, that, though the superiority [of the right hand] is acquired, the tendency to acquire the superiority is natural [i.e. hereditary]" (cited by Merrell, 1957). This conclusion summarises very well the analysis made in Chapter 1 of the complementary roles of genetic and developmental influences on growth. But most theoreticians since the time of Sir George have looked for specific genes for right- and left-handedness.

Jordan (1911) was the first to collect information on the handedness of students and their relatives and to attempt to interpret the distribution in the light of Mendelian principles. He concluded (Jordan, 1914) that the data were overwhelmingly in accord with Mendelian theory; there were certain real exceptions to Mendelian expectations, but these could be reconciled with the theory, "By the aid of the suggested hypothesis of degrees of intensity of bias, and mild dominant and intense recessive strains of left handedness." In other words, left-handedness looks as if it might be a Mendelian recessive character, but a quantity of "fudge" factors must be invoked to blur the rules governing its appearance. Most subsequent genetic theories of handedness have involved variations on the theme of the dominant/recessive gene pair, with differing interpretations of the "fudge" factors. These are summarised in Table 3.5. Each theory will be considered in relation to the findings for handedness in families.

The first description of a large sample of families where percentages of left-handed children could be assessed for each type of parental mating was that of Ramaley (1913). Table 3.6 summarises Ramaley's data and also gives the corresponding percentages for three later series, each based on several hundred students and their families. In each series, the proportion of left-handed children was greater for L × R families than for R × R families, and greater still for L × L families (except for Annett, 1973a). The numbers of L × L families (sibships) were small in each study, and the proportions therefore liable to error. It is clear, however, that contrary to expectations for the classic gene pair model (see Table 3.5), in all series there were some right-handed children when both parents were left-handed. Among the 48 children observed in all the L × L families of the four series combined (ignoring the variations in incidence between series for the moment), only 20 (41.7%) were recorded as left-handed. Chamberlain (1928) reported on 24 additional L × L families contacted through newspapers, whose 75 children included 39 (52.0%) left-handers. Similarly, Annett (1973a) found 64 additional L × L families with 35% left-handed children; in 17 families where both parents were *consistent* left-handers (reported using the left hand for *all* of 12 actions of a questionnaire), 44% of the children were left-handed. Thus, there can be no doubt that families of L × L parents include many right-handed children, even when the parental left-handedness is very strong indeed. The classic model will not do.

The fact that there are wide variations in the incidence of left-handedness as assessed in these several studies is evident from inspection of the percentages of left-handers in R × R families in Table 3.6. In fact, the incidences over-all varied in the parents between 3.5 and 8.0% and in the children between 4.8 and 15.7%. Variations in the assessment of incidence present a problem that has to be faced before handedness becomes fully amenable to study (Chapter 13). For the moment, it must be pointed out that *despite the differences of incidence* for parents and children, Trankell (1955) was able to show that the three studies available at that time (those of

TABLE 3.5

Predictions for Handedness Phenotypes from the Classic Mendelian Single Gene Pair Model and Variants of the Model

	Possible Genotypes			
	rr	*rl*	*ll*	
Genetic Model	*(Dominant Homozygote)*	*(Heterozygote)*	*(Recessive Homozygote)*	*Children Expected of Left × Left Matings*
A. Classic pattern	right	right	left	left only
B. Imperfect penetrance of recessive gene (Trankell, 1955)	right	right	right and left	right and left
C.1. Variability in heterozygotes (Annett, 1964)	right	right, mixed, and left	left	right, mixed, and left
C.2. If heterozygote = mixed handedness (Annett, 1967)	right (consistent)	mixed	left (consistent)	if consistent left × consistent left, left only

Note: *r* = dominant gene for right-handedness; *l* = recessive gene for left-handedness.

TABLE 3.6

Incidences of Left-Handedness in Families According to the Handedness of Parents

Data Source	Parents' Handedness		
	Right × Right	Left × Right	Left × Left
Ramaley (1913)			
No. families	258	45	2
No. children	953	143	7
Percentage left-handed	12.2	38.5	85.7
Chamberlain (1928)			
Percentage left-handed	4.3	11.4	28.0
Rife (1940)			
Percentage left-handed	7.7	19.5	54.5
Annett (1973a)			
Percentage left-handed	9.7	21.0	20.0

Ramaley, Chamberlain, and Rife) gave almost identical estimates of the frequency of the recessive gene (l) on the hypothesis he proposed of imperfect penetrance in recessive homozygotes (see Table 3.5). That is, if it is argued that some natural left-handers fail to express their left-handedness (presumably because of cultural pressures) and if the extent of imperfect penetrance is estimated from the proportion of right-handers in L × L families, then the other proportions of left-handers in each family type are consistent with a gene frequency in the range of 40–43% (in nine estimates from the three family types of three series). This remarkable consistency suggests that the differing incidences of left-handedness in the three series depend on relatively superficial differences in methods of measurement, and that there is an underlying regularity in the transmission of handedness in families. The main problem with Trankell's (1955) solution to the genetic question is that more than half of the children of L × L families (all of whom should be natural left-handers) become right-handers, and further that the chance of being a right-handed shifted sinistral is the same in families where both parents are left-handed as in families where both parents are right-handed. Surely, if social pressures are the main agent of shifted sinistrality, the pressures on natural left-handers to shift must be smaller when both parents are left-handed. There are other problems with Trankell's model in accounting for handedness in twins (Section 3.4.4).

The third variation on the classic gene pair theme (Table 3.5C1) is the suggestion that the recessive gene might not be fully recessive but partly expressed in heterozygotes to give mixed-handed tendencies; the majority of so-called "left-handers" actually have mixed right- and left-hand preferences (Annett, 1964). Ramaley (1913) suggested that, "Possibly some heterozygote

... persons may easily learn to use the left hand." Expressed in this way, heterozygote variability becomes another "fudge" factor, which makes it impossible to make strict tests of the model against real data. Rife (1950) used the idea of heterozygote variability to account for the occurrence of identical twins pairs with one right- and one left-handed twin. The main point of the Annett (1964) hypothesis was to explain the occurrence of mixed-hand preferences and to suggest that cerebral dominance for speech might also be *either* right or left in the heterozygote. Variability of brainedness and handedness in heterozygotes would allow for all the combinations of hand and brain laterality observed above (Section 3.3). The model does *not* imply, as suggested by Levy and Nagylaki (1972), that left-handers would not have persistent dysphasia from left hemisphere lesions, as heterozygotes could vary in both the direction and strength of cerebral dominance.

The second and more precise version of the heterozygote variability model (Table 3.5C2) followed studies of the distributions of hand preferences in large samples (Section 13.3), which suggested that all heterozygotes might be mixed handers; if this were true, then all *rr* homozygotes would be consistent right-handers and all *ll* homozygotes consistent left-handers. This strict interpretation of the model can be tested against family data. All parents identified as consistent right-× consistent right-handers should have only right-handed children and consistent left-× consistent left-handers should have only left-handed children. The family data I had collected from families of R × R and L × L parents (when parents and children each completed their own questionnaires) showed that the strict interpretation of the model could be rejected.

3.4.2. A Two-Gene, Four-Allele Model

Levy and Nagylaki (1972) suggested that the cerebral lateralisation of language and handedness might depend on two pairs of alleles at two independent gene loci. It was hypothesised that one gene pair governs whether language is on the left or right (*L* or *l*, dominant and recessive, respectively) and that one pair governs whether the preferred hand is contralateral or ipsilateral to this hemisphere (*C* or *c*, dominant and recessive, respectively). The genes were said to be completely penetrant. The model assumed that the dominant hemisphere for speech always controls the preferred hand; in most cases the preferred hand is opposite to the speech hemisphere, but left-handers with left-hemisphere dominance and right-handers with right-hemisphere dominance were hypothesised to control the preferred hand from the ipsilateral hemisphere, via uncrossed pyramidal tracts (Section 2.2).

The model was shown to fit the family data reported by Rife (1940) when the proportions of left-handers with right- and left-hemisphere speech were as estimated by Goodglass and Quadfasel (1954), about 47% and 53%, respectively. A glance at Table 3.6 shows that the incidences of left-handedness obtained by Rife (1940) for the three types of families (R × R, L × R, and L × L) were broadly similar to those of Ramaley (1913), Chamberlain (1928), and Annett (1973a), but they differed considerably in detail. Levy and Nagylaki (1972) did not test their model against Ramaley's data on the grounds that he did not state his criterion of left-handedness, nor against that of Chamberlain because of certain inconsistencies in the numbers and percentages given in his paper. Annett (1973a), in addition to reporting a large new series of family data from students, used the data of Rife and Chamberlain to estimate heritabilities of handedness, after correct-ing one error of number in Chamberlain's Table 1 (the other errors were of percentages). Hudson (1975) tested the Levy–Nagylaki (1972) model against the data of Chamberlain as reconstructed by Annett and the new Annett data and found highly significant departures from the numbers predicted.

Levy (1976, 1977) argued that Hudson's tests of the model were inappro-priate because of the uncertainties of Chamberlain's data and because the writing hand was the criterion used in the Annett study (writing hand being subject to change through cultural pressures). Rife's criterion was use of the left hand for any of 10 actions, which should allow those with strong sinistral tendencies to be detected. Annett (1978a) responded to these criticisms and showed that a reanalysis of her family data for the more generous "any left" preference criterion yields percentages that still do not fit the Levy–Nagylaki predictions. Any repetition of Rife's study in the United States today would come up with larger percentages than those obtained in the late 1930s. McGee and Cozad (1980) have reported such a study of students at the Universities of Minnesota and Texas, with incidences of "any left" prefer-ence in the children of R × R, L × R and L × L families of 20, 32, and 42%, respectively; these and other recent data (to be considered in relation to the genetic predictions of the RS theory in Section 16.3) also differ from those of Rife. Trankell (1955) has shown, as mentioned above, that the three sets of data of Ramaley, Chamberlain, and Rife were highly consistent when differences in incidence were taken into account, but Levy and Nagylaki made no provision for differences in incidence. If no such allowance is made, the untenable position must be adopted that the data of Rife (1940) represent the first and last word on the distribution of handedness in families.

To account for the idea that left-handers might be bilateral in hemisphere speech and recover more often from dysphasias, Levy and Nagylaki sug-gested that strong cerebral dominance might occur only in those with the dominant alleles L or C, or perhaps both together. Thus right-hemisphere dominance was expected to be weak, and although genes were said to assort independently, there might be interactions between them. Such qualifications make any model even more difficult to test and allow scope for considerable further speculation. An additional postulate to which Levy has remained committed (Levy & Gur, 1980; Levy & Reid, 1976, 1978) is that ipsilateral hand–hemisphere relationships give rise to the practice of writing with the pen pointing towards the self. Inverted writing is thus claimed to be an *index* of cerebral dominance. The status of inverted writing will be considered later (Section 8.2) in the context of other tests and techniques psychologists have devised in the hope of elucidating patterns of cerebral specialisation in normal subjects. It is not germane to the present assessment of the genetic model.

3.4.3. Polygenic Inheritance

Human characteristics such as height, weight, and possibly intelligence are more likely to depend in the general population on the effects of several relatively minor genes rather than on a few major genes (Carter, 1962). The risk of suffering certain illnesses (such as peptic ulcer, diabetes, and perhaps also schizophrenia) have been hypothesised to depend on a scale of liability that varies continuously in the population, together with certain environmental factors that contribute to the susceptibility to breakdown (Falconer, 1965). Imagine a line of camels, ordered from small to large in a continuous series of gradations; it is then easy to see that if the same load is put on each camel's back, there is some point along the line where the last straw will break the back of that particular camel. The backs of smaller camels will probably have been broken already, whereas the larger camels will probably remain unbroken. This point, known as the threshold, governs what proportion of the population is likely to be assessed as affected by the disorder in question. This is exactly analogous to the decision to classify people as tall or short, perhaps for recruitment to the police force or a special regiment of guards; although height varies continuously, some threshold has to be reached if people are to be accepted as "tall". Perhaps handedness is a continuously varying characteristic, and being classified as left-handed depends on a fairly arbitrary threshold that can be raised or lowered according to different criteria appropriate for different purposes. The utility of such a varying threshold is evident as a release from the barren controversy of the last section over the correct criterion for family studies.

Is there evidence that lateral asymmetries vary continuously? When objective measurements were made of the differences in lengths of the right and left halves of the skull by Hoadley and Pearson (1929—Figure 3.1), the distribution took the form of a continuous, unimodal, and roughly normal curve. These are the characteristics that might be expected if asymmetries depended on the effects of several minor genes; it does not prove the polygenic hypothesis, of course, but it is compatible with it. When Woo and Pearson (1927) examined differences in strength between the hands in some

7000 males, in data collected at the instigation of Sir Francis Galton from visitors to a Health Exhibition in 1884, they found a continuous and unimodal curve. They concluded that "Lateralism . . . is a continuous variate, and that dextrality and sinistrality are not opposed alternatives, but quantities capable of taking values of continuous intensity and passing one into the other." It was not demonstrated, however, that asymmetries of skull length or of strength of grip were directly related to hand preference. A distribution that is also continuous and unimodal *and* reliably related to hand preference (Annett, 1976a) is the difference in time taken by each hand on a peg-moving task (Section 11.2). If the continuous difference between the hands in peg-moving time did depend on many genes of small effect, we would expect to find correlations between relatives for L–R differences on this task. In 63 families, Annett (1978a) found nonsignificant correlations for 6 out of 7 sets of pairs of relatives, as shown in Table 3.7. The only significant correlation was for mothers × daughters, and this was based on only 1 of 3 subsamples. (The question of association for left-handedness between mothers and daughters is considered further in Section 16.3.) These data offer no substantial support for the hypothesis of polygenic inheritance for differences between the hands in skill.

TABLE 3.7

Correlations Between Relatives for L–R Peg-Moving Time in Personally Visited Families

	L × L Hull			R × R Bedfordshire			R × L Coventry			All families		
	N	r	SE	N	r	SE	N	r	SE	N	r	SE
Fathers × sons	25	−.11		16	.03		26	.23		79	.08	±.11
Fathers × daughters	20	.13		19	−.12		21	−.44[a]	±.21	80	−.19	±.11
Mothers × sons	25	.22		20	−.02		29	−.11		86	.17	±.11
Mothers × daughters	20	−.07		24	−.18		24	.44[a]	±.19	88	.28[b]	±.10
Brothers × brothers	10	−.09		13	−.12		13	.79[b]	±.18	36	.21	±.16
Sisters × sisters	3			11	.13		5	—		24	−.01	±.21
Brothers × sisters	19	.13		29	−.45[b]	±0.17	25	.07		74	.08	±.12

[a] $p < .05$.
[b] $p < .01$.

Note: Annett (1978a).

3.4.4. The Problem of Twins

Identical (monozygotic or MZ) twins carry identical genes. Nonidentical (dizygotic or DZ) twins have, on average, one half of their genes in common. If handedness were fully determined genetically, then MZ twin pairs should be identical for handedness; if there were a strong genetic influence on handedness, MZ twins should be more often alike than DZ twins. Table 3.8 shows the numbers of RR, RL, and LL pairs in a large twin study in the United States (Loehlin & Nichols, 1976). The table also shows the numbers of pairs of each type expected if the handedness of each twin were independent of that of the other twin. (The chance or binomial proportions are of some importance in later analyses of the distribution of handedness, so it is worth making clear what this means. Taking the observed proportion of left-handers in individual MZ twins, 14.1%, as p, and the proportion of right-handers, 85.9%, as q, the proportions of LL, RL, and RR pairs expected by chance are predicted by p^2, $2pq$, and q^2 respectively; these are the proportions expected if 14 white and 86 black marbles were placed in a bag and were drawn out in pairs at random.) Clearly the numbers of pairs of each type are very close to those expected by chance, for both MZ and DZ pairs. A review of 19 studies of twins showed that this has been true of almost every study (McManus, 1980a). McManus demonstrated, however, that there have been fairly consistent trends for MZ series to include fewer RL and more LL pairs than would be expected for a true chance assortment. DZ pairs fit the chance distribution more closely.

Another feature of the data in Table 3.8 is the slightly higher proportion of left-handers in MZ than in DZ twins. The difference is barely significant statistically ($\chi^2 = 3.218$, $df = 1$, $p = .069$), but it is a trend that has occurred in several previous studies. In a survey of 10 studies including over 1000 pairs of each kind of twin, Zazzo (1960) found 16% left-handers in MZ and 13% left-handers in DZ twins. McManus (1980a) has pointed out that this difference was exaggerated in some early studies, when investigators were influenced by information on handedness in their decision whether the twins should be classified as identical or nonidentical—RL pairs were thought to be identical but mirror images. However, the trend is still apparent in several recent series.

TABLE 3.8
Distribution of Twin Pairs for Handedness; Numbers of Pairs Observed for Monozygotic and Dizygotic Twins, With Numbers Expected by Chance (Binomial Proportions)

	Right–Right	Right–Left	Left–Left	Left-Handed individuals
Monozygotic pairs				
observed	380	123	11	14.1
expected	379.2	123.9	10.2	
Dizygotic pairs				
observed	261	70	2	11.1
expected	263.1	65.8	4.1	

Note: Data from Loehlin and Nichols (1976).

Do MZ pairs resemble each other more often than DZ pairs? From data such as that represented in Table 3.8 there is no obvious difference in degrees of resemblance. A close examination of LL pairs finds a slightly higher proportion in MZ (2.1%) than in DZ (.6%) pairs. Zazzo (1960) found more LL pairs in MZ (3.9%) than DZ (1.8%) twins. The differences are small, but the trends are consistent.

What is to be made of the virtually chance assortment of right- and left-handers in twins of both kinds? Collins (1970) showed that the twin data is incompatible with the classic gene pair model, the imperfect penetrance model (Trankell, 1955), and the suggestion that one twin becomes right- and one left-handed when they are of heterozygote geneotype (Rife, 1950). Collins' view was that left-handedness arises from some unknown environmental mechanism. To account for family resemblance, the environmental mechanism would have to be common to certain families. Nagylaki and Levy (1973) argued that the twin data cannot be used to rule out genetic influences on handedness, since twin birth itself is associated with so many special factors. However, if handedness in twins were greatly affected by special factors, the incidence of left-handedness should be very much greater in twins than in singleborn, which is not the case (McManus, 1980a; but see Chapter 16).

Does the twin data rule out genetic mechanisms? There is an observation that strongly supports the view that there is a genetic influence on handedness. Rife (1950) showed that families that included a RL pair of twins were more likely to have another singleborn left-hander in the family than families with RR twins. Whatever the effect of twin birth itself, the chance of left-handedness in twins is affected by the presence of left-handed relatives.

3.4.5. Is There Any Genetic Influence On Human Handedness?

The evidence reviewed above shows that handedness cannot be *fully determined* by any of the proposed genetic mechanisms. Would it be sensible to agree with Collins that some unknown environmental agent produces a certain proportion of left-handers in each generation? There are several reasons for rejecting the view that there is *no* genetic influence on handedness.

The first and most important is a study of children in adoptive families. Such a critical study has been needed since genetic theories of handedness were first proposed, but it is difficult to do in countries where information on adoption is treated as confidential. Table 3.9 summarises data collected by Carter-Saltzman (1980) for a large number of biological and adoptive families, assessed by the same methods and examined for both a fairly strict and a generous criterion of non-right-handedness. For both criteria, the

TABLE 3.9

Incidences of Left-handedness in Families of Biological and Adoptive Parents

	Parents' Handedness							
	Right × Right		Left × Right		Right × Left		Left × Left	
	N	Left (%)	N	Left (%)	N	Left (%)	N	Left (%)
Stricter criterion								
Biologically related children	340	10.9	60	25.0	—*	—*	—*	—*
Adoptive children	355	13.5	53	11.3	—*	—*	—*	—*
More generous criterion								
Biologically related children	194	46.9	170	52.9	39	71.8	—*	—*
Adoptive children	228	45.6	145	53.1	42	45.2	—*	—*

Note: Data from Carter-Saltzman (1980).
* Not given as N small.

trends in the biologically related families resemble those of previous studies. For adoptive families, there is no significant increase with increasing parental sinistrality in the proportion of left-handed or not completely right-handed children. This study is of major importance in ruling out the possibility that the increased proportions of left-handers in L × R and L × L families are due to experiences associated with being reared by a left-handed parent.

From the data on handedness in families in Table 3.6 it was clear that hand usage is not specifically taught or acquired by imitation of parents, in most cases, since some 80% of all left-handers in the population are born to R × R parents, and the children of L × L parents include more right- than left-handers. Levy (1976) reviewed several sources of evidence that showed that hand preferences could not be due only to "cultural conditioning". These include the observations of structural asymmetries of the brain (Section 3.3.2) that are present from fetal life and several asymmetries of posture and perceptual sensitivity that can be observed in the newborn. Such early asymmetries, though unlearned, may still not be of genetic origin unless it can be shown that they differ in families. One characteristic mentioned by Levy (1976) that is inherited, laid down early in fetal life, and associated with handedness is finger-print pattern. There are very small but statistically significant differences between right- and left-handers in the distribution of certain patterns (Rife, 1955, 1978). This demonstrates some genetic influence on handedness. Eye preferences (Section 12.1), of which most of us are unaware and which in most people are unlikely to be influenced by specific training, are correlated with hand preferences. Eye preferences may show some correlation between relatives (Merrell, 1957; Table 12.3).

Asymmetries of the skull vary in left-handers according to the presence or absence of left-handed relatives. Table 3.10 shows the findings of LeMay (1977) for left-handers who were the only left-handers in their families, and those who reported sinistral relatives. Comparison with Table 3.4 shows that the left-handers without left-handed relatives were intermediate between right-handers and left-handers with left-handed relatives, in percentages having right frontal and left occipital petalia. Chui and Damasio (1980) have not confirmed this distinction, but their number of left-handers with a left-handed relative was too small for effective comparison.

TABLE 3.10

Asymmetries of the Skull in Left-Handers With and Without Left-Handed Relatives: Percentages Showing Protrusions of the Frontal and of the Occipital Bones on Each Side

	Frontal			Occipital		
	↑L	=	↑R	↓L	=	↓R
Sinistral relatives absent (N = 39)	28	21	51	59	15	26
Sinistral relatives present (N = 41)	41	24	34	29	32	39

Note: Based on LeMay (1977).

3.5 SUMMARY

There is no clear evidence available as to hand preferences in fossil hominids. To the extent that structural asymmetries of the brain in modern man are associated with handedness, the evidence for similar structural asymmetries in hominids suggests that these precursors of modern man included more right- than left-handers. Evidence from early artefacts, works of art, and biblical references to sinistrality give no indications of a time when the distribution of human handedness differed from the modern pattern.

No associations have been discovered between hand preferences and asymmetries of the circulation or internal organs. *Situs inversus* is independent of handedness and of twinning. There are associations between hand preference and the functional asymmetry of the brain for speech, but the nature of this asymmetry is unclear. Similarly, there are associations between anatomical asymmetries of the brain and handedness, but these also are not close. Whereas groups of right-handers show characteristic biases (which are not present in all right-handers as individuals), groups of left-handers show reduced or absent biases. The incidence of left-handedness is higher in the families of left-handed parents than of right-handed parents, for biological but not for adoptive families. Several versions of the theory that left-handedness is due to a recessive gene have been proposed, but none is fully satisfactory. Twins pose a particular problem for genetic theories of handedness as the combinations of right- and left-handed MZ and DZ twin pairs are close to those expected by chance. There are several indications of a genetic influence on handedness, but the nature of this influence is obscure.

4 Questions About the Development of Handedness

This chapter continues the search for the causes of handedness begun in Chapter 3. There can be no absolute divisions between types of cause, as discussed in Chapter 1, but whereas Chapter 3 looked at the possible origins of handedness in structural and antecedent asymmetries, this chapter asks whether left- and right-handedness can be associated with influences on the process of development.

4.1. HOW EARLY DO ASYMMETRIES ASSOCIATED WITH HANDEDNESS APPEAR?

The prenatal physical asymmetries of the planum temporale and of finger-print patterns have been mentioned in Chapter 3. Another prenatal asymmetry occurs in the direction of the spiral of the umbilical cord. Malcolm and Pound (1971) found in 100 consecutive deliveries that the cord rotated anticlockwise in 81 and clockwise in 10, and it changed direction in 9. Subsequent follow-up studies of these children found no association between direction of umbilical spiral and handedness (Pound—personal communication).

The earliest observable asymmetry that might be called behavioural is the orientation of the head at birth. Among births with the usual head-first (vertex) presentation, about 58% of fetal occiputs present towards the mother's left and about 42% to the mother's right (Myles, 1972). Churchill, Igna, and Senf (1962) reported a consecutive series of deliveries in a Detroit hospital where birth position was recorded, and the children were invited for follow-up examination at 2 years of age. Those with presentations other than occiput anterior and any with abnormal neurological signs were omitted. Handedness was assessed by asking the child to pick up and throw a ball several times, the examiner being unaware of the birth information. Data for the cohort of 1102 cases, of whom 54.4% were born left occiput anterior (LOA), are given in Table 4.1. The majority of children born in either orientation became right-handed, but there is a statistically significant association between birth position and handedness ($\chi^2 = 14.224$, $df = 2$, $p < .001$—my calculation). Of 836 right-handed children, 42.7% were born ROA, whereas of 93 left-handed children 62.4% were born in this position; of 173 ambidexters, 49.1% were born ROA. The left-handedness of these children was unlikely to be due to brain damage at birth, as the births were under expert supervision and any neonates with abnormal signs were treated separately. Studies of birth position in children with focal motor epilepsy (Churchill, 1966) and children with hemiplegia and epilepsy (Churchill, 1968) found that in those with epilepsy the side of the brain lesion was more often opposite the side of presentation. In hemiplegics without epilepsy, lesion laterality and side of presentation were not related. This last negative evidence should warn us to beware of simplistic assumptions about the role of birth stress in the causes of handedness (Section 4.3). In another study of normal birth position and handedness, 62% of 21 left-handed and ambidextrous children were also found to present with occiput to the right (Grapin & Perpère, 1968).

When the newborn infant is placed supine, the head tends to turn to one side, with the arm and leg on that side extended, whereas the opposite arm and leg are flexed. This attitude, referred to as the tonic neck reflex (t.n.r.) by Gesell and Ames (1947) was found partially predictive of later handedness. Their data for 19 infants is given in Table 4.2, in which I have classified any

TABLE 4.1
Distribution of Handedness of Two-Year-Old Children Born With the Left or Right Occiput Anterior

Handedness	Position at Birth					
	LOA		ROA			
	N	%	N	%	N	Total %
Right	479	79.6	357	71.4	836
Both	88	14.6	85	17.0	173
Left	35	5.8	58	11.6	93
Total	602		500		1102

Note: Based on Churchill, Igna, and Senf (1962).

TABLE 4.2

Neonatal Head Orientation and Hand Preference at 5 to 10 Years

Head Orientation	Handedness			
	Left	Mixed	Right	Total
Right	—	1	6	7
Mixed	—	2	1	3
Left	4	2	3	9

Note: After Gesell and Ames (1947).

child described as "R or L" at 5 or 10 years as "mixed". All the right-head turning infants became either right- or mixed-handed, and about a half of the left-turning infants became left-handed.

Michel (1981) observed 150 infants 16 to 48 hours after birth for head orientation and followed up 10 strongly left-biased and 10 strongly right-biased infants for voluntary reaching at about 22 weeks. Table 4.3 shows the distribution of neonatal head orientation preference. About two thirds showed the head-right bias, and a substantial proportion were not clearly biased to either side. The rightward bias was stronger in females than in males. At 22 weeks, only 1 of the 10 right-biased infants was more likely to reach with the left than the right hand, and only 2 of the strongly left-biased infants were more likely to reach with the right hand than with the left. Michel (1981; Michel and Goodwin, 1979) argued that head orientation in infancy is a cause of hand preference, since the infant is more likely to see the hand that is extended on the same side and hence likely to develop better visuomotor co-ordination on that side.

Greater auditory and tactile sensitivity on the right than the left side in most infants has been shown to be related to head orientation, as these

TABLE 4.3

Distribution of Neonatal Head-Orientation Preference

	Head Orientation Preference			
	Right or Right-Bias (%)	Mixed (%)	Left or Left-Bias (%)	N
Males	56.8	27.2	16.0	81
Females	73.9	13.0	13.0	69
Total	64.7	20.7	14.7	150

Note: After Michel (1981).

asymmetries are abolished if the infant's head is held in the midline for 15 minutes before testing (Turkewitz, 1977). The question whether head orientation bias is caused by head position at birth was investigated by observation of infants born by Caesarian section. Turkewitz (1977) found a distribution of neonatal head biases like that of normally born infants. He then suggested that both head position at birth and in the neonatal period might be caused by position in utero. This possibility has not been tested in humans, but relations between uterine position and paw preference have been studied in rats, with negative results (Section 9.2).

The quest of psychologists for the causes of human behaviours in their earliest manifestations was discussed in Chapter 1. In the case of head turning in the neonatal period, a genetic influence may be involved: Liederman and Kinsbourne (1980) have shown that a rightward bias in newborns was present in infants with two right-handed parents, but that infants with one non-right-handed parent were not systematically biased to either side; there was a similar lack of bias in the infants with a non-right-handed father as in those with a non-right-handed mother, suggesting that whatever is transmitted from one generation to the next is unlikely to depend on the maternal cytoplasm (Section 3.2) or on conditions in utero. Whether or not this genetic bias is confirmed, it is not impossible that head orientation in the early weeks of life contributes to the development of hand preferences, but it is unlikely to be a primary cause. The structural asymmetries of the skull (Section 3.3.2) suggest that gravity may be sufficient to make an infant's head turn to the right if the left occiput is protruding.

Studies of the infant's use of the hand in the first year have not led to any clear conclusions about the development of handedness. Perhaps this was to be expected from consideration of the anatomy and development of the motor system (Section 2.2). Darwin noted that the hand first able to reach successfully was not necessarily the one ultimately preferred (cited in Harris, 1980a). Gesell and Ames's (1947) description of their data is too vague to bear close examination; their conclusion that there are alternating stages of dextral, sinistral, and bilateral hand use is difficult to understand, as their graphs show predominantly right-handed reaching from 40 weeks of age. Their stage account appears like a hardy perennial in the literature but should be rooted out as thoroughly misleading. Young's (1977) re-examination of published data on early hand use led him to conclude that the right hand was the more active at most periods and that supposed trends to left-handedness were not substantial.

An analysis of the reaching of infants at 17 to 40 weeks of age distinguished several kinds of movement (Bresson, Maury, Pieraut-Le Bonniec, & Schonen, 1977). When both hands approached a target, the left sometimes arrived first to touch the support on which the object was presented, while the right hand then approached the object directly. This suggests that the left hand may have a localising function, whereas the right hand grasps. Ramsay (1980) observed infants holding the base of a toy with the nonpreferred hand while the preferred hand attempted to manipulate. It was usually clear that one hand was the more active (Ramsay, 1979). Insufficient analysis of the differing roles of the two hands may have led to the emphasis on bilaterality in accounts of the hand use of infants. Some infants are predominantly dextral or sinistral from 6 to 7 months of age (personal observation). Part of the confusion in accounts of infant handedness may be due to lack of recognition of the variability of handedness at all ages. About one third of adults have mixed hand preferences (Section 13.1). Uncertainty in some infants does not imply bilaterality in all.

4.2.   IS HANDEDNESS A PRODUCT OF TRAINING?

Questions about the role of training in the development of hand preference have usually been approached either from an environmentalist or from a nativist stance. Neither extreme position will do, and we must try to reach some understanding of the interaction of nature and nurture in the development of hand preference.

The suggestion that hand preferences are due to early handling by mothers and nurses has been attributed to Plato, but the source of this attribution is uncertain (Harris, 1980a). The belief that hand preferences must arise from early training, either unwitting or deliberate, in the behaviour of nurses, parents, and teachers, agrees with the environmentalist *zeitgeist* that has dominated most of twentieth-century psychology, psychoanalytic and behaviourist alike. The contrasting view, that hand preferences depend on "natural" or inborn predispositions assumes that the effect of training is to force natural left-handers to adopt dextral habits, as demanded by social convention. Assumptions about "shifted sinistrals" have played an important part in theories of the genetics (Section 3.4.1) and the neurology (Chapter 7) of laterality.

The extreme environmentalist view, that all hand preferences are due to social pressures, is exemplified by John Watson (1924, cited in Harris, 1980a). Watson concluded from his own research on infants that there are no fixed preferences until, "Society ... steps in and says, 'Thou shalt use thy right hand.' ... We force it to eat with the right hand. This is a potent enough conditioning factor to account for handedness." (Watson, in Harris, 1980a).

Two main questions follow from the theory that hand preferences are entirely arbitrary before social conditioning occurs. First, why has every human society chosen the right hand, and, second, why are there left-handers? On the question why all societies choose the right hand, Watson speculated about *physical* influences, such as the position of the fetus in utero and the weight of the liver. If physical factors such as these influence handedness, they must affect individuals within societies and offer a source of behavioural differences. Watson also speculated whether our primitive ancestors *learned* to carry their shields on their left arm and hurl their spears with the right, since they observed that those who did so were more likely to come back bearing their shields than being borne on them. Thus Watson adapted the famous musing of Thomas Carlyle, who noted in 1871, "Why that particular hand was chosen is a question not to be settled, not worth asking except as a kind of riddle; probably arose in fighting; most important to protect your heart and its adjacencies, and to carry the shield in that hand." (Cited in Harris, 1980a.) I had always assumed that Carlyle had in mind a mechanism akin to evolutionary selection, which might have a genetic basis, rather than observational learning. However, Carlyle's speculation is not very helpful on either interpretation as, as has been pointed out many times, the heart is only slightly to the left of the midline, and a wound on the right is as likely to be fatal as one on the left. Further, right-handedness is more common in modern females than males (Section 4.4).

The question of why there are left handers is answered neither by the primitive warfare theory, nor by the pure conditioning theory. If preferences depend only on social training, then left-handedness becomes a form of deviance. Burt (1937), whose long chapter on left-handedness has been extremely influential, especially in the field of education, reported that his case summaries of left-handed children often included descriptions such as stubborn, wilful, contra-suggestible or "just cussed". "Even left-handed girls ... often possess a strong, self-willed and almost masculine disposition" (Burt, 1937). Burt recognised, however, that these character traits could be the result of having to put up with constant corrections of hand use, rather than being the cause of left-handedness. An extreme form of the social deviance view was taken by the American psychiatrist Abram Blau (1946) who argued that, "Sinistrality is ... nothing more than an expression of infantile negativism and falls into the same category ... as contrariety in feeding and elimination."

An extreme version of the "natural" theory, which said that training has no effect on hand preferences, would be untenable since there are differences in incidences of left-handedness between cultures and between generations within cultures, which are most probably due to variations in social pressures. Less than 1% of Japanese school-children were reported by Komai and Fukuoka (1934) to use the left hand for writing, but incidences of left-handed throwing, cutting with scissors, striking a match, and kicking a football (5–8.5%) were comparable to those found for English children today (Chapter 10). Chinese children were found to use the left hand rarely for eating (1.5%) or writing (.7%) in Taiwan but more often (6.5%) in the United States (Teng, Lee, Yang, & Chang, 1976). A population sample of parents and children in Hawaii is especially interesting because differences in incidences of left-handed writing were found between parents of different ethnic origin (Japanese versus European) but not between their children, presumably because of an easing of social sanctions against left-handedness in Japanese families living in Hawaii (Ashton, 1982).

A difference between generations, with more left-handers among children than parents, has been found in all studies of the families of university students (Tables 3.6 and 16.7). It was also found for both ethnic groups in Ashton's (1982) sample, which was not university-based. A questionnaire given to Londoners attending a dental hospital for treatment found about 10% left-handed writers in younger respondents (15–44 years) but only about 3% in older respondents (55–64 years) (Fleminger, Dalton, & Standage, 1977). Burt (1937) reported incidences of 3–4% in his studies of 1913 and 1923, at about the time the older Londoners were at school.

Studies of trends in adult populations in the United States (Porac, Coren & Duncan, 1980) and in Australia (Brackenbridge, 1981) have documented falling incidences of left-handedness with increasing age. All of these studies were cross-sectional, examining different individuals in different age groups (as opposed to longitudinal study of the *same* individuals as they grow older). When Porac, Coren and Duncan (1980) say that hand preferences "become" more right-sided over the adult life span, it is surely not being implied that adults switch the writing hand. Searches for evidence of changing incidences with age in school samples have found no evidence for such changes (Annett, 1970b; Hardyck, Goldman, & Petrinovich, 1975; Roszkowski, Snelbecker, & Sacks, 1980; see Sections 17.1.1 and 20.1). There is no evidence that the hand used for writing is changed, once this skill has been well established. It has been suggested that the difference between generations in incidence of left-handedness could arise if there were differential mortality of left-handers (Brackenbridge, 1981), but there seems to be no direct evidence for this suggestion (but see Section 19.4). This review has shown marked variations of incidence of left-handedness between cultures and generations for actions such as writing and eating, which are subject to social constraints, but the constraint seems to operate at the time the child learns the activity. There is no reason to suppose that people become more often right-handed for specific actions such as writing once the skills have been learned.

If children are studied while in the process of learning, there is a sense in which they might be said to become more right- (or left-) handed with increasing age. Hand preferences can only develop in the context of the individual's experience of using the hands to grasp, pull, shake, and throw, and to use spoons, hammers, and pens. Some of the confusing reports of alternating left, right, and bilateral stages in early childhood discussed in the last section probably depended on observations of children who were in the process of discovering how to perform certain actions and who were not certain which hand would "feel best." When children first use new toys and tools, some may try with one hand and then with the other. After increasing practice it is probable that one hand will come to be preferred, so that the child appears consistent where he formerly appeared inconsistent. Unusually high incidences of "mixed" handedness reported for some groups of children are probably a function of lack of experience of the activities tested, rather than a true mixture of preferences. In the sense that hand preferences have to be discovered through use, they must be a function of experience, and the number of actions for which one hand is preferred may well increase with age.

The key question for theories of the causes of hand preference is whether there are constitutional biases for the use of one hand that are present *before* experiences of hand use begin. If there are such constitutional biases, can they be countermanded by forced practice with the nonpreferred hand? Experiments with mice allowed to reach with one paw only for food, in right-biased or left-biased worlds, found evidence of constitutional biases that predated the early experience and were not overridden by the forced practice (Collins, 1975; see Section 9.2). I believe that the evidence for humans points to the same conclusion.

To say that there may be a congenital basis for hand preference does not imply that there must be genes for right- or left-handed writing. It would be difficult to see how such genes could have evolved, as writing seems to have been invented only a few thousand years ago, and evidence of human right-handedness is very much older (Section 3.1). While learning to write, specific pressures may be placed on the child to use the right hand, and in this respect handedness is clearly influenced by training. But does it make sense to say that the training *causes* hand preference? It would make sense only if those forced to use the right hand for writing then found that the right hand had become superior for other unimanual actions. Among the left-handed parents in families I have personally examined there were some who were forced to learn to write with the right hand and continued to use that hand for writing; in all other actions they were strongly left-handed, and they were clearly superior with the left hand on a test of peg-moving skill. If handedness were simply a matter of training, individuals who had been trained successfully to use the right hand should have generalised this skill to other actions, and the right hand should have become more skilled than the left. That this did not happen after some 40 to 50 years shows that preference is not caused by the use of one hand for a highly skilled action such as writing.

The inference that differences in performance are due to differential training of the two hands seems to have been drawn from a study of typing skills. Provins and Glencross (1968) showed that trained typists type at least as fast, and perhaps faster, with the left hand than the right, while novice typists perform more quickly with the right than the left hand. It was concluded that, "The level of performance achieved by an individual in a motor task appears to depend on the extent of his training ... and in so far as the training of the two sides has been dissimilar, then the levels of performance achieved on the two sides are dissimilar" (Provins and Glencross, 1968). In typing, both hands have to work in synchrony, and there would be no point in the right hand racing ahead of the left; perhaps the training enables the left hand to reach an acceptable level of skill, but there is no certainty that the right hand (of right-handers) worked at its maximum rate.

Efforts to train the nonpreferred hand to equal the skill of the preferred hand have been made for peg moving and for repetitive tapping. The peg-moving task was practised by three subjects for 130 trials with each hand, spread over four weeks. Subjects became faster with both hands, but the difference between the hands was unchanged in two and reduced but by no means eliminated in the third (Annett, Hudson, & Turner, 1974). Peters (1976) practised tapping as fast as possible with the index finger of each hand, until both hands became equally fast. It took 1300 trials of 10 seconds each, performed over some 70 days. A further study of the effects of prolonged practice of finger tapping in 14 subjects found that while both hands improved, the relative difference between hands remained stable for most subjects (Peters, 1981). Forced practice can lead to considerable improvements in the performance of the weaker hand, but it does not change the underlying natural asymmetry.

4.3. IS HANDEDNESS A PRODUCT OF DEVELOPMENTAL PATHOLOGY?

In considering this question it is essential to make a basic distinction between "some" and "all". There can be no doubt that in *some* cases, hand usage is influenced by abnormal developmental events. Children suffering severe lesions involving the motor tracts on one side are obliged to use the better side for skilled actions. Their hand use can hardly be described as a "preference", as they have no choice. The effects of early brain lesions on intellectual development will be considered in Section 6.2.

Controversies about the pathological origins of sinistrality revolve around the possibility that *all* left-handedness is due to minimal brain damage, even when there is no other evidence of such lesion. This possibility will be considered first in relation to cases of probable brain lesion and second in normal samples.

4.3.1. The Effects of Early Brain Lesions on Hand Preference

To what extent is the incidence of left-handedness increased by early brain lesions that are not associated with specific motor weakness? Some epileptics have brain lesions of long standing, but in many the cause of the epilepsy is unknown. Bingley (1958) reviewed several studies that reported incidences of left-handedness of 14 to 18% in epileptics, in contrast to 8 to 9% in controls. Not all studies found an excess of left-handers in epileptics. In Bingley's (1958) series of 90 cases of temporal lobe epilepsy, the incidence was the same (6.7%) as for other cases operated for temporal lobe tumour (6.5%). In an unpublished study of adult epileptics, I found no evidence of an excess of left- or mixed-handers.

McManus (1980b) examined the relationship between hand preference and epilepsy in the 12,000 children of the National Child Development Survey (NCDS). All children born in England, Wales, and Scotland in one week in 1958 were included in a survey of perinatal mortality and subsequently followed up at 7 and 11 years of age. The records include the response of the mother to a question about the child's handedness for writing and also observations by the examining doctor of the child's hand use in throwing. No association was found between hand preference and epilepsy.

In one study a raised incidence of left-handedness was found in the relatives of epileptics (Steiner, 1911, cited in Bingley, 1958) which suggests the possibility that left-handedness might be one of the antecedents rather than one of the consequences of epilepsy. Annett (1973b) found recurrent epilepsy more frequent in right-hemiplegic children with a left-handed parent or sibling than in those without a close left-handed relative. Perhaps families liable to left-handedness are at a slightly greater risk of epilepsy. Another related alternative suggested by Trankell (cited in Bingley, 1958) is that the rate of manifestation of left-handedness is increased in certain populations. Trankell's genetic theory of handedness (Section 3.4.1) implied that over 50% of *ll* genotypes become phenotypic right-handers as a result of social pressures. Perhaps the effects of pressures towards dextrality are reduced in certain mildly abnormal populations, so allowing left-handedness to be more often expressed.

The other main subgroup of the population found to have a raised incidence of left-handedness is the mentally handicapped. Gordon (1921) found 18.2% children throwing with the left hand in schools for mental defectives in London, in comparison with 7.3% in normal schools. He attributed the increased proportion of left-handers to left-brain lesion in some cases, which produced both mental deficiency and a shift of hand preference to the other side. The view that the excess of left-handers in the mentally handicapped is a consequence of early pathology has been widely accepted (Brain, 1945).

Satz (1972, 1973) examined statistical aspects of assumptions concerning pathological handedness. Changes from left- to right-handedness can be expected, of course, as well as changes from right- to left-handedness, if pathology is a result of lesions of the cerebral motor cortex. It is important to notice that pathological right-handers would be a very small proportion of all right-handers, whereas pathological left-handers could form a much larger proportion of all left-handers. This inequality of proportion is due to the differing base rates of right- and left-handedness in the population. This difference has important consequences for the assessment of relationships between handedness and other characteristics (Chapter 5). Differences between groups of right- and left-handers might be due to the higher proportion of pathological cases in the latter. Hence, conclusions that seem to apply to *some* left-handers do not necessarily apply to *all*.

When Silva and Satz (1979) examined incidences of left-handedness in a population of mentally handicapped persons with abnormal EEG recordings, they found that left-handers were more likely to have left-hemisphere dysfunction than right-handers, as the pathological left-handedness hypothesis would predict. However, they also found a raised incidence of left-handedness in those with bilateral EEG dysfunction. Clearly, pathological left-handedness is not only associated with unilateral left-brain lesions. The raised incidence in bilateral cases is in accord with the possibility of a *changed manifestation rate* in certain developmental conditions, as suggested by Trankell (cited in Bingley, 1958).

4.3.2. Is All Left-Handedness Caused by Abnormalities of the Brain?

The argument that *all* left-handedness is pathological rests on the assumption that humans are naturally predisposed to left-hemisphere dominance for speech and control of the right hand, and that these characteristics are universal in humans in the same way that upright walking, the precision grip, and speech itself are human characteristics. All departures from the typical pattern would then depend on pathological distortions of growth. These pathologies need not be severe enough to give rise to frank neurological symptoms, but they might have involved "minimal brain damage" of a kind that has been associated with the concept of a continuum of reproductive casualty (Pasamanick & Knobloch, 1960). Bakan, Dibb, and Reed (1973) suggested that "left-handedness and ambilaterality may be added to this continuum as one of the minor effects of birth stress". Bakan (1971) reported that a higher proportion of left-handed male university students were born first or fourth plus than were born second or third. Arguing that first and late pregnancies carry a higher risk of birth stress and hence minimal brain damage, Bakan suggested that there is a relationship between left-handedness and neurological insult. There was no significant association between left-handedness and birth order in female students in Bakan's original report. Hubbard (1971) replied to Bakan with a report of a larger student sample, in which there was a mildly significant tendency in the opposite direction, more left-handers being second- and third-born than first or fourth plus. In the same year, another student survey found no relationship between birth order and left-handedness (Gray, Hentschke, Isaac, Mead, Ozturk, Rieley, Smale, & Stern, 1971). These authors asked how many other negative findings remain unpublished, and how the scientific world is to be kept informed of the weight of negative evidence. This query is especially apposite for the handedness and birth-stress hypothesis since a large amount of journal space has continued to be devoted to this issue. The great majority of findings are negative, but any trends in the positive direction are given disproportionate attention.

Positive support claimed by Bakan (1977) includes a study of university students who gave information by questionnaire on their own birth histories and handedness: 40% of left-handers and 41% of ambilaterals reported stressful births, in contrast to 22% of right-handers (Bakan, Dibb, & Reed, 1973). A report by Leviton and Kilty (1976) supporting Bakan's hypothesis gave insufficient details of the sample, and since some 60 to 70 left-handers were divided between four birth order categories, numbers within groups were almost certainly inadequate for statistical test.

Negative evidence after the initial studies cited above includes those of Schwartz (1977), Hicks, Pellegrini, and Evans (1978), Dusek and Hicks (1980), Searleman, Tsao, and Balzer (1980) and Tan and Nettleton (1980). An especially powerful test of the birth order effect was made in Taiwan on 2101 elementary–school-children whose birth orders could be classified from 1 to 9; the mean laterality quotients of the 534 children who were first-born and 21 children who were ninth-born were identical, and there were no significant trends in the data (Teng, Lee, Yang, & Chang, 1976). McManus (1981) analysed the data for over 12,000 children in the British National Child Development Sample. There were no significant effects for birth order in children of either sex. A very large number of variables associated with the state of the mother and that of the infant were examined for differences in handedness, and the very few found to be associated with higher incidence of left-handedness in the child should be regarded as chance effects when so many variables were examined.

A prospective study of 1094 children born in Manchester in 1971 examined relationships between birth conditions and handedness (Smart, Jeffery, & Richards, 1980). There were no effects for birth order. Of the many variables tested, only two gave small positive findings. These were, first, that in 15 boys delivered by breech, 6 (40%) were classified as non-right-handers, in comparison with 19% of children with vertex and 13% of children with caesarian delivery; the difference is barely significant statistically. In the NCDS survey, breech presentations were recorded for 82 males and 121 females, and in neither sex was the incidence of left-handedness elevated (McManus, 1981). The other finding in the Smart sample concerned children of 21 mothers who had their first-born child at 39 years or older; 9 (43%) of the children were non-right-handed. In the NCDS survey there were no significant effects for maternal or paternal age (McManus, 1981).

Coren and Porac (1980) distributed 10,000 questionnaires on hand, eye, and foot preference, with questions about birth order, maternal age, and birth stress; the latter questions were addressed to the mothers of college-age students. The response rate was 28%. Of the many comparisons made, there was a small effect of maternal age in males but not females and a small effect of birth stress, again in males only (both effects significant at the 5% level). Will these small positive findings among a mass of negative findings, in a sample liable to unknown volunteer effects, keep alive this issue?

Two factors that must be considered in relation to the birth stress hypothesis are socioeconomic status and the association of left-handedness in families. The risks of perinatal mortality and of birth complications are higher in families of low socioeconomic status. Bakan (1977) argued that some of the failures to replicate his findings could be due to lack of control of this variable. In the NCDS survey there were no significant differences in the proportion of left-handed children between social classes 1 to 5 for either sex. Leiber and Axelrod (1981b) examined data for 1869 undergraduates and 762 university faculty members in relation to the birth-stress hypothesis; the only significant birth order effect was in the direction contrary to that expected, and in females only. Parents of students were classified for educational level and also for occupational level. Among *parents* of higher educational and occupational levels, incidences of left-handedness were higher than in parents of lower levels, but parental level did not affect the incidence of left-handedness in the students.

To account for the association of left-handedness in families, Bakan, Dibb, & Reed (1973) suggested, "Perhaps the familial tendency to left handedness is mediated by a familial tendency to birth stress." Annett and Ockwell (1980) considered this possibility in a series of personally visited families of left-handed and right-handed parents. If left-handers are more likely to experience stress in giving birth, left-handed mothers should report more stressful births for their children than right-handed mothers. On the contrary, left-handed mothers reported stressful births for 23% of their children and right-handed mothers for 30%. Other analyses for birth order and birth stress in this sample gave no substantial support for the pathology hypothesis.

In addition to these several empirical tests of the association between handedness and perinatal variables, the hypothesis that all left-handedness is a result of left hemisphere pathology can be regarded as unlikely on other grounds. First, the hypothesis implies that right-hemisphere speech laterality only occurs as an abnormal condition. The alternative view, that right-hemisphere speech occurs as a natural variant, is strengthened by the occurrence of dysphasias following acute *right*-sided brain lesions suffered as war wounds by young service men (Conrad, 1949; Russell & Espir, 1961). Although it cannot be proved that their brains had not suffered minimal early damage sufficient to alter speech laterality, there is no ground for believing that they had done so. Second, left-handedness occurs as a natural variant in man's primate cousins (Section 9.2); to say that left-handedness is always pathological in man implies that this natural primate variation was lost in man and then re-introduced as pathological variation. It is more economical to assume that handedness varies naturally in all primates. Third, reports of birth stress are most common for first-borns, and yet first-borns have higher average IQs than later-born children (Bee, 1981). A fourth reason for doubting that left-handedness is caused by birth stress is the possibility that some slightly greater difficulty might be experienced in the birth of a fetus that does not adopt the typical left occiput anterior (LOA) position, and it was shown that children who were left-handed at 2 years of age were less likely to have presented in the LOA position than right-handers (Section 4.1). Thus it is possible that the potential left-hander is a little less likely to adopt the most advantageous position at birth. The observation of Barnes (1975) that left-handers were a little slower to establish regular breathing immediately after birth may be due, as she suggested, to some characteristic of the nervous system of the potential left-hander rather than that left-handedness is caused by damage consequent on cerebral hypoxia. Respiratory distress was not associated with increased incidence of sinistrality in the NCDS sample (McManus, 1981). Finally, left-handers are often found among those with the highest levels of achievement in the arts, music, sport, and theatre (Barsley, 1966). The proposition that all these people suffered early brain damage, however minimal, seems most implausible.

4.4.   SEX DIFFERENCES IN HAND PREFERENCE

Reports of incidences of left-handedness that distinguish sex usually, but not always, find a higher incidence in males than in females. Table 4.4 lists incidences for several samples with numbers exceeding 1000 for each sex. Several samples are not included in the table because information was not obtained in the same way for each sex. (For example, the assessment of females in the filial generation of Chamberlain, 1928, presumably relied on the reports of student brothers, while the filial males included a large proportion giving self-report.) The table shows a larger proportion of lef-

TABLE 4.4

Incidences of Left-Handedness in Males and Females in Large Samples Where Both Sexes Were Assessed by the Same Method

	Males		Females			
	N	Left (%)	N	Left (%)	χ^2	p
School children						
Hardyck, Goldman, and Petrinovich (1975) California	3960	10.5	3728	8.7	7.25	<.01
National Child Development Survey U.K. (McManus, 1981)	6495*	12.8	6173*	9.6	31.84	<.001
Komai and Fukuoka (1934) Japan	9072	12.3	7875	10.6	12.02	<.001
Parents of Undergraduates						
Chamberlain (1928)	2177	4.2	2177	2.9	4.88	<.05
Annett (1973a)	3644	4.4	3644	3.7	2.21	NS
Undergraduates						
Annett (1973a)	2151	11.8	1493	11.4		NS

*Estimated from Ns given for parity in Table 8 in McManus (1981).

handed males than females in all studies, but the differences were small in absolute size and not significant in undergraduates, when both sexes were students who completed their own questionnaire (Annett, 1973a). In that same sample, when brothers and sisters were included, on the evidence supplied by the students, there were more male left-handers (11.3%) than female left-handers (9.8%) ($\chi^2 = 4.48$, $df = 1$, $p < .05$). Other samples have found small but statistically significant sex differences when the data were transformed into laterality quotients (Bryden, 1977; Longstreth, 1980; Old-field, 1971). When the small absolute size of the differences between the sexes in Table 4.4 is noted, it will be readily understood that in smaller samples (hundreds rather than thousands) the sex difference may be statistically insignificant, absent, or even reversed. However, there can be no reasonable doubt that males are more likely to be left-handed than females, but by a small margin.

In her survey of 11- to 12-year-old Glasgow school-children, Clark (1957) noticed a curious sex difference in the association between left-handedness in children and parents. In her sample of 330 children there were approximately equal numbers having a left-handed father and a left-handed mother; but of 32 strongly left-handed children, 5 had a left-handed mother and none had a left-handed father. Falek (1959) noticed that in his small sample of personally visited families there was a higher proportion of left-handed children in families with a left-handed mother (37.5%) than in families where the left-handed parent was the father (12.8%). Table 4.5 summarises the findings for this comparison for five studies with large Ns in each group. The trend is consistent though not always statistically significant. This trend was not found by Carter-Saltzman (1980) in her biological families, but Ns were smaller.

Sex differences in families are more complicated if the sex of children is taken into account. The stronger effect of maternal left-handedness on children's handedness was more noticeable for daughters than sons in several sets of data (Annett, 1973a; Chamberlain, 1928; Rife, 1940) but not in that of McGee and Cozad (1980). (Leiber and Axelrod, 1981a, did not differentiate sex of children.) It would be wrong to conclude that left-handedness in the father has *no* effect on the handedness of daughters, but it seems to have a lesser effect on daughters than sons and a lesser effect than left-handedness in the mother on children of *both* sexes. An interaction between sex of parent and sex of child was noted in two studies that presented the data in terms of laterality quotients rather than incidences (Hicks & Kinsbourne, 1976; Longstreth, 1980). Further analyses of the distribution of handedness for sex of parents and sex of children are given in Section 16.3.

TABLE 4.5

Comparison of Left-Handed Fathers and Left-Handed Mothers for Percentages of Left-Handed Children

| | Sinistral Parent | | | |
| | Father | | Mother | |
	No. Children	Left-Handed Children (%)	No. Children	Left-Handed Children (%)
Chamberlain (1928)	268	9.7	196	13.8
Rife (1940)	99	18.2	75	21.3
Annett (1973a)	308	14.0	288	28.5
McGee and Cozad (1980)	261	29.5	214	34.1
Leiber and Axelrod (1981a)	212	16.0	132	22.0

4.5.   SUMMARY

Behavioural asymmetries associated with later hand preference can be found from birth, in the orientation of the fetal head in the birth canal and in the tendency of most infants to lie with the head facing towards the right side.

These asymmetries, and reaching in the first year, are correlated with but not fully predictive of later hand preference.

Cultural pressures against sinistrality may greatly reduce the incidence of left-hand use for socially monitored actions such as writing and eating, but for actions under lesser social control incidences of left-handedness are similar between cultures. There is no evidence that forced use of the right hand leads to greater relative skill in that hand. Practice of specific tasks may lead to greater skill in both hands, but it is difficult for most people to reduce the difference between hands. Smaller incidences of left-handed writing in older than younger age groups are probably mainly due to the gradual easing of cultural pressures towards right-handedness.

Some left-handedness is probably due to developmental pathology. Some of these developmental pathologies may be of the left motor cortex, but more generalised abnormal influences on development also lead to increased incidences of sinistrality. The argument that *all* left-handedness is of pathological origin has generated a very large literature. It is supported by weak trends in a few studies, which seem to outweigh in the psychological imagination the substantial mass of negative evidence. There are very good theoretical as well as empirical grounds for rejecting the view that pathology is a main cause of left-handedness.

There are sex differences in the incidence of left-handedness that are small but consistent and statistically significant in large samples. There are reports also of sex differences in the association of left-handedness between relatives.

Considering developmental influences on handedness as a whole, it seems that the expression of left- and right-handedness can be modified by factors associated with sex, physical disruptions of normal development, and training for socially significant actions. All these effects are relatively slight and do not change the general pattern of a majority of right-handers and a minority of left-handers.

5
Questions About the Psychological Implications of Handedness

The last two chapters have investigated the origins and development of left- and right-handedness. This chapter asks whether right- and left-handedness have implications for other aspects of human performance—for language, motor skills, intelligence, or personality. These questions could be interpreted as questions about what handedness "causes" rather than what it "is caused by". However, recalling the discussion in Chapter 1 of the concept of balanced polymorphism, it must be remembered that if there are any detectable differences between handedness groups, these could be "causes" in the sense of promoting the persistence of certain genes in the population. This chapter examines the evidence for associations between handedness and a variety of characteristics, trying to avoid presumptions about what is "cause" and what is "effect". The possibility that handedness variation could be associated with certain differences but not be the cause of those differences is an important point to bear in mind.

5.1.   THE DEVELOPMENT OF LANGUAGE

5.1.1. Speech Disorders

The discovery that most people depend on the left hemisphere for speech and other language functions led very soon to speculation about the role of the right hemisphere and whether reversed or mirror image traces of letters might be established in the two hemispheres (Ireland, 1881, cited in Harris, 1980a). If there are competing "centres" in each of the two hemispheres, perhaps some problems of language development such as confusions between letters and their mirror images, mirror writing, and stuttering might be a result of the failure of one side to dominate the other. In the 100 years since Ireland's speculation, there have been innumerable further speculations and research enquiries on this theme, without any clear answer to the original question being found. Rather it seems as if the original questions are being posed again and again and with some changes in method of enquiry but little tangible progress.

The report of Ballard (1911–1912, cited in Harris, 1980a) that stuttering was four times as common in "dextro–sinistrals" as in other children led to a theory that has become part of current popular wisdom that stuttering can be caused by forcing a naturally left-handed child to write with the right hand. In my visits to families of right- and left-handed parents I was asked about the relationship between stuttering and handedness more often than any other topic. One left-handed mother told me that she had been *forced to use her left hand* for writing at school because her teachers noticed she had some left-handed tendencies and were anxious she should not stutter. She was of the opinion that she should have used her right hand, and on the peg-moving measure of hand skill she was about equally fast with both hands. The hypothesis of a link between handedness and stuttering was elaborated by Travis in the 1920s and 1930s, but negative findings led him to abandon the hypothesis in the 1940s (Beech & Fransella, 1968; Travis, 1959).

What have surveys of children with speech difficulties shown about incidences of left- and mixed-handedness? Morley (1957) reported tests of the hand, eye, and foot preferences of some 600 children with a variety of speech difficulties in comparison with a control group of similar size. The incidences of left- and mixed-handedness were 6% and 8%, respectively, in controls, whereas the corresponding incidences in 362 stutterers were 11% and 9%. The differences are small in absolute values, but highly significant statistically given such large numbers of cases ($\chi^2 = 8.406$, $df = 2$, $p < .025$, my calculation). Morley found no increased left-handedness in children classified as dyslalic. In some other smaller groups of children there were higher incidences of sinistral preferences, but these were groups where neurological complications would be probable.

Ingram (1959a) studied laterality in 80 children classified as having "specific developmental disorders of speech" (that is, excluding cases where the problem was attributable to any other disorder) and found that about half were not consistently right-sided, in contrast to 22% of controls. The sex ratio in the children with speech disorder was 2.64 to 1 (boys to girls). Stutterers included many with inconsistent handedness (Ingram, 1959b). In an unpublished study I made in the early 1960s of children attending a clinic for speech therapy in Sheffield, the incidence of left-handedness was 13.2% in

53 stutterers and 5.7% in the rest of the 228 children. This difference is just short of statistical significance (on 2-tail but not on 1-tail χ^2 test).

This pattern of findings is typical of many others investigating the laterality of children with speech and reading problems—the incidence of left-handedness is about twice as high as in controls, but the absolute difference is not large enough to be *statistically* significant unless the number of cases is very large. But even if results are statistically significant, what *theoretical* significance could there be in an increase of left-handedness from about 6 to 12%? It is clear that stuttering and other developmental disorders of speech cannot be *caused* by left- and mixed-handedness, as there are many children with such speech problems who are consistently right-handed (and right-sided for eye and foot preference, too), and because there are many left- and mixed-handers in the general population who do not have developmental speech problems.

The belief that stuttering might be associated with anomalies of cerebral dominance was revived by Jones's (1966) report of four stutterers, ages ranging from 13 to 50 years, whose speech laterality was studied before brain operation by the intracarotid amytal technique. All were found to have bilateral speech, and after operation on one hemisphere stuttering ceased. A study of four further cases (Andrews, Quinn, & Sorby, 1972) by intracarotid amytal testing found three to have left-hemisphere and one bilateral speech representation. Since the latter is unusual (see Table 3.23), its presence in one case supports the hypothesis of bilaterality in stuttering, although not as dramatically as Jones's original report. Measurements of cerebral blow flow during stuttering speech in two individual stutterers found higher flows in Wernicke's area on the left and Broca's area on the right; when the stutterers were speaking normally under medication, higher flows in both of these cortical areas were on the left (Wood, Stump, McKeehan, Sheldon, & Proctor, 1980). If these observations are replicable in more stutterers, it will suggest that there might, indeed, be anomalies of cerebral control in stutterers. It is possible to make normal speakers stutter by delaying the auditory feedback of the speaker's voice. It seems possible, therefore, that stutterers could have a feedback problem if the self-produced feedback has to travel by the indirect route (via association areas—Section 2.1) from one hemisphere to the other. However, it would be premature to accept this explanation without further support.

5.1.2. Reading Difficulties

There are several confusions and controversies in the literature on reading difficulties and laterality, and we must make some important distinctions before attempting to assess possible relationships. The first main confusion concerns the children under discussion: Is it being suggested that *all* children who are slow to learn to read are more likely to be left- or mixed-handed (or eyed, or footed, or any mixture of these) or only a subgroup of slow learners who have been described as "congenitally word blind" or "dyslexic" (meaning "defective reading")? Is there such a syndrome as "dyslexia"? This question has been highly controversial. Some paediatricians and neurologists have recognised the syndrome, but most teachers have not. If there is a subgroup of poor readers meriting the label "dyslexia", is it sufficient for investigations of laterality to compare the best and poorest readers in school? Other confusions concern the assessment of laterality, a topic to be considered in detail later (Chapter 10). The point to be made here is that it does not matter, within wide limits, how laterality is assessed, provided a control group is assessed in the same way as the poor readers.

Reports of children who seem to have a specific disability in reading in spite of good intelligence, reasonable progress in other subjects like mathematics, and the usual educational opportunities for learning have been made since the turn of the century (Critchley, 1970b). Samuel Orton (1937) used a variety of tests of handedness, eyedness, and footedness on children referred to his clinic for developmental problems of language, and he was struck by the large proportion who were not consistently right-sided but showed varying degrees of "motor-intergrading". Orton elaborated the idea of confusions between the traces of symbols laid down in the two cerebral hemispheres as being the result of incomplete cerebral dominance. This theory would make the uncertainty of laterality a *cause* of the reading problem. Orton recognised that many children were consistently right-sided but noted that they often had left-handed relatives, and he had no doubt of a genetic influence on laterality. Children referred to clinicians for medical advice on delay in learning to read are likely to be highly selected; they are likely to belong to families with relatively high levels of academic performance, where brothers and sisters are doing well at school, and where the child's failure to learn to read is out of step with all reasonable expectations. Clinicians seeing such children have accepted for a long time that they have specific problems in learning to read.

Teachers and educational psychologists (Burt, 1937, Crabtree, 1976) were highly sceptical of the existence of "dyslexia". Among the very large number of slow readers in school whose problems range from slight delay to lifelong illiteracy, there seemed no ground for distinguishing a small select subgroup and giving them a probably pseudomedical label. This longstanding controversy has now been resolved by statistical analyses of the findings of large-scale surveys of reading progress and intelligence in general populations of school-children (Rutter, Tizard, & Whitmore, 1970; Rutter & Yule, 1975). When reading attainments were compared with those predicted from the child's age and IQ, a significant excess of poor readers was found in five epidemiological surveys. The children who were poor readers in relation to age and IQ, termed "specific reading retardates", were compared with children who were poor readers in relation to age but not in relation to IQ, termed "backward readers". They differed on several counts. The sex ratio differed such that there were 3.3 boys to 1 girl among the specific reading retardates and only 1.3 boys to 1 girl in the backward reading group. Signs of neurological disorder were more common in the backward readers, together with clumsiness and poorer performance on constructional tests (such as making shapes from matches). The groups also differed in educational progress as assessed at a follow-up examination 4 to 5 years after the initial assessment. The specific reading retardates had made *less* progress than the backward readers in reading and spelling, but they had made better progress than backward readers in an arithmetic-maths test. These findings demonstrate that the children with specific reading retardation were distinguishable from other backward readers on three sets of evidence—statistical, clinical, and prognostic (Rutter & Yule, 1975). There can be no further reasonable doubt that there are children with specific difficulties in learning to read among the many backward readers. Whether the term "dyslexia" or "specific reading retardation" should be applied to this subgroup is a matter for further dispute. The latter might avoid some of the controversies associated with the former, but it is clumsier to use. "Dyslexia" will be used below as a convenient short term for *specific* (not general) reading retardation.

If it is accepted that there is such a condition as "dyslexia", it can then be asked whether dyslexics include more left- and mixed-handers than nondyslexics. Among the 86 children with specific reading retardation identified by Rutter, Tizard, and Whitmore (1970) there were 8 (9.3%) classified as left-handers, whereas among 147 controls there were 7 (4.8%) left-handers. This difference was not statistically significant, and the authors concluded that laterality of hand and other preferences is not a significant variable in specific reading retardation (also in Rutter, 1978). As seen above for stuttering, the incidence of left-handedness was about twice as high in the group with reading delay as in controls, but the difference was not statistically significant for a relatively small number of cases.

Evidence as to whether there are more left- and mixed-handers among children with reading problems is conflicting. Reports finding a significant excess of non-right-handers almost invariably depend on samples carefully selected as exemplifying specific reading difficulties and excluding all cases where the delay might be due to identifiable causes. Hallgren (1950) found 18% of dyslexics and 9% of controls left-handed in Sweden. Naidoo (1972) also found 18% left-handers among children attending a Word Blind Clinic in London and 9% in controls. In a study in Paris, Granjon-Galifret and Ajuriaguerra (1951) found more clinic children than controls with mixed laterality in a younger (7–10 years) group but not in an older group (11–13 years). In a study of a large clinic sample in the United States Harris (1957) found more of the children with reading disabilities to be mixed-handed than controls. A study often cited as negative for laterality effects in poor readers is that of Belmont and Birch (1965). The comparison was made between 150 poor readers and 50 normal readers in Aberdeen schools. However, these children were not matched for intelligence, and it is not certain than the poor readers would have qualified for the label "specific reading retardate".

In contrast to the studies of clinic children, studies of children in the general school population do not find any association between reading progress and laterality. Clark (1970) described a complete population of 1544 Scottish children tested for reading progress at 7 years of age. The reading test scores of children classified for right, mixed, or left hand, eye, and foot use were almost identical. This finding demonstrates very clearly that lateral preferences cannot be used to predict reading progress in school. However, among 19 severely backward readers of normal intelligence studied further at 9 years of age, 15.8% were left-handed in contrast to 8.8% for the total sample. As in several instances, above, the incidence of left-handedness was about twice as high in the children with special language disability as in controls. There are several other studies that have classified normal school-children for laterality and then looked for differences in reading progress, with negative results (Lyle & Johnson, 1976; Richardson & Firlej, 1979; Stephens, Cunningham & Stigler, 1967; Zeman, 1967). Further, studies that have classified mentally retarded children for laterality and then compared the laterality groups for scholastic progress have found no differences (Capobianco, 1966).

The distinction made above between clinical and educational experience of dyslexia extends to the evaluation of laterality effects—none in the general school population and small but consistent trends in clinic samples. There is an apparent paradox here which the right shift theory offers to resolve. It is important to be clear at this point how the paradox arises. When children in the general (or retarded) school population are classified for handedness and tested for progress in learning to read, no differences are found. Annett and Turner (1974) examined a random sample of school-children selected according to birthday (Appendix I 9.b) and also all left-handed children in the same classes to give more than 100 right- and 100 left-handed children. There were no significant differences between the groups on several tests, including school assessment of reading progress. However, when children with reading quotients 30 points or more below their IQ on a vocabulary test were considered separately, they were found to be 6.1% of the right-handers and 15% of the left-handers. (As extra left-handers were included in the sample, the *numbers* of cases cannot be compared, but the percentages suggest that there could be an excess of left-handers among children identified as having a reading problem.) These findings are in accord with the possibility that one cannot argue from laterality to reading skill—but one can argue from poor reading skill to laterality (see further Section 18.1).

A parallel analysis was made by Porac and Coren (1981) for reading speeds in 1912 college entrants in Canada. No differences were found between the students when they were classified for laterality. (This can be inferred from the fact that most of Porac and Coren's analyses take this form, but none were reported for reading speed.) When the students ranked in the top and bottom 25% for reading speed were compared for handedness, the former included 8.1% and the latter 12.2% left-handers. The difference was small, but statistically significant for this large number of cases. There were no effects on either type of analysis for comprehension or vocabulary. It is worth noting that a difference for handedness was found for an aspect of speech production (reading speed) but not for comprehension or word knowledge (as in hemiplegic children in Section 6.2).

Hardyck (1977b) attempted to check the report of Annett and Turner (1974) using records of some 14 measures of scholastic attainment. There were no children with reading scores more than 1 SD below the mean in grades 1 to 3, so there was no group on which the specific hypothesis of an excess of left-handers among poor readers could be tested. Slow readers tend to remain poor spellers. Examination of Hardyck's tables suggests an excess of left-handers among children in grades 4 to 6 with spelling scores more than 2 SDs below the mean, and an excess of right-handers with spelling scores more than 2 SDs above the mean. The significance of this apparent difference cannot be evaluated, as the numbers of individuals at each extreme were not given. See Section 20.2 for further instance of the Annett and Turner effect, absence of difference in the general sample classified for laterality and presence of an effect for laterality in children classified for language disability.

What have previous theories suggested about the possible relevance of laterality to reading progress? Vernon (1957) reviewed the early literature on laterality in relation to backwardness in reading and concluded, "the relationship of all these (asymmetries) to cerebral dominance, or lack of cerebral dominance, is extremely obscure" but that, "it is of course possible that incomplete lateralization is a sign of a general lack of maturation in the development of cortical functions, which also affect reading". Recent proponents of the maturational theory of reading delay and uncertain laterality are Satz and Sparrow (1970), and Satz, Taylor, Friel, and Fletcher (1978). The idea that mixed- and left-handedness are signs of immaturity depends on the assumption that the incidence of right-handedness increases with increasing age. Sections 4.2, 17.1.1, and 20.1 find no evidence for this assumption.

5.2.   ABILITIES

5.2.1.   Motor Abilities

It is often said that we live in a right-handed world and that left-handers have an inherent disadvantage in using tools designed for right-handers. When right- and left-handers are compared on tasks in which levers or knobs have to be manipulated to control target displays, it is important to be sure that each handedness group has equal opportunity to move the controls in the preferred direction. For example, Bradley (1957) found right-handers more likely to turn knobs clockwise and to expect clockwise rotations to increase and counterclockwise relations to decrease the level of the variable controlled; left-handers did not show a clear directional preference. On a motor task reported by Davis, Wehrkamp, and Smith (1951) on which right-handers were faster than left-handers, the manipulations were all clockwise, which might have given the right-handers an advantage.

Chapanis and Gropper (1968) compared 32 right-handers and 32 left-handers in setting dials where movements had to be made in either direction, by either hand, and when the relationship between direction of turn and changes in display were either in accord or discord with the usual expectation (clockwise movements associated with display changes from left to right or upward, and anticlockwise movements with changes from right to left or downward). The errors made by right- and left-handers using each hand varied considerably with the differing display control relationships. Over-all there was not much difference between right- and left-handers in using their preferred hand. However, left-handers were considerably *better* than right-handers in using their nonpreferred hands. When the direction of display-control relationship was opposite to that generally expected, left-handers did better than right-handers with both hands, and right-handers did relatively better with their left hands than for the usual relationship. Annett and Sheridan (1973) also found that right-handers were better at using the left hand than the right hand when the display control relationship was reversed for moving a lever to control a visual display. Grant and Kaestner (1955) found that right-handers tracked right-to-left targets better than left-to-right targets and left-handers vice versa, but there was no over-all difference between them. Simon, De Crow, Lincoln, and Smith (1952) found no difference between right- and left-handers in tracking with a hand-wheel control.

Two studies of speed of writing by right- and left-handed children found no significant differences (Reed & Smith, 1962; Smith & Reed, 1959). Flowers (1975) compared right, left, and ambilateral handers (any mixture of preference for the left and right hands) on two tasks, one of visually controlled aiming between targets and one of rhythmical tapping. There were no differences between handedness groups for the nonpreferred hand on the aiming task and no difference for either hand on the tapping task. The one significant difference between groups was that ambilaterals were slower than consistent handers (right and left) with their preferred hand on the aiming task. Peters and Durding (1979) compared right- and left-handers for speed of tapping by each hand. The handedness groups were virtually identical for the preferred hand, but left-handers were significantly faster than right-handers with their nonpreferred hand.

Comparisons of right- and left-handers for hand control found no difference between groups for steadiness (Simon, 1964) or for capacity for independent finger movement by each hand (Parlow, 1978). Kimura and Vanderwolf (1970) found right-handers better than left-handers in tasks of independent finger movement in one experiment but did not confirm this difference in a second experiment.

In contrast to the above laboratory-based tasks, motor skills in sports performance can also be compared between handedness groups. Way (1958) asked whether women enrolled in college physical education programmes differ in motor ability between groups classified as mixed or consistent for hand, eye, and foot preferences. She reported the mixed group superior for skill in archery, bowling, badminton, and tennis. Porac and Coren (1981) collected questionnaire data on the hand, eye, and foot preferences of 2611 athletes in a variety of sports. They found, like Way, that athletes rated as in the top levels of proficiency differed from controls in being less consistently right-sided.

The analyses for particular sports must be interpreted cautiously, as the numbers of respondents for each sport were not given. Further, when nine comparisons were made for each of 15 sports, some differences at the 5% level of significance would be expected by chance, as Porac and Coren acknowledged. Comparisons for left- and right-sidedness of hand, foot, and eye found that the only advantage for a handedness group occurred for left-handed boxers. Advantages for eyedness were found to be left for basketball and gymnastics and right for bowling. Comparisons for mixed versus consistent preferences (for a questionnaire asking 4, 3, and 3 questions about hand, foot, or eye preference, respectively) and for crossed versus congruent preferences (for hand–foot, hand–eye, and foot–eye) found other significant effects. Very few of these were in favour of consistent sidedness (mainly shooting and racquet sports), and the remainder favoured *not* consistent sidedness (including baseball, basketball, soccer, field and ice hockey, and gymnastics).

5.2.2. Intellectual Abilities

Is there any evidence that left-handers differ from right-handers in general intelligence or in special abilities such as verbal, spatial, or numerical skills? If there are differences, are left-handers worse or better than right-handers in all or some of these skills? Before attempting to examine such questions, there is a quantity of preliminary ground to be cleared. What do psychologists mean by intelligence and by special abilities? Are special abilities uniformly distributed in the population, or do levels of relative ability (for instance verbal in comparison with visuospatial ability) differ between the sexes or between subgroups such as the subnormal and university undergraduates? If all left-handedness should turn out to be a result of early brain pathology, would it not be expected that all left-handers must have some disadvantage, perhaps slight but detectable in large samples, in comparison with right-handers? But if only *some* and *not all* left-handedness is a result of early pathology, it would be important to recognise that studies of school-children, for example, might find left-handers slightly less able than right-handers because of the undue influence of a few brain-damaged individuals.

With regard to the nature of intelligence and its component special abilities, we can adopt the useful and operational definition (even if some regard it as 'cynical) that "intelligence is what the tests measure". When large numbers of tests are administered to substantial samples of people and the common factors of the tests are explored through analyses of their intercorrelations, it has been shown many times that tests are broadly divisible into two main groups: those that are language-based and those that are not directly language-based. The latter are variously described as requiring spatial, mechanical, perceptual, visuospatial, or performance abilities. This broad division between two main types of intelligence (Butcher, 1968) and the construction of tests to reflect this division in the Verbal and Performance Scales of Wechsler (1941) and the Vocabulary and Progressive Matrices tests of Raven (1958a; 1958b) occurred long before general acceptance of the idea that these two types of intelligence might be differentially served by the two sides of the brain. Indeed, it might be suggested that the readiness of the psychological world to adopt the left brain/verbal and right brain/nonverbal formula depended on the prior existence of this verbal/spatial distinction through factor analysis. Once this conjunction of ideas was effected, it became a firmly fixed intellectual Gestalt. The left brain/verbal and right brain/spatial formula is probably grossly oversimplified—but have we tools to prize apart such an apparently self-evident combination? This question is mainly rhetorical but will be taken up later (Section 8.1). The main point to be made here is that the question of whether handedness groups differ in intelligence is usually asked in the form of whether left-handers are better or worse than right-handers in verbal and/or visuospatial abilities, although occasionally Full Scale Wechsler IQs are thrown in for good measure.

With regard to differences within the population, aside from handedness, it must be noted that there are differences between the sexes and between ability levels. Girls have an early advantage over boys in rate of language acquisition and verbal fluency (Hutt, 1972; Sherman, 1978). There does not seem to be any significant sex difference in verbal skill in adulthood (Wilson, De Fries, McClearn, Vandenberg, Johnson, & Rashad, 1975). Males almost invariably gain higher mean scores than females on tests of spatial reasoning from late childhood (Harris, 1978). This spatial advantage for males persists at least until age 50 years (Wilson et al., 1975). How these sex differences arise and how they should be interpreted in terms of psychological significance is in contrast to their statistical significance is controversial (Section 8.5). Relative advantages and disadvantages in verbal and spatial test performance differ also with overall level of intelligence. Among those who are classified as mentally handicapped on verbal tests, there are many who score in the normal range on nonverbal tests. At the other extreme of the ability range, students in higher education who are selected for high verbal intelligence are typically not quite so high on performance scale tests. Given these differences in patterns of test scores between the sexes and between levels of ability, there are many potential sources of ambiguity for studies of handedness.

During the 1960s, I collected several sets of data on the test scores of students and others in order to examine possible relationships between ability and handedness. This followed up a finding of Annett, Lee, and Ounsted (1961) that mixed-handed children with unilateral brain damage (EEG foci) had better-developed performance scale than verbal scale IQs (on the Wechsler Intelligence Scale for children, Wechsler, 1949). Annett (1959) had found that children's early explanations of conceptual relationships depended heavily on knowledge of the places where objects are to be found. Piaget's studies of the growth of number concepts (Piaget, 1952) showed that early reasoning was in terms of spatial extent. Further, Piaget's analysis of the growth of intelligence suggests that verbal and symbolic capacities grow from a basic sensorimotor knowledge of how to "perform" in the spatial world.

It seemed reasonable to suggest that nonverbal spatial knowledge might be an essential substrate for intellectual development. If there were any choice of developmental pathways in the specialisations of the two hemispheres, it seemed possible that nonverbal concepts would have priority over verbal ones. The idea that mixed-handers are heterozygotes who have such a choice of cerebral specialisation (Table 3.6) seemed in accord with the observations for children with EEG foci. Of course this was all highly speculative. I had no opportunity to replicate the original study with a further sample of epileptic children. The question I asked was whether a similar advantage could be found for normal mixed-handers in visuospatial skills.

At the University of Aberden, a vocabulary test (Mill Hill Scale, Raven, 1958a) and a spatial test (the Shapes Test, Morrisby, 1955), along with an 8-item handedness questionnaire (Questionnaire 1 of Annett, 1967; Section 10.1), were given to the first-year psychology class of over 300 students.

Students in other years had been given routine tests of cognitive abilities (Moray House, 1952), and response to the handedness questionnaire could be obtained for a further 411 students in these years. The data were analysed for the effects of consistent versus mixed-handedness, for left- versus right-handed writing, and for right versus non-right preference in both groups. There was a highly significant male superiority on the spatial test, but no significant effect associated with handedness. Some years later, a colleague at the University of Hull who routinely tested entrants to one of the armed services offered to include a handedness questionnaire in the examination. Scores on several tests of ability, including verbal and nonverbal reasoning, were available for over 400 recruits. No relationships between handedness and ability could be found. These uniformly negative findings were not published, because the train of ideas that led me to look at the data was highly speculative and also because there was no general interest in laterality and ability at that time. These findings for adults, together with further studies of school-children (Annett, 1970b; Annett & Turner, 1974), which also found no substantial differences, convinced me that normal left-, mixed-, and right-handers are essentially equal for intellectual abilities.

When Levy (1969) published her findings for 15 right- and 10 left-handed graduate science students at CALTEC (Table 5.1), I fully expected her suggestion that left-handers are inferior to right-handers for visuo-spatial abilities to be quickly disproved. Reports of larger samples of students with negative findings were published very soon (Gibson, 1973; Roberts, 1974), but the idea of visuo-spatial deficit in left-handers seems to have become firmly fixed in the literature. Inspection of Levy's findings for her very small and highly selected sample (never replicated by Levy herself to my knowledge) shows that the performance IQs of the left-handers were at about the level expected in students (and found by Gibson for both handedness groups). What was odd about Levy's data was the high performance IQs of the 15 right-handers. Without independent replication, this should be treated as being due to sampling variation, and not as the starting point of a further pursuit of high spatial ability in right-handers.

TABLE 5.1
Data for CALTEC Graduate Science Students

	N	Verbal IQ	Performance IQ
Right-handers	15	138	130
Left-handers	10	142	117
		$p > .10$	$p < .002$

Note: Based on Levy (1969).

Early support for Levy's thesis was given by Miller (1971), but this sample was not controlled for sex. Nebes (1971a) reported that left-handers were worse than right-handers in matching segments of circles that were explored with the fingers but without vision to visually presented whole circles. This was interpreted as being due to an inferiority of left-handers on perceptual tasks. Nebes and Briggs (1974) reported that the superiority of right-handers over left-handers included memory for visuo-spatial relations. Several attempts to replicate Nebes's findings for tactile perception have found no significant differences between left- and right-handers (Gardner, English, Flannery, Hartnett, McCormick, & Wilhelmy, 1977; Hardyck, 1977a; McKeever & VanDeventer, 1977a; Nilsson, Glencross, & Geffen, 1980; Thomas & Campos, 1978).

Two studies of Wechsler test scores in undergraduates have found only slight and differing effects for handedness. Briggs, Nebes, and Kinsbourne (1976) compared right-, mixed-, and left-handed students, selected for handedness score and for presence or absence of sinistral relatives, on the Wechsler verbal and performance tests as well as on several tests of specific cognitive factors. There were 17 subjects of each sex in the six handedness/family handedness groups. Analyses for verbal and performance IQs and for tests showing high loadings on a verbal and a spatial factor found no significant differences related to handedness or familial handedness. There were statistically significant differences for full-scale IQ associated with presence of left-handed relatives and with personal handedness, but the actual differences were at most about 2.5 IQ points; statistical significance for such small differences must have depended on extremely narrow variances (not given). Several further analyses were made of the nine tests of cognitive factors, with uniformly negative results for handedness and familial handedness. Among all these negative findings there was only one that matched the usually accepted minimum level of significance (at the 1 in 20 or 5% level of significance for handedness), and this is the finding referred to when the Briggs' data are cited in support of the hypothesis that left-handers differ from right-handers in intelligence. Of course such a finding could itself be due to chance when so many comparisons are made.

Bradshaw, Nettleton, and Taylor (1981) made a similar analysis of Wechsler IQ scores in groups of undergraduates matched for sex, strong left- or right-hand preference, and the presence or absence of at least one left-handed parent or sibling. Significant effects were found between handedness groups on all comparisons; this was due almost entirely to the familial sinistrals, who were poorer than the rest on verbal and especially on performance IQ in males. The subjects were not matched for over-all IQ except in so far as they were all university entrants; it is possible that the poorer scores of the male familial sinistrals are a result of chance sampling factors when $N = 12$ per group. Unlike Briggs and colleagues' (1976) sample, there was no general deficit in Full Scale IQ in the left-handers since nonfamilial sinistrals were at the same level as familial and nonfamilial dextrals. The fact that these two studies of Wechsler IQ in undergraduates differ in the significant differences obtained suggests that neither set of results can be accepted without independent replication.

The studies considered so far have been of students. Questions about differences between handedness groups in intelligence need to be answered through studies of large samples of the general population. One such sample was drawn from a group of villages near Oxford (Newcombe, Ratcliff, Carrivick, Hiorns, Harrison, & Gibson, 1975). The WAIS verbal and performance scale IQs of 462 males and 466 females were compared between those showing right, left, and various types of mixed and either hand preference. There were no significant differences between groups and certainly no trend to poorer scores by left- or mixed-handers. A second population study included a variety of psychological tests on over 3,000 people in Hawaii (Wilson, De Fries, McClearn, Vandenberg, Johnson, & Rashad, 1975). Kocel (1980) reported that "Comparisons of all left and right handers on the 4 cognitive factors and the 15 cognitive tests revealed no significant differences between the left handed group of 246 subjects and the right handed group of 3,005 subjects."

A third population sample included 7,688 children in general community schools in California (Hardyck, Petrinovich, & Goldman, 1976). Left- and right-handed children were compared on several tests of ability and educational attainment in each grade from 1 to 6. Some 50 comparisons were made between right- and left-handers when the numbers of left-handers were very large (70+ for each comparison). No significant differences were found. A survey of visuo-motor ability in 8- to 9-year-old children in schools near Cambridge (UK) included 82 left-handers and 728 right-handers (Brenner & Gillman, 1966). There were no significant differences between handedness groups. Tests of the spatial deficit hypothesis in kindergarten children also found no significant differences between handedness groups (Fagan-Dubin, 1974; Keogh, 1972). This great weight of negative evidence should surely be sufficient to counter the left-handers' spatial disability hypothesis. However, as seen for the pathological handedness theory, slight positive trends seem to be more attention-worthy than substantial negative ones. Perhaps this is part of the inequality that cognitive psychologists have demonstrated in the uses made of positive and negative evidence (Wason, 1960).

The most effective way to supplant an erroneous hypothesis is to replace it with a more attractive one. It must now be admitted that there are a number of indications that left- and mixed-handers might have a special *advantage* over right-handers in handling certain types of nonverbal tasks. One such finding is for numerical ability (treated as part of the verbal–educational factor in some factor analyses but as a separate factor in others). Heim and Watts (1976) examined the 2,165 children and young adults of the standardisation sample of the AH2/3 test for differences associated with handedness. There were no systematic differences due to handedness in either sex for total test performance. When each of the 203 left-handed writers was individually matched for sex and total score with a right-handed writer and compared for scores on each of the three subscales (verbal, numerical, perceptual), there were significantly more left-handers who scored higher than their paired right-handers on the *numerical* scale; because of the matching for total score, higher marks on one scale entailed lower marks for left-handers and on the other scales, but the differences were not statistically significant for the verbal or perceptual scales. The left-handers' superiority on the numerical test was clear and highly significant for males but not clear for females, who showed only a slight trend in this direction. A high incidence of left-handedness (20%) has been found in mathematically gifted children, most of them boys (Kolata, 1983).

Herrmann and Van Dyke (1978) found left-handers faster than right-handers in evaluating perceptual patterns as same or different when they were presented in various orientations. Porac and Coren (1981) found better performance on a test of mental rotation of 3-D patterns by left-preferent than right-preferent individuals in a large student sample. Further evidence that left-handers might have advantages over right-handers in imagining the rotations of figures comes from a reanalysis of a subset of the Hawaii sample (Sanders, Wilson, & Vandenburg, 1982). A left-handers' superiority was found in males. Female left-handers were *worse* than female right-handers for the sample tasks, but the numbers of left-handers were relatively small in all groups (24 of each sex). Carter-Saltzman (1979) reported a superiority on perceptual tasks in individuals with at least two left-handed relatives. Further indications that left-handers might have special skills in nonverbal pursuits come from comparison of the handedness of students in faculties. Peterson and Lansky (1974) reported a higher incidence of left-handedness in architects, but their study did not include a control group. Mebert and Michel (1980) found more students of art left-handed than non-art controls.

There are a number of suggestions that musical abilities might be associated with non-right-handedness. Oldfield (1969) found that almost 20% of staff and students of university schools of music answered yes to the question "have you ever had any tendency to left handedness?"—but found a similar response rate in his psychology student controls. Byrne (1974) reported a higher incidence of mixed-handedness in instrumentalists. Deutsch (1978) found that mixed-handers (mildly rather than strongly left-handed as assessed by questionnaire) made fewer errors than strongly right- or left-handed subjects on a test of pitch identification. The advantage was confirmed in a second experiment (Deutsch, 1980), Craig (1980) found left-handers superior to right-handers for identifying rhythms when beats were presented to both ears simultaneously.

5.3.   DO LEFT- AND RIGHT-HANDERS DIFFER IN PERSONALITY?

As outlined in Section 4.2, left-handedness has been regarded as a sign of social deviance originating in "negativistic" personality traits. Two sorts of evidence can be examined with regard to personality: (1) scores on personality tests and (2) findings for groups of subjects referred for penal or psychiatric care. My comparisons of handedness groups for personality test scores were uniformly negative (and unpublished). They included MMPI (Hathaway & McKinley, 1948) scores for psychology undergraduates at the University of Hull and EPI (Eysenck & Eysenck, 1963) scores for about 800 Open University students attending summer schools.

Reports of relationships between personality test variables and handedness include associations between ambilaterality and poorer "ego-strength" (Palmer, 1963; 1964), mixed-handedness and stronger internal locus of control (Hicks & Pellegrini, 1978b), and right-handedness and lesser anxiety (Hicks & Pellegrini, 1978a). Wienrich, Wells, and McManus (1982) found 19 mixed-handers less anxious than 28 right- and 23 left-handers. They point out that this apparent association could be due to a tendency to give moderate rather than extreme responses on the tests of anxiety and of handedness. Mascie-Taylor (1981) found that right- and left-handers did not differ in mean scores on personality tests; he felt it was worth drawing attention, however, to a trend in right-handed males to be slightly less neurotic than other groups, though this trend was not apparent in females. My own view is that there is nothing of substance in any of these reports.

With regard to groups referred for penal care, Cesare Lombroso (1903) reported higher incidences of left-handedness in criminal men (13%) and especially in criminal women (22%) compared with controls (4–8%). More recent reports of similar trends have been based on groups too small to carry weight, so that Lombroso's findings have not been replicated, to my knowledge, in modern samples. Bakan (1973) reported that 15% of 47 male patients in a ward for alcoholics were left-handed writers, and Fitzhugh (1973) found 32% of 19 juveniles referred to the courts to be left-handed. In both studies, the *numbers* of cases are too small for serious consideration. Orme (1970) described the handedness and the scores for a test of emotional instability of 300 girls passing through an approved school classifying centre (for delinquents). The incidence of left-handedness (7.7%) was not excessive. Both right-handers and left-handers gained high scores for emotional instability, and the scores were more extreme for left- than for right-handers.

Turning to psychiatric disorders in children, Pringle (1961) reported finding high incidences of left-handedness in boys and girls who were residents in special schools for maladjusted children, but it is not clear that a control sample was assessed in the same way as the school sample. Psychoses in childhood are fortunately too rare for large-scale studies of the handedness distribution of child psychotics. In small samples of autistic children there is no convincing evidence of an excess of non–right-handedness, but there are trends that keep this possibility open (Boucher, 1977; Colby & Parkinson, 1977; Prior & Bradshaw, 1979).

For adult psychiatric patients, there is no evidence of an unusual distribution of hand preference. Fleminger, Dalton, and Standage (1977) compared questionnaire findings for 800 Londoners attending Guys Hospital for dental treatment (Section 4.2) and for 800 attending Guys Hospital Psychiatric Department. The groups resembled each other closely over most of the age range. A trend toward an excess of *right*-handers among the schizophrenics was checked in a second sample in which a significantly higher proportion of fully right-handed individuals was found in 272 schizophrenics than in controls (Taylor, Dalton, & Fleminger, 1980). Further evidence has been found of an excess of consistent right-handedness in schizophrenics and also in prisoners with a history of violence (Taylor, Brown, & Gunn, 1983). In all of these studies an "either"-hand response to questions about hand preference was taken to be evidence of nondextrality. Hence the groups classified as fully dextral were those who did not give "either" responses. Whether the difference between groups reflects some true difference in strength of dextral preference or a difference in willingness to give "either" responses to questionnaires remains to be determined.

Lishman and McMeekan (1976) reported handedness questionnaire data for 65 psychiatric inpatients of each sex at the Maudsley Hospital. A slight excess of left-handers was found in younger psychiatric males. These were *not* schizophrenic but rather classified as having affective or schizo-affective disorders. Apparent differences between the Guys and Maudsley series were shown to be due to different classifications of "either" responses (Taylor, Dalton, Fleminger, & Lishman, 1982). When these superficial differences were clarified, it was concluded that "There was no significant excess of left-handed subjects among schizophrenics in either sample by either classification." Neurotics did not differ from controls in either study. Oddy and Lobstein (1972) are often cited as having found evidence of greater nondextrality in schizophrenics, but how such a belief gained ground is difficult to understand when incidences of consistent right-hand and right-eye dominance were 56.5% for controls and 58.6% for male and 57.1% for female schizophrenics.

Although the findings reviewed above find no evidence of an association between left-handedness and schizophrenia, there are some intriguing and unexplained observations that are noted here and commented upon later (Section 19.4). First, there was the observation of Gottesman and Shields (1972) for their sample drawn from the Maudsley Hospital twin register, and for an earlier sample of Slater (1953), that MZ twins who were discordant for schizophrenia were also more often discordant for handedness than MZ twins concordant for schizophrenia. The combined data are given in Table 5.2. The total incidence of left-handedness is 31.25%. No excess of left-handers both became schizophrenic is 31.25%. No excess of left-handers was found in MZ twins discordant for schizophrenia in another series (Luchins, Pollin, & Wyatt, 1980), and further study of the Maudsley twin series seems to be finding no excess of left-handers in MZ twins where one or both are schizophrenic (Reveley, personal communication).

A second finding concerns patients with intractable epilepsy who were treated by temporal lobectomy. In rare cases, temporal lobe epilepsy is associated with a schizophrenia-like psychosis. This psychosis was found most frequently (23%) in a group whose temporal lobe pathology proved to be "alien tissue", defined by Taylor (1975) as "a small locus of cells alien from their context". These lesions were unsuspected before surgery and were presumably due to some abnormality of fetal brain growth. Among 11 psychotics with this pathology, six were left-handed (Taylor, 1975); four of the left-handers had left-sided and two right-sided operations, and there were three of each sex.

A third finding suggesting a link between anomalies of laterality and schizophrenia is the observation of Luchins, Weinberger, and Wyatt (1979) that physical asymmetries of the cerebral hemispheres detected by CAT scans (Table 3.4) are less often biased in the normal direction in schizophrenics. Table 5.3 shows the distribution of occipital skull asymmetries of 28 schizophrenics with evidence of brain atrophy (to which their symptoms might be attributable) and of 29 schizophrenics without atrophy; all were right-handed. The distribution of skull asymmetry in patients with atrophy

TABLE 5.2
Concordance for Schizophrenia and for Handedness in Monozygotic Twins

Schizophrenia	Handedness in Twin Pairs						
	RR	%	RL	%	LL	%	No. Pairs
Both twins	12	75.0	3	18.7	1	6.3	16
One twin	3	18.7	11	68.8	2	12.5	16

Note: Combined data of Slater (1953) and Gottesman and Shields (1972) after Shields (1974, personal communication).

TABLE 5.3

CAT Scan Assessments of Asymmetries of Widths of Occipital Lobes in (a) Schizophrenics With and Without Brain Atrophy and (b) in Mentally Retarded and Autistic Children

	N	Left Lobe Wider (%)	L=R (%)	Right Lobe Wider (%)
a. *Luchins et al. (1979)*				
Schizophrenics with brain atrophy	28	64	25	11
Schizophrenics without brain atrophy	29	41	21	38
b. *Hier et al. (1979)*				
Mentally retarded children	44	59	18	23
Autistic children	16	31	13	56

resembles that found for normal right-handers, and that for schizophrenics without atrophy resembles that of 118 normal left-handers in having no systematic bias to either side. Table 5.3 also gives the findings for occipital brain asymmetries in 16 autistic children contrasted with 14 mentally retarded children (Hier, LeMay, & Rosenberger, 1979). Whereas the mentally retarded children show the typical overall bias to a wider left lobe, the autistic children do not show this but rather a trend to the opposite asymmetry. Further studies have not consistently replicated these findings (Luchins, 1983).

A fourth lateral difference said to be associated with schizophrenia is Blau's (1977) report that 9-year-old children who draw circles in the clockwise (atypical, Section 3.1) direction are at a greater risk of being diagnosed schizophrenic by 21 years of age than children who draw circles consistently anticlockwise.

A fifth observation concerns EEG synchrony while thinking about a problem requiring visual imagery, compared with resting EEG. Shaw, Colter, and Resek (1983) found that EEG coherence increased in healthy right-handers and in neurotic patients during cognitive activity but decreased in healthy left-handers and in schizophrenic patients.

5.4.   SUMMARY

Raised incidences of left-handedness have been found in children with certain types of speech disorder, especially stuttering and specific developmental speech delay. Raised incidences have also been found in children with specific reading retardation, but not in children with general reading backwardness. Incidences of left-handedness in children with specific delays in speech and reading are about twice those of controls. It is important to notice that the increased incidences are found only in clinic samples of children identified as having specific developmental language delays. There is no evidence that left- and mixed-handers in the general school population differ from right-handers in language skills.

There is little evidence that hand preference groups differ in motor abilities. Very few significant differences were found for laboratory-based studies of motor control or for sports performance. Where significant differences have been found, they suggest that left-handers are better than right-handers in the control of the nonpreferred hand. In several sports, the advantages seem to lie with those who are not consistently right-sided.

With regard to intellectual abilities, there is no convincing evidence that left-handers differ from right-handers on tests of general intelligence or scholastic progress. Reports of such differences have been based on very small numbers of subjects or on small differences that were barely statistically significant among a mass of insignificant comparisons. There is no substantial support for the idea that left-handers have a specific disadvantage in visuo-spatial tasks. On the contrary, there are indications that left- and mixed-handers might include some who have slight advantages in visuo-spatial thinking, numerical ability, and musical perception.

It seems unlikely that handedness is related to personality traits as assessed by questionnaires in the normal population. Schizophrenia is *not* associated with excess sinistrality in general psychiatric samples, even if there might be an excess of left-handers among rare types of schizophrenia with temporal lobe pathology. The association of left-handedness with criminality, as suggested by Lombroso, does not appear to have been checked with substantial modern data. On the contrary, there are suggestions that violent offenders are more fully dextral than controls. There seems to be very little here to account for the persistence of a small proportion of left-handers among a majority of right-handers.

III

QUESTIONS ABOUT THE LEFT AND RIGHT CEREBRAL HEMISPHERES

6 The Typical Pattern of Hemisphere Specialisation

This chapter considers the typical pattern of cerebral specialisation in the majority of the population, most of whom, of course, are right-handers. Patterns of cerebral specialisation are variable, even among right-handers, as seen in Section 3.3.1. The nature and origin of the predominant pattern is the topic of this chapter. Chapter 7 asks about the cerebral specialisation of left-handers. Chapter 8 looks at more speculative issues about patterns of cerebral organisation and the interrelations between the hemispheres. Chapter 8 also considers evidence for sex differences in cerebral asymmetry.

For about 100 years after the recognition of the dependence of speech on the left hemisphere, research and theory on hemisphere asymmetries was the province of a small and highly specialised branch of neurology. Since the Californian series of operations to separate the cerebral hemispheres by cutting the corpus callosum (the split-brain operation) there has been a large amount of publication in this field. Speculation about cerebral specialisation quickly outran the facts, so that mythologies of laterality have become established before the evidence could be properly evaluated.

That most popular accounts of hemisphere specialisation are exaggerated and erroneous was pointed out by Gazzaniga and LeDoux (1978), and later reviewers have agreed. Beaumont (1982) described his aim as to plant a few landmarks in the *bog* of visual laterality research. Bryden (1982) hoped to give a balanced view that would counter the extravagant claims that have been made about lateralisation. Bradshaw and Nettleton (1983) acknowledged that findings have not always been verifiable and consistent. The reader is referred to these reviews for fuller accounts than can be given here.

The purpose of this chapter is to outline the main evidence as to cerebral specialisation in the majority of the population, with a view to discovering what might be the *minimum* difference between the hemispheres. What difference between the right and left half-brains might lead to the development of speech and language skills on the left side? What might nudge development toward the pattern found in most people?

6.1.   EVIDENCE
FOR HEMISPHERE SPECIALISATION

6.1.1.   Clinical Evidence

With regard to the left hemisphere, evidence from all sources confirms, and none gives reason to doubt, that for most people, speech and other language skills depend mainly on the left side. As language is involved in many aspects of human cognition, lesions on the left give rise to many disabilities. Among the symptoms associated more often with left- than right-sided lesions in right-handers are disorders of speech production and comprehension, reading, writing, and calculation (Hécaen & Sauguet, 1971). Intelligence test scores are more affected by left- than right-sided lesions (Meyer & Yates, 1955; Smith, 1966). In addition to these tasks with an obvious dependence on language, left-sided lesions are also associated with disorders of right–left orientation, recognition of colours, and the ability to perform certain complex learned actions (apraxia). The analysis of the apraxias is complex and controversial (Geschwind, 1975; Heilman, 1979). It seems clear, however, that learning how to perform actions such as using a hammer, brushing the teeth, or making a cup of coffee depend for most people on the left hemisphere. Thus the popular description of the left hemisphere as "verbal" grossly oversimplifies its role.

Electrical mapping studies (outlined in Chapter 2) have demonstrated that different aspects of language function, such as naming, short-term verbal memory, reading, and phoneme discrimination may depend on discrete locations in the left hemisphere. Naming in different languages may also depend on different locations. Lesions outside the speech cortex may lead to subtle deficits in aspects of verbal functioning. Left temporal lobectomies are associated with defects of verbal memory (Milner, 1962), and left frontal lesions are associated with loss of verbal fluency (Milner, 1964).

Lesions of the right hemisphere are not associated with dramatic losses of function comparable to the loss of speech for lesions on the left, and the idea that the right hemisphere might have its own special skills was not given wide credence before the 1960s. One of the few symptoms associated with right cerebral lesion is neglect of the left half of space, such that the patient may ignore food to the left side of the plate, draw a clock with numbers on the right side only, or even deny that the paralysed left arm or leg belong to him. Unilateral neglect extends to all sensory modalities and even affects the imagined representation of space. Bisiach, Capitani, Luzzatti, and Perani (1981) asked their patients to imagine that they were standing in the great square facing Milan cathedral and to describe what they saw. The patients described features on the right only. They were then asked to imagine that they had walked to the other side of the square and, with the cathedral behind them, describe what they saw. The descriptions again included features only from the *new* right-hand side. The problem for the patient with unilateral neglect has been described as a "mutilated representation of space" (De Renzi, 1978). Patients with left-hemisphere lesions very rarely show neglect of the right half of space, and all of those recorded by Hécaen and Sauguet (1971) were described as left-handed.

A second dramatic but infrequent symptom associated with right-hemisphere lesions is dressing apraxia. The patient may be found helplessly looking at his clothes, not knowing how to put them on. Another symptom noted by Brain (1941) was difficulty in localising objects in space. Some of the tasks that have detected greater impairment in patients with right-sided than left-sided lesions are the location of a point in space, reproducing the angle of a hinged rod, and discriminating the shape of blocks by touch (De Renzi, 1978, 1982). A review of effects of right-hemisphere lesions led Benton (1979) to conclude that the right hemisphere plays a special role in the apprehension of spatial relations, independently of sensory modality.

Visual imperception was noted by Hughlings Jackson (1876), the English neurologist contemporary with Broca, in a patient with a right-hemisphere lesion. There have been several demonstrations that patients with right posterior lesions have difficulty in recognising pictures of letters, objects, and faces when the representation is degraded in various ways, or when the picture is confused by overlapping of drawings (De Renzi & Spinnler, 1966b; Warrington, 1982). Warrington and her colleagues have also shown that patients with right-sided lesions have special difficulty in recognising pictures of objects from unusual viewpoints or when lit from unusual angles; they also had difficulties in matching pairs of photographs of the same face, or the same building, when taken from different angles (Warrington, 1982). The recognition of faces is a task for which most of us take for granted a high level of skill. Loss of ability to recognise faces of members of one's own family is an exceedingly rare disorder and probably depends on bilateral damage to the occipito-temporal visual system (Geschwind, 1979). The ability to recognise pictures of strange faces seems to be associated with right- more often than left-sided lesions (De Renzi & Spinnler, 1966a; Yin, 1970). Newcombe and Russell (1969) showed that both spatial deficits and visual perceptual deficits were associated with posterior right-hemisphere lesions, but that the two disorders did not necessarily go together. Thus the visual and spatial aspects of right-hemisphere function are partly dissociable.

Comparisons of the effects of surgical lesions of the right and left sides have found patients with right temporal lesions impaired on tests of spatial learning and memory (Milner, 1954, 1974), and also on tests of musical perception (Milner, 1962). Lesions to the right frontal lobe were associated with difficulties in the planning of movement sequences and also of keeping track of the order in which pictures were seen (Milner, 1982).

6.1.2. Split-Brain Evidence

The general effects of the split-brain operation seem to be remarkably few. Basic movement patterns such as walking depend on bilaterally represented systems. Some deficits have been found in capacities for sustained attention (Dimond, 1976; Ellenberg & Sperry, 1979) and for tasks requiring fast co-ordinated movements by both hands (Preilowski, 1972; Zaidel & Sperry, 1977). There have been occasional instances when the two hands of split-brain humans seem to be in competition with each other. In commissuro-tomised monkeys, competition between the hands was rare and occurred only in early stages after operation (Lehman, 1972; Trevarthen, 1978).

Sperry (1974) summarised his conclusions as to human cerebral specialisa-tion, drawn from studies of split-brain patients, in the schematic map reproduced in Figure 6.1. The left hemisphere is described as the main language centre, while the right hemisphere is credited with only simple language comprehension. In the early stages after operation, all patients could talk about stimuli presented to the left hemisphere but not about those presented to the right hemisphere, although the right hemisphere could demonstrate, by other means, that it had recognised the stimuli. Smell is lateralised to each nostril, but the olfactory nerves are uncrossed, so that patients can talk about smells presented to the left but not the right nostril. Each hemisphere is aware of the contralateral hand and visual field. Auditory messages are received from both ears, but those of the contralateral ear take precedence when there is competition. Calculation is assigned to the left hemisphere, which is not surprising since counting relies on verbal symbols.

The right hemisphere is assigned spatial abilities and nonverbal ideation (Fig. 6.1). Simple figures, such as triangle and rectangle, were drawn better by the right hand in the right-handed split-brain patients, but the spatial relationships of more complex figures, such as a house or a cube, were better represented by the left hand (Gazzaniga & Sperry, 1967). The left hand (right hemisphere) was able to arrange three-dimensional blocks to match a pictured design when the right hand could not (Gazzaniga, 1967). Nebes (1971b, 1972) developed tests requiring tactile manipulation of arcs of circles or other geometrical shapes that had to be matched to the whole presented visually (or vice-versa from whole to segment). In these tests, and in the

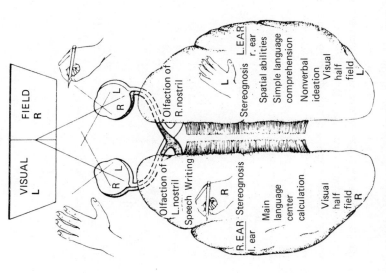

VISUAL L FIELD R

Olfaction of R.nostril

L.EAR
r. ear
Stereognosis
Spatial abilities
Simple language
comprehension
Nonverbal
ideation
Visual
half
field
L

Olfaction of
L.nostril
Speech Writing
Stereognosis
R.EAR
l. ear
Main
language
center
calculation
Visual
half
field
R

FIG. 6.1. Sperry's 1974 schema summarising inferences about cerebral specialisation.

perception of the orientation of lines (Nebes, 1973), the left hand/right hemisphere was found to be superior to the right hand/left hemisphere. Milner and Taylor (1972) asked split-brain patients to manipulate patterns made from bent wire and match them with visually presented shapes. The right hemisphere showed evidence of nonverbal memory: It could match patterns after a two-minute delay, but the left hemisphere could not. Later research demonstrated that the right hemisphere has a special role in solving geometrical problems (Franco & Sperry, 1977).

What has the study of split-brain patients contributed to the understanding of the nature of the difference between the hemispheres? A possibly important clue was found in experiments that tested the hemispheres simultaneously by presenting the two halves of different stimuli, juxtaposed in the midline to make chimeras, as illustrated in Figure 6.2. After each presentation, the patient was asked to point to what had been seen by selecting it from a set of pictures, words, shapes, or faces that included the wholes of the stimuli presented in each half field. In the four right-handed patients tested, there was some variability of response. For most types of stimuli, the *right* hemisphere tended to dominate the selection. The propor-

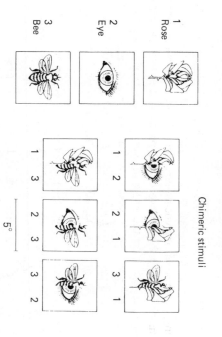

Chimeric stimuli

1 Rose

2 Eye

3 Bee

5°

FIG. 6.2.   Examples of chimeric stimuli used by Levy, Trevarthen, & Sperry, 1972.

tion of left-hemisphere selections increased when the response required was naming of the stimulus seen (Levy, Trevarthen, & Sperry, 1972). The shift to RVF stimuli was especially clear when the task was to choose from one set of pictures (toes, pie, or key) the one whose name rhymed with pictures presented chimerically (rose, eye, or bee) (Levy & Trevarthen, 1977). That is, only the left hemisphere, of most patients tested, could match the pictures presented for the *sound of their names*. This experiment seems to pinpoint a critical difference between the hemispheres, in that only the left hemisphere could generate an internal representation of the word sound.

Further tests of right-hemisphere language were made using a contact lens technique that made it possible to present stimuli for a longer period than a brief flash. Stimuli remained in the LVF while the patient moved the eyes freely (Zaidel, 1976, 1977, 1978). Sets of pictures could be presented in the LVF, from which the patient was required to select the answer by pointing. On the Progressive Matrices Test (Raven, 1958b), a measure of nonverbal intelligence, the left hand/right hemisphere performed almost as well as the right hand/left hemisphere in the small group of split-brain and hemispherectomy patients tested. A test of word comprehension found right-hemisphere performances equivalent to the norms for 8- to 16-year-olds. When tested for an understanding of associations such as pen-envelope or gun-holster, the right hemisphere was again able to perform the task, but not quite to the level found for single words. Right-hemisphere performance was poor in the Token test, which requires following a sequence of instructions such as "Put the yellow square under the green circle." Zaidel also confirmed the observation of Levy and Trevarthen that the right hemisphere is weaker than the left hemisphere in making phonetic discriminations. Zaidel's analysis of these and other findings led him to suggest that the right hemisphere has its own pattern of language skill which cannot be likened to that of an immature or an aphasic left hemisphere. It has a surprisingly rich auditory vocabulary, and it can understand grammatical and semantic relationships in words and phrases. It is weakest in analysing long sentences in which the order of words is important and the context unhelpful. This difficulty with long instructions might be due to the right hemisphere's inability to generate words so as to maintain the subvocal rehearsal, which for most people is important for short-term or working memory (Baddeley, 1976; Hitch, 1980).

In a small number of patients, a capacity to generate language has developed some time after the commissurotomy. A young man, P.S., was able to make verbal responses in writing soon after operation and 2.5 years later developed the capacity to speak from that hemisphere (Gazzaniga, Volpe, Smylie, Wilson, & LeDoux, 1979). A female patient, V.P., showed a similar pattern of right-hemisphere language, speaking from the right hemisphere about 1 year after operation. Both patients were right-handed. Reviewing the evidence for right-hemisphere language in cases of brain bisection, Gazzaniga (1983) reports that of 44 split-brain cases in the United States, only 5 (11.4%) have shown clear evidence of language processing in the right hemisphere. The language capacities of these 5 vary from rudimentary naming to skills comparable to those of the left hemisphere. Hence, differences between the hemispheres in language capacity could be regarded as continuous, rather than as a discrete all-or-nothing dichotomy. Of course, all of these patients had brain damage of long standing, which may have contributed to some reorganisation of hemisphere function. It is worth noting, however, that there is substantial individual variability within the split-brain sample.

Do the split-brain studies imply that the right hemisphere is dominant for shape perception? LeDoux, Wilson, and Gazzaniga (1977) and Gazzaniga and LeDoux (1978) suggested that the difference between the hemispheres for visuo-spatial functions has been greatly exaggerated. They argue that it is unlikely that each hemisphere would have become endowed, through evolutionary adaptations, with unique patterns of neural organisation, each incompatible with the types of processing occurring in the other half-brain: "We prefer the view that what has become uniquely specialized and genetically specified in the course of human neural evolution is a potential for the expression of linguistic functions ... Where linguistic functions finally settle down in the brain during development alters the prototypical primate brain plan so that homologous areas in opposite hemispheres come to carry out different functions" (Gazzaniga & LeDoux, 1978, page 72). According to this view, it would be unnecessary for genetic codes to specify the differing functions of each hemisphere; the differences would arise in the course of development as a result of the localisation of linguistic mechanisms. Both hemispheres may have capacities for visuo-spatial skills, but these capacities may be diminished on the left by the need to serve language. These speculations will be considered further in Section 6.4.

6.1.3. Normal Subjects

Asymmetries have been found in the response of normal subjects to stimuli presented to each side of the body in several experimental situations. The dichotic listening technique (Broadbent, 1956; Cherry, 1953) involves playing different messages to each ear simultaneously, usually from a two-channel tape recorder through headphones. Kimura (1961) found greater accuracy in the report of messages received at the right ear than at the left ear. Kimura's initial studies were done at the Montreal Neurological Institute, where the hemisphere speech laterality of patients had been assessed by the Wada method (Chapter 2). Her findings, given in Table 6.1, show that the differences between ears were related to hemisphere speech laterality more than to hand preference. The mean differences were not large for any group, and subsequent studies have shown that there is considerable individual variability within groups. However, the group trends are clear and the right-ear advantage (REA) has proved extremely reliable in later research.

Kimura (1964) was the first to demonstrate in normal subjects, by the dichotic listening technique, a left-ear advantage (LEA) in the perception of melodies. Knox and Kimura (1970) reported that nonverbal environmental sounds, such as running tap water and car engines starting up, are correctly identified more often when presented to the left than the right ear. These differences between ears in normal subjects—REA for normal speech and LEA for musical sounds and nonverbal noises—parallel the findings for the effects of brain lesions reviewed above. The agreement between findings for asymmetries in normal subjects with expectations derived from clinical

TABLE 6.1
Left and Right Ear Scores for Dichotic Listening in Patients Classified for Speech Hemisphere
and Handedness

Handedness	N	Left Ear	Right Ear	R–L
Left speech hemisphere				
Right	93	77.03	83.73	6.7
Left	10	72.50	77.00	4.5
Right speech hemisphere				
Right	3	83.67	81.67	−2.0
Left	9	85.00	71.44	−13.6

Note: After Kimura, 1961.

studies, together with the interest generated by the split-brain operation, led to an explosive growth of research on laterality in normal subjects.

In the visual modality, letters, words, lights, or shapes can be presented briefly to either side of a visual fixation point and provided the subject maintains this fixation, stimuli in the left visual field will be transmitted to the right hemisphere and stimuli in the right visual field to the left hemisphere (Fig. 2.5). A right-visual-field advantage (RVA) is almost invariably found for words, and left-field advantages (LVA) have been found for the perception of certain nonverbal stimuli such as lights, shapes, and faces. Asymmetries of perception between the visual fields had been noted many years earlier, but Bryden (1964) was the first to show that the asymmetries found in right-handers are absent in left-handers and to suggest that the visual asymmetries might be related to cerebral dominance for speech, like the auditory asymmetries found by Kimura. As far as I have been able to discover, there has been no direct check on Bryden's suggestion, by testing patients of known hemisphere speech for visual asymmetries. This omission seems extraordinary in view of the weight of publication premised on the assumption that visual asymmetries reflect cerebral ones.

On tests of tactile perception, advantages for the left hand have been found in normal right-handers, in accord with the left-hand advantages reported for split-brain patients. Sensitivity to pressure was found greater for the left than the right thumb (Ghent, 1961) and for the left side in most subjects tested for palms, forearms, and soles (Weinstein & Sersen, 1961). Harris (1980b) has reviewed the considerable evidence of left-hand superiority for reading braille, in blind subjects and in normal children taught to recognise braille characters. Witelson (1976) asked children to palpate two shapes simultaneously in each hand (dichaptically) and found left-hand superiority in boys but no difference between the hands in girls.

These perceptual asymmetries of hearing, vision, and touch are in accord with expectations for asymmetries of hemisphere function, as deduced from clinical studies. The important question, however, is whether they have contributed anything new to the understanding of cerebral specialisation. As Bryden (1982) put it with regard to visual studies, "More conclusive evidence that these procedures really tap functional cerebral asymmetries is needed." I believe that there may be individual differences in visual directional perception that are not necessarily due to hemisphere specialisation for speech (Annett & Annett, 1979; Annett, 1983b). Hence, I am not confident that the literature on visual asymmetries is directly relevant to questions of cerebral dominance. As mentioned above, the reader is referred to other reviewers of this literature (Beaumont, 1982; Bradshaw & Nettleton, 1983; Bryden, 1982). For the purpose of this chapter, which is to try to reach an understanding of the nature of the differences between the hemispheres, there are two main points to be made.

First, one of the recurring themes of the literature is that the right hemisphere is specialised for "holistic" or "gestalt" processing, while the left hemisphere is specialised for "analytic" or "sequential" processing. LEA and LVA are often found when stimuli must be responded to quickly, in a direct global fashion, whereas REA and RVA are often found (even for the same stimulus material) when more complex judgements that take time have to be made. This contrast has been found for judgements of nonverbal stimuli as well as verbal ones, leading to the inference that the essential difference between the hemispheres does not relate to the verbal or nonverbal nature of the stimulus material but rather to the holistic or analytic nature of the processing required. The point here is that sequential and analytic processing must involve mechanisms for holding information over time, which depend, in turn, on the symbolic representation of the material to be analysed. The symbols used are probably verbal for most types of material. Hence, the characterisation of the left hemisphere as sequential or analytic does not add significantly to the original inference that it is specially adapted for carrying information in verbal symbols.

The second point to be made from the perceptual asymmetry literature concerns the nature of the difference between the ears in dichotic listening. Since Studdert-Kennedy and Shankweiler (1970) recommended the use of the dichotic listening technique to "pull the speech signal apart", consider-able research effort has been devoted to trying to discover what it is about certain speech sounds that induces REA, whereas other speech sounds do not. Consonants give reliable REAs but not vowel sounds (Shankweiler & Studdert-Kennedy, 1967), unless the difficulty of the vowel discrimination task is increased (Darwin, 1971).

Liberman (1974) suggested that the REA depends on stimuli being perceived in the "speech mode". This would make the ear difference a consequence of the speech processing advantage of the left hemisphere. It is possible to take the opposite view and suggest that the development of speech processing in the left hemisphere depends on some fundamental difference in the perception of sounds at the two ears. In this case, the REA would be the cause rather than the consequence of the specialisation of the left hemisphere for speech.

Many experiments have compared the perception of synthetic speech sounds at the two ears when distinctive features were mutilated in differing ways. The consensus seems to be that the typical REA depends on a capacity to detect very fine differences in the timing of sounds (Allard & Scott, 1975; Bryden, 1982; Lackner & Teuber, 1973; Schouten, 1980; Schwartz & Tallal, 1980). For example, the difference between /ga/ and /ka/ depends on a very small difference in the timing of voice onset. Divenyi and Efron (1979) showed that subjects can be left-ear dominant for the pitch of dichotically presented musical sounds, and for vowel-like sounds but switch to REA when a fine time discrimination is required. They concluded that speech may be special (among other sounds) only in its temporal complexity.

The idea that only a very small difference between the two hemispheres is involved, a capacity to make finer time discriminations on the left side, supplies a hypothesis as to just the sort of developmental nudge that might, in normal circumstances, be sufficient to induce the left hemisphere to serve speech.

6.2. THE EFFECTS OF EARLY BRAIN LESIONS ON CEREBRAL SPECIALISATION

Children with severe early unilateral lesions of either hemisphere do learn to talk (unless profoundly retarded due to other handicaps). Clearly, the right hemisphere is capable of serving speech if the left hemisphere is impaired early in life, an example of an alternative developmental pathway. The ball on the epigenetic landscape (Fig. 1.4) can take the right-hemisphere route to speech if the left-hemisphere route is blocked. But are the right and left hemispheres fully equal in their capacities to serve speech? Is it possible to detect differences between children with early damage of the left and right sides that might suggest that there is some inherent advantage in developing speech on the left side of the brain, even if this inherent advantage can be overridden if necessary?

Lenneberg's (1967) analysis of the literature on the effects of early unilateral lesions has strongly influenced subsequent discussions of this topic. Lenneberg believed that it is not possible to distinguish between the effects of early lesions on the left and the right, and he concluded, therefore, that the hemispheres are fully equipotential for language at birth; this would imply that there is no inherent advantage to the left side. He noted that the time to recover from dysphasias acquired in childhood becomes longer with increasing age and that whereas the chances of recovery from lesions sustained before puberty are fairly good, recovery after puberty is often incomplete. These two main features of Lenneberg's analysis should be kept distinct. The hypothesis of absence of inherent left-hemisphere advantage and the hypothesis of a critical period for language development extending up to puberty could either or both be true or false.

Lenneberg's analysis relied mainly on a report by Basser (1962), which depended, in turn, on 102 cases of severe hemiplegia of early onset seen at the National Hospital, London. Some were treated by the removal of the affected hemisphere (hemispherectomy). Basser's sample was a highly selected group of severely handicapped patients. Basser found no evidence of differences between the speech capacities of patients with lesions of each side.

There have been several other studies of children with hemiplegias of early onset that have found differences between left- and right-sided cases. Dennis and Whitaker (1977) reviewed nine studies reported in the nineteenth century and five in the twentieth century. Most of these found a higher incidence of *speech disorder* in children with lesions of the left than the right hemisphere. The differences are highly significant for the combined series ($\chi^2 = 28.3$, $df = 1$, $p < .001$, for the nineteenth-century series, and $\chi^2 = 25.37$, $df = 1$, $p < .001$ for the twentieth-century series—my calculations). Hécaen's (1983) reappraisal of his cases of acquired aphasia in childhood led him to conclude that the hypothesis of equipotentiality was mistaken. Thus, Basser's sample was not representative of children with early unilateral lesions, and Lenneberg's inference that the hemispheres are fully equipotential for language was probably incorrect.

Lenneberg's conclusion that there is a critical period for recovery of language impairment may also need qualification in the sense that there is considerable individual variability in adults for the recovery from aphasias. Evidence that this variability is related to handedness is considered in Chapter 7.

In what ways do children with early right- and left-hemisphere lesions differ? This is a critical question for an understanding of the nature and development of cerebral dominance for speech. Annett (1973b) made individual personal examinations of a complete population sample of children diagnosed as hemiplegic at four paediatric centres in Yorkshire. It was expected that careful testing of a population sample would reveal differences in verbal and nonverbal intelligence, reading, and spatial perception that might have remained undetected in earlier selected samples. The degree of physical impairment of the hand was measured by a peg-moving task (Chapter 11), norms for peg moving having been established in school-children (Annett, 1970b; see Appendix III). The peg-moving task demonstrated that 39% of the children referred for examination with a diagnosis of hemiplegia were in fact disabled in *both* hands.

When children were equated for degrees of physical disability, there were no differences for intelligence test scores between right- and left-sided cases. Table 6.2 shows that for children with a normal better hand, the mean verbal IQ of 36 children with left-sided lesions was 88.1, and for 29 children with right-sided lesions it was 88.0. The groups were also virtually identical for performance-scale IQ. This remarkable similarity, which was *not expected*, convinced me that both hemispheres are equally capable of developing intellectual skills, verbal and nonverbal. In children with slight-to-moderate impairment of the better hand there were dramatic falls in mean IQ, to the level bordering on mental handicap. This fall was especially great for performance-scale IQ, suggesting that nonverbal skills might be especially sensitive to bilateral brain lesions. Other comparisons of children with right

TABLE 6.2
Verbal IQ and Verbal Minus Performance IQ in Children With Right and Left Hemiplegias, Classified for Three Grades of Peg Moving by the Better Hand

Better hand	Side of Hemiplegia	N	Affected Hand z Score[a]		Better Hand Standardised Score[b]		Verbal WISC IQ		Verbal Minus Performance IQ	
			Mean	SD	Mean	SD	Mean	SD	Mean	SD
Normal										
Within 2 SDs of normal mean	Right	36	26.0	27.2	96.4	12.9	88.1	17.7	−2.6	12.5
	Left	29	26.7	28.7	91.0	13.2	88.0	16.3	−2.8	10.9
Slightly impaired										
Between 2.0 and 6.7 SDs below the normal mean	Right	16	51.2	37.5	45.9	20.8	70.9	19.5	7.6	16.4
	Left	12	46.5	34.5	49.7	16.4	74.1	14.0	7.3	13.4
Severely impaired										
More than 6.7 SDs below the normal mean	Right	7	73.1	37.6	< 1		49.7	9.2	1.7	7.8
	Left	6	76.9	36.2	< 1		57.5	9.9	5.8	8.3

Note: Annett (1973b).

[a] z score = the difference between the time for the affected hand and the mean time of normal children of similar age divided by the normal standard deviation.

[b] Standardised score = mean 100, SD = 15 in normal children.

and left hemiplegias have also found no significant differences for intelligence (Cruikshank & Raus, 1955; Hammil & Irwin, 1966; Perlstein & Hood, 1957; Reed & Reitan, 1969).

In contrast to the similarity of right- and left-sided cases for intelligence, there was a clear difference for history of speech disorder, as noted above. Children with right hemiplegias (left-hemisphere lesions) were delayed in learning to talk or experienced problems of articulation significantly more often than children with left hemiplegias. Among children with normal better-hand speed, 39% of left-lesion and 7% of right-lesion cases had a history of speech problems. These findings suggest that the two half-brains are equally capable of serving verbal intelligence, but that the left has some special role in facilitating speech production. The speech difficulties of the hemiplegic children had cleared, in most cases, at the time of testing, suggesting that the difference between the sides affects early stages of speech acquisition but not later development. As noted earlier (Section 1.1), it is necessary to distinguish between speech and language; left-brain-lesioned children may suffer some transient handicap in the sensorimotor control of the speech apparatus without subsequent language impairment.

In contrast to the findings for childhood hemiplegia, differences have been reported between right- and left-sided cases of childhood hemispherectomy in verbal and nonverbal skills (Dennis & Whitaker, 1977; Griffith & Davidson, 1966; Kohn & Dennis, 1974). The differences in patterns of disability associated with the laterality of the remaining hemisphere were subtle and not likely to be found without special testing. This evidence for lateral differences of function must be regarded as tentative pending further studies.

Rasmussen and Milner (1977) described the laterality of cerebral speech, as assessed by the Wada technique, in patients who probably suffered lesions of the left hemisphere before the age of 2 years. If the hemispheres were fully equipotential, it might be expected that all of these cases of early lesion would depend on the right hemisphere for speech. In Table 6.3, the patients show increased incidences of bilateral and right-sided speech, in comparison with

TABLE 6.3
Cerebral Speech Laterality in 134 Cases With Definite Evidence of Early Left Hemisphere Lesion

Handedness	No. cases	Speech Representation (%)		
		Left	Bilateral	Right
Right	42	81	7	12
Left or mixed	92	28	19	53

Note: Based on Rasmussen and Milner (1977).

cases without early lesion (Table 3.2). However, the majority of right-handers, and even some left-handers, continued to depend on the left hemisphere for speech, despite the early left-sided lesion. These observations suggest that the left hemisphere does not easily give up its role in speech.

Is it possible that the right hemisphere should serve speech, despite an early right-sided lesion? Milner, Branch, and Rasmussen (1964) described a right-handed man with extensive *right* posterior pathology presumed to date from soon after birth, who became dysphasic after removal of the damaged area. Later Wada testing confirmed the right hemisphere's role in speech. This case is especially interesting because it suggests that the range of variability of speech laterality that is resistant to change following early brain lesion includes right-hemisphere speech in right-handers.

In conclusion, the hypothesis of full cerebral equipotentiality at birth must be regarded as untenable. There is some difference between the hemispheres in readiness to serve speech. The difference is probably slight, concerns speech rather than language, and can normally be compensated for in the course of growth. It has all the characteristics expected for a hypothetical "nudge" in the developmental pathway. How long the alternate hemisphere remains capable of serving speech is uncertain. For some people this capacity may persist into adulthood and contribute to the recovery from dysphasias.

6.3.   WHAT IS SPECIAL ABOUT THE LEFT HEMISPHERE?

In asking what is special about the left hemisphere, it is important to distinguish between the special features that *follow from* a lifetime's development of verbal capacities on the left side and those that *lead to* the development of those capacities. In asking what *causes* left-hemisphere specialisation, we are looking for a developmental nudge of the kind hypothesised in the last section. Here, it is proposed to argue that some slight advantage to the left hemisphere in the sensorimotor control of the speech apparatus would suffice to channel the growth of language to that side.

In the typical adult brain, the left hemisphere is responsible not just for speech, but also for maintaining a large word store and for combining words in the propositions through which meanings are conveyed to other people and to ourselves. A full understanding of the role of the left hemisphere must wait upon an understanding of normal language, thinking, and associated cognitive functions. Current analyses suggest that human languages can be analysed into sets of propositions (Clark & Clark, 1977). Propositions are sequences of symbols, with publicly agreed meanings, which represent aspects of the world. When higher apes are taught to use symbols, they combine them into sequences. Although ape sentences such as, "Tickle

Washoe", or "Nim eat" fall far short of fully developed human language (Terrace, Petitto, Sanders, & Bever, 1979), they do parallel the earliest two-word utterances of human children. In my view, this is sufficient to suggest that the capacity to use symbols propositionally is an inherent feature of an intelligent brain. The fact that human adults tend to rely on the left hemisphere in constructing such symbolic sequences is a consequence of the development of the word store on that side. The ability to construct propositional sequences is not the cause of left-hemisphere specialisation.

Evidence from several sources reviewed in Sections 6.1 and 6.2 points to the conclusion that what is distinctive about the left hemisphere is a special capacity for the perception and production of speech sounds. The electrical mapping studies of Ojemann (Section 2.4) found that discrimination between phonemes depends on sites at which stimulation also disrupts mimicry of sequences of mouth movements. This suggests an intimate link between the sensory and motor aspects of sound perception and production. In split-brain patients, a difference between the hemispheres was found in capacities to generate the sounds of words in rhyming tests. In dichotic listening studies, the REA was inferred to depend on a superior capacity to detect fine time differences at the right ear, presumably by the left hemisphere. In hemiplegic children, the only evidence of a special handicap in left-compared with right-lesion cases was in early developmental problems of speech acquisition. What do these observations suggest about the ontogeny of left-hemisphere specialisation?

Speech sounds are produced by complex patterns of movement involving the lips, tongue, and vocal cords. The quality of the sounds depends on variables such as the size of the vocal tract, the shape of the palate and nasal cavities and the control of breath; all of these differ with body size, age, and sex. Males and females, children and adults differ in the sounds produced, and yet infants learn in their first year to produce most of the speech sounds used in their native language. Human languages use subsets of the sounds it would be possible to use to carry meaning in the language (the phonemes of the language). Infants in their babbling produce the same range of sounds in all cultures, so that it is not possible to distinguish the babbling of babies in Europe, Africa, or Asia. Towards the end of the first year, infants can produce many of the phonemes used in their own language and combine them into simple words. The acquisition of speech sounds is a beautiful example of the interaction of a genetically programmed developmental sequence that relies on the experience of the individual child in the family for its fulfilment. How is the acquisition achieved?

It must be presumed that for most infants voice play is fun, and the fun depends upon mechanisms that enable the infant to listen to the sounds it produces. As for other repetitive games (the "circular reactions" of Baldwin, cited by Piaget, 1950), the game consists of trying to reproduce what just happened. The acquisition of control depends on being able to "do that again". It is fun to be able to reproduce the sounds spontaneously produced, but even more fun to be able to reproduce the sounds made by papa and other members of the family. Piaget's (1951) descriptions of imitation at about 1 year of age include accounts of how his children discovered how to say the new words he produced, through trial-and-error combinations of the required phonemes, which were already in their speech repertoire. This must have required a selection and matching process in which the infant produced trial sounds, listened to their effects, and judged whether they were sufficiently similar to the sound produced by papa (somehow compensating for the fact that papa's word would differ in pitch and many other qualities and matching for essential features of the pattern).

There is an important point to be made about this feedback process with regard to brain organisation. The brain of the infant is analogous, in some respects, to that of a split-brain adult because the cerebral commissures are largely unmyelinated (Yakovlev & Lecours, 1967). In discovering how the mouth must be shaped to produce the fine differences between /b/ and /p/, or between /l/ and /r/, it would be advantageous to have a close link between the somatosensory feedback from the mouth and the auditory feedback from the ear. If the mouth were being controlled from one side and the sound analysed on the other, this intimate link would be absent. Subcortical pathways might be available, but they would involve some delay, in comparison with the virtually instantaneous link if motor production and auditory analysis were controlled from the same cerebral hemisphere. The conclusion seems obvious that there would be great advantages for the acquisition of speech if the control of the speech apparatus and auditory analysis were on the *same* side. The side could be the right or the left, but the evidence from hemiplegic children, dichotic listening, and split-brain patients suggests that there is something special about the left hemisphere of most people, which makes it more fitted than the right to serve speech acquisition. Summarising the argument, it may be said that the advantages of having the motor and sensory aspects of speech control located on the same side of the brain are sufficient to account for the evolution of some mechanism that attempts to ensure this concordance. The concordance could have been for the right or the left hemisphere, but it happens to have evolved for the more efficient control of speech from the left side.

The nature of the mechanism that promotes the control of speech by the left hemisphere is unknown. It must have productive and receptive components. On the receptive side, the larger planum temporale (Fig. 3.2) seems to be associated with left-brainedness for speech and right-handedness (Witelson, 1983). As far as I know, no one has looked for an enlargement of the somatosensory mouth areas on the left; it is not clear whether such an enlargement would be necessary, provided the auditory cortex were larger on the left. On the productive side, Wada, Clarke, and Hamm (1975) were unable to demonstrate that Broca's area is larger on the left. Falzi, Perrone, and Vignolo (1982), however, estimated the areas of the anterior speech regions in 12 brains and found larger areas on the left side. The brains were also examined for the planum temporale, and there was no clear association between the two asymmetries. The three brains with larger Broca's area on the right differed from the two brains with larger planum on the right. However, the observation that exceptional cases are independent does not rule out the possible existence of some common influence on the growth of the frontal and posterior areas in most brains.

6.4.   WHAT IS SPECIAL ABOUT THE RIGHT HEMISPHERE?

It has been argued that the right hemisphere has the capacities to be expected of a large primate brain but without the capacity, in most people, to generate speech. Gazzaniga and LeDoux (1978) argued that functional differences between the cerebral hemispheres depend mainly on modifications to left-hemisphere processes associated with speech acquisition. Gazzaniga's (1983) further argument that a human cerebral hemisphere without speech has a level of intellectual ability inferior to that of a chimpanzee does not necessarily follow. The human right hemisphere could have a rich capacity for intellectual activity but, having delegated to the left side the acquisition of generative speech in the interests of over-all economy of function, be disproportionately handicapped, in comparison with the left, when the corpus callosum is divided. In the few split-brain patients who managed eventually to generate language from the right hemisphere, the concepts expressed seem to be not markedly different from those of the left hemisphere.

The analysis of right-hemisphere function is impeded by the fact that most right hemispheres cannot talk, and also by the rudimentary state of psychological theories of nonverbal cognition. In the growth of human intelligence a critical transition is made from a level at which all interactions with the world are in an immediate and direct mode (sensorimotor intelligence) to a level that can handle representations. Piaget (1951) noticed that several behaviours that depend on representative capacities are acquired at about the same time: the imitation of absent models, pretend play, using words symbolically, and recognising pictures as representations of objects. Neuropsychological comparisons of the right and left hemispheres for direct sensorimotor interactions with their respective halves of space have revealed no evidence of differences in function or efficiency. Questions of levels of intelligence concern capacities for representations of the world. The human right hemisphere can certainly respond to pictures, drawings, and photographs—most psychological tests depend on these materials. The unresolved questions concern the level of symbolic skill that the right hemisphere can bring to bear on these nonverbal representations.

It is possible, though difficult, to demonstrate conclusively that the right hemisphere is *more* efficient than the left in recognising and generating representations of reality in nonverbal modes. There are many skills that cannot be fully explained in words, such as recognising faces, dressing, tying shoelaces, manipulating three-dimensional objects, and travelling to distant places. The representations made to guide these activities in sketches, plans, and maps could owe as much to the right hemisphere as to the left. Accurate representations of sizes and distances involve measurement and counting. The construction and use of number systems requires the invention and application of verbal symbolic means of representing spatial relationships. Such symbolic systems, the basis of mathematical thinking, must depend on the cooperative activity of both cerebral hemispheres.

The characterisation of the right hemisphere as serving visuo-spatial functions is now firmly based on a wealth of neuropsychological evidence (De Renzi, 1982). It has been suggested above that the level of visuo-spatial reasoning in humans could demand high levels of nonverbal symbolic ability—while admitting that cognitive psychology has not yet elucidated what this might mean. But is this ability more than would be expected of an intelligent primate? I believe that there is no need to look for a mechanism of right-hemisphere specialisation. The differentiation of cerebral function in the typical human brain could depend on the single nudge that induces the left hemisphere to serve speech and subsequently to store words and their meanings, which the symbolic use of speech requires. Both hemispheres are probably capable of serving visuo-spatial processes, but the right is led to take the major role as the left becomes specialised for language.

6.5.   SUMMARY

Evidence is reviewed for a typical pattern of functional specialisation of the human cerebral hemispheres. Clinical studies of the effects of unilateral lesions, comparisons of the right and left hemisphere functions of split-brain patients, and research on the perceptual asymmetries of normal subjects consistently support the conclusion that in most people speech and other language skills depend on the left hemisphere, whereas the right hemisphere has some special role in tasks that require an appreciation of features of the spatially extended world. The special role of the left hemisphere encompasses many aspects of intellectual activity that depend on the use of verbal symbols. The special role of the right hemisphere has been detected in the appreciation of nonverbal patterns presented visually (in degraded drawings and pictures from unusual angles), auditorily (in environmental sounds and melodies), and tactually (in haptic perception and reading braille). It should be noted that the advantages of the right hemisphere for such tasks have been more difficult to identify and to substantiate than the advantages of the left hemisphere for verbal tasks.

Early unilateral brain lesions are associated with moderate impairments of intelligence but no specific deficits of verbal or nonverbal abilities. Children with comparable degrees of physical disability on the two sides were found to have virtually identical mean verbal and performance-scale IQs. Evidence for limitations in the capacities of each hemisphere to serve the intellectual functions normally served by the other is slender. There is a significant difference between the hemispheres in readiness to serve *speech*. Children with early left-hemisphere lesions are more likely than children with early right-hemisphere lesions to have transient problems of speech acquisition. Early lesions affecting the motor control of one hand force the child to use the other hand for fine movement, but in many cases of early unilateral lesion the damaged hemisphere continues to serve speech and the preferred hand.

Analysis of the *special* features of the left hemisphere, which might be responsible for directing the development of speech to that side, suggests that the left hemisphere is better fitted than the right hemisphere for making the fine temporal discriminations required for decoding speech sounds. In the development of speech, it is probably advantageous to have motor and sensory aspects of speech production on the same side of the brain. It seems possible that in most people the development of speech on the left side could be due to some mechanism that increases the probability that motor output and its associated somatosensory and auditory feedback are on the same side.

The capacity to construct symbolic propositions is probably an intrinsic feature of a large primate brain. The human dependence on the left hemisphere for verbal propositionising is probably a consequence rather than a cause of the capacity of that hemisphere to generate words. There is no need to postulate special mechanisms to account for right-hemisphere functions; they are probably the functions to be expected of a human brain that does not have the capacity to serve speech.

7 Hemisphere Specialisation in Left-Handers

7.1. CLINICAL STUDIES

7.1.1. Theories of Hemisphere Specialisation in Left-Handers

As outlined in Chapter 3, all possible patterns of cerebral specialisation have been suggested for left-handers. Table 7.1 summarises the alternatives and the authors mainly associated with each. The classic contralateral rule, that the speech hemisphere is opposite to the preferred hand, is one that is popularly believed *ought* to hold. The fact that it does not hold for left-handers was discovered soon after Broca adduced the left-hemisphere speech

TABLE 7.1

Hypotheses Concerning the Speech Laterality of Non-Right-Handers

	Cerebral Speech Representation	
1	right	Classic contralateral rule
2	left	Goodglass and Quadfasel (1954); Penfield and Roberts (1959)
3	either	Bingley (1958); Chesher (1936); Humphrey and Zangwill (1952)
4	both	Conrad (1949); Hécaen and Piercy (1956)
5	some combination of the above	Zangwill (1960); Roberts (1969)

rule for right-handers (Zangwill, 1960). In popular writings the idea continues to be reiterated. Psychologists look assiduously for evidence of the opposite rule, and recent theories (Levy & Nagylaki, 1972) have tried to preserve the rule for certain cases (left-handers who write with the pen in the normal orientation).

The observation that the majority of left-handers have *left*-hemisphere speech, like right-handers, led to questions about the relevance of handedness for hemisphere speech. It is true that more left-handers have left-sided speech than have right-sided speech, but the proportion with right-sided speech is significantly larger than in right-handers. Chesher (1936) was the first to suggest that *either* hemisphere could serve speech in some cases, but this flexibility was restricted by Chesher to mixed-handers, while the contralateral rule was expected to hold for strong left-handers. Humphrey and Zangwill (1952) found that a group of left-handers with unilateral cerebral lesions included some with evidence of left-sided and others of right-sided speech. Bingley (1958) reviewed the literature and described a new study of patients with temporal lobe lesions. He concluded that left-handers may develop cerebral speech in either hemisphere and suggested that about 50% develop speech on each side.

The theory that *both* hemispheres are involved in the cerebral speech of left-handers was stimulated by Conrad's (1949) observation of a slightly greater frequency, but also slightly greater transience, of aphasias in left-handers. The findings of Hécaen and Piercy (1956; see Section 3.3.1) led to the widely held belief that hemisphere speech is typically bilateral in left-handers. This view has taken so firm a hold that a recent case of a left-hander with right-sided speech was reported as a surprising departure from the expected bilaterality (Delis, Knight, & Simpson, 1983). In fact, the grounds for believing that left-handers are typically bilateral for cerebral speech are weak (Sections 7.1.3 and 14.3). Table 3.3 shows that only a small proportion of left-handers were affected by injections of sodium amytal on both sides. Further analysis of these cases showed that only about one-half (about 8% of left-handers overall) were fully bilateral for the speech functions tested (Rasmussen & Milner, 1975). In the remainder there was a cerebral division of labour such that one hemisphere was responsible for naming objects and the other for the semi-automatic speech required for saying the days of the week or months of the year.

Some combination of the above possibilities seems to be the most frequently used working hypothesis. In other words, left-handers may use either or both hemispheres for speech. In what proportions are these varieties of cerebral speech found? Here, there is great diversity of opinion. Zangwill (1960) estimated that about 40% of sinistrals could be bilateral (or indeterminate). Roberts (1969) suggested that a very small proportion are bilaterals, and about 30% of left-handers are right-brained. A study of transient dysphasias following unilateral ECT found 5% of left-handers affected by treatments on both sides and 24% by right-sided treatments only (Warrington & Pratt, 1973). Carter, Hohenegger, and Satz (1980) suggested that 76% of left-handers could have bilateral speech, but the methods used to reach this assessment are questionable (Bryden, 1982; Hammond and Kaplan, 1982; see Chapter 14).

Are "atypical" patterns of cerebral specialisation exclusive to left-handers? Right-handers with evidence of right cerebral speech have been reported as rare exceptions to the typical pattern described in Chapter 6 (Ettlinger, Jackson, & Zangwill, 1956; Hécaen, Mazars, Ramier, Goldblum, & Merienne, 1971; Zangwill, 1979). Wada testing has confirmed that right-sided and bilateral speech can occur in right-handers (Ratcliff, Dila, Taylor, & Milner, 1980). The proportion in which they occur in right-handers is as difficult to determine as for left-handers. A major source of the difficulty is shown to depend on the classification of handedness (in Sections 7.1.3 and 14.3).

If some people, including left- and right-handers, depend on one side of the brain for speech and on the other for the control of the preferred hand, how do they manage to write? EEG measures during writing have found greater suppression of alpha rhythms on the side opposite to the writing hand in right- and left-handers writing in the normal and the hooked position (Section 8.2), suggesting that writing is typically controlled from the contralateral hemisphere (Herron, Galin, Johnstone, & Ornstein, 1979). There are clinical reports of patients who lost the ability to write and to perform other learned actions without significant loss of speech, as would be expected if speech and writing sometimes depend on opposite sides of the brain. This pattern was observed in a left-hander who had been taught to write with the right hand and who lost the ability to write when the *left* arm became paralysed (Heilman, Coyle, Gonyea, & Geschwind, 1973). It was inferred that the patient had depended on his right hemisphere for skilled movements, including writing, and when forced to write with the right hand had controlled that hand via the corpus callosum; the cross-callosal route was used for writing, even though speech was on the left side. A similar but reversed pattern was reported in another patient who was right-handed but had right-hemisphere speech and lost the ability to write, but not to speak, when the left hemisphere was impaired (Heilman, Gonyea, & Geschwind, 1974). These observations suggest that although the control of the preferred hand and speech go together in the "typical" case, there is no necessary connection between these asymmetries.

7.1.2. Are Dysphasias More Transient In Left-Handers?

The transitory nature of some dysphasias in left-handers was noted by Subirana (1958) and by Gloning, Gloning, Haub, and Quatember (1969), as well as by Conrad (1949). Zangwill (1960) reported data of Luria (1947/1970) for the persistence of aphasias in groups of patients classified for handedness, as shown in Table 7.2. Whereas almost all the patients classified as right-handed continued to show some disability on follow-up examination, only about one third of left-handers and ambidexters did so. This comparison suggests greater capacity for recovery of speech in non-right-handers than right-handers following unilateral lesions. Evidence that recovery depends on the "other" hemisphere in some cases (Kinsbourne, 1971; Pettit & Noll, 1979) suggests that the alternative hemisphere may be more ready to serve speech in non-right-handers than in right-handers. Of course, either hemisphere can serve speech in children with severe early lesions of one side (Section 6.2); the either hypothesis for left-handed adults would imply a greater persistence of this readiness of the alternative hemisphere in mature left-handers than in mature right-handers.

The further observation of Luria (Table 7.2) that right-handers with sinistral tendencies or a left-handed relative showed capacities for recovery almost equal to those of left-handers could be interpreted as showing that some right-handers also retain the capacity to use the other hemisphere for speech. If the presence of left-handed relatives significantly affects the prognosis for aphasia, then a genetic influence on cerebral speech would be indicated. Subirana (1969) wrote that in his experience, "The aphasics with a left handed sibling are nearly always the champions of the rehabilitation division."

No support for the theory of relative transience of dysphasias in left-

TABLE 7.2
Persistence of Aphasia in Left- and Right-Handers

Handedness	N	Aphasia (Severe or Mild)	
		Initial Stage (%)	Residual Stage (%)
Pure right	64	100	97
Right with left tendencies or sinistral relative	73	77	37
Left-handed or ambidextrous	23	83	35

Note: Data of Luria (1947/70) based on Zangwill (1960).

handers was found by Newcombe and Ratcliff (1973). Table 7.3 compares the proportions of right- and left-handers who were recorded as dysphasic on admission to hospital and also on discharge in the British war wound series. No evidence was found of differential recovery rates between the two handedness groups (but see further Table 14.7).

TABLE 7.3
Persistence of Aphasia in Left- and Right-Handers

	N	Aphasia Present	
		Admission (%)	Discharge (%)
Right-handers	704	34	24
Left-handers	63	30	21

Note: Adapted from Newcombe and Ratcliff (1973).

7.1.3. Clinical Symptoms Associated With Unilateral Cortical Lesions in Left-Handers

Hécaen and Sauguet (1971) compared right- and left-handers with left- and right-sided cerebral lesions for over 50 symptoms recorded on clinical examination and by special tests. For almost all of these symptoms there were statistically significant differences within the right-handed group between those with left-sided and those with right-sided lesions; that is, for almost all symptoms in right-handers it is possible to say which hemisphere is associated with greater risk for that symptom. Comparisons within the left-handed group were also made for lesion side. Further comparisons were reported between left-handers and right-handers for the effects of left-sided lesions, right-sided lesions, or lesions on either side. Hécaen and Sauguet's report is difficult to follow because of the number of symptoms and also the number of different kinds of comparison made.

Table 7.4 lists the percentages of patients showing certain symptoms in pairs of columns. Columns 1 and 2 compare right- and left-handers having lesions of either side; columns 3 and 4 compare the effects of left- and right-sided lesions in right-handers, and columns 5 and 6 the effects of left- and right-sided lesions in left-handers. The symptoms listed include all those associated with significant differences in left-handers; the symptoms associated with left-hemisphere lesions in right-handers are listed first, followed by those associated with right-hemisphere lesions in right-handers. The

TABLE 7.4
Comparisons of Right- and Left-Handers for the Effects of Unilateral Cerebral Lesions[a]

Side of unilateral lesion	(a) Comparisons Between Handedness Groups, Irrespective of Lesion Side		(b) Comparisons Between Left- and Right-Sided Lesions in Each Handedness Group			
	Right-Handers	Left-Handers	Right-Handers		Left-Handers	
	Left or Right	Left or Right	Left	Right	Left	Right
N^b	487	73	293	194	47	26
(cases as % of N) Deficits associated with left-hemisphere lesions in right-handers						
Oral language						
Articulation	8	12	13*	0	18	4
Naming	23	23	38*	0	31	12
Comprehension	20*	10	33*	0	11	8
Reading						
Words	10	12	16*	0	14	8
Complex commands	20	23	33*	1	31*	8
Text	29	45*	38*	16	58*	23
Writing						
Sentences	28	34	44*	4	44*	16
Copy	13	19	20*	3	26	10
Numbers	18	22	30*	1	29*	8

(continued)

TABLE 7.4—*continued*

	1	2	3	4	5	6
Calculation						
Anarithmetia	39	41	53*	18	56*	15
Mental calculation	34	29	54*	5	38	10
Recognition of position of digits within a number	34	26	44*	18	25	29
Verbal designation of the fingers	9	4	14*	1	3	9
Ideomotor apraxia	6	1	10*	0	2	0
Deficits associated with right-hemisphere lesions in right-handers						
"Spatial" dyslexia	9	15	1	22*	7	31*
"Spatial" dysgraphia	12	16	4	25*	9	31*
Constructional apraxia	33	37	25	45*	26	59*
Dressing apraxia	6	9	0	16*	9	9
Unilateral spatial agnosia	12	14	0	31*	5	32*

Note: Data from Hécaen and Sauguet (1971).

[a] An asterisk (*) indicates a significant difference in percentage (at the .10 level or smaller) in comparison with the paired column; that is, between right- and left-handers in columns 1 and 2, or between left and right lesions in columns 3 and 4, or 5 and 6. The * denotes the greater impairment.

[b] N denotes the maximum number, but not all patients were included in all comparisons; the percentages in columns 3–6 are taken from Hécaen and Sauguet (1971), but the percentages in columns 1 and 2 are estimated, where not specifically given by Hécaen and Sauguet.

percentages in columns 3 to 6 are taken directly from Hécaen and Sauguet's (1971) report, but the percentages in columns 1 and 2 are estimated where not given directly; since the percentages in columns 1 and 2 are estimated where not estimates are approximate. Some important points should be borne in mind about the numbers of cases. The very large numbers of right-handers imply that relatively small differences in percentage are likely to be statistically significant, whereas the very much smaller numbers of left-handers, especially left-handers with right-sided lesions, imply that statistically significant differences are unlikely to be obtained *even when absolute percentages in right- and left-handers are similar.*

When Hécaen and Sauguet's (1971) findings are set out as in Table 7.4, certain features become readily apparent. First, substantial differences between left- and right-handers for the risk of psychological deficits were found for only two of the large number of comparisons made. Left-handers were less likely to suffer defects of oral language comprehension, but they were more likely to have difficulties in reading from text than right-handers. The risks of disorders of naming were identical in the two handedness groups; there is no reason to believe that left-handers are more or less likely than right-handers to suffer disorders of speech and other language functions.

With regard to comparisons for lesion side within handedness groups, all symptoms listed show statistically significant differences for right-handers. Some of the comparisons for lesion side within left-handers are also statistically significant, and in all cases the significant findings are *in the same direction as for right-handers.* There is no instance of a statistically significant result that goes the "opposite way" in left-handers and right-handers. Inspection of the percentages for left- and right-handers suffering symptoms associated with left- and right-sided lesions shows a remarkable similarity between handedness groups for most symptoms. The chief difference between handedness groups is that whereas almost no right-handers were recorded as having language disturbances following right-sided lesions, a small percentage of left-handers were so recorded. This is as would be expected from the data given in Table 3.1. Two or three of the left-handers with right-sided lesions in Hécaen and Sauguet's sample appear to have right-hemisphere speech; the majority of left-handers appear to depend on the left hemisphere, like the majority of right-handers. Examining the symptoms associated with right-hemisphere lesions in right-handers, the same conclusion seems warranted as for left-hemisphere symptoms. The majority of left-handers resemble right-handers, but a few do not.

Hécaen and Sauguet examined a subset of their data in relation to the presence of left-handed relatives (familial sinistrality or FS) and also in relation to the strength of sinistral tendencies, as assessed by questionnaire. It should be noted that these two variables were not independent. Of FS− left-handers, 34% were classified as weak, and of FS+ left-handers, 65% were weak ($\chi^2 = 4.43$, $df = 1$, $p < .05$). The possibility that there might be a relationship between FS and strength of sinistrality was examined in a student population by McKeever and Van Deventer (1977b) and not supported. The association in Hécaen and Sauguet's series could be accidental, or it could have arisen if patients with weak personal tendencies to sinistrality were more likely to be classified as sinistral if they had left-handed relatives.

With regard to cerebral laterality, the FS+ left-handers and the weak left-handers were more likely to show atypical patterns of deficit than the FS− and the strong left-handers. The finding for strength of handedness looks paradoxical, but it is not unexpected if knowledge of the patients' symptomatology influenced the classification of handedness. If patients with language disturbances associated with *right* hemisphere lesions were more likely to be classified as left-handed on the basis of *weak* personal sinistrality *and the presence of sinistral relatives*, the association would follow. The possibility that a weak criterion of sinistrality was adopted for dysphasics, especially for dysphasics with right-sided lesions, will be supported by the analysis in Section 14.2.

Hécaen, De Agostini, and Monzon-Montes (1981) reported findings for a smaller number of symptoms in groups of right-handers and left-handers classified for the presence or absence of sinistral relatives. Table 7.5 summarises their findings in paired columns, to facilitate comparisons between groups. For FS− right-handers almost all comparisons were statistically significant, with certain symptoms being clearly associated with left-hemisphere lesions and others with right-hemisphere lesions. As Hécaen and colleagues acknowledge, the lack of statistical significance for FS+ right-handers was largely due to the small numbers. What was found for left-handers? As in the data of Hécaen and Sauguet, fewer of the comparisons for left-handers were statistically significant than for FS− right-handers, but in all cases where statistically significant differences occur they are in the *same direction* as for right-handers. Looking across the rows, the similarities between groups are more striking than the differences. In comparison with FS− right-handers, left-handers (both FS− and FS+) are a little more likely to suffer disorders of language functions in association with right-sided lesions. They are also a little more likely than right-handers to suffer disorders of nonverbal functions in association with left-sided lesions. In the majority of left-handers deficits of all kinds are associated with lesions on the same side as typical of right-handers.

With regard to the issue of bilaterality of cerebral speech, Hécaen and Sauguet (1971) concluded that "cerebral ambilaterality is not a characteristic of all left handers, but only of those who belong to the familial type". Hécaen, De Agostini, and Monzon-Montes (1981) suggested that their new

TABLE 7.5
Comparison of the Effects of Left- and Right-Sided Unilateral Cerebral Lesions in Right- and Left-Handers Without (FS−) and With (FS+) a Left-handed Relative (First Degree)[a]

Familial Sinistrality	Right-Handers								Left-Handers							
Laterality of Lesion	FS−				FS+				FS−				FS+			
	Left		Right		Left		Right		Left		Right		Left		Right	
	(%)	(Score)	(%)	(Score)	(%)	(Score)	(%)	(Score)	(%)	(Score)	(%)	(Score)	(%)	(Score)	(%)	(Score)
N (maximum)	46		34		24		26		38		32		46		21	
Nonfluency	22*		3		8		19		37*		13		37		19	
Articulation	17		6		4		0		34*		13		35*		10	
Naming		84.6*		100		86.9*		100		82.7*		97.5		71.2*		89.8
Auditory comprehension		80.1*		97.9		84.3*		97.8		79.9*		95.0		80.4		88.6
Visual verbal comprehension		75.5*		97.8		84.8		96.1		70.6*		92.2		72.6		87.6
Writing		2.9*		3.8		3.3		3.7		2.6*		3.7		2.8		3.4
Spatial dysgraphia	17		41*		13		31		30		34		33		62*	
Unilateral spatial agnosia	2		21*		0		12		16		9		4		43*	
Constructional apraxia	17		35		4		23		34		16		17		48*	
Spatial agnosia	4		24*		0		4		26		13		4		29*	

Note: Data from Hécaen, De Agostini and Monzon-Montes (1981).

[a] An asterisk (*) indicates a significant difference (at the .05 level or smaller, on the calculations of Hécaen et al.) between left and right lesion cases for each group; the * denotes the side associated with more frequent impairment.

analysis confirmed the greater cerebral ambilaterality of FS+ left-handers. However, the observation that the risks of language disorder are more evenly spread between the left and right hemispheres in groups of left-handers having lesions on each side does not necessarily imply that representation of language functions is evenly spread between the left and right hemispheres of individuals. This argument rested, in the Hécaen and Piercy (1956) analysis, on the observation of greater risk of language disorder in left-handers than in right-handers, *whichever the lesion side*. There is no sign of this greater risk in the data reported by Hécaen and Sauguet (1971) or Hécaen and colleagues (1981). In my view the most impressive feature of Hécaen's data is the similarity between right- and left-handers in patterns of deficit. Left-handers differ from right-handers as would be expected from the distributions in Table 3.1, namely, that left-handed individuals are a little more likely than right-handed individuals to show "reversed" patterns of cerebral representation, but this reversal is by no means typical of left-handers.

The fact that *some* reversals of cerebral organisation occur in left-handers is confirmed by recent case reports (Brust, Plank, Burke, Guobadia, & Healton, 1982; Delis, Knight, & Simpson, 1983; Poeck & Lehmkuhl, 1980). The fact that these are infrequent is confirmed by the absence of aphasias in 13 left-handers with right-hemisphere lesions (Kimura, 1983b) and the absence of instances of visuo-spatial deficit in 7 left-handers with left-hemisphere lesions (Kimura, 1983b). In Kimura's sample, the incidence of aphasia in 27 left-handers with left-hemisphere lesions was smaller than in right-handers with left-sided lesions, not larger, as in the series on which the bilaterality in left-handers hypothesis was founded. This close look at symptoms associated with cerebral lesions in left-handers supports the conclusions drawn in Chapter 3, that a majority of left-handers have left-hemisphere speech, a substantial minority have right-hemisphere speech, and some small proportion (yet to be determined) have bilateral speech.

7.2.   STUDIES OF NORMAL LEFT-HANDERS

7.2.1.   Perceptual Asymmetries in Left-Handers

As mentioned in Section 6.1.3, Kimura's (1961) demonstration that digits played in dichotic pairs tend to be reported better at the ear opposite to the known speech hemisphere led to an explosion of studies of perceptual asymmetries in normal subjects. Can ear differences be used to diagnose hemisphere speech in normal right- and left-handers? To answer this question, one would need to know how often the ear difference score would predict the *wrong* side for cerebral speech. If the differences between ears

(Table 6.1) are expressed as proportions of the total score correct, the largest difference is about 9%; given some individual variability about this difference, some misclassification would be expected. Does left-handedness have any significance for ear differences? Bryden (1978) reanalysed Kimura's data to show that within each hemisphere speech group, left-handers are less biased to the right ear than right-handers. Kimura omitted ambidexters from her report. It seems probable that they would have diluted the difference between groups.

Other problems for individual diagnosis concern reliability. Correlations between scores on test and retest are statistically significant but give considerable scope for reclassification of subjects between test sessions (Fennell, Bowers, & Satz, 1977; Pizzamiglio, Pascalis, & Vignati, 1974; Repp, 1977; Teng, 1981). Satz (1977) drew attention to the doubtful status of inferences about hemisphere speech from ear differences on dichotic listening tests, since many more subjects obtain LEAs than would be expected to have right-hemisphere speech, on clinical evidence. Is this because ear asymmetries are poor predictors of cerebral speech laterality or because testing methods are not sufficiently sensitive?

When differences between the scores for each ear on dichotic listening tests are plotted for several subjects, the distribution is found to be continuous (Orlando, 1972; Shankweiler & Studdert-Kennedy, 1975). This implies that all classifications are to some extent arbitrary. Modifications of the dichotic listening technique have been developed that report findings more in accord with clinical expectations (Geffen, Traub, & Stierman, 1978; Wexler & Hawles, 1983). Figure 7.1 shows the distribution of ear difference scores for subjects of differing handedness, tested by a dichotic monitoring technique (in which the listener gives a manual response when a target word occurs in

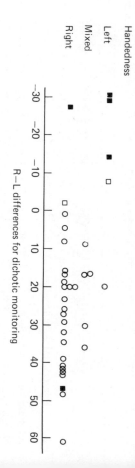

FIG. 7.1.   The relations between handedness, brainedness and R–L differences between ears on a dichotic monitoring test. Data of Geffen, Traub, & Stierman, 1978.

the streams of words played to either ear). The majority of subjects were psychiatric patients being treated by unilateral ECT, and the speech hemisphere was inferred from differences in numbers of errors to questions following treatment of each side. Except for one patient, there was a remarkable concordance between the classification of speech hemisphere and extent of ear difference. Ear differences were continuously distributed between strong REA and strong LEA. Of the 10 mixed- and left-handers, 3 showed LEA, 6 REA, and 1 no difference between ears.

Table 7.6 summarises data from several studies of normal subjects. They are studies for which the proportions of subjects with REA were given or could be inferred for right-handers and for left-handers who were assessed by the same procedures (differences between the studies do not matter for this comparison). The percentages of right-handers with REA range from 72 to 86% and for mixed- and left-handers with REA range from 53 to 65%. In all studies, there were fewer left- than right-handers with REA, but in no case did a majority of left-handers show LEA. Other studies agree in finding left-handers to have REAs like right-handers, but at a reduced level (Briggs & Nebes, 1976; Curry & Rutherford, 1967; Searleman, 1980) or no significant bias to either side (Fry, 1975).

Have any studies found left-handers with significant LEA? There are none with a convincing difference in this direction. Bryden (1965) found a nonsignificant trend to LEA in 20 left-handers. Zurif and Bryden (1969) found 10 FS+ left-handers unbiased to either side. Knox and Boone (1970) reported a significant mean LEA, but their subjects were 11 very strong left-handers selected from a subject pool of 80, who were asked to listen to digits

TABLE 7.6

Right-Handed Versus Mixed- and Left-Handed Subjects Showing Right-Ear Advantage in Dichotic Listening Studies

	Right-Handers		Mixed and Left-Handers	
	N	REA (%)	N	REA (%)
Lake and Bryden (1976)	72	72	72	61
McGlone and Davidson (1973)	49	84	50	64
Geffen and Traub (1980)	43	84	62	61
Lishman and McMeekan (1977)	22	86	20	65
Dee (1971)	49	77	70	53

against a background of white noise. Satz, Achenbach, and Fennell (1967) examined ear differences for 33 strong left-handers who were clearly superior with the left hand on measures of skill; the proportion with REA (54%) was as found in other studies (in Table 7.6; see further Table 14.9).

The possibility of a genetic influence on REA has been explored in a twin study and a family study. Springer and Searleman (1978) tested 75 MZ and 47 DZ same-sex twin pairs. The pairs were concordant for right-handedness in just over 70% of twins of each type. Considering the data for individuals, the proportions of subjects showing REA were in accord with those above, about 80% for right-handers and 64% for left-handers. Considering the data for pairs, MZ pairs were not more alike than DZ pairs. Bryden (1975) tested parents and children in 49 families. All correlations between relatives were very small. It seems that the differences between relatives for dichotic listening measurements are more impressive than the similarities, and there is no evidence here for a genetic influence on variations in ear asymmetry.

Asymmetries of visual perception using the divided visual field technique have been reviewed for differences between handedness groups by Annett (1982). Studies varied in the tasks used, methods of analyses, and the classifications of handedness, but these details need not concern us here as it is being asked what was found for non-right-handed subjects when they were tested by the same methods that gave significant RVA in right-handers. Table 7.7 lists findings for right- and left-handers in several studies using letters or words as stimuli. The direction of difference is recorded for significant comparisons; differences of unreported significance are indicated with a query. Only three studies reported significant biases in left-handers, and two of these were for RVA, as for right-handers. The majority of studies found no significant bias in left-handers. The one report of a significant LVA in left-handers (Haun, 1978) was based on 12 subjects.

Table 7.8 compares the visual fields of right- and left-handers for several kinds of nonverbal stimuli. Some of the most systematic comparisons found no significant bias in right- or left-handers (Bryden, 1973). Others found significant LVA in right-handers, and, among these, only one found a significant opposite RVA in left-handers. This one exception depended on a group of 12 left-handers.

Table 7.9 summarises findings for right- and left-handers distinguished for absence of left-handed relatives (FS −) or their presence (FS +). There is no substantial evidence of a reversal of asymmetry between right- and left-handers, whether FS − or FS +. The two studies finding such a reversal depended on FS + left-handers in groups of $N = 4$ and $N = 12$. Thus, distinctions for family handedness do not lead to the discovery of reversed visual asymmetries.

Differences between handedness groups have been sought in asymmetries in the facial expression of emotion. Right-handers tend to express emotions

TABLE 7.7

Summary of Findings for Visual-Field Asymmetries for Verbal Stimuli in Right- and Left-Handers

	Right-Handers		Left-Handers	
	N	Asymmetry	N	Asymmetry
Bryden (1964)	108	RVA	27	NS trend RVA
Bryden (1965)	20	RVA	20	None
Zurif and Bryden (1969)	20	RVA	20	NS trend RVA
Bryden (1973)	32	RVA	32	None
Cohen (1972)	6	RVA	6	NS trend LVA
McKeever and Gill (1972)	20	RVA	9	NS trend LVA
McKeever et al. (1973)	24	RVA	24	NS trend RVA
McKeever et al. (1975)	20	RVA	20	NS trend RVA
McKeever and Van Deventer (1977c)	44	RVA	71	?RVA
Dimond and Beaumont (1974)	18	RVA	12	RVA
Holmes and Marshall (1974)	30	RVA	18	NS trend RVA
Hines and Satz (1974)	60	RVA	30	?RVA
Fennell et al. (1977a)	16	RVA	—	—
Fennell et al. (1977b)	—	—	20	RVA
Haun (1978)	12	RVA	12	LVA

Note: From Annett, 1982.

TABLE 7.8

Summary of Findings for Visual-Field Asymmetries for Nonverbal Stimuli in Right- and Left-Handers

	Stimuli	Right-Handers		Left-Handers	
		N	Asymmetry	N	Asymmetry
Bryden (1964)	Geometrical forms	47	NS trend RVA	15	None
Bryden (1973)	Nonsense forms	32	None	32	None
Bryden (1973)	Dot location	32	NS trend RVA	32	NS trend RVA
Beaumont and Dimond (1975)	Abstract shapes	20	LVA	10	LVA
McGlone and Davidson (1973)	Dot enumeration	35	NS trend LVA	44	NS trend LVA
Smith and Moscovitch (1979)	Dot location	16	LVA	16	LVA
Gilbert and Bakan (1973)	Faces	34	LVA	29	None
Gilbert (1977)	Faces	32	LVA	32	LVA
Lawson (1978)	Faces	130	LVA	68	None
Davidoff (1975)	Lightness (greys)	12	LVA	12	RVA
Davidoff (1975)	Lightness (red/grey)	12	LVA	12	None
Jeeves and Dixon (1970)	Lights for RT	?40	LVA	?20	LVA
Jeeves (1972)	Lights for RT	10	LVA	10	None

Note: From Annett, 1982.

TABLE 7.9

Summary of Findings for Visual-Field Asymmetries in Right- and Left-Handers, With and Without Left-Handed Relatives

	Right-Handers				Left-Handers			
	FS−		FS+		FS−		FS+	
	N	Asymmetry	N	Asymmetry	N	Asymmetry	N	Asymmetry
Alphanumeric stimuli								
Bryden (1965)	20	RVA	—		16	NS trend RVA	4	LVA
Zurif and Bryden (1969)	20	RVA	—		10	RVA	10	NS trend LVA
Bryden (1973)	16	?RVA	16	?RVA	16	?NS trend RVA	16	?NS trend RVA
McKeever and Gill (1972)	13	RVA	7	NS trend RVA	—		—	
McKeever et al. (1973)	24	RVA	24	NS trend RVA	9	NS trend RVA	14	NS trend RVA
McKeever et al. (1975)	—		—		13	RVA	7	None
McKeever and Van Deventer (1977c)	44	RVA	36	NS trend RVA	34	NS trend RVA	37	RVA
McKeever and Jackson (1979)	12	RVA	12	RVA	—		—	
Hines and Satz (1974)	30	RVA	30	RVA	—		—	
Higenbottam (1973)	32	RVA	—		28	RVA	26	RVA
Holmes and Marshall (1974a)	30	RVA	—		18	NS trend RVA	—	
Marshall and Holmes (1974)	48	?RVA	48	?RVA	—		48	?RVA
Bradshaw et al. (1977)	24	RVA	—		—		24	NS trend RVA
Bradshaw and Taylor (1979)	24	RVA	—		24	NS trend RVA	24	RVA
Haun (1978)	12	RVA	—		—		12	LVA
Piazza (1980)	16	?RVA	16	?RVA	16	?RVA	16	?RVA
Non-alphanumeric stimuli								
Bryden (1973) (Nonsense forms)	16	None	16	None	16	None	16	None
Bryden (1973) (Dot location)	16	?NS trend RVA	16	?NS trend RVA	16	?NS trend RVA	16	?NS trend RVA
Piazza (1980) (Faces)	16	LVA	16	None	16	?NS trend RVA	16	None

Note: Annett, 1982.

more strongly with the left side of the face and to judge the left sides of perceived faces as more expressive (Campbell, 1978). As in the comparisons reviewed above, left-handers were found to resemble right-handers (Borod, Caron, & Koff, 1981; Heller & Levy, 1981; Koff, Borod, & White, 1981) or to show no consistent asymmetries to either side (Moscovitch & Olds, 1982).

Reports of greater sensitivity of the left than the right hand in right-handers to tactile stimuli have been supported in some studies (Rhodes & Schwartz, 1981; Witelson, 1976) but not in others (Fennell, Satz & Wise, 1967). Left-handers have been reported to show differences in the same direction as right-handers (Weinstein & Sersen, 1961) or no difference between sides (Fennell, Satz, & Wise, 1967; Harris, 1980b). Thus studies of tactile asymmetries resemble those for auditory and visual field asymmetries in finding that for left-handers, differences between sides are like those of right-handers, but often smaller.

7.2.2. Motor Asymmetries in Left-Handers

The tendency to gesticulate, to make spontaneous hand movements while conversing, was studied by Kimura (1973a, 1973b). While speaking, right-handers made more free movements (not touching the self or other objects) with the right hand than with the left hand. Self-touching movements, such as rubbing the chin or pushing back hair, were made equally often with both hands. Left-handed and ambidextrous subjects made free movements while speaking equally often with either hand, as they did for self-touching movements. When the left-handers and ambidexters were classified for dichotic listening performance, those with REA behaved like right-handers, and those with LEA made more free movements with the left hand. This would suggest that the hand used to gesticulate during speaking is contralateral to the speech hemisphere, as if the activity of speaking "overflows" to the hand on the same side. Dalby, Gibson, Grossi, and Schneider (1980) confirmed that right-handers make more gestures with the right hand than the left during speech and that there is no lateral bias of self-touching movements. The observation that self-touching movements tend to be made by either hand accords with findings for nursery-school children (Brown, 1962; Ingram, 1975). It is clear that not all types of unilateral movement are more often performed by the hand preferred for tasks of skill. This is to be expected from the hierarchical organisation of the motor system (Chapter 2).

Movements of the eyes to the left or right have been hypothesised to reflect greater activation of the right or left hemisphere, respectively, and there seems to be some support for this theory from regional blood flow studies (Gur & Reivich, 1980). Several studies (reviewed by Kinsbourne, 1974) found significantly more rightward gaze when subjects were solving verbal problems. This result has not been universal (Erhlichman, Weiner, &

Baker, 1974; Erhlichman & Weinberger, 1978). Berg and Harris (1980) concluded that the reliability of gaze shifts as a measure of hemisphere activation needs further study. There seem to have been few comparisons of right- and left-handers for lateral gaze, but in conditions where right-handers were found to show the expected bias, left-handers showed no systematic bias to either side (Gur, Gur, & Harris, 1975).

Movements of the mouth during speaking were compared for extent of activity on the right and left side by Graves, Goodglass, and Landis (1982). The lower right half of the face has stronger links with the left than the right hemisphere. In four experiments involving nearly 200 subjects, greater right-sided mouth opening was recorded for about three-quarters of the time. The asymmetry was greater in male right-handers (86%) than in male left-handers (67%). Findings for females differed between tasks and were less clear.

7.3. SUMMARY

There is no generally agreed theory as to the brainedness of left-handers. Clinical studies demonstrate that some left-handers depend on the right hemisphere for speech and on the left hemisphere for visuo-spatial skills, but this reversal is relatively infrequent. Some left-handers have bilateral speech representation, but this also is infrequent. The majority of left-handers show the typical pattern of cerebral representation considered in Chapter 6. It must be recognised that all possible patterns of cerebral lateralisation can occur in right-handers also. Estimates of the proportion of people having each type of cerebral speech have varied widely.

Comparisons of left- and right-handers for symptoms following unilateral lesions of each hemisphere found left-handers a little more likely than right-handers to have difficulties in oral reading but less likely to have defects of oral comprehension. When the frequency of symptoms associated with lesions of each side was examined, all significant effects for left-handers were in the same direction as for right-handers. That is, there was no indication of a reversal of cerebral asymmetry between handedness groups. The interpretation of analyses for the presence of sinistral relatives and for the strength of hand preferences is complicated by the fact that these variables were not independent.

The theory that most left-handers have bilaterally represented speech has no substantial foundation. The fact that some left-handers have reversed asymmetry would be sufficient to make group means smaller for left-handers than for right-handers on measures of asymmetry. The fact that *groups* of left-handers appear to show little bias does not necessarily imply that lack of bias is characteristic of individual left-handers. Comparisons of right- and left-handers with and without left-handed relatives, for the clinical effects of unilateral lesions, find very few significant differences between groups. There are a number of indications that left-handers are more likely to recover from dysphasias than right-handers, but one test of a large sample found no evidence for such a difference.

Some measures of perceptual and motor asymmetries in normal subjects are probably associated with cerebral speech laterality. There is no certainty at present that these asymmetries can be used for the diagnosis of cerebral laterality in individual cases. The group data are surprisingly consistent between studies in showing that for measures on which 70 to 80% of right-handers are biased in a particular direction, 50 to 60% of left-handers are also biased in the *same direction*. In other words, groups of left-handers usually show weak biases in the same direction as found in groups of right-handers, or no bias at all. Studies finding reversal of bias in groups of left-handers are exceptional, and all are based on small numbers of cases. As argued previously for the clinical evidence, weak or absent biases in group data do *not* imply weak or absent biases in individuals. Classifying subjects for the presence of left-handed relatives has not led to any substantial clarification of the evidence.

8 Speculations About Patterns of Cerebral Specialisation

Speculations that lead to testable hypotheses are essential for scientific progress, but speculations that do not threaten to drown us in a sea of conjecture. Much of the literature on hemisphere asymmetry seems to be of the latter kind, but an attempt must be made to navigate these dangerous waters.

It was seen in Chapter 6 that there is a pattern of cerebral specialisation that may be regarded as typical of the majority and in Chapter 7 that some people differ from this pattern. Unless all departures from the typical case are accidental, and there is reason to believe that they are not (Section 14.1), it may be asked how and why people differ in cerebral asymmetry. The fact that left-hemisphere speech is predominant in *Homo sapiens* suggests that it must have conferred some advantage in the past, whether or not it continues to do so. If it conferred an advantage, why is it not universal in the population? These questions parallel the questions that may be asked about handedness: Why are most people right-handed, and if right-handedness is advantageous, why is it not universal? The causes of brain asymmetries and of hand asymmetries could be independent or related. If evolutionary mechanisms are involved, patterns of laterality must have *implications* for individual differences in human performance, in the sense discussed in Chapters 1 and 5. This chapter gives a selective review of issues concerning individual differences in hemisphere specialisation, including sex differences in cerebral organisation.

8.1.   HOW MANY PATTERNS OF CEREBRAL SPECIALISATION?

If speech can depend on the left, or right, or both hemispheres, as suggested for left-handers in Table 7.1, these alternatives give three possible patterns of hemisphere specialisation. Are visuo-spatial functions similarly variable? If so, there are nine possible patterns of hemisphere specialisation. Logically, the null hypothesis (absence of specialisation) should be included, to give 16 possible patterns, as set out in Fig. 8.1. Are the specialisations of one hemisphere independent of those of the other, or are they interactive? Is there competition for hemisphere-processing capacity? Are specialisations all-or-none or graded variables? Perhaps people differ in the proportions of each hemisphere's capacity given to verbal or visuo-spatial functions. Clearly, the range of possibilities is enormous, and the problems of generating testable predictions are similar in scale.

Certain patterns are identified in Fig. 8.1 as possible representations of certain theoretical positions. Pattern 1, V/S (verbal left/spatial right) is the commonly accepted "rule" for the typical right-handed adult. VS/VS indi-

Left hemisphere	Right hemisphere			
	Verbal (V) L R	Spatial (S) L R	Verbal & Spatial (VS) L R	Neither (O) L R
Verbal	V – V[5]	V – S[1]	V – VS	V – O
Spatial	S – V	S – S[4]	S – VS	S – O
Verbal & Spatial	VS – V	VS – S[3]	VS –VS[2]	VS – O[6]
Neither	O – V	O – S	O – VS	O – O

Some hypotheses

[1] Typical right-handed adult.
[2] Normal potential at birth. Lenneberg, 1967.
[3] An alternative view of the typical pattern (Gazzaniga & LeDoux, 1978) or typical for males only (Buffrey & Gray, 1972).
[4] Mixed handers with unilateral EEG foci. Annett, Lee & Ounsted, 1961.
[5] Left-handers and females. Levy, 1973.
[6] Females, Inglis & Lawson, 1982.

FIG. 8.1.   Some hypotheses about verbal and spatial cerebral specialisation by the left and right hemispheres (specialisation, in all cases should be considered relative rather than absolute). v = verbal; s = spatial; o = neither.

cates that the hemispheres might be equipotential. VS/S reflects the view of Gazzaniga and LeDoux (1978) that both hemispheres serve spatial skill in the primate brain, while verbal specialisations are superimposed on the left side. S/S represents speculations advanced by Annett, Lee, and Ounsted (1961) on the basis of findings for mixed-handed children with EEG foci of either hemisphere (Section 5.2.2). V/V represents Levy's (1969) hypothesis that verbal abilities might take precedence over visuo-spatial ones in the development of abilities in left-handers (Section 5.2.2). This hypothesis was later extended to females (Levy, 1973) and has been widely accepted (see Bradshaw & Nettleton, 1983, p. 265). Pattern V/V was also implied in Teuber's (1974) suggestion that in hemiplegic children visuo-spatial skills were likely to be more impaired than verbal skills. Annett (1973b), however, found evidence of visuo-spatial impairment only in hemiplegic children with disabilities of the better hand also (see Section 6.2). Pattern 6, VS/O, represents the view of Inglis and Lawson (1982) on the cerebral specialisation of females (Section 8.5).

The authors referred to above might object that the patterns in Table 8.1 represent their views in a very rough fashion. But if refinements are to be introduced, the complexity must be increased. Further complications arise when it is asked whether patterns apply to typical right-handers, or to left-handers, or to those of mixed hand preferences? It was considerations such as these that led me to suggest (Annett, 1980) that there are as many patterns in the laterality literature as in the Rorschach literature and as little likelihood of making testable predictions.

8.2.   ARE THERE INDICES OF CEREBRAL SPECIALISATION?

The only variable shown so far to be relevant to hemisphere specialisation is hand preference, and it has been evident that this is a very poor guide to cerebral laterality. In Chapter 5 the evidence concerning the implications of hand preference for intelligence, abilities, and personality was reviewed, and in so far as hand preference indexes cerebral specialisation, we can conclude that there are weak and unclear associations between left-handedness and developmental problems of speech and reading; left-handers may have advantages in a variety of "right-hemisphere" skills, not disadvantages as postulated by Levy (1969).

If hand preference is such a poor guide to cerebral laterality (even when other lateral preferences such as those for eye and foot are taken into account), can any other clues be found as to cerebral asymmetry? A frequent suggestion has been that classification for the presence or absence of sinistral relatives (FS+ or FS−) should improve the differentiation between laterality groups. This variable appeared to distinguish usefully between sub-groups of left-handers in Hécaen and Sauguet's (1971) clinical studies, but it was shown in Section 7.1.3. that this was not necessarily to be taken at face value. It has become common practice to classify normal right- and left-handers studied for perceptual asymmetries into FS+ and FS− subgroups. Table 7.9 showed that this practice did little to clarify findings for studies of asymmetries of visual perception.

McKeever and VanDeventer (1977c) reviewed studies of perceptual asymmetries in normals for the effect of classifying subjects for sex, personal handedness, and familial handedness. Many inconsistencies were found between studies, but it was concluded, "that both FS and sex may moderate the degree of 'cerebral dominance' for language processing". A replication of findings for a sex–FS interaction seems to be based on differences that depend on 1 or 2 subjects whose results "go the other way" (McKeever, Seitz, Hoff, Marino, & Diehl, 1983).

On theoretical grounds, if FS+ reduces the chances of the presence of the typical pattern of cerebral specialisation, groups should be ordered as follows: The strongest asymmetries should be found in FS− right-handers, followed by FS+ right-handers, then FS− left-handers, and FS+ left-handers. Bryden (1982) calculated verbal–nonverbal differences from scores for two verbal and two nonverbal tasks in data of Piazza (1980). The predicted order of size of laterality effect held except for small and almost certainly trivial reversals for FS− and FS+ left-handers. However, this study is but one of many where effects are less clear. It is not certain that FS+ has any detectable effect.

The strongest claims for an Index of Cerebral Dominance have been made for the manner of holding the pen, either in the normal or inverted orientation (Levy, 1974; Levy & Reid, 1978; Levy & Gur, 1980). The hypothesis derives from the Levy–Nagylaki (1972) model of the inheritance of handedness (Section 3.4.2), which suggested that some people have ipsilateral control of the preferred hand from the speech hemisphere. Those holding the pen in the normal orientation, pointed away from the body, were suggested to have the usual contralateral relation between hand and hemi-sphere, while those holding the pen in an inverted position, pointing towards the body, were predicted to have ipsilateral hand/hemisphere relations (Section 2.2). Thus left-handed inverters (LI) should be left-hemisphere dominant for speech and right-handed inverters (RI) right-hemisphere dominant for speech. RI are rare, but LI are relatively common. Compari-sons of left normal writers (LN) with LI should find opposite advantages on tasks of perceptual asymmetry. This hypothesis has been examined in five studies of dichotic listening, and none found significant differences or even noteworthy trends in the predicted directions (Beaumont & McCarthy, 1981; Herron, Galin, Johnstone, & Ornstein, 1979; McKeever & VanDeventer,

1980; Searleman, 1980; Smith & Moscovitch, 1979). There were differences between right- and left-handers of the sort seen in Table 7.6 but no differences between left-handers writing in the normal and inverted orientations.

Several authors have looked for opposite visual directional asymmetries between LN and LI writers and failed to find the predicted difference (Bradshaw & Taylor, 1979; Lawson, 1978; McKeever, 1979; McKeever & VanDeventer, 1980). Smith and Moscovitch (1979) found a trend in the predicted direction for verbal stimuli but no difference for dot location. Attempts have been made to test the hypothesis of contralateral versus ipsilateral hand hemisphere control by measuring reaction time with either hand to stimuli in each visual field. Smith and Moscovitch (1979) reported substantial differences in the expected directions, but McKeever and Hoff (1979) did not. In the first study, very much larger differences between sides were found than the reaction time literature would lead us to expect.

Another test of the hypothesis that inverted writing indexes ipsilateral cerebral control has been based on EEG measures of alpha suppression. Herron, Galin, Johnstone, and Ornstein (1979) measured the suppression of the alpha rhythms at central, parietal, and occipital leads in RN, LN, and LI writers while subjects wrote or performed several other tasks. For all three groups there was greater suppression on the side contralateral to the writing hand at the central and parietal leads. Right-handers showed greater alpha suppression during writing than left-handers, but there were no differences between the two groups of left-handers. At the occipital leads there was a small difference between LN and LI writers. The LI were unbiased to either side, while some of the LN group showed reversed asymmetry in comparison with right-handers. The number of subjects in group LN was 9.

In addition to this wealth of negative evidence for the idea that the hooked writing position is an index of cerebral dominance, there is a fundamental problem in the variability of ascertainment. In my observations of students writing examination papers I found 0.65% of 460 right-handers and 8.82% of 68 left-handers writing in the hooked position. Other studies reported 30 to 60% of left-handers using the inverted position (Peters & Pederson, 1978; Coren & Porac, 1979; McKeever, 1979). In Australian left-handers examined by Bradshaw and Taylor (1979), about 23% were inverted writers. The ascertainment of writing position seems to be very variable between observers. Presumably the criterion of inversion can be set at any point through about 180°. Levy (1982) tried to account for the difference between North American and Australian incidences in terms of pressures of the school system on conformity for writing position; if that is the cause of the differences in incidences, the pressures in British schools must be tremendous, but such pressures have escaped notice. My own view is that a variable subject to such vagaries of training or ascertainment cannot "index" anything. It may well be that the practice of writing with the hand inverted will turn out to be related to interesting psychological variables, but it cannot be an index of cerebral dominance.

8.3.   WHAT IS LATERALISED?

In studies of perceptual asymmetries in normal subjects, it soon became evident that the verbal–nonverbal dichotomy was not always sufficient to predict what would be heard or seen better on each side. For example, letter stimuli are associated with faster responses in the LVF than RVF when judgements have to be made about their physical identity, whereas faster responses are made to RVF than LVF presentations of the same stimuli when judgements have to be made about their names (Cohen, 1972; Geffen, Bradshaw, & Nettleton, 1972). A similar dissociation was demonstrated for responses to the same figures presented in the two visual fields when they were to be judged for global spatial organisation (LVF faster) or for a small difference in a particular feature (RVF faster). Observations such as these have led to several reformulations of what is lateralised in terms of new dichotomies, such as analytic–holistic, serial–parallel, sequential–gestalt. These various dichotomies have in common the idea that the left hemisphere is more likely to be involved if stimuli must be examined systematically for detail over a period of time, whereas the right hemisphere will be faster than the left in making rapid global judgements on the basis of immediate impressions. As pointed out in Section 6.1.3, analytic, sequential, and serial processing may all require the symbolic mediation that depends on the left hemisphere's verbal skills, whereas holistic, parallel, and gestalt processing do not. Hence these redescriptions of hemisphere differences are not necessarily explanatory.

Evidence for individual differences in perceptual asymmetries has been found to vary with levels of skill. This could arise in two ways. First, it is possible that skilled operators have developed specific codes that enable them to process material more systematically than novices. This is the probable explanation of the findings for morse code operators; novices were better in reporting short sequences of code presented to the right ear than to the left, but better for longer sequences presented to the left ear than to the right, whereas skilled operators were superior at the right ear in all conditions (Papcun, Krashen, Terbeek, Remington, & Harshman, 1974). These observations are consistent with the possibility that when sequences are processed symbolically (short sequences for novices and all sequences for skilled operators), the superiority depends on the left hemisphere, but that for sequences that cannot be handled symbolically (long sequences for novices), perception depends on the global impressions of the right hemisphere.

A second possible explanation for variations in patterns of asymmetry with levels of skill is that individuals having certain types of cerebral specialisation are better fitted to acquire certain skills. This would imply that cerebral laterality has implications for ability. Findings for lateral perception of musical material in musicians and non-musicians could depend on either or both of these explanations. Bever and Chiarello (1974) reported that non-musicians showed an LEA for the perception of melodies (as did Kimura, Section 6.1.3), while musicians showed REA for the same material. In this experiment, the more experienced group seemed to depend on the left hemisphere, as for morse code operators. Other studies of dichotically presented music (reviewed by Bradshaw & Nettleton, 1983; Gordon, 1983) include several that have supported the possibility that musical perception is lateralised differently in musicians and non-musicians, although the *direction* of difference has not always been as found by Bever and Chiarello.

The possibility that patterns of lateral specialisation might be related to musical *aptitude* rather than musical experience was suggested by findings of Gaede, Parsons, and Bertera (1978). Subjects classified for low and high musical experience and low and high musical aptitude (assessed through tests of musical memory and aptitude) were compared for the perception of musical chords and musical sequences presented monaurally to either ear. Over all subjects, errors were fewer for chords presented to the left ear and for melody sequences presented to the right ear. The most interesting aspect of these findings was that low-aptitude subjects (even if they had had 5 or more years of music lessons) showed *larger differences between ears* than high aptitude subjects. They conclude by suggesting, "that low aptitude for music may be the result of adherence to a rather rigid hemispheric strategy whether analytic or sequential (left hemisphere) or 'holistic and synthetic' (right hemisphere). Conversely, high aptitude for music may be based on the brain's ability to use both strategies flexibly" (Gaede, Parsons, & Bertera, 1978). If they are correct in these inferences, Gaede and colleagues are suggesting a way in which differing patterns of cerebral specialisation, in the sense of a capacity for the hemispheres to cooperate rather than to compete, may have implications for ability. Other studies have found musicians to have no over-all bias to either side but to be more variable than nonmusicians (Gordon, 1980; Morais, Peretz, Gudanski, & Guiard, 1982).

Further speculations as to what is lateralised have concerned the role of attention in asymmetries of perception. Clearly each hemisphere is in most direct contact with its own half of space, and there are many indications that representations of the left and right halves of the external world are more relevant to perceptual asymmetries than the ear of entry of auditory stimuli

(Morais & Bertelson, 1973; Pierson, Bradshaw, & Nettleton, 1983). Similarly, in visual perception, subjects with tilted heads seemed to be influenced by left and right with respect to *gravity*, not only as stimulated on the retina (Corballis, Anuza, & Blake, 1978).

Speed of response to simple stimuli (reaction time, RT) has offered a rich source of experimental variations. **RT** is strongly affected by the compatibility of the locations of stimuli and responses. A critical variable appears to be consistency in space rather than consistencies between right and left hands and visual fields or ears (Broadbent, 1974; Nicoletti, Anzola, Luppino, Rizzolatti, & Umilta, 1982; Simon, Hinrichs & Craft, 1970). These findings raise interesting questions about how far the asymmetries observed in clinical and normal experimental studies depend on differences between sides "inside the head" as opposed to how the brain codes the world "outside the head". The example of Milanese patients with unilateral neglect failing to report the left half of an imagined cathedral square (Bisiach, Capitani, Luzzatti, & Perani, 1981) suggests that "inside" the head asymmetries also may depend on space as represented as well as experienced. Asymmetries of perception and performance could have a physical basis in subcortical systems, or in structural differences between the hemispheres, or they could depend on subtleties of the codes for left- and right-sided information. There is evidence for directional biases in the perception of lateralised visual stimuli that are independent of the visual fields (Sekuler, Tynan, & Levinson, 1973). Further, there may be individual differences in these directional biases that are independent of handedness and also independent of direction of learning to read and write (Annett, 1983b). These observations are offered here only to make the point that lateral asymmetries do not necessarily arise from cerebral specialisation for speech.

Kinsbourne (1970, and in subsequent papers reviewed by Bryden, 1982, and Bradshaw & Nettleton, 1983) has suggested that asymmetries of perception and performance depend on relative levels of arousal in the two hemispheres such that one or the other dominates processing. On this view, visual field and auditory asymmetries depend on the priming of the hemisphere better adapted to deal with the verbal or nonverbal stimuli presented. But how did this better adaptation arise? Kinsbourne's model offers no explanation, as far as I am aware, of the origins of left-hemisphere specialisation for speech, nor for individual differences in left-handers. It is a theory premised on these asymmetries as given. Kinsbourne is probably correct in suggesting that there are reciprocal interactions of relative arousal and inhibition between the hemispheres, but the question remains as to *what* is lateralised and so affected by these relative states of arousal.

As acknowledged already, a full understanding of what is lateralised must wait upon a fuller understanding of cognitive mechanisms and their neural foundations. One of the important issues in cognitive psychology concerns the nature of coding systems, whether single or dual. The existence of verbal coding is not in dispute, but is there also another code that operates through imagery (Paivio & Begg, 1981) or through some spatial analogue system (Anderson, 1980)? Could both verbal and nonverbal coding depend on a more abstract propositional system such that both are translated into a common symbolic language presumably mediated by the left hemisphere? If there is a spatial—imaginal—analogue code distinct from the verbal code, is the former mediated by the right hemisphere? Attempts to test this possibility by comparing the lateral perception of concrete and abstract words have met with variable success (Bradshaw & Nettleton, 1983). Perhaps this was not a good test of right-hemisphere coding.

One way of attempting to handle individual differences in asymmetry effects that has recently become fashionable is to invoke strategy effects. Perhaps some subjects use "verbal" or "analytic" strategies when others use more "holistic" ones, and perhaps subjects vary the strategies adopted between tasks (Bryden, 1978, 1982). The idea that subjects tend to adopt the *same* strategy over several tasks leads fairly directly to the idea of hemisphericity (Bogen, DeZure, Tenhouten, & Marsh, 1972), the possibility that some individuals are left-hemisphere or right-hemisphere processors. This would imply that some people tend to try to solve problems verbally, and others try to solve them nonverbally. Alternatively, if strategy effects are supposed to vary within individuals between tasks, it is very difficult to see how experiments could be designed to disentangle strategy and laterality effects (Bryden, 1982). The argument seems to be intrinsically circular.

8.4. RELATIONSHIPS WITHIN AND BETWEEN HEMISPHERES

We now move into the realm of metaspeculation. It has been shown that there are certain differences between the left and right cerebral hemispheres the nature, origins, and implications of which are not known. There may be small differences between left- and right-handers in some psychological characteristics (in addition to the obvious difference of writing hand). The source of these differences is also unknown. Attempting to link together two sets of barely understood phenomena and using them as foundations for further edifices can only lead to castles in the air. However, some of these metaspeculations are firmly entrenched in the laterality literature. Some of them may turn out to be fruitful when new techniques such as CAT scans and regional cerebral blood flow studies give a firmer foundation for the study of hypothesised asymmetries (e.g., Gur & Reivich, 1980).

The idea that relationships within the hemispheres might differ on a diffuse–focal dimension was suggested by Semmes (1968). This suggestion was based on a comparison of impairments of the somatosensory sensitivity of the right and left hands in U.S. veterans some years after sustaining war wounds to the right and left hemispheres. Impairments of sensitivity of the right hand tended to be associated with lesions of the left hemisphere sensorimotor cortex, whereas impairments of the left hand were more often associated with lesions outside the right-hemisphere sensorimotor cortex. In a few cases left-hand impairments seemed to be associated with left-hemisphere lesions, suggesting some significant ipsilateral link between the left hemisphere and left hand for somatosensory sensitivity. Semmes speculated that a more focal representation of functions in the left hemisphere could be advantageous for the fine sensorimotor control presumably required for manual skills and speech; diffuse representation in the right hemisphere was suggested conversely to be useful for the "multimodal" coordination presumed necessary for spatial abilities. These ideas grew from findings for a relatively small population of brain-impaired cases, and they have not been specifically checked in another sample as far as I am aware. They were professed to be speculative at the time they were put forward, but they have nevertheless been assimilated into the current hemisphere lore.

The focal–diffuse distinction has been generalised to hypotheses about differing patterns of cerebral representation in right- and left-handers. Hécaen and Piercy's (1956) argument that speech was likely to be represented bilaterally in left-handers seems to imply that speech representation should be "diffuse" in left-handers. Dimond and Beaumont compared right- and left-handers on several perceptual and performance tasks (reviewed by Beaumont, 1974). It is not clear how far right- and non-right-handers had absolute advantages and disadvantages for specific tasks. In a summary overview it was suggested that the system of cerebral organisation of the right-hander might be "a well defined system of relatively disparate but larger units" and that of the non-right-hander "a homogenous matrix of small functional units". The former was hypothesised to have advantages for rapid simple communication, but the latter to have advantages for complex integrative activity. The right hemisphere is described by Bryden (1982) as the "integrative" hemisphere.

Hardyck (1977c) reviewed several models and attempted to construct a general model to account for individual differences in cerebral function. The principal assumption was that there are two types of human cerebral organisation, one highly lateralised for the processing within each hemisphere of its special skills (verbal–left and visuo-spatial–right) and the other type bilateral, having multiple specialisations in each hemisphere. The types were suggested to be at the extremes of a continuum, with considerable individual variations between the extremes. Hardyck also attempted to formulate specific postulates about personal handedness and familial handedness as relevant to individual variation. As a synthesis of speculations,

Hardyck's model gives a good summary of prevalent notions. However, as all these notions are tenuous, the result has to be characterised as metaspeculation.

Almost every dichotomy the human mind has been able to generate seems to have been linked at some time with the dichotomy of left and right. Bogen (1969) reviewed the dichotomies associated with the left and right brains in the neurological literature and added a suggestion of his own, that right-hemisphere thinking is "appositional". Hughlings Jackson (1915—first published 1874) pointed out that the chief impairment associated with left-hemisphere lesions is not loss of speech (the right hemisphere can utter words in swearing or singing) but the capacity to formulate propositions. "Appositional" was suggested by Bogen as a term for those "capacities as yet unknown to us" in which the right hemisphere excels. As a term, then, it had no specific content, but it created an apparent vacuum that others rushed to fill. In that same paper Bogen (1969) listed a "pot-pourri" of dichotomies, which, he suggested, might be of appositional interest though *not* related to cerebral lateralisation. Many of them—such as abstract–concrete, digital–analog, successive–simultaneous, rational–metaphoric—have been taken up in the experimental and popular literature. Ornstein (1972) speculated about the duality of the brain alongside speculations about dualities of consciousness. Is the rational and scientific to be associated with the left brain and the irrational and intuitive with the right brain? Are Western and Eastern modes of thought to be characterised and "explained" as associated with differential hemisphere function? Or is this speculation run riot?

The observation that some people have relatively better-developed verbal skills and others have relatively better-developed visuo-spatial skills is supported by factor analytic studies of intelligence test scores. There is an obvious temptation to say that some people "use" their left hemisphere more than others (and are therefore more verbally orientated) and others "use" their right hemisphere more than others (and try to solve problems visuo-spatially). We all know some people who are compulsive talkers and some whose words have to be dragged from them. Some people can fix motorbikes and other machines, others cannot imagine how to begin (Pirsig, 1974). There is no difficulty in speculating about individual differences in hemisphere-related function. The point at issue, however, is whether it can ever be more than speculation. Attempts to identify cognitive styles or cognitive modes of functioning and relate them to other variables such as field-dependence or independence (Witkin, Goodenough, & Oltman, 1979), or patterns of verbal–spatial scores (Arndt & Berger, 1978), or to dichotic asymmetries (Caplan & Kinsbourne, 1982) do not seem to me to have any secure foundation. However, improvements in theory and measurement may give this security in future (Section 8.5 for a possible example).

Questions about the nature of the relationships *between* the hemispheres stem from Jackson's description of the left hemisphere as "leading" rather than "dominant". At one extreme it may be believed that only the one hemisphere—the language hemisphere—can sustain those aspects of human intelligence and personality that are associated with a sense of self and consciousness (Eccles, in Popper & Eccles, 1977). This implies extreme dominance in the sense that only one hemisphere is fully human. Gazzaniga (1983) also implies that the right hemisphere might be subhuman. If both hemispheres are allowed to support consciousness, the possibility arises that consciousness may be split (Pucetti, 1981). Our brain may even support a republic of consciousnesses (Gazzaniga & LeDoux, 1978), and multiple personality may then be a problem, not because it happens but because it does not happen more often.

The possibility that certain psychopathologies may be due to failure in the transfer of information between the hemispheres was suggested by Dimond and Beaumont (reviewed by Dimond, 1979). Schizophrenia was hypothesised to be functionally equivalent to a split-brain-operated patient, on account of poor cross-callosal connections. (The term "schizophrenia" implies a split between thought and emotion, not a split between two half-brains. However, the suggestion that the right hemisphere is more "emotional" than the left introduces the possibility that the split between thought and emotion is partially dependent on a lack of communication between the hemispheres.) Green, Glass, and O'Callaghan (1979) review evidence for callosal dysfunctions in schizophrenia and cite evidence that schizophrenics who learn to make a tactile discrimination with one hand have to *relearn* the discrimination when tested with the other hand, whereas normals seem to transfer this information between sides without need for further learning. Schizophrenics also seem to have poor perception of material presented auditorily to the left ear, both monaurally and dichotically. The evidence points to a lack of integration between the hemispheres, but the hypothesis of callosal dysfunction is only one of many possible explanations (Frith, 1979).

Normal human intellectual activity depends on the cooperative function of both cerebral hemispheres, not just on one. There is considerable evidence from experimental psychology that the integrated use of two hemispheres is better than one (Broadbent, 1974). For example, in RT studies, responses are much faster when alternative stimuli (Dimond, 1970) or alternative responses (Annett & Annett, 1979) involve different rather than the same hemispheres. Split-brain patients, as well as normal subjects, can report more auditory inputs when the type of input differs between ears (tone versus digit) than when both ears receive digits (Teng, 1980) which suggests that different or complementary processing mechanisms could be engaged simultaneously. The cerebral hemispheres probably work more efficiently as a cooperative team rather than as competitive individualists. Hypotheses about the nature of this interaction in experimental tasks (Friedman & Polson, 1981; Sergent, 1982) must inevitably be highly speculative.

In hemiplegic children with one normal hand and presumably one normal hemisphere, equivalent verbal and performance-scale IQs were achieved regardless of which hemisphere was damaged, and for both groups IQs were in the dull normal range (Table 6.2). These findings make it clear that two "good" hemispheres are needed for the normal development of intelligence, even if one does usually take the lead in the verbal sphere. The right hemisphere is as important as the left for the growth of normal verbal and nonverbal skills. In the evolution of the human brain, it would have been a wasteful strategy to allow only one hemisphere to develop sufficient power to support human intelligence. The data for childhood hemiplegia show that both hemispheres make an equal contribution to intellectual growth in childhood. For superior intellectual power, two very good half-brains must be required. Several versions of the analogy of a pair of horses harnessed side-by-side in the shafts have been used to illustrate possible relationships between the cerebral hemispheres (Beaton, 1979). In such a pair of horses accustomed to working together, one would normally lead and the other follow. This need not imply that the "following" horse is weak, stupid, or lazy, but only that for the smoothness of operation of the pair it is a good strategy not to pull against the other. If the horse that normally leads becomes unable to do so, it may be possible to reverse roles. In the case of human left-hemisphere injuries, it seems that a reversal of roles presents little problem if the handicap to the left side occurs early in life. It presents more problems later, as though in the course of a lifetime of working together only the left hemisphere has troubled to learn the codes by which certain activities should be guided, and the right has difficulties in learning these later in life. There are many variations on the theme of this analogy that can be imagined, concerning possible relationships between the two horses. The main point it is wished to make here is that two good horses are likely to be much more efficient than one good and one indifferent one.

8.5.   ARE THERE SEX DIFFERENCES IN PATTERNS OF CEREBRAL SPECIALISATION?

Evidence was cited in Chapter 5 for sex differences in the risk of developmental language problems and also in patterns of intellectual ability. Boys outnumber girls by 3 or 4 to 1 in clinic samples of children referred for problems of speech or reading. The trend for girls to be slightly earlier than boys in speech acquisition is well documented. The tendency of males to outperform females on tests of spatial reasoning in adolescence and adulthood is one of the most reliable of psychological test findings. Accepting that these sex differences exist, it may be asked, first, whether they are substantial enough to be worth notice, and, second, how they arise. Fairweather (1976) has argued that comparisons of the sexes in the general school population find only trivial differences, and Sherman (1978) has calculated that the proportion of the variance accounted for by sex difference ranges between 1 and 4%. There have been genetic, environmental, and hormonal explanations offered for sex differences in spatial ability; the most recent speculations concern lateral specialisation of the cerebral hemispheres (reviewed by McGee, 1979).

Evidence for sex differences in patterns of cerebral specialisation has been sought in studies of perceptual asymmetries in normal subjects and also in the effects of brain lesions. The literature for normal subjects has been reviewed by Bradshaw and Nettleton (1983), Bryden (1979, 1982), and McGlone (1980). The predominant recent view has been that females are less lateralised for verbal processes than males. This has been taken to imply that the female brain is more bilaterally organised than the male brain and that verbal processes in females (as in left-handers, see Section 5.2.2) invade right-hemisphere space to the detriment of spatial abilities. Figure 8.1 showed how many possible patterns must be differentiated to sustain such an argument. Fairweather (1976) and Sherman (1978) have argued that there is no substantial foundation for the view that there are sex differences in cerebral processing. They draw attention to the poor quality of experimental procedures, small numbers of subjects, and inadequate statistical comparisons that have characterised studies claiming to find significant effects. Bryden (1982) and Bradshaw and Nettleton (1983) suggest that there is support for the hypothesis of cerebral bilaterality in females, but both give a catalogue of weak, ambiguous, conflicting, and negative evidence. In Bradshaw and Gates (1978), for example, RVF superiorities were as large in females as in males for most of the experimental conditions but weaker only in *early* stages of the experiment in one of the response conditions. For more than 20 studies of nonverbal stimuli, Bradshaw and his colleagues found no sex differences (Bradshaw & Nettleton, 1983).

In the clinical field, the possibility of sex differences in cerebral specialisation was not considered in the studies summarised in Tables 3.1 and 3.2. (Males were probably overrepresented in the studies summarised in Table 3.1, since two of the five series included were of war wounds.) The clinicians and researchers making these reports presumably believed that the effects of brain lesions are similar between the sexes.

McGlone (1977) analysed a consecutive series of neurological patients with unilateral cerebral lesions seen in London, Ontario, for sex differences. Of 29 males and 16 females with left-sided lesions, 48% and 13%, respectively, were aphasic. Why were there so few females in comparison with males?

McGlone suggested that "some degree of bilateral speech representation is more common in adult females than adult males". No instances of aphasia associated with right-hemisphere lesions were recorded in females, as might have been expected if females were, indeed, bilateral. Comparisons of the verbal and performance-scale IQ scores of these patients (McGlone, 1978) found clear differences between the effects of left- and right-sided lesions in males but not in females. McGlone's (1980) review of evidence for stronger hemisphere specialisation in males than females depended heavily on these clinical data. She agreed with Bryden (1979) that studies of asymmetries in normals point only weakly in this direction. McGlone's findings for neurological patients have been followed up with respect to incidences of dysphasia and patterns of IQ scores.

Incidences of dysphasia have been re-examined in an enlarged sample of patients from London, Ontario, by Kimura (1983a). The difference between the sexes was now reduced; 41% males and 31% females with left-sided lesion were dysphasic. No significant sex differences were found in independent series examined by De Renzi, Faglioni, and Ferrari (1980) or Kertesz and Sheppard (1981).

The patterns of IQ scores in males and females with unilateral cerebral lesions have been analysed in a series of papers by Inglis and Lawson (1981; 1982) and their colleagues (Inglis, Ruckman, Lawson, Maclean, & Monga, 1982). First, Inglis and Lawson (1981) reanalysed reports in the literature of all studies that measured Wechsler Verbal and Performance Scale IQs in patients with unilateral left- and right-hemisphere lesions where the sex composition of the sample was also known. They plotted the difference between mean verbal and performance IQs for each lesion group against the proportion of males in the sample. A rank order correlation of $+.51$ ($p < .01$) was found between the difference and the proportion of males in the sample. The evidence seems clearly to support McGlone's observations that larger specific deficits are associated with unilateral lesions in males than females.

Inglis et al. (1982) reported a new study of the psychological test scores of patients suffering unilateral cerebrovascular accidents. The findings are shown alongside those of McGlone in Fig. 8.2. As in McGlone's sample, the males show the expected pattern of deficits, which differ for lesions on each side. Also as in McGlone's sample, females show small V–P differences for lesions of either side. However, while McGlone's female patients with left-hemisphere lesions showed average verbal and performance scale IQs, the female patients of Inglis and colleagues show lower means on both scales. This suggests that females may not be immune to psychological deficit after left-hemisphere lesion, but that *they are globally impaired in all psychological functions.*

Inglis and Lawson (1982) returned to a further analysis of reports in the literature. They found evidence of an interaction of lesion side and

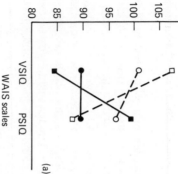

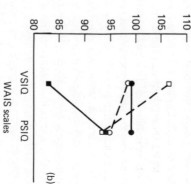

FIG. 8.2.   Mean I.Q. scores for neurological patients on the Wechsler verbal and performance scales: (a) study of Inglis *et al.*, 1982; (b) McGlone, 1978. From Inglis, Ruckman, Lawson, MacLean, & Monga, 1982.

psychological deficit in males. In females the trends are in the same direction, but much less marked. Females with right-hemisphere lesion are relatively little impaired on either verbal or performance scales. Females with left-hemisphere lesion are impaired on both scales.

How are these observations to be explained in terms of sex differences in hemisphere processing? Inglis and Lawson (1982) note that both sexes are about equally impaired for verbal IQ following left-hemisphere lesions. Both sexes seem to depend on the left hemisphere for verbal intelligence. The chief difference between the sexes concerns performance-scale IQ. The pattern of findings is consistent with the possibility that males depend on the right hemisphere for performance-scale items, whereas females tend to process performance-scale tasks *verbally.* In other words, females tend to use left-hemisphere processes for *both* types of task. Females with right-hemisphere lesions are relatively spared on both types of task, and females with left-hemisphere lesion are impaired on both types of task.

As Inglis and Lawson acknowledge, Sherman (1978) had already suggested that female priority in language development might serve to "bend the twig" toward verbal processing for all cognitive problems and lead to greater reliance by females on the left hemisphere for verbal and visuo-spatial tasks. The "bent-twig" hypothesis is an example of a "developmental nudge" theory (Chapter 1). The outcome of such a developmental bias, it seems, is to make females *more* dependent on the left hemisphere. Whether this sex difference has a structural or a developmental-functional basis, the outcome is that females appear to depend on the left hemisphere for tasks that in males would be shared between the hemispheres.

An example of a differentiation between sides for a spatial task in males and absence of differentiation in females is to be found in data for normal right-handed children studied by Witelson (1976). As mentioned in Section 6.1.3, children were asked to identify shapes palpated one by each hand simultaneously. There was a clear superiority for the left hand in boys throughout the age range but no clear advantage to either hand in girls.

Perhaps this new interpretation of clinical data will lead to a new interpretation of sex differences in normals studied for perceptual asymmetries. The weaker lateral differences observed in females could result from the use of more consistent verbal strategies for the processing of material presented to both hemispheres in females than in males. The weight of evidence points, in my view, to the conclusion that females are more dependent on the left hemisphere than males, not less. This conclusion is consistent with the evidence of female advantage in the early acquisition of language skills. It is also possible that female weaknesses in spatial reasoning result from attempts to solve all problems verbally, as suggested by Sherman (1978). This analysis of sex differences suggests that patterns of cerebral specialisation may, indeed, have implications for the development of psychological functions.

Is there evidence of sex differences in physical asymmetries of the brain? The asymmetries of the skull reported by LeMay (1977) are similar between the sexes. Wada, Clarke, and Hamm (1975) compared male and female brains for size of the planum temporale and found similar asymmetries in the sexes; in the brains showing reversed asymmetry (right planum larger) for which sex was known, there was an excess of females, but the number in this group was small.

A comparison of male and female right, left, and ambidextrous subjects for various EEG (electroencephalographic) measures of asymmetry of hemisphere function found no over-all difference between the sexes (Galin, Ornstein, Herron, & Johnstone, 1982). There were no significant sex differences in right-handers; there were some differences in left-handers, with more females (46%) showing reversed asymmetry during verbal tasks than males (26.7%). Reversed asymmetry was found in 10% of right-handers.

In studies of cerebral blood flow, differences between sex and handedness groups were found in measures that were interpreted as reflecting percentages of grey matter (in relation to white matter) and in rates of blood flow (Gur, Gur, Obrist, Hungerbuhler, Younkin, Rosen, Skolnick, & Reivich, 1982). However the pattern of increased flow to the left hemisphere during verbal tasks and increased flow to the right hemisphere during spatial task performance was found for both sexes. The pattern was clearer in right-handed females than right-handed males, suggesting that females may be *more* rather than *less* asymmetrical in the cerebral representation of functions.

In summary it may be concluded that there are differences between the sexes in patterns of cerebral specialisation, when group trends are considered (which do not necessarily apply to all individuals). The suggestion that females are bilateral or unspecialised (pattern VS/VS in Fig. 8.1) does not hold up on further examination. Females are biased to the left hemisphere at least as much and possibly more than males. The apparent lack of asymmetry in female groups might be due to overdependence on the left hemisphere for both verbal and visuo-spatial thinking (pattern VS/O, perhaps, in Fig. 8.1).

8.6. SUMMARY

Theories about patterns of cerebral specialisation have considered several alternatives, and others are logically possible. It is much easier to speculate about such patterns than to formulate testable hypotheses. There are no external indices or signs that give reliable indications of the laterality of cerebral speech. Personal handedness, familial handedness, and orientation of the pen in writing do not offer reliable guides to the speech hemisphere in individual cases.

The question "What is lateralised?" has led to several redescriptions of hemisphere differences in terms of analytic-synthetic and sequential-parallel processing or in terms of differing attention biases. It is argued that none of these redescriptions goes significantly beyond the basic observation that the left hemisphere tends to serve speech functions. Differences in manner of processing and in attention are more likely to be consequences than causes of the fundamental asymmetry for cerebral speech.

A mythology of differences within and between hemispheres has grown from originally tentative speculations about focal versus diffuse cerebral representations and about propositional versus appositional modes of function. The extension of such notions to theories of individual differences in terms of cognitive styles seems quite unwarranted on present evidence. Similarly, suggestions that some of the problems associated with the schizophrenias are analogous to those of split-brain patients depend on speculative leaps that owe more to imagination than logic. However, some of these surmises may become testable when improved methods of studying structural and functional asymmetries become available.

It is argued that the most important point to be made about the relationship between the hemispheres is that two good hemispheres working together are very much better than one. Whatever the relative advantages of either hemisphere for specific tasks, the cooperation of both hemispheres is required for the most efficient performance of laboratory-based tasks such as choice reaction time, and also for the development of normal levels of intelligence.

The existence and the nature of sex differences in patterns of cerebral specialisation are controversial. It has been argued and widely accepted that the female brain is more bilaterally symmetrical than the male brain. There is evidence that the pattern of deficits expected for the "typical" brain, on suffering unilateral lesions of each side (left lesion with verbal and right lesion with visuo-spatial deficits) is more often found in males and females. An alternative explanation to the female bilaterality hypothesis is that females tend to depend on the left hemisphere for *both* types of intellectual activity; that is, females are more likely than males to use the left hemisphere in trying to solve verbal *and* nonverbal problems.

IV

THE SEARCH FOR ANSWERS: EXPERIMENTAL STUDIES OF LATERAL ASYMMETRIES

9

Lateral Asymmetries in Nonhuman Species

9.1. ASYMMETRIES OTHER THAN HANDS AND BRAINS

There is a multitude of asymmetries in physical and living things (Gardner, 1967; Mason, 1984). These asymmetries include the direction of spin of subatomic particles and speculations about whether the bathwater should drain clockwise in the southern hemisphere and counterclockwise in the northern hemisphere. Pasteur discovered that certain crystals have right- and left-handed forms. Solutions of right-handed crystals rotate polarized light in one direction, whereas solutions of left-handed crystals rotate the light in the opposite direction. Mixtures of right- and left-handed crystals are called "racemic" and do not rotate light. (The term "racemic" will be useful later.)

The basic molecules of life that carry the genetic code deoxyribosenucleic acid (DNA) and ribosenucleic (RNA) take the form of a helix that normally turns to the right, but some left-handed forms have been discovered (Scott, 1984). Most plants have more than one plane of symmetry (that is, they can be divided into symmetrical mirror halves by cuts in more than one plane), but asymmetries appear in the coil of tendrils of climbing plants. Some species vary in the direction of coil, but most have a definite handedness, like the bindweed, which coils to the right, and the honeysuckle to the left, a difference that was presumably known to Shakespeare when he wrote *A Midsummer Night's Dream* where Queen Titania promises to wind Bottom the weaver in her arms, "so doth the woodbine and sweet honeysuckle gently entwist". It was noted in Section 4.1 that the human umbilical cord may have a clockwise, counterclockwise, or alternating spiral. There are coils in the shells of molluscs and in the single tooth of the Narwhal, which grows into a spear 8 or 9 feet long.

What relevance, if any, do these many natural asymmetries have for human handedness and brainedness? The answer may well turn out to be "none", but until all these asymmetries are understood, including the human ones, we cannot be sure. This review of nonhuman asymmetries will be mainly concerned with studies of hand and paw preferences in nonhuman mammals and with the search for analogues of human brainedness in other species, including birds. But before turning to these topics, a few examples of experimental studies of other asymmetries will be considered for the light they throw on the sorts of mechanisms that may govern asymmetries in nature. Convergent evolution is said to have occurred when similar mechanisms evolve independently in widely separated living things, presumably in response to similar selection pressures. It is quite possible that mechanisms governing very primitive lateral asymmetries *resemble* those of human handedness and brainedness without necessarily implying that the *same* mechanism has been transmitted in a direct line from the primitive to the human form.

An attempt has been made to formulate comprehensive generalisations that would include human handedness and brainedness, with a wide range of more primitive animal asymmetries, as being due to a general left–right maturational gradient (Morgan, 1977; Corballis & Morgan, 1978; Morgan & Corballis, 1978). Some of the difficulties of this generalisation have been considered with respect to *situs inversus* and twinning (Section 3.2). The left–right maturational gradient hypothesis originated with a doubt that genes could encode left–right directional information, a belief that genes are "left–right agnosic" (Morgan, 1977). Morgan and Corballis suggest that directional asymmetries arise from some fundamental nongenetic bias, possibly coded in the cytoplasm of the egg. Individuals showing atypical asymmetries must then arise from developmental accidents. This position entails the view, considered in Section 4.3.2, that all human left-handedness is a pathological aberration of a human species bias to the left brain and right hand. To counter the Morgan and Corballis position it would be necessary to show not only that *some* atypical individuals occur (because they could be accidental), but also that the atypical asymmetry is transmitted between generations. There are examples of asymmetries in some species that suggest that there can be genetic transmission of right- *and* left-handed forms, and there are other examples where only one directional bias seems to be genetically transmitted.

The fresh water mollusc *Limnaea peregra* was studied for the inheritance of sinistrality by Boycott, Diver, Garstang, and Turner (1930). The spiral twist of the body shell is normally dextral and a sinistral twist is very rare, but samples were found in a Yorkshire pond. Cross-breeding showed that sinistrality was inherited like a classic Mendelian recessive gene, except that the 3:1 dominant–recessive proportion appeared in the third generation, not the second as in Mendel's experiments (Section 1.2). Boycott and colleagues (1930) suggested that the direction of coiling depends on the first division of the egg, but this depends on *genetic* information carried by the mother, not on a universal directional bias. The genes that determine the laterality of the offspring do not determine the mother's own laterality (Gardner & Snustad, 1981). Another example of the same pattern of inheritance has been found for the coiling of the shells of a Pacific islands snail: *left* coiling is dominant over right in this species (Murray & Clarke, 1966, cited by Dawkins, 1982).

Male crabs have front claws of unequal size, and the larger claw may be on the left or right. Early studies (cited by Corballis & Morgan, 1978) suggested that if the larger claw were removed, it would regenerate at the next moult as a small claw, while the originally small claw regenerates as a large one. Experimental studies of handedness in fiddler crabs did not confirm this but found that the large claw regenerated in every case on the same side as before (Vernberg & Costlow, 1966). The proportions of left- and right-large-clawed males were similar, and in a small number large claws developed on both sides. Vernberg and Costlow (1966) were of the opinion that, "These data form the basis for suggesting that handedness is genetically determined."

Flounders swim like other fish early in life but as adults lie on one side on the sea floor, the eye on the lower side migrating over the top of the head so that both eyes look upward. There are some 500 species of flounder, grouped in several families. Figure 9.1 illustrates the presumed evolutionary relationships among the several families. Some families consist of right-eyed species (which lie on their left sides, like halibut), some consist of left-eyed species (like turbot), other families include left- or right-eyed species (left or right in the figure). In L, R, and L or R families all individuals in a species lie on the same side except for rare and presumably accidentally changed individuals. In some species, however, there can be variations between members; these are called "racemic" or left *and* right in the figure. For example, the starry flounders off the coast of California are about 50% left-eyed. The relationships given in Fig. 9.1 suggest that from a presumably racemic ancestor, left- or right-sided asymmetry evolved at least four times (Policansky, 1982b). Where whole families of species are consistently asymmetrical, the asymmetry must be coded in fixed genes (universal to the species—Section 1.2). There is no single universal directional asymmetry, as both right and left directionality have become fixed in different species.

Policansky (1982a, 1982b) investigated the genetics of the asymmetry of starry flounders, which differ in the proportions of left-eyed forms in different parts of the Pacific ocean. Less than 1% of those in Japanese waters are right-eyed, whereas Californian flounders are about 50% right-eyed, as already mentioned. Figure 9.2 shows the proportion of left- and right-eyed

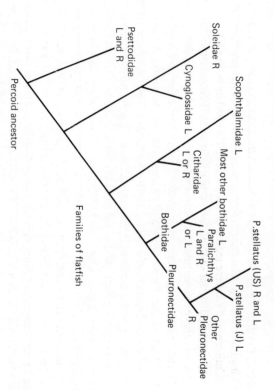

FIG. 9.1. Evolution of laterality in flounders. The letters **L** and **R** indicate the side of the head bearing the eyes; "**L and R**" means that species are racemic; "**L or R**" means that some species are sinistral and others dextral. Policansky, 1982b.

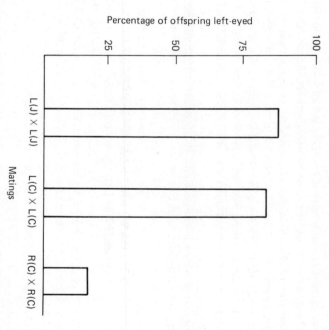

FIG. 9.2. Matings of starry flounders: Percentages of left-eyed offspring when left- or right-eyed fish, of Japanese (J) or Californian (C) stock, were mated experimentally. Adapted from Policansky, 1982a.

offspring from a few of several matings. It shows a majority of left-eyed offspring from matings between left-eyed Japanese fish. When pairs of same-eyed Californian fish were mated (both parents left-eyed or both right-eyed), the majority of offspring showed the same eyedness as their parents. The fact that there are some exceptions in each family type shows that the directionality is not under full genetic control, but in all cases there are significant biases to one side or other and not a racemic mixture. In other experiments Policansky showed that directionality does not depend only on the mother, but that the father's genes also contribute to the asymmetry. These experiments are continuing with the aim of further elucidating the mechanisms involved. The example of the starry flounder is important for showing that asymmetries in the *left* and the *right* directions can be coded genetically. A universal asymmetry in the first division of the egg will not do here.

Other studies of directional biases have found either no transmission between generations or evidence of transmission of a bias in one direction only. Duckweeds (*Lemnaceae*) may take right- or left-handed forms, and during vegetative reproduction the daughter fronds are always of the same handedness as the parent. Sexual reproduction of left- or right-handed plants in all possible combinations always yields 50% right- and 50% left-handed offspring (Kasinov, 1973). A mutant strain of mice in which *situs inversus* of the viscera is common was studied by Hummel and Chapman (1959) and again by Layton (1976). In both series the proportion of mice with anomalies of *situs* was about 50%. *Situs inversus* has been produced experimentally by several techniques in newts and salamanders since the classic experiments of Spemann (reviewed by Wehrmaker, 1969). Layton (1976) reports that a review of this literature found no instances where the proportion of animals with *situs inversus* significantly exceeded 50%. Layton suggested that there is a dominant allele that normally induces the arrangement of the viscera in the typical direction, but in the absence of this allele asymmetry is determined in a random fashion (it is racemic).

9.2.   HAND AND PAW PREFERENCES IN NONHUMAN MAMMALS

There have been several very thorough studies of the hand and paw preferences of mammals. Among the higher apes, the largest study was made by Finch (1941) of 30 chimpanzees, observed making a total of 800 reaches each on 4 different tasks. Finch's graph of his findings is given in Fig. 9.3. Taking a criterion of 90% reaches with one hand, 9 animals can be described as left-handed and 9 as right-handed. The figure shows a roughly continuous distribution of degrees of right and left preference. There are no studies of comparable scale of other apes. In a study of the feeding behaviour of six

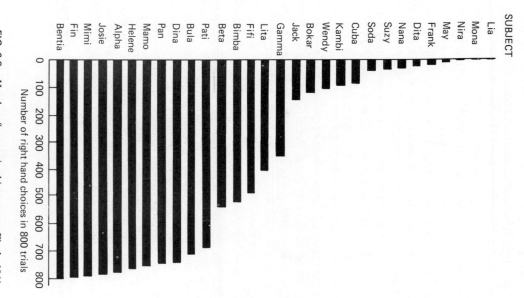

FIG. 9.3.   Hand preferences in chimpanzees. Finch, 1941.

gorillas and five orang-utans at Twycross Zoo, the hand used to convey food to the mouth was recorded for a minimum of 65 observations each for gorillas and 25 for orang-utans. The findings, in Fig. 9.4, give no reason to doubt that the distributions are like that of chimpanzees, but of course more extensive observations would be required to substantiate this opinion. A family group of Siamangs was observed feeding on several occasions over a period of 6 months by Chivers (1974). As Siamangs are fully monogamous and strongly territorial, it is highly probable that the young apes were the offspring of the adult pair. Both adults used the left hand predominantly. A subadult male and an infant both appeared to prefer the right hand, while a juvenile was significantly left-preferent. It would be interesting to know which hand apes use to perform actions requiring greater skill than conveying food to the mouth. Self-touching and feeding behaviour involve so little skill that humans often use the nonpreferred hand (Section 7.2.2). Schaller (1963) detected a bias to use the right hand first in the chest-beating displays of gorillas. This is a highly automatic ritualised behaviour that need have no relevance to hand skill.

Data on the hand preferences of monkeys are more extensive than for apes. The findings of several studies, summarised in Table 9.1, are essentially like those for chimpanzees. About as many animals are strongly left-preferent as strongly right-preferent. Depending on criteria of classification, up to about 50% are described as "mixed" or ambilateral. The three nonprimate groups studied for paw preferences, cat, rat, and mouse (Table 9.1) show a similar distribution. Figure 9.5 shows the distribution of numbers

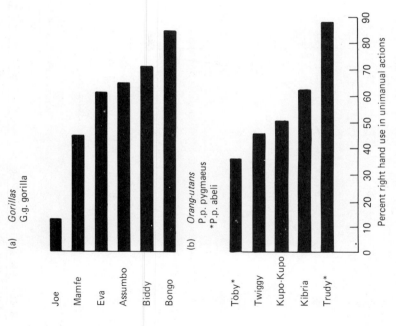

FIG. 9.4. Hand preferences in gorillas and in orang-utans: Personal observations at Twycross Zoo.

TABLE 9.1

Incidences of Left-, Mixed-, and Right-Hand and Paw Preferences in Nonhuman Mammals

	Criterion of R or L (%)	No. Animals	Left	Mixed	Right
Ape					
Chimpanzee (Finch, 1941)	90	30	30.0	40.0	30.0
Monkey					
Rhesus (Warren, 1953)	90	84	27.4	45.2	27.4
(Milner, 1969) Criterion task I	90	58	25.9	50.0	24.1
(Gautrin and Ettinger, 1970, Criterion Task I)	90	28	35.7	32.1	32.1
(Lehman, 1978)	90	171	24.0	53.2	22.8
Bonnet (Brooker et al., 1981)	$\chi^2 p < .05$	67	31.3	35.8	32.8
Cat (Cole, 1955)	75	60	38.3	41.7	20.0
Rat (Harper, 1970)*	100	149	26.9	53.0	20.1
Mouse (Collins, 1969) C57 BL/6J	c. 88	858	26.3	43.8	29.8

*Personal communication.

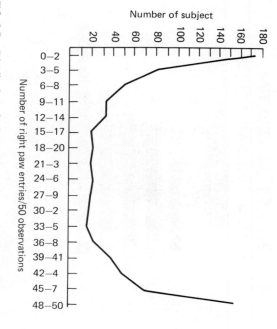

FIG. 9.5.   Distribution of mice making right-paw reaches. Collins, 1969.

of mice making various numbers of right-paw reaches into a feeding tube (illustrated in Fig. 9.6). If the data were plotted for individual animals as for Finch's chimpanzees, the picture would be essentially similar. In both cases there is a gradual and continuous progression between strongly left-preferent and strongly right-preferent animals, with all possible gradations between the two extremes, and each extreme equally represented. The only vertebrate for which an unequal distribution of limb preferences seems to have been reported is not a mammal but a bird. Parrots often prefer the left claw in holding food (Friedman & Davis, 1938, cited in Walker, 1980).

These data are of great importance in considering the origins of human hand preference. It is clear that mammals can show strong side preferences. The development of handedness in individuals is part of the mammalian (including primate) pattern. There is a major difference from the human distribution of handedness, however, in that no species bias has been discovered to the right side (or to the left side) in any mammal other than man.

Does the lack of species bias in other mammals make the study of hand preferences in monkeys or mice irrelevant to an understanding of human handedness? The answer to this question cannot be known until we understand the origins of handedness in all species, including our own. Several experiments have been performed on other species with a view to answering questions raised in Part II about the origins and development of hand preferences.

FIG. 9.6.   Feeding tube for testing paw preferences in mice. Collins, 1969.

The most fundamental hypothesis considered in Part II was that handedness is determined genetically. Peterson (1934) bred 30 litters of rats from various combinations of right, left, and ambidextrous parents. There was no discernible effect on the paw preferences of offspring. Collins (1969) bred mice from R–R and L–L parents for three generations of selection and found 50% left-handers in both breeding lines. These experiments conclusively rule out the hypothesis that paw preferences in rats and mice depend on genetically transmitted information.

Does handedness depend on position in utero? Peterson (1934) delivered rats by caesarean section and noted from which horn of the uterus each animal was taken; this aspect of fetal position had no effect on subsequent handedness. Peterson also examined the mode of origin of the carotid arteries and concluded this was not relevant. Is handedness influenced by the dominant eye? Peterson removed one eye in infancy and found no effect on handedness. What about the role of practice? Peterson concluded that practice cannot altogether account for handedness as ambidextrous animals remained ambidextrous after greater practice with one hand. The only experimental manipulation that Peterson found would change hand preference depended on first identifying the area of the motor cortex of the brain that produces hand and arm movements when electrically stimulated and then destroying this area. Very small lesions of the brain, which destroy all of this cortical area, cause permanent changes of hand preference, but if the area is not completely destroyed the animal may transfer back to its original hand preference after recovery from the operation. Destruction of 50% of the hemisphere outside this cortical area does not affect hand preference (Peterson, 1934). These observations agree with those for humans (Section 4.3.1) in suggesting that hand preferences are not easily changed by brain lesions but that definite shifts must occur when there is an injury that gives a motor weakness on the preferred side. Peterson and Chaplin (1942) explored the effects of extra-pyramidal lesions on handedness in rats. Destruction of one half of the cerebellum did not influence the handedness of a rat with intact cortex.

The role of developmental influences on the paw preferences of cats was investigated through observations of preference on eight tasks given to cats between the ages of 6 months to 1 year; some cats were retested after 2 years (Warren, Ablanalp, & Warren, 1967). Correlations between performances on the several tests and between performances after 2-year intervals were highly significant, showing that preferences were both consistent and enduring. Extensive early practice in manipulation in kittens did not affect paw preferences. Forcing cats to use the nonpreferred paw in a specific situation increased the chances that the animal would use the nonpreferred paw in that situation, but did not generalise to other situations. Experimentally placed lesions in the sensorimotor area of the brain contralateral to the preferred side induced changes in paw preference in cats, but lesions elsewhere in the brain, including section of the corpus callosum, did not (Warren, Cornwell, Webster, & Pubols, 1972).

Warren, Ablanalp, and Warren (1967) studied the consistency of hand preferences for five tasks and changes with age in 81 immature and adult rhesus monkeys. Hand preferences were consistent over a 2-year interval, and no evidence of systematic change with age was found. Figure 9.7 shows a re-analysis of the data of Warren and colleagues to show consistency between tasks (Passingham, 1982). Nearly 50% of animals showed no clear bias to either side, and the remainder were about equally divided between those biased to the right and those to the left.

In a later analysis of correlations between the preferences of 14 rhesus monkeys tested on several tasks, Warren (1977) drew attention to the variability between the correlations obtained when tests were given on three separate occasions. On all three occasions one set of measures was highly intercorrelated, whereas another set showed almost no intercorrelation. A third group showed intermediate levels of intercorrelation that became stronger over the three sessions. These differences implied that some tests were fairly good predictors of hand use on other similar tests, and others were not. These findings are not unexpected in the light of knowledge of the organisation of the motor system (Section 2.2). The hands can be used in a variety of actions that require varying degrees of fine or gross motor control, and there is no intrinsic reason why we should expect lateral preferences to

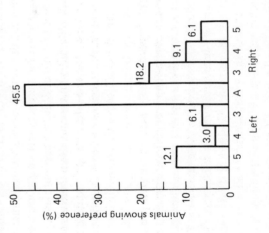

FIG. 9.7.   Distribution of hand preferences in rhesus monkeys. A = ambidextrous; the numbers 3, 4 and 5 along the bottom refer to animals showing the same hand preferences on three, four and five tasks. Warren et al., 1967, reworked by Passingham, 1982.

affect all levels of control equally. With regard to the development of preferences in individual monkeys, Warren (1977) points out that ''The initial performance of inexperienced monkeys is somewhat unstable, inconsistent and largely task specific . . . (but) . . . as monkeys become experienced . . . they develop skills and strong hand preferences for dealing with limited classes of manipulanda'' (as discussed for humans in Section 4.2). Clearly the consistency of hand preferences varies between tasks, with the animal's age, and with the animal's experience of a task. It also varies, as shown in Table 9.1, between animals. Does all this variability imply that it was mistaken to study handedness in monkeys? Surely not. The mistake is more likely to be in overreliance on the correlation co-efficient in a search for consistency and a reciprocal lack of recognition of the intrinsic variability of handedness.

Does hand preference depend on eye preference? Vision plays an important role in the activities of cats and monkeys, and reaching for food or other experimental targets depends heavily on vision in normal circumstances. Some experimental findings suggested that monkeys might prefer to use one hand for reaching in the light and the other hand when trained to reach in the dark (Ettinger, Blakemore, & Milner, 1968), but this alternation was not found in subsequent experiments (Gautrin & Ettinger, 1970). The hand preferences and eye preferences of 19 monkeys were tested prior to brain operations by Kruper, Patton, and Koskoff (1971). The data were given for individual animals, in terms of percentage right and left responses in 300 trials for handedness tests and 140 trials for an eyedness test (looking down a tube at raisins or sugar pellets). Animals varied continuously between 91% preference for the left hand to 85% preference for the right hand and between 98% for the left eye to 91% preference for the right eye; there was a slight bias over-all toward the left hand and the left eye, but the important point to be made here is that hand and eye preferences were *independent*. Eleven animals used the hand and eye on the *same* side and eight animals used *different* sides for hand and eye. Thus, there is no reason to believe that the preferred hand is determined by the preferred eye, or vice versa.

Can bias to one hand be induced by rearing animals in right-handed or left-handed worlds? Collins (1975) found that when young mice were first tested for reaching from a feeding tube (Fig. 9.6) that was placed flush with a right (or left) wall, so that it was difficult to reach into except with the right (or left) hand, about 90% of animals used the easier paw. These same animals that had been ''reared'' in right-handed or left-handed ''worlds'' were then tested in ''worlds'' of the opposite handedness (that is, mice experienced in reaching into the tube flush against the right wall were tested with the tube flush against the left wall). Some animals were found to adapt to the new arrangement easily, and some did not. The ones who adapted easily turned out to be the ones that had found it hard to adapt to their original biased world, whereas the ones that did not adapt to the new world had adapted easily to the old. This very important finding shows that though the *expression* of paw preference in mice could be influenced by environmental circumstances, the *origin* of the preference predated the animals' first experience of reaching. The paw preferences were not *caused* by training. The expression of preference was clearly modified by the environment, but the modifications did not persist in a changed environment. Collins (1975, 1977) reported a sex difference in the expression of paw preferences in mice, but this was inconsistent between animals in unbiased and biased worlds. Collins argued that there is a genetic influence on hand preference in the sense that preferences are more strongly expressed in females, but that the direction of preference is independent of sex.

9.3.   BRAIN ASYMMETRIES IN NONHUMAN SPECIES

The search for precursors or analogues of human brain specialisation in other species has met with very limited success. The only convincing analogue has been found in certain song birds. Nottebohm (1970) reported the effects of cutting the hypoglossal nerves to either the right or left sides of the syrinx, the avian vocal organ, in chaffinches. Lesion on the right side was followed by the loss of a few elements of song, whereas lesion on the left side led to a severe disruption of almost all elements of song. Subsequent research in canaries and other species (Nottebohm, 1977, 1981) has confirmed this asymmetry and explored its basis in brain anatomy and development. There are several analogues between the human and songbird asymmetries for vocalisation. Birds whose left syrinx innervation is cut before song learning begins develop normal song under right-sided control, and the left nerve atrophies; this resembles the human capacity to develop speech in the right half of the brain if the left is damaged early in life. Humans with left brain lesions in adulthood have variable and limited ability to relearn speech, but birds develop new song under right-sided control in the following season, showing that they retain functional equipotentiality. When the left hypoglossus was cut 2 to 4 weeks after hatching and allowed to regrow, the left-sided dominance was reduced, and the birds became ambisinistrous (Nottebohm, 1981). Ambisinistrality or reverse dominance do *not* seem to occur readily in the wild, since in 81 songbirds tested from four different species only one failed to show clear left dominance; this bird was instead fairly evenly balanced on the two sides (Nottebohm, 1977). Left hypoglossal dominance has been demonstrated for four species tested (chaffinch, canary, white-throated sparrow, and Java-sparrow); it also appears to be true of the domestic fowl. Zebra finches are thought to show right-sided control of song.

The imprinting process first studied systematically by Lorenz (Section 1.3) has been found to depend, in chicks, on developmental processes that occur at different rates on the two sides of the brain (Bradley & Horn, 1981; Bradley, Horn, & Bateson, 1981). Lesion studies suggest that homologous structures on the two sides may have different roles in the learning process (Cipollo-Neto, Horn, & McCabe, 1982). In rats there is also evidence of differential rates of development between the hypothalamic regions of the two sides, as judged from the differing effects of sex hormones placed on each side (Nordeen & Yahr, 1982). Glick, Jerussi, and Zimmerberg (1977) have found differences in rats between the quantity of dopamine (a neurotransmitter) in the left and right pathways to the basal ganglia. Animals were found to turn spontaneously more often in the direction opposite the side with more dopamine. Rats were said to turn more often to the right, but gerbils turned equally to the left or right. Turning biases toward the left have been noted in horses. Williams (1972) observed foals in three studs and in wild New Forest ponies to see whether there was a bias to suckle with the head turned to the right or left; no significant bias was found. It has also been said that cattle prefer to rest on one side. Uhrbrock (1969) reported three sets of observations of several hundred cattle and found a slight bias to the left side (52–61% for three samples). Asymmetries of these kinds could conceivably depend on inequalities of transmitter substances in subcortical pathways. They are not necessarily relevant to functional asymmetries of the cortex.

Cunningham (1902) described his searches for inequalities in the development of the two sides of the brain in man and higher apes. He noted that the left sylvian fissure tended to be larger than the right in apes as in man (Fig. 3.3). Assuming that the human inequality might be related to right-hand preference, he searched for evidence of right-hand preferences in apes but could not find any, as we saw for later studies (Table 9.1). Greater length of the left sylvian fissure has been confirmed in subsequent studies of apes but not of monkeys (LeMay, 1976; Yeni-Komshian & Benson, 1976). Groves and Humphrey (1973) measured the internal lengths of gorilla skulls and found species differences in asymmetry. There was no systematic bias to either side in 138 coast gorillas (*Gorilla, gorilla, gorilla*); the majority of measurements were equal on both sides. But in 55 skulls of other species (*Gorilla, gorilla, gruaeri* and *Gorilla, gorilla, beringei*) there were significant biases to greater length on the left side, opposite to the bias in man (Fig. 3.1).

Studies of the structural asymmetries of the skull (the left–occipital, right–frontal protrusions discussed in Section 3.3.2) found these asymmetries in apes but not monkeys (LeMay, Billig, & Geschwind, 1982). Ape, modern human, and fossil hominid (including australopithecus, *Homo erectus*, and *Homo neanderthalis*) brains were examined by Holloway and LaCoste-Lareymondie (1982) for several measures of skull asymmetry. There were clear trends toward the typical human asymmetries in apes, but the asymmetries were not as clear as for hominids. Table 9.2 summarises the findings for

TABLE 9.2
Left Occipital and Right Frontal Petalia in Apes, Humans, and Hominids

Group	N	%
Gorilla gorilla	40	32
Pan[a] troglodytes	34	12
Pan paniscus	41	34
Pongo[b] pygmaeus	20	15
Homo sapiens	14	79
Hominid fossils	24	83

Note: Adapted from Holloway and LaCoste-Lareymondie (1982).
[a] Pan = chimpanzee; two species represented here.
[b] Pongo = orang-utan.

percentages of skulls showing *both* left occipital and right frontal petalia. Whereas about 80% of humans (modern and fossil) showed this pattern, about 33% of gorilla and one species of chimpanzee brains did so. These observations suggest that there are precursors of human brain asymmetries in apes but not in monkeys. The ape asymmetries are far less clear than those of man.

There are structural asymmetries in the skulls of whales that are most probably unrelated to human asymmetries but worth noting as whales are large mammals that are known to communicate by making sounds that travel over long distances. Ness (1967) reported measurements of 317 skulls from several varieties of whales and found the majority show a leftward bias for the blow hole; none showed the opposite asymmetry.

What evidence is there for *functional* brain asymmetries in mammals? Webster (1977) reviewed the evidence for brain asymmetry in cats and found none convincing. Functional asymmetries have been searched for in monkeys with almost entirely negative results (Hamilton, 1977; Warren, 1977). Butler and Francis (1973) reported the directional preferences of 8 female baboons for clockwise and counterclockwise rotation of discs by each hand, and suggested there might be some cerebral asymmetry involved; however the 8 monkeys showed between them three of the four patterns found in 100 normal children and no evidence of the human bias to one pattern (Reed & Smith, 1961). Dewson (1977) reported an auditory memory task that was disrupted in monkeys by left-sided more than by right-sided lesions. It has also been reported that five Japanese macaques could discriminate sounds relevant to communication with other monkeys better when these were presented to the right ear than to the left ear, as for humans in the dichotic listening situation, but other old-world monkeys could not (Petersen, Beecher, Zoloth, Moody, & Stebbins, 1978). These two reports of positive findings for functional asymmetries in primates are exceedingly rare amid a wealth of negative evidence. To accept these slender positives and reject the mighty negatives as evidence of functional hemisphere specialisation in nonhumans (Denneberg, 1981) requires an act of faith that is beyond this author.

9.4. SUMMARY

There is a multitude of asymmetries in nature, most of which are probably irrelevant to the determination of human asymmetries of hand and brain, but of course it is not possible to be sure of this irrelevance until the mechanisms are understood. Genetic influences that code for right- and left-handed forms (that is, genes that code for each of both alternatives) have been found for the coiling of snail shells and for the laterality of some flat fish. Among the many species of flounders, some are typically right-eyed, some typically left-eyed, some show apparently random mixtures of left- and right-eyed individuals, and some appear to be genetically coded for left- or right-eye laterality within the species. In mice, a mutant strain has been studied in which right and left arrangements of the viscera (*situs sollitus* and *situs inversus*) each occurs with 50% probability; this suggests that the arrangement typical in vertebrates, including man, is genetically determined but that when the gene inducing this pattern is absent, the arrangement depends on chance.

Hand and paw preferences are found in many mammals, and in all species studied there are as many right- as left-handed animals. It is especially important to notice that careful studies of monkeys and apes have found no evidence of group biases to one side. These observations show that handedness is a primate characteristic, but species bias to the right (or left) hand is *not* a general feature of primates.

Experimental studies of paw preferences in mice and rats make it possible to eliminate several hypotheses. Preferences in these animals are not determined by genes, by positions in utero, by dominant eye, by early practice, or by forced use of one hand. Paw preferences in rats and cats were changed by lesions in the motor cortex controlling the preferred paw, but not by lesions elsewhere in the cortex. Cats and monkeys show considerable individual variation in patterns of hand preference for different tasks. This implies that preferences do not depend on some single unitary mechanism but vary in ways that could depend on the different levels of the motor system involved in specific tasks.

Mice reared in right-biased and left-biased worlds used the most adaptive paw in about 90% of animals. Reversing the world bias showed that animals readapted at differing rates that were related to their initial readiness to adapt to the first world bias. It can be inferred that the main determinants of paw preference are *congenital* but not genetic.

Asymmetries of brain function have been found for certain song birds, in which the *left* neural control system appears to be responsible for producing most of the song elements. Several parallels can be drawn between the effects of lesions in birds and lesions in humans, but there are important differences since birds re-develop their song each season. Asymmetries in bird and mammal brains have been found in rates of development on the two sides and in levels of biochemically active substances. Behavioural correlates of these asymmetries have been found in tendencies of rats to turn to one side.

The question whether nonhuman primates show asymmetries of the brain and skull like those of man cannot be answered unequivocally. Apes but not monkeys show asymmetries in the length of sylvian fissure and in protrusions of the left occiput and right frontal regions like those of humans. These asymmetries are found in apes less consistently than in modern man and in fossil hominids. In a series of measures of internal skull length, an asymmetry was found in some species of gorilla opposite to that reported for humans.

The search for *functional* asymmetries in nonhuman primates has been almost entirely negative. Advantages for the left hemisphere have been reported for monkeys (in whom structural asymmetries are *not* found), but these were for small numbers of animals in isolated experiments. Independent replication is necessary before the idea that there are nonhuman precursors of human asymmetries for language is accepted.

10 A Close Look at Human Hand Preferences

Handedness has been taken to mean, above, whatever the author under discussion understood it to mean. Now we must try to analyse the concept, discover its empirical bases, and face the problem of trying to pin down what seems to be a rather elusive characteristic. The elusiveness of handedness can be illustrated by Hécaen and Ajuriaguerra's (1964) summary of findings of previous investigators, in Table 10.1. Incidences range from 1 to 30% and take almost all possible values in between. This diversity of assessments of incidence is a major problem for the scientific study of handedness. How can laws be discovered for something that is present in some studies in 1% and in other studies in 30% of the population?

Variations in incidence could arise in at least three ways. First, there could be genuine differences between the groups studied; incidences could vary

TABLE 10.1
Percentages of Left-Handedness Recorded in 48 Studies

Left-Handedness (%)	No. Studies
0–4	15
5–9	18
10–14	5
15–19	3
20–24	3
25–30	4

Note: Studies listed by Hécaen and Ajuriaguerra (1964).

with characteristics such as sex, race, level of education, or social status. A second source of variation could be differences in methods of enquiry, whether by objective observation, by self-report, or by report of relatives or teachers. Third, given standard groups of subjects and standard methods of enquiry, differences could be due to differing criteria of handedness, such as consistent left preference for all important activities, or any left preference for less skilled activities. Wile (1934), for example, observed people in the street carrying cases, handbags, parcels, and umbrellas. Closed umbrellas were carried on the left in 70% of instances but open umbrellas on the left in 20%. Perhaps it was for actions such as these that incidences of 20 to 30% were obtained in Table 10.1. Standard methods of enquiry and agreed criteria of classification are necessary before questions about differences due to age, sex, or other variables can be investigated.

This chapter takes a close look at methods of assessment of hand preference because these provide the basic data from which inferences about the nature of handedness are drawn. An analysis of data already available can lead to a useful approach to questions about handedness. It is hoped to show that the search for an elusive "essence" of handedness is a mistake. In biology, little progress was made while efforts were concentrated on the search for the "essence" of each species; this entailed a search for an ideal species type amid the "noise" of variation. Progress was made when it was realised that the variability is fundamental and the ideal species type an abstraction (Mayr, 1970). Similarly, for handedness, it is necessary to recognise the genuine variability of hand preference patterns before the elusive phenomenon can be pinned down.

10.1.   TYPES OF HAND PREFERENCE ASSESSMENT

10.1.1.   The Right–Left Dichotomy

The question "Are you right- or left-handed?" implies a simple dichotomy between two types of handedness. Most people are prepared to describe themselves and others as left- or right-handed, usually on the basis of the writing hand. Direct classification can be used for one's own handedness (self-report) or for the handedness of others (the data for relatives in most family studies).

Table 10.2 gives examples of right–left classifications from three sources. The first is the incidence of left-hand use depicted in works of art (data of Coren & Porac, 1977, mentioned in Section 3.1). In this example, there are only two possibilities, as the artist must have depicted either the left or the right hand in use. Similarly, for any single observation of human hand preference, one or other hand is involved. The second example of dichoto-

TABLE 10.2

Incidences of Left-Handedness by Right–Left Classification

	N	Left-Handed (%)	Range
A. *Left-hand use as depicted in works of art* (Coren and Porac, 1977) 16 periods from pre-3000 BC to 1950	1180	7.4	2.0–14.0
B. *Self-report in U.S. army registrants* (Karpinos and Grossman, 1953)			confidence interval (0.99%)
1. Qualified	6040	7.9	6.9–8.8
2. Disqualified	6119	10.1	9.0–11.2
3. Total U.S. males (adjusted by K & G)	12159	8.6	7.9–9.3
C. *Report of relatives* Report by OU students of parents' handedness	1540	5.0	left + mixed 6.2

mous classification is taken from data for men examined for military service in the United States in 1952 (Karpinos & Grossman, 1953). The men were asked, "Are you (check one) □ right handed □ left handed." Table 10.2B gives the percentage for men who qualified and were disqualified for military service, separately and together (adjusted by Karpinos and Grossman for inequalities in the proportions of men from the several U.S. Army geographical areas). The proportion of left-handers was significantly higher in those disqualified than qualified for army service, presumably because the former included some pathological left-handers (Section 4.3.1). The estimate of the confidence level for this very large sample implies that the true prevalence of left-handedness for men of this age group in the United States in 1952 had a 99% probability of being within the range 7.9–9.3%.

The third example is a report by Open University students of their parents' handedness, by questionnaire (Annett, 1979). Fathers and mothers are combined because they had identical incidences in this sample. Very few parents were described as "both" or "mixed" handed (1.2%). Even when these are included with those called left-handed, the total incidence for parents is smaller than for other samples in Table 10.2.

Evidence that students under-report the handedness of their parents was obtained by Porac and Coren (1979). High-school students were asked about their parents' handedness, and the reports were then checked against questionnaires sent directly to the parents. Whereas the students described

4.1% of their parents as left-handed, the parents themselves reported a 9.1% incidence of sinistrality. McGuire and McGuire (1980) found that when students and school-children were asked to describe themselves, very few mentioned their hand preferences, but of those who did, almost all were left-handers. These studies imply that handedness does not seem to be a noteworthy characteristic for most right-handers and that under-reporting of left- and mixed-handedness in relatives is more likely to occur in right-handed than left-handed informants. Biases such as these must be considered when analysing data for handedness in families (Chapter 16).

10.1.2. Questionnaire Enquiries About Various Actions

Questionnaires give scope for the amplification of information about handedness in two ways: First, enquiries can be made about several actions, and, second, answers other than left or right are possible. Some "either" (E) responses were always given in my student samples, even when right (R) or left (L) were asked for. Perhaps the service registrants in Table 10.2B were more conforming. Some questionnaires invite respondents to rate the strength of their preferences for the right or left hand, as will be considered further below.

Figure 10.1 lists the 12 items used in most of my questionnaires and observational studies of hand preference. Table 10.3 gives the proportions of L and E questionnaire responses given to each item, by 2,321 young adults, students, and service recruits (Annett, 1970a; see Appendix I for details of samples). Table 10.3 shows considerable variation between actions in the likelihood that subjects will respond in these two ways. The two sets of ranks are not closely related (Spearman rank correlation, $\rho = .475$, $N = 12$, NS). Many deal playing cards left-handed (17%) but few claim the ability to deal either way (3%). Writing is half-way down the ranked list of L preferences but at the bottom of the list of E preferences. Only 3 to 4 per 1,000 claim to write with either hand. That is, true ambidexterity is very infrequent and much less common than changes of preference between tasks.

Cutting with scissors has the smallest proportion of L responses (6%), but relatively many claim to be able to cut with either hand (7%). When questionnaire responses were compared with observed performance in 113 students (Section 10.2) 7 changed the response for scissors, 4 from either to right, one from either to left, and 2 from left to right. This suggests that questionnaire-based claims to use scissors in either hand may be a little optimistic. Normal scissors are made for right-hand use and are difficult to use in the left hand because of the position of the cutting edge. I was informed by a psychologist colleague early in my studies of handedness that *all* left-handers have to learn to use scissors in the right hand. I found,

Handedness research

Name...Age.........Sex.........
Were you one of twins, triplets at birth or were you single born?...............

Please indicate which hand you habitually use for each of the following
activities by writing R (for right), L (for left), E (for either).*

Which hand do you use:

1. To write a letter legibly?..
2. To throw a ball to hit a target?...
3. To hold a racket in tennis, squash or badminton?...........................
4. To hold a match whilst striking it?..
5. To cut with scissors?..
6. To guide a thread through the eye of a needle (or guide needle on
   to thread)?...
7. At the top of a broom while sweeping?..
8. At the top of a shovel when moving sand?.....................................
9. To deal playing cards?..
10. To hammer a nail into wood?...
11. To hold a toothbrush while cleaning your teeth?............................
12. To unscrew the lid of a jar?...

If you use the *right hand for all of these actions*, are there any one-
handed actions for which you use the *left hand*? Please record them
here ....

....

If you use the *left hand for all of these actions*, are there any one-
handed actions for which you use the *right hand*? Please record them
here ....

* This instruction was omitted in some versions with the intention of dis-
couraging 'E' responses.

FIG. 10.1   The questionnaire used for studies of hand preference. Annett, 1970a.

however, that some left-handers discover how to use normal right-handed
scissors in the left hand.

Questions about criteria arise when it is asked which of these several items,
or combinations of items, should be used for classifying individuals as right-
or left-handed. What rules are to be adopted for transforming the questionnaire data into the right/left classification discussed above? It can be seen at
once that the percentages of left-handers would be very different if the
criterion were dealing playing cards than if it were cutting with scissors.
Should it be required that subjects perform *all* the actions with the left hand

TABLE 10.3

Percentages of 2,321 Subjects Responding "Left" and "Either" to 12 Items of a Hand-Preference Questionnaire

	"Left" Responses			"Either" Responses	
I*	Dealing cards	17.0	L	Unscrewing jar lid	17.5
L	Unscrewing jar lid	16.5	G	Sweeping	16.9
H	Shovelling	13.5	H	Shovelling	11.9
G	Sweeping	13.5	F	Threading needle	9.7
F	Threading needle	13.1	D	Striking match	8.7
A	Writing	10.6	K	Toothbrush	8.5
D	Striking match	10.0	E	Scissors	6.8
B	Throwing ball	9.4	I	Dealing cards	3.3
J	Hammering	9.2	C	Racquet	2.6
K	Toothbrush	8.1	J	Hammering	2.5
C	Racquet	8.1	B	Throwing ball	1.3
E	Scissors	6.2	A	Writing	0.3

Note: From Annett (1970a).
*Letters refer to order of presentation of items.

(4.3% of subjects in Table 10.3) or that subjects perform *any* action with the left hand (32.9%), or perhaps that they perform any action with *either* hand (55.2%). On this last criterion, only about 45% of the sample would be counted fully right-handed. This seemed to me to be extending the concept of non-right-handedness so far as to make it probably meaningless. E responses were noted, of course, and used in some analyses (Section 10.3.3) but never used as a criterion of non-right preference. The subjects classified as "mixed"-handers in my samples always showed a definite preference for the left hand for at least one of the actions listed in Figure 10.1. (That is, R + E combinations were counted consistent right, L + E were counted consistent left, and R + L, with or without E, were counted as mixed.) The only possible ambiguity arises for those who claim to perform all actions with either hand; this response is so infrequent that the ambiguity is of no practical signifi-cance.

Some questionnaires invite respondents to quantify the strength of their hand preferences as mentioned above. Crovitz and Zener (1962) asked subjects, for each action, whether they preferred to use the right hand always (score 1), or mostly (2), either hand (3), left hand mostly (4), or left always (5). Gedye (1964) provided a scale labelled at one extreme "Nothing to it" and at the other "Impossible" and asked subjects for each item how easy it would be to use the other hand. Oldfield (1971) invited subjects to indicate preference by placing a "+" in columns labelled "right" and "left", with two crosses to indicate strong preference for one hand and a single cross in both columns to indicate either hand preference; this amounts to a rating scale such as that of Crovitz and Zener (right always $= + +$ R, right mostly $= +$ R, either hand $= +$ R $+$ L, left mostly $= +$ L, and left always $= + +$ L). Since the Edinburgh Handedness Inventory (EHI), as Oldfield called his question- naire, was given mainly to university undergraduates, the rating system was probably well enough understood. Response to this scale probably demands a good level of intelligence.

Before using the questionnaire in Figure 10.1, I used an earlier version (questionnaire I of Annett, 1967), which included items 1–8 only and asked subjects to indicate how easy it would be to change the hand used for each item. This followed the example of Gedye, but the scale was divided into three sections labelled "easy", "slightly difficult", and "difficult", thus giving a 3-point rating scale. Data were collected from 730 undergraduates at the universities of Aberdeen and Hull. The analysis of ratings seemed to add nothing of value to the classification of right-, mixed-, and left-handedness given above. This experience, together with the finding that more than 50% of subjects indicate some non-right preference if E responses are included in the criterion, led me to believe that subjective ratings of strength of preference were not likely to be informative. When questionnaire responses are checked against objective observations of performance, E-hand responses are often changed (Table 10.6). It seemed probable that claims to be able to use either hand for unimanual skills might depend more on an optimistic approach to the task than on any solid foundation in reality. Hence, the claim of Briggs and Nebes (1975) to have *improved* the Annett questionnaire (Figure 10.1) by adding a rating scale is not one with which I would concur.

Whether or not "either hand" or "strength of preference" self-reports are allowed in questionnaires, is it possible to transform the responses into a numerical scale? The Crovitz and Zener and the Oldfield questionnaires are commonly used to provide laterality indices by assigning numerical values to the self-assessed ratings. Examination of the items listed in Table 10.3 shows that the proportions of subjects giving L and E responses differs between items. Laterality indices take no account of such differences, which probably depend on differences in the levels of skill required. Laterality indices are considered further in Section 10.3.1.

Questionnaires can include short or long lists of items. Porac and Coren's (1981) handedness questionnaire was of 4 items, that of Raczkowski, Kalat, and Nebes (1974) used 23 items, and Beukelaar and Kroonenberg (1983) included 39 items. Provins, Milner, and Kerr (1982) compared responses to three questionnaires and concluded that, "A larger and more wide-ranging questionnaire, with self-weighting of items may provide an alternative to the 10–12 item inventory usually employed." My own view is that "larger" might mean "better" only if the problems of how to interpret what the shorter questionnaires are telling us had been solved. The fundamental issue of how to use the information in Table 10.3 remains. Increasing the number of items does not solve the problem. The uses of factor analysis and association analysis will be considered in Section 10.3.

10.1.3. Observations of Hand Use

Instead of relying on questionnaire reports, subjects may be observed performing actions such as those considered above. Observation is essential for studies of young children, the mentally handicapped, and others unable to respond to questionnaires. It is also essential for intelligent adults when confidence in the data is required, since many subjects are surprised to find, on objective testing, that they perform certain actions in the left-handed manner. Most of the data considered for my samples from Chapter 11 onwards depends on observation, not questionnaire (Appendix I).

Observational studies suggest how certain ambiguities may arise if subjects show uncertainty about the hand to use. If the subject tries the action using the R and the L hand and is confident that both feel equally comfortable, an E can be recorded. As explained above, E responses alone were not regarded as evidence of mixed-handedness in my samples. Nursery-school children, when given a child's sand spade and asked to show how they would dig at the seaside, were sometimes unsure what was wanted and tried out the action in different ways as though trying to discover what would feel most comfortable. Changes of this kind should not be regarded, in my view, as indicating "either" or "mixed" preferences, but rather as examples of the preliminary trial and error required to "get the feel" of a new action. I believe that some reports of high incidences of bilateral or mixed preferences in

TABLE 10.4

Observation of Left and Either Hand Preferences in School-Children Aged 6 to 15 Years

Item	Left (%)	Either (%)
Unscrewing lid of		
a jar	24.8	1.4
Pointing to pictures[a]	17.4	14.3
Drawing	15.5	0.4
Placing buttons in		
a narrow-necked bottle[b]	13.7	34.2
Throwing a ball	12.2	0.7
Cutting with scissors	10.4	0.4

Note: N = 278.
[a] N = 161.
[b] N = 117.

young children may depend on such trial and error, rather than genuine bilaterality (Sections 4.2 and 20.1).

Table 10.4 gives examples of hand preference items observed in two samples of school-children (Annett, 1970b; Annett & Turner, 1974; see Appendix I.A.9). As for the questionnaire reports in Table 10.3, there were large differences between the percentages of L and E hand use recorded for the several actions. E responses were rarely noted, except for pointing and for placing buttons in a narrow-necked bottle. L responses were often observed for unscrewing the jar lid, as reported by questionnaire.

10.2.   RELATIONS BETWEEN TYPES OF HAND PREFERENCE ASSESSMENT

As a first step in trying to interpret hand preference data, it may be asked how data collected by one method relates to that of another method, and whether retests by the same method give consistent information. These questions are usually considered under the headings of validity and reliability.

10.2.1. The Self-Classified Dichotomy Versus Questionnaire

Humphrey (1951) gave a 22-item questionnaire to 35 right-handers and 70 left-handers (the latter including 35 left- and 35 right-handed writers). The subjects were male, aged 17 to 46, and mostly of university status. The initial selection of subjects depended on "reputation" as to handedness, so the starting point of the enquiry was a dichotomy, depending mainly on self-classification. The outstanding finding was that the right-handers were very much more consistent in their preference for the right hand (93% out of 735 actions recorded) than non-right-handers (71% for left-handed writers and 50% for right-handed writers). The greater inconsistency of left-handers is a recurring theme in the laterality literature. Humphrey's study shows that it is evident in the basic pattern of hand use.

Whenever groups are classified for handedness by self-report, the non-right-handers are found to be less consistent than the right-handers. Does this imply that *all* so-called left-handers would be better described as mixed-handers? Are there no left-handers who are as consistent as most right-handers? This was not clear from Humphrey's report, and it was one of the first questions I asked in my studies of handedness. Here, the important point must be emphasised that the inconsistency of self-classified left-handers should no longer be reported as a new discovery but recognised to be a consequence of this method of definition of groups.

10.2.2. Questionnaire Versus Observation: Validity

How do questionnaire reports relate to observed hand usage? Raczkowski, Kalat, and Nebes (1974) asked 47 students who had completed a hand preference questionnaire about 1 month previously to perform the actions under observation. Subjects were selected to include a majority of *left-handers*, so they did not represent an unbiased sample. Any item for which a "both" response was given to the questionnaire was omitted on the objective test, so that the actual numbers of subjects included in the several comparisons range between 15 and 41. Table 10.5 lists the percentages of subject changing between R and L responses (in either direction) between questionnaire report and actual performance, the items being listed in order of

TABLE 10.5

Validity of Hand Preference Questionnaire Responses: Changes Between Questionnaire and Objective Test for Students Selected as Predominantly Left-Handed ($N=27$) or Predominantly Right-Handed ($N=14$)

Items Ordered for Frequency of Change	Subjects making a change between R and L* (%)
1. Drawing	0
2. Writing	0
3. Dealing cards	0
4. Bottle opener	0
5. Throwing baseball	2
6. Hammering	3
7. Toothbrush	3
8. Screwdriver	3
9. Eraser	5
10. Tennis racquet	5
11. Scissors	6
12. Striking match	6
13. Stirring liquid	6
14. Shoulder for resting bat before swinging	7
15. Foot for kicking	14
16. Carrying books	15
17. Salt or pepper shaker	15
18. Threading needle	16
19. Foot first in shoes	17
20. Pouring liquid	20
21. Holding drinking glass	20
22. Arm first in coat sleeve	21
23. Top of broom	22

Note: After Raczkowski, Kalat, and Nebes (1974).
*Both or either responses omitted.

frequency of change. Items 1 to 10 can be regarded as fairly consistent, with 5% change or less. Items 15 to 23 show poor consistencies, with 14% change or more.

Table 10.6 shows similar previously unpublished data for 113 students of psychology at the University of Hull, who were unselected for handedness. They were all students available at the time the analysis was made who had been given the questionnaire in Figure 10.1 and who were then observed by fellow students performing the actions listed in laboratory classes some weeks later. This analysis shows that changes between R and L were infrequent for all actions except unscrewing the lid of a jar (10.6%). Changes involving E responses were relatively more frequent but less than 8% over all items. The direction of changes involving E responses, shown at the bottom of the Table 10.6, were mainly between E on questionnaire and R on test. This analysis for an unselected sample of students suggests that question-naire reports of hand preference are valid for most items of this question-naire. Most inconsistencies are associated with E responses and mainly due to an over-estimation by right-handers of their capacity to use either hand.

TABLE 10.6

Validity of Hand Preference Questionnaire Responses: Changes Between Questionnaire and Objective Test for 113 Undergraduates Unselected for Handedness

Items Ordered for Frequency of Change	Subjects Making Any Change Between R, E, L (%)	Subjects Making Any Change Between R and L (%)
1. Writing	0	0
2. Hammering	0.9	0
3. Racquet	1.8	0.9
4. Throwing	5.3	3.5
5. Toothbrush	5.3	0.9
6. Scissors	6.2	1.8
7. Dealing cards	6.2	4.4
8. Match	7.1	0.9
9. Shovelling	8.8	1.8
10. Threading needle	11.5	3.5
11. Sweeping	15.0	4.4
12. Unscrewing lid	23.9	10.6
Total change for 1356 responses	7.7	2.7
Direction of change		
from either to right	3.3	
from either to left	1.0	
from right to either	0.4	
from left to either	0.3	

10.2.3. Questionnaire Versus Questionnaire Retest: Reliability

How reliable are questionnaire reports when retested after an interval? Raczkowski, Kalat, and Nebes (1974) asked 27 of their selected subjects to repeat the questionnaire after an interval of about 1 month (and after having tried the items on the objective test). Agreements were 92 to 100% for the first 10 items of Table 10.5 but were poorer for several of the items lower in the list. Coren and Porac (1978) obtained retest questionnaire data after an interval of 1 year, also in 27 subjects, on 8 items drawn from the most reliable on the scale of Raczkowski *et al.*; they found consistencies of 96 to 100%.

McMeekan and Lishman (1975) asked 73 subjects, selected so as to include a majority of left-handers (41), to repeat the Annett (1970a) questionnaire (Fig. 10.1) and the Oldfield (1971) Edinburgh Handedness Inventory (EHI) after intervals of 8 to 26 weeks. Table 10.7 shows the percentages of items changed between any of the R, L and E responses, and also changes between R and L responses. As in Table 10.6, the majority of changes involved E responses, and there were relatively few changes between R and L. The direction of change here is toward fewer E responses on second testing, in contrast to the change to more E responses between questionnaire and observation (in Table 10.6). (Could this be due to impatience at being asked to repeat a boring task?) It should be recalled that McMeekan and Lishman's subjects, like those of Raczkowski *et al.*, were selected to include a

TABLE 10.7

Reliability of Handedness Questionnaires: Changes Between Test and Retest

	Any Change Between R, L, E (%)	Any Change Between R and L (%)
Annett (1970a)		
all items	9.25	3.9
primary items	7.5	3.4
Oldfield (1971)	12.9	2.6
Direction of change (both questionnaires combined)		
No. items = 1606	(%)	
from either to right	1.2	
from either to left	1.8	
from right to either	2.6	
from left to either	2.0	

Note: Based on McMeekan and Lishman (1975).

majority of left-handers, making the changes observed not necessarily representative of those in general samples.

McMeekan and Lishman (1975) distinguished six classes of hand preference (consistent right, inconsistent right, right ambidexters, left ambidexters, inconsistent left, and consistent left-handers). The consistent right-handers were the most stable and the inconsistent left-handers the least stable on retest. Hence, it is probable that those reliability studies that include a majority of left-handers find levels of consistency lower than would be expected in a sample unselected for handedness.

It has been demonstrated above that the most frequent changes of response, between questionnaire retests and between questionnaire and observation, involve E responses. What of the reliability of judgements for strength of right and left hand preference, as shown by placing "++" for strong or "+" for less strong preference? Out of 730 responses to the EHI, 18.2% showed some change; in terms of the proportion of subjects, 82.7% made such a change on at least one item.

10.3. THE CONTINUITY
OF THE HAND PREFERENCE DISTRIBUTION

The above account of studies of hand preference makes it plain that the more questions subjects are asked about their handedness, the more complicated the picture becomes. It has long been remarked that there is no absolute distinction between left- and right-handers. "Right-handedness and left-handedness are relative terms" (Burt, 1937), and "Handedness . . . is nothing absolute; it is a question of degree" (Brain, 1945). For practical purposes, however, Burt's recommendation to teachers was that the best single test is to ask a child to cut paper with loosely riveted scissors, and Brain advised neurologists that elaborate tests were probably of not much more value than simple ones such as the hand used for throwing. Is there any way of converting the hand preference data considered above into a simple, useful measure of degree of preference?

Perhaps the simplest count that can be made is of how many actions are performed with the left hand. Figure 10.2 gives an analysis of the questionnaire responses of 241 service recruits, showing how many claimed to perform between 0 and 12 actions with the left hand. The distribution is J shaped, with the majority (66.8%) reporting no use of the left hand for these actions, and a small proportion (3.7%) reporting left preference for all 12 actions. First impressions on looking at the graph suggest that there are relatively few individuals of intermediate preference. Porac and Coren (1981, p. 16), commenting on the J shape of the preference distribution, wrote, "Ambilaterality is relatively rare in preference distributions." If "ambila-

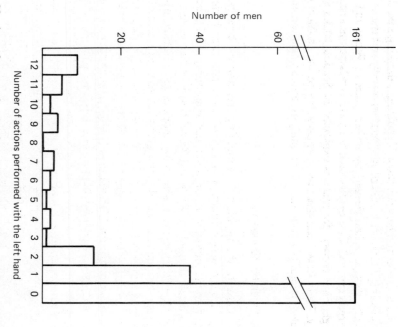

FIG. 10.2.   Numbers of men performing from 0–12 actions with the left hand in 241 service recruits. Redrawn from Annett, 1972.

teral" refers to the 2–3% of the sample performing 5 to 6 actions with the left hand, it might be considered rare. However, 29.5% fall between the extreme right and extreme left in this sample; similar proportions of subjects were found, by questionnaire or observation, to show mixed hand preferences in all of my samples for the actions in Figure 10.1.

What to do with the 30% of subjects who are inconsistent in hand preference presents a fundamental problem. The treatment of this group has implications for the further analysis of problems of lateral asymmetry. There are two main alternatives. Either hand preferences are regarded as basically discrete, or they are regarded as basically continuous. The discrete argument suggests that there are two main types of handedness, right and left, and apparent mixtures of preference are due to the imperfections of our measuring instruments or to social pressures on natural left-handers to conform to the habits of the right-handed majority. The continuity argument suggests that right and left are extremes of a range of preferences, with many shades of intermediate expression between them. Typological thinking runs through all of the laterality literature reviewed in Chapters 3 to 9, and the evidence for continuity, though acknowledged by writers such as Brain and Burt, has been largely ignored. Continuous variability is a fundamental assumption of the Right Shift theory, for reasons explained in Section 10.3.3 and subsequently. There have been three main approaches to the problem of subject variability: laterality quotients, factor analysis, and association analysis.

10.3.1. Laterality Quotients

One response to the problem of variability has already been partly considered. This is to assign numbers to the various responses and convert them by some formula into an index of preference. Humphrey (1951), for example, used a formula devised by Witty and Kopel (1936), which gave a dextrality index as $(R+1/2E)N$, and a sinistrality index as $(L+1/2E)N$, where R, E, and L mean the numbers of right, either, and left responses, respectively, and N is the total number of responses. The Crovitz and Zener (1962) rating scale (above) gives scores ranging from 14 for the fully right-handed to 70 for the fully left-handed. For the EHI, Oldfield (1971) recommended that a "Laterality Quotient" be derived using the formula $100(R-L)/(R+L)$, where R and L refer to the number of crosses placed in each column. The formula gives quotients ranging from -100 to $+100$, however many crosses are used.

The possibility of quantifying otherwise messy data is attractive, especially to psychologists for whom messy data is more often the rule than the exception, and many studies report their findings in terms of laterality quotients. The two fundamental objections to laterality quotients have been mentioned already. First, they give the same numerical value to actions involving differing levels of skill, such as writing, cutting with scissors, and sweeping. This is like counting together oranges, tomatoes, and cabbages—necessary perhaps on some occasions, but these are not likely to be frequent. The second objection is that the scores also depend, in many scales, on subjects' estimates of degrees of strength of preference. The use of E responses on questionnaires was seen above to be not very reliable and probably inflated (only 45% of subjects *not* giving some L or E response). The use of E responses probably depends upon an optimistic and extraverted attitude as often as upon a genuine equality of hand use. (This objection applies as much to the attempts to study associations between laterality and personality through laterality indices, discussed in Section 5.3, as to the interpretation of hand preference data itself.)

Bryden (1977) gave the Crovitz and Zener questionnaire and the EHI to 1107 undergraduates at the University of Waterloo. Comparing responses to the same items on the two scales, he found that subjects were more likely to use the ratings 1 or 5 than they were to use the "++" response for designating strong preferences. Some items were given E responses more often than not (holding a glass of water for drinking, sweeping, and opening a box lid). There were sex differences in that females were more likely than males to claim they "always" rather than "usually" performed actions with one hand. These observations underline the conclusion above, that self-ratings of strength of preference cannot necessarily be taken at face value.

10.3.2. Factor Analyses of Handedness Questionnaires

A second response to the messy questionnaire data has been to search for dimensions of handedness through factor analyses of questionnaire responses. Bryden (1977) asked how far the 24 items of the two questionnaires mentioned above depend on a single dimension of hand preference. Three factors were obtained, as shown in Table 10.8. The highest loadings for the first factor were for writing, drawing, using a tennis racquet, and using a toothbrush—actions expected to be dependent on the preferred hand. Factor 2 identified items that had been designed to make subjects stop and consider their responses carefully, by being scored the "other" way; for example, the hand that holds the *nail* when hammering, or the *bottle* when opening it. This requirement for reversed responses seems to lead to ambiguity, and suggests that students cannot be assumed to be as attentive as necessary to cope with these items. Factor 3 depended mainly on three items of the EHI, for match, broom, and box lid; these are two-handed actions that right-handers often claim to do with the left hand. Bryden's findings suggest that there is only one substantial dimension accounting for the correlation between items, a single dimension of hand preference. Other factor analyses using smaller numbers of items or smaller numbers of subjects agree in finding only one major factor in hand preference data (Porac, Coren, Steiger, & Duncan, 1980; White & Ashton, 1976).

What conclusions can be drawn from the factor analyses of hand preference data? Certain actions needing two-handed responses seem to

TABLE 10.8
Factor Analysis of Questionnaire Items: Highest Loadings on Three Factors

Factor 1		Factor 2		Factor 3	
write	.86	bottle	.71	broom	.70
draw	.86	dish	.68	box lid	.62
racquet	.76	needle	.66	match	.56
toothbrush	.72	potato	.58	spoon	.51
ball	.71	pitcher	.55	knife (w/o fork)	.51

Note: adapted from Bryden (1977). (N = 984.)

require special consideration, especially if there is any ambiguity as to the hand that does the more skilled work. The main outcome is that items such as writing, drawing, and using a tennis racquet seem to be closer to the "essence" of handedness than other items such as drinking from a glass and opening a box lid. The former are clearly actions that require more skill than the latter. Should the less skilled actions be ignored? Or might it be possible to discover a method of scaling items, or discovering patterns of hand use along the dimension of right–left preference?

10.3.3. Association Analysis

The data summarised in Table 10.3 shows great diversity between subjects in claims to use one or the other hand for a number of actions. When patterns of preference are considered for individual subjects, it is evident that there is an enormous number of possible combinations of R, L, and E responses. How can sense be made of this diversity? Perhaps somewhere in the multitude of patterns there are meaningful distinctions to be drawn between types of preference pattern.

Association analysis is a technique developed by botanists for analysing ecological patterns in the distribution of species (Williams & Lambert, 1959, 1960, 1961). The terrain to be investigated is divided systematically into plots, and the numbers of plants of each species is noted within each plot. For any pair of species it is possible to count how often they go together in the same plot and to express this association as a chi square or a phi coefficient. This first stage is like that of a factor analysis. The coefficients are calculated for all possible pairs of species. The next step is to sum the correlations for each species, to discover which species is most highly correlated with all others. This species is then used to divide the plots into those in which it is present and those where it is absent. Within each subgroup, the calculations are repeated to find the species most highly correlated with all others in the subgroup, and further subdivisions are made. Whereas factor analysis tries to discover what is common to a set of individuals, association analysis looks for meaningful differences. Botanists studying the ecological relationships between plants and their environment have been able to identify the features of the terrain relevant to the distribution of species; sometimes they discovered features such as old railway tracks that had previously been unmarked. If subjects are taken as analogous to plots and hand preference items are analogous to species, association analysis can ask whether it is possible to identify ways of making meaningful distinctions between individuals on the basis of patterns of hand preference.

Association analyses were run for several subsets of questionnaire samples (for sex, generation, and source of subjects). The outcomes were substantially

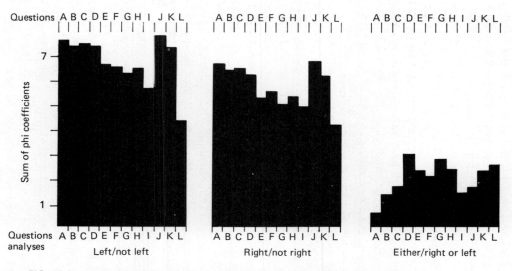

FIG. 10.3. Association analysis: Histograms of sums of phi coefficients for three analyses of total sample ($n = 2321$). Annett, 1970a.

alike for all analyses, and the data published (Annett, 1970a) was for the 2,321 young adults already referred to in Table 10.3.

As responses to the questionnaire could be R, L, or E, the two-way classification needed for the association analysis could be achieved in any of several ways (L versus R + E, R versus L + E, and E versus R + L). Figure 10.3 shows the sums of phi coefficients for each item in each of these three analyses. The sums of phi coefficients are larger for the left versus not left analysis than for the other two, suggesting that this might be the most informative analysis. Second, the pattern of items is very similar for the first two analyses. The highest sums were obtained in each case for question J (hammering), but A (writing) was only just smaller. Six items stand out well above the others: writing, throwing, tennis racquet, striking a match, hammering, and toothbrush, while the other six items are much less informative (in the sense of the association analysis). The similarity of the first six items in levels of phi coefficient suggests they should be treated for some purposes as a group. They were designated "primary" actions and used together in later classifications of hand preference (Chapter 11).

The third analysis, E versus R + L, was very much less informative than the other two in levels of phi coefficients. The item with the highest phi coefficient for E was striking a match, followed by sweeping with a long-handled broom, unscrewing a jar, and shovelling with a long-handled shovel. All of these actions involve the coordinated use of two hands. Their similarity here might mean that humans are genuinely able to reverse the patterns of hand use for these items; when sweeping or shovelling, it may well be helpful to be able to change hands from time to time. It is possible, however, that respondents are not well aware of their actual preferences for bimanual actions and are relatively inaccurate on these questions. Factor 3 in Table 10.8 was highly loaded on broom and match.

Figure 10.4 shows the outcome of the full association analysis based on left versus not left responses. It gives the action used as a basis for the division and the percentages of subjects involved. The first division distinguished between the 9.2% left-handed hammerers and the 90.8% right-handed hammerers. The second division separated out the 1.94% of right-handed hammerers who wrote with the left hand. The height of the division on the graph (the ordinate) depends on the largest chi square at each division (range 5–500, transformed to a logarithmic scale). Having made these major divisions for hammering and writing, the majority of subsequent divisions depend on the bimanual actions: shovelling, striking a match, unscrewing the lid of a jar, and sweeping. There are also several divisions lower in the hierarchy for throwing. Thus there were 9 subjects (0.39%) identified as left-handed for hammering, striking matches, unscrewing the lid of a jar, and sweeping who were right-handed for throwing. There were also 9 subjects on the other side of Fig. 10.4, who were right-handed for hammering, writing,

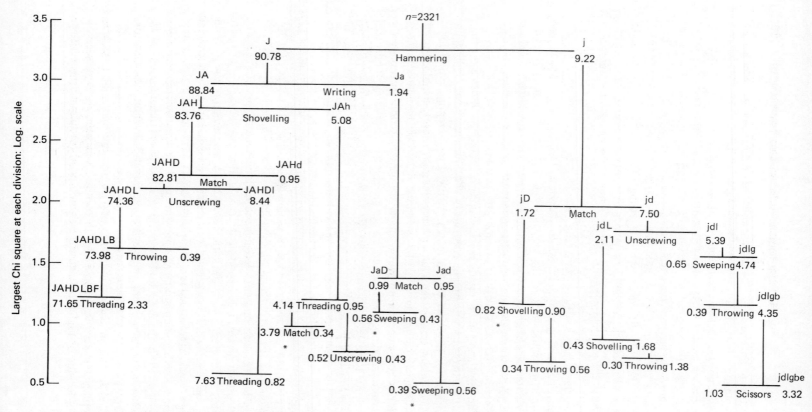

FIG. 10.4. Association analysis of "left" responses showing response used for each division
and percentage of subjects in each subgroup. Annett, 1970a

shovelling, striking matches, and unscrewing the lid of a jar, but left-handed for throwing. Thus, it seems there is some genuine independence between sidedness for throwing and these other activities. There are some 24 subgroups identified in Fig. 10.4. Each distinguishes a relatively small percentage of subjects, except at the extreme right, where about 72% remain without further division. The conclusions to be drawn from the association analysis are:

1. About 30% of the population are not consistently right-sided.
2. There are all shades of preference between strong right and strong left.
3. There are no absolute divisions to be drawn, but if distinctions are required, hammering and writing offer the best criteria.

The association analysis did not reveal any formerly unsuspected source of variation analogous to the botanists' old railway tracks, but it was interesting that hammering was even more informative than writing as a criterion of hand preference. Skilled control of the hands to make tools through hammering must have an evolutionary history spanning millions of years (Section 1.1). Writing was invented, as far as we know, only a few thousand years ago. The strong association between hammering and other items for hand preference suggests that the need to make controlled movements with precisely specifiable outcomes is an important feature of human hand preference. Tasks such as sweeping, shovelling, opening box lids, and drinking from a glass have more loosely specifiable outcomes than do hammering and writing. Questions about hand skill are considered in Chapter 11.

The main conclusion drawn from the association analysis (Annett, 1970a) was that hand preferences are continuously variable. All subdivisions of the continuum are to some extent arbitrary.

10.4. SUMMARY

Hand preferences can be assessed by self-report, by the report of relatives, by questionnaire, and by observation. They can be classified in a right–left dichotomy, in a right, mixed, left trichotomy, or they can be recognised to form a continuum with many degrees of mixed preference between the right and left extremes.

When hand preferences are observed for several actions, considerable variability is found between actions in the percentage of subjects preferring the left hand or using either hand. Some 30% of subjects show mixtures of definite right- and left-hand preferences, and over 50% claim to use the left or either hand for at least one action. The problems posed by this variability have been largely ignored, and it will be argued in later chapters that failure to consider variations in patterns of hand preference is the source of many confusions about laterality.

One misleading assumption about mixed hand preferences is that they are a sign of developmental immaturity and that they become less frequent with increasing age. It is important to distinguish the uncertainty shown by a child (or adult) on first trying a new action as to which hand "feels best", from the established preferences for *different* hands between differing actions found in 30% of young adults. Another misleading assumption is that variability is characteristic of left-handers; of the 30% with mixed-hand preference, about 6% are left-handed writers and 24% right-handed writers. Thus mixed-handers form a higher proportion of left- than right-handers, but the *numbers* are greater in right-handers by about 4:1.

Attempts to quantify the variability of hand preferences through indices that give equal weight to actions such as writing and sweeping ignore the different levels of skill involved. Quantifications of subjective estimates of strength of preference have not been shown to have any objective foundation. The reliability and validity of questionnaire responses is high for some items but low for others, especially when two-handed actions and judgements of strength of preference are involved.

Factor analyses find only one substantial factor in questionnaire data for handedness. An association analysis confirmed that there are many patterns of hand preference and no objective grounds for dividing the preference continuum at any point. The item most highly correlated with all others was hammering, with writing a close second. Actions such as throwing, which involve hand and limb rather than hand and finger control, and two-handed actions such as striking matches and threading needles may be done with the "other" hand both by right-handers and by left-handers.

11 | Hand Preference and Hand Skill

The idea of hand preference implies some greater skill for the preferred hand. "We say that a person is right handed if he for preference uses his right hand rather than his left to carry out the more skilled kinds of movement and is more skilful at such movements with the right hand than with his left. The converse is true of a left handed person" (Brain, 1945). It is currently fashionable to stress the weakness of the relationship between hand preference and hand skill (Bradshaw & Nettleton, 1983; Porac & Coren, 1981). An evaluation of this judgement depends on questions about the nature of skill and whether psychologists have succeeded in measuring it, as well as questions about whether psychologists have been successful in measuring hand preference.

While attention is focused on hand preference alone, there are no independent criteria against which to judge the significance of particular patterns of preference. If hand preference could be systematically and reliably related to *something else*, then we would have an objective standard against which to evaluate preference data. This point is fundamental, in my view, to the problem of analysing handedness. It is analogous to the problem of how to define a point in space. This was not possible until the system of coordinates was invented. If hand preference can be coordinated with an independent measure of hand skill, then the elusive phenomenon can be regarded as pinned down.

This chapter considers the relationship between hand preference and skill in three sections. The first considers the surprisingly few analyses of the nature of the difference between the hands in skill. The second examines the distribution of differences between the hands and shows how patterns of hand preference, as identified by the association analysis, are systematically related to differences between the hands in peg-moving time. The third section examines previous studies that have treated measures of skill as objective tests of handedness.

11.1   HOW DO THE HANDS DIFFER IN SKILL?

Relationships between handedness and skill can be examined from several points of view, and it is important to be clear about the objectives of the several possible enquiries. The question whether left-handers are at a general disadvantage in comparison with right-handers was considered in Section 5.2.1, where it was shown that there is no evidence that left-handedness is a handicap to skilled performance (see further Section 17.1.2). The chief question to be considered here is how the two hands differ in skill when one is described as preferred and the other as nonpreferred. This question leads to two further questions: "What is skill?" and "Have psychologists succeeded in measuring it?"

There have been two main approaches to the first question, what is skill, and both make similar suggestions with regard to handedness. One approach, exemplified by the work of Fleishman and his colleagues (Fleishman, 1958; Fleishman & Ellison, 1962; Fleishman & Hempel, 1954) is to measure the performance of a number of individuals on a large variety of tasks involving the use of the arms and hands, to intercorrelate them all, and to submit them to a factor analysis. A great many factors have been identified, such as finger or fine dexterity, manual dexterity, aiming, arm-hand steadiness, and reaction time. Barnsley and Rabinovitch (1970) gave 100 subjects (50 of each sex) some 32 tasks, based largely on Fleishman's work, to be performed with each hand in turn (but randomised for order between subjects). Details of hand preference were not reported, but it seems that subjects were drawn from general groups of students and hospital staff and were unselected for handedness. The scores were then factor analysed for the preferred hand and for the nonpreferred hand separately in each sex. Some 10 factors were identified, and for each one there were no noteworthy differences between the preferred hand and nonpreferred hand in factor loadings. Whatever it was that the factor analyses were identifying as dimensions of skill applied equally well to each hand. As Barnsley and Rabinovitch put it, "It can be stated with confidence that the same skills are involved in non-preferred hand performance as in preferred hand performance." The preferred and nonpreferred hand scores were then compared for each test and in all cases except RT, the preferred hand was better than the nonpreferred. The absence of consistent differences between the hands for RT was evident in the work of Poffenberger (1912). Barnsley and Rabinovitch conclude that, "Handedness appears to be a single dimension characterised by the superior performance of the preferred hand." In other words, the hands resemble each other in all essential respects except that one tends to be better than the other.

A second approach to the analysis of skilled movement began with the experiments of Woodworth (1899) on the relations between speed and accuracy for hitting targets or drawing lines of certain length. While the left and right hands were equally accurate at slow rates, the left hand became less accurate than the right as speed increased; differences between the hands for rapid movements were observed with visual control and with eyes shut. Woodworth concluded, for subjects who were presumably right-handed, "While not capable of greater precision than the left when plenty of time is allowed, it (the right hand) can be controlled much more rapidly. . . . The seat of this superiority of the right hand is probably in the motor centres." Woodworth's experiments show that the left hand is less accurate than the right when acting under time constraints.

The relations between accuracy and speed of movement were suggested by Fitts (1954) to depend on the capacity of the motor system to transmit information (see Howarth and Beggs, 1981, for review). The time taken for movements between specified targets was shown to depend both on the distance to be moved and on the size of the target. The difficulty of a visually guided movement depends mainly on the size of the target to be hit. This was confirmed in a frame-by-frame analysis of the placement of pegs of constant size in holes varying in width; the increase in time taken for smaller holes occurred almost entirely for the last $\frac{1}{2}$ in. of an 8-in. movement (Annett, Golby, & Kay, 1958). This suggested that the "skill" of the movement might depend on the visuo-motor control required for the final approach to the target.

During the 1960s I needed a manual task with which to assess the severity of impairment of children with hemiplegia (Section 6.2). As a clinical psychologist, I knew that putting pegs in holes is an inherently attractive task for small children; often when a child would perform no other psychological test s/he would transfer the pegs of the Merrill Palmer Scales (1931). A peg-moving task like that used by Annett, Golby, and Kay (1958) was devised, with parallel rows of holes 8 in. apart but with larger pegs ($\frac{3}{8}$ in. × 2 in.) to be transferred between $\frac{1}{2}$-in. holes (Fig. 11.1). The task was a success in that every hemiplegic child was eager to try it, often with the "bad" hand as well as the "good". The task was given to normal school-children (Annett, 1970b) as controls for the hemiplegics and also to psychology undergraduates in laboratory classes. These data led to the analyses of hand preference in relation to skill to be described in Section 11.2. But, first, what could be discovered about the *nature* of the difference between the hands in skill?

Annett, Annett, Hudson, and Turner (1979) compared the performance of each hand in two experiments. In the first, subjects were asked to transfer pegs from one row of holes to another as in the standard task (Fig. 11.2) and also for boards with larger hole sizes, and for boards where the holes were farther apart. When the target holes were large, there was relatively little difference between hands in time taken, but when target holes were small the nonpreferred hand was at a greater disadvantage than the preferred hand. These results resemble those of Woodworth except that he varied speed and Annett and colleagues varied accuracy. When the task is easy, there is little difference between the hands, but as it becomes more difficult, the advantage of the right hand becomes evident. The question about skill is a question about what is meant by "difficulty". Difficulty for Woodworth's subjects meant a requirement to make faster movements, and for Annett's subjects it meant smaller target holes. The main findings of Annett and colleagues relevant to the difference between the hands in skill was that increasing the distance between the holes made both hands slower to about the same extent; decreasing the hole size increased the relative difference between the hands. These findings showed, as expected, that hand preference is relevant to the precise control needed to hit a small target, not the grosser movements of the arm involved in travelling towards the target.

Annett et al.'s (1979) second experiment made a frame-by-frame analysis

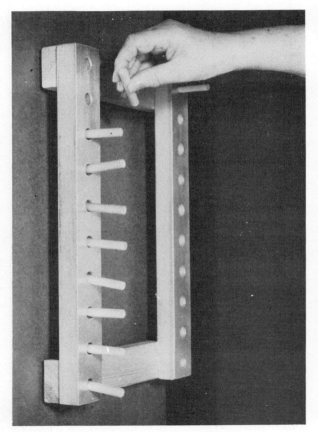

FIG. 11.1.   The peg-moving task.

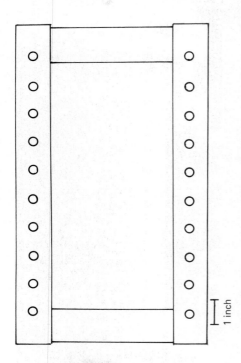

1 inch

FIG. 11.2.   Dimensions of the peg-moving apparatus.

of high-speed film recordings of the standard peg-moving task performance of four subjects, one of whom was a left-hander. We assumed that the greater difficulty of hitting small targets (and by implication the greater difficulty for the nonpreferred than the preferred hand) would be found to depend on some difference in capacity for monitoring the hand visually as it approached the target and made the small corrective movements necessary for a hit (that is, it would be a function of feedback control). On the contrary, it was found that the preferred and nonpreferred hands moved at similar speeds and corrected errors (hitting the board in the vicinity of the hole) equally fast. There was no evidence of differing patterns of feedback control. Differences between the hands were examined for several variables, but there was no substantial difference except that the preferred hand made *fewer mistakes*. Table 11.1 shows the numbers of corrective movements made by each hand.

TABLE 11.1
Peg-Moving Task Errors by Each Hand: Total Numbers of Peg Transfers Requiring 0 to 3 or More Corrective Movements for Four Subjects, 200 Transfers With Each Hand

No. Corrective Movements	Preferred Hand	Non-preferred Hand
0	54	33
1	94	87
2	37	51
3 or more	15	29
Total trials	200	200

Note: From Annett, Annett, Hudson, and Turner (1979).

The preferred hand hit the target either directly (hole-in-one) or with 1 further movement 74% of the time, whereas the nonpreferred hand did this only 60% of the time. The preferred hand needed to make 3 or more attempts only 8% of the time, while the nonpreferred hand needed 3 or more attempts 15% of the time. The findings for the left-handed subject resembled those of the right-handers, except that the more accurate hand was the left.

These differences look rather small for accounting for a difference as subjectively important as hand preference. They imply, however, that the preferred hand is likely to hit the target before the nonpreferred hand would do so. The preferred hand does not move faster, but it has a better aim and hence it is likely to do what its owner wants done more quickly than the other hand. Like the factor analysis, this study suggests that there is no substantial difference between the hands in the components of skilled performance except that the preferred hand is better!

The very simple manual skill of tapping the index finger as rapidly as possible differs between the preferred and nonpreferred hands (Peters, 1976). Peters (1980) sought to discover how the hands differ on this task. In three experiments he showed that the differences are not due to fatigue or to the time taken in travel for the up-and-down movements; the difference between the hands seems to lie in the reversal phase when the direction of movement is to be changed. Peters concluded that sensory feedback was not an important factor so much as precision of force modulation.

Both Annett *et al.* (1979) and Peters (1980) independently reached the conclusion that the superiority of the preferred side is not due to a better capacity to process feedback but rather to more efficient control of the motor output. This implies that the advantage to one side is not due to more efficient sensorimotor control loops, while a specific action is in progress. It is rather due to a more efficient plan at the start of the action, or a plan that can be put into effect more efficiently. The association analysis of hand preference questionnaire responses identified hammering as the action most highly discriminating between right and left preferences. In hammering, efficiency depends on the "skill" of each single strike; it seems intuitively unlikely that one could correct a hammer blow in mid-flight. Similarly, the analysis of peg-moving performance suggests that each "stab" at the hole with a peg is a single blow. Why is one hand better than the other? Woodworth found the preferred hand better than the nonpreferred in moving to a target when subjects closed their eyes, as well as with eyes open. There is also evidence for differing capacities to use visual information to direct the movement of each hand. Honda (1982) found that movements of the right hand towards small targets on the right were greatly dependent on eye movements towards the right. Left-hand movement towards small targets on the left were little affected by the absence of eye movements to the left, and little improved by eye movements specifically directed to the left. In Honda's right-handed subjects there seemed to be a clear difference between capacities to utilise visual information for the control of each hand.

When considering the nature of the difference in skill between the sides, it seems clear that there need be no fundamental difference in patterns of motor organisation, no difference in movement speed or in the capacity for making gross arm movements to large targets. When some precise hand or finger movement has to be made to a small target, the nonpreferred hand is a little more likely to miss. This could be because the cerebral hemisphere controlling the nonpreferred side is less able to use sensory information about the target, or it could be due to some small difference in the efficiency of motor output control. The main point being made here is that the difference between sides could be very small and depend on minor inequalities in the sensorimotor capacities of the two sides.

11.2. THE CO-ORDINATION OF MEASURES OF HAND PREFERENCE AND HAND SKILL

It is shown in Chapter 10 that hand preferences vary through so many fine gradations that the distribution can be regarded as continuous. What is found when differences between the hands in strength or skill are examined? Differences between the hands in strength were measured at the suggestion of Francis Galton, when men attending a health exhibition in 1884 were invited to try the strength of each hand by pressing a dynamometer. The data were analysed some 40 years later by Woo and Pearson (1927). The distribution of differences for 6,992 males was found to take the form of a regular normal curve with the mean at 3.34 and standard deviation at 7.261b, the mean favouring the right hand. There was no negative skew, but otherwise the distribution resembled that for differences in internal lengths of the left and right halves of the skull (Fig. 3.1). Subjects were grouped for age from 6 to 81 years "to enquire if there is the supposed change from sinistrality to dextrality" (Section 4.2). About 65% were superior with the right hand at all ages. The visual acuity of each eye was also measured (Section 12.1), and differences between the eyes were not associated with differences between the hands. Woo and Pearson concluded, "Dextrality and sinistrality are not opposed alternatives, but quantities capable of taking values of continuous intensity and passing one into the other." No wonder left-handedness seemed elusive.

Figure 11.3 shows the distribution of differences between the hands in peg-moving time for 617 males and 863 females (Annett & Kilshaw, 1983; see Appendix I.B.10). The totals include all subjects drawn from complete nonvolunteer samples (that is unselected for handedness) who were observed

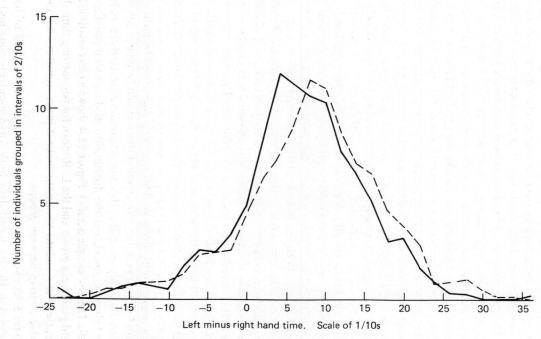

FIG. 11.3.   The distribution of males (——) and females (– – –) for L–R difference between the hands in peg-moving time. Based on Annett and Kilshaw, 1983.

performing the 12 actions of the handedness questionnaire (Fig. 10.1) and measured for peg-moving time on the task described in the last section. The usual procedure was to give five trials for each hand, alternating hands between trials and alternating the starting hand between subjects. The great majority of subjects were students testing one another during laboratory practical classes, so there can be no danger of experimenter bias influencing the results. The data represent differences between the means for each hand, measured to 1/10 s, subjects being grouped here at 2/10-s intervals. The graphs show continuous distributions of differences in skill that approximate to normal curves. They are more peaked and negatively skewed (longer left-hand tail) than expected for true normal distributions. The sexes differ in that the female distribution is slightly to the right of the male distribution except at the left-hand tail. These features are considered in Chapter 16. The point being made here is that the distribution of differences between the hands in skill is continuous, roughly normally distributed, and with no sign of a dip in the curve at 0 to indicate a natural division between right-handers and left-handers. The proportions of subjects at 0 or no difference between hands are about as expected for unimodal normal curves. It is clear that the distributions of differences between hands for strength and for peg-moving skill are very different from the J-shaped distribution of preference.

Despite this difference in the shape of the preference and skill distributions, I had strong evidence that asymmetries in preference and skill are related. When a sample of school-children was classified into groups of pure left-, mixed left-, mixed right-, and pure right-handers and the mean differences between hands (L–R) on the peg-moving task were plotted for each group, the relationship was clear and linear (Annett, 1970b). Figure 11.4 gives similar data for a second sample of school-children (Annett & Turner, 1974). Children were selected according to date of birth to obtain a sample random with respect to handedness. This was then augmented by testing all other left-handed writers in the class, so that there would be a large number of left-handers for analyses such as this one, where the characteristics of left-handers are being examined, not the distribution in the general population (see Appendix I.9b for sample details). Figure 11.4 shows a clear relationship between hand preference group and the L–R mean for peg-moving time. The bars representing the standard deviations make it plain, however, that there is considerable overlap between groups.

At the time I received the results of the association analyses of hand preference (Section 10.3.3), I had data both for peg-moving time and for observed hand preference for the 12 actions listed in Fig. 10.1 on 283 subjects. These were in two groups: 188 psychology students who had tested one another in laboratory practical classes, and 165 twelve-year-old children tested by myself and my assistants as a complete year group in a comprehensive school (LS sample). Both samples should be free from volunteer effects

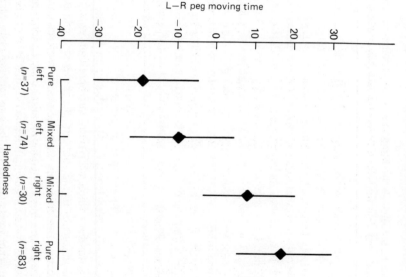

FIG. 11.4.   Left minus right peg-moving times (1/10s) in children classified for hand preference; means ± 1 standard deviation.

and hence reasonably representative of students and school children. What could these data for hand preference and hand skill in the same subjects reveal about the relationship between these two variables?

One simple analysis was to find the mean L–R peg-moving times for subjects who performed each of the actions with the left hand. This was done for each sample separately, but as Ns were small for some actions, the samples are combined in Table 11.2. As in the association analysis (for 2,321 subjects by questionnaire only), the hand used to hold a hammer was the most discriminating item. The hand used for scissors was close to hammering in terms of left-hand skill, but fewer people used scissors in the left hand (as was seen for the questionnaire sample in Table 10.3). Writing, toothbrush, match, racquet, and throwing were all associated with a significant bias to the left hand in peg-moving skill. The other five actions are all bimanual in that they involve the co-ordinated use of both hands. Dealing cards in the left-

TABLE 11.2

Mean L–R Peg-Moving Times for Subjects Performing Each Action With the Left Hand

Action	N	L–R mean	S.E.
Hammer	19	−7.0	1.8
Scissors	12	−6.8	2.0
Writing	24	−6.5	1.5
Toothbrush	21	−6.3	1.7
Match	23	−5.6	2.1
Racquet	18	−4.6	2.3
Throwing	23	−4.3	2.0
Dealing cards	56	−1.1	1.4
Shovelling	36	0.6	1.9
Sweeping	35	1.0	1.9
Unscrewing lid	59	1.8	1.3
Threading needle	46	2.1	1.8

Note: Total N=283.

handed fashion was found in a substantial number of subjects. This was the action with the largest percentage of "left" responses in Table 10.3, and this might have been taken to imply that the manner of dealing cards is a relatively trivial action, not especially significant for handedness classifications. The analysis for peg-moving time shows that it is of greater significance than the other four actions. All actions from playing cards to needle threading are associated with L–R differences whose means are not significantly different from 0 or L = R. These varying means for L–R skill between the several actions support the view expressed above that to combine all the actions in a single "index" of preference is to lose a great deal of possibly useful information. The analysis in Table 11.2 is not directly useful for the classification of hand preference in meaningful categories, because one needs to know what *combinations* of actions occur and to evaluate their significance. I needed to co-ordinate the findings of the association analysis and the data for L–R peg-moving speed. Of course there were over 2,000 subjects in the association analysis and only 283 with peg-moving times, so there were insufficient data to test all the subgroups shown in Fig. 10.4. My method of analysis was to make successive divisions of the sample of 283 subjects, to give an inverted tree as in the association analysis, and to test for the significance of differences in L–R peg-moving times between groups at each division.

Figure 11.5 shows the classification achieved. The first decision was made for writing, instead of hammering, since the writing hand is easier to ascertain and seemed of greater practical value for teachers and others who

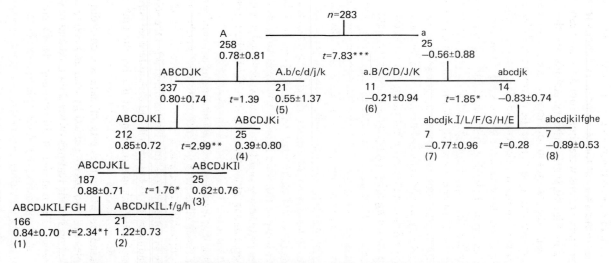

FIG. 11.5.   The classification of hand preference patterns: The coordination of information on hand preference and L–R peg-moving time (in seconds). Left minus right hand mean in seconds in preference classes. A = writing; B = throwing a ball; C = using a racquet; D = striking a match; E = using scissors; F = threading a needle; G = sweeping; H = shovelling; I = dealing playing cards; J = hammering; K = using a toothbrush; L = unscrewing a jar. Capital letters = right-handed; lower-case = left-handed; . = and; / = or. Figures in parentheses are the classes defined in Table 11.3. *** indicates $p < .001$; ** indicates $p < .01$; $p < .05$ (one-tailed). † indicates difference in the unpredicted direction. Annett, 1970a.

might want to use the system of classification. The next decision on each side was between those who performed any of the other primary actions with the nonwriting hand. (The primary actions were those found to have especially high sums of coefficients in Fig. 10.3; the primary actions are the top 6 actions in Table 11.2, with the exception of scissor use.) This gave a significant t for left writers (one-tailed test since the direction of difference is predicted in all comparisons), but not for right-handed writers. The division for right-handers was retained, however, for the sake of consistency and because the lack of significance might be due to chance factors in the samples being used. It will be seen later that class 5 continued to be out of line in many subsequent samples. Among left-handers who perform all primary actions with the left hand, one further division was made between those who were consistently sinistral for all actions and those who were not. The comparison for L–R times was not significant statistically but in the expected direction. Between right-handers performing all primary actions with the right hand, further divisions were made chiefly on the empirical ground that the distinctions gave significant t comparisons. The first was for dealing playing cards (I), the second was for unscrewing the lid of a jar (J), and, finally, for left-hand response to any of the three actions, needle threading (F), sweeping (G), and shovelling (H). This category produced a highly significant t test with means in the *opposite* direction to that expected. That is, subjects performing these actions left-handed were more strongly *dextral* than the remaining subjects on the peg-moving task. The groups identified at the end of the analysis are numbered in parentheses in Fig. 11.5. Table 11.3 lists them with their definitions.

Figure 11.6 shows the L–R means of the Hull undergraduate and school samples, when they were classified in the 8 preference groups identified in the above analyses. Both groups show the trend to greater *dextrality* for class 2 than for class 1. Class 5 was more dextral than classes 3 and 4 for the school-children but for undergraduates it was between 4 and 6. A difference between classes 7 and 8 was clear for the school-children but not for the undergraduates.

An analysis of this kind, in which two sets of data are co-ordinated, following certain principles but also partly guided by trial and error, could turn out to have depended on specific features of the data used and have no value for subsequent studies. The real test of this 8-group classification of hand preference came when, some years later, I was able to collect data from 804 Open University students attending psychology summer schools. A practical class on laterality included the observations of hand use for the 12 actions in Fig. 10.1 and the measure of peg-moving time, as performed by the Hull samples. Written instructions for the class were supplied by me, but the classes were run by several summer school teachers at a number of locations. All observations and measurements were made by the students working as

TABLE 11.3

The Definition of the Classes of Hand Preference Identified in Fig. 11.5 and Percentages of Combined Main Sample Subjects
in Each Class

Actions Observed	Preference Classes	Females (%) (N=617)	Males (%) (N=863)
A. Writing*	1. Right (or R+E) for all actions	64.7	61.4
B. Throwing*	2. Left for any of F, G, H only	6.5	12.7
C. Using a racquet*	3. Left for L and no others except above	7.6	6.9
D. Striking a match*	4. Left for I and no others except above	9.7	5.8
E. Cutting with scissors	5. Right writing but left for any other primary action	4.1	4.4
F. Threading a needle	6. Left writing but right for any other primary action	2.4	3.0
G. Sweeping with broom	7. Left for all primary actions but right for any others	2.4	2.1
H. Shovelling with long-handled shovel	8. Left or (L+E) for all actions	2.6	3.6
I. Dealing playing cards			
J. Hammering a nail into wood*			
K. Using a toothbrush*			
L. Unscrewing a jar			

Note: Revised from Annett (1976a).

*Primary actions: those most highly intercorrelated (Annett, 1970a).

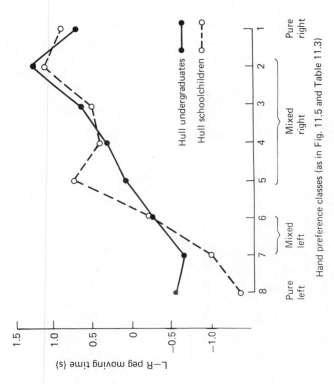

FIG. 11.6. The coordination of hand preference and skill in undergraduates (——●) and schoolchildren (○--○) in Hull. Redrawn from Annett, 1970a.

experimenters and subjects in pairs. Students were asked to make a copy of their data, and these were collected and sent to me. I checked all the arithmetic, excluded students who reported any physical problem concerning the hands and arms, and classified the remainder in the 8 preference groups defined above. Figure 11.7 shows the mean L–R peg-moving times for each hand preference group of the new sample and the means of the former Hull samples, combined. It was quite astonishing to find such close agreement between two large sets of data. Apart from class 2 (which was now in line) and class 8 (which was not more sinistral than 7), the means were almost identical. There was the same "bump" for class 5. This finding convinced me that not only are hand preference and hand skill related, but they are related in a highly reliable and systematic manner.

Further groups of undergraduates and school-children have been observed performing the 12 actions of the standard questionnaire (Fig. 10.1) and measured for peg-moving time. These several samples have been examined for the homogeneity of findings and combined to give a substantial quantity of data with which to examine aspects of the laterality distribution (Annett & Kilshaw, 1983; Kilshaw & Annett, 1983). The combined sample data are considered later. The L–R distributions of the combined sample

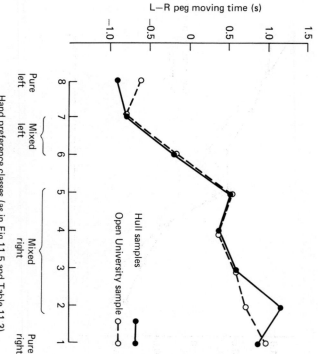

FIG. 11.7.   The coordination of hand preference in skill in the Hull samples of Fig. 11.6 (●——●) and Open University students (○--○). Redrawn from Annett, 1976a.

males and females are given in Fig. 11.3. Figure 11.8 gives the mean L–R times in hand preference groups for the total ($N = 1,480$), along with findings for 129 pupils attending a dyslexia clinic, who were tested in the same way as the normal samples for hand preference and hand speed (Appendix I.A.3). The numbers of dyslexics in some groups were small (only 1 in class 3 and 6 in class 7, otherwise 9 or more) so a very close fit could not be expected. There is no doubt, however, that over-all there is a remarkable agreement between the dyslexic and normal samples. This finding demonstrates that the various degrees of sinistrality found in dyslexics have similar significance in terms of L–R skill as the corresponding degrees of sinistrality in control populations (Chapter 18).

The means and standard deviations of L–R times for the combined samples are listed for each preference class in Table 11.4. The sexes are combined here but are listed separately in Table 16.1, where it is shown that there are no statistically significant sex differences except for class 1. Table 11.4 shows a fairly orderly progression of L–R means in relation to preference class, except for class 5, which gave a "bump" in the data for most samples. Class 5 also has a larger standard deviation than other classes, which suggests it is most heterogeneous and might be worth redefinition. I

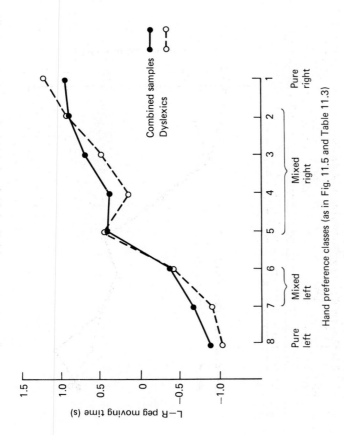

FIG. 11.8. The coordination of hand preference and skill in combined sample controls (●——●) and dyslexics (○--○). Revised from Annett, 1981.

listed all class-5 subjects over the several samples, noting the hand preference responses and L–R times. It was found that for subjects who performed only 1 primary action with the left hand (and did not deal playing cards with the left hand), the L–R mean was like that of class 3 (unscrewing the lid of a jar). For subjects who performed at least 2 primary actions with the left hand, the L–R mean was similar to class 4 (dealing playing cards with the left hand). A redefinition of classes is suggested on the right of Table 11.4, with rules specified at the bottom. This reclassification would reduce the number of classes to 7. It has the advantage of identifying a group of right-handers with strong left-hand preferences (any two primary actions "left" and/or dealing playing cards "left") who match for L–R skill left-handed writers who perform any primary action with the right hand.

The revised class 3, like the original one, identifies a small but clear departure from full dextrality. This is a little surprising as class 3 mainly consists of those who unscrew the lid of a jar left-handed, and this action would seem to require little skill. In so far as this requires "power" or strength, it is worth noting that tests of strength by dynanometer press show positive but weak associations with self-classified handedness (see Table 11.5). Class 2 (left-handed sweeping, shovelling, and needle threading) has

TABLE 11.4
L–R Times in Hand Preference Classes and a Possible Re-definition of Classes 3, 4, and 5

Hand Preference Class	Original Classification (as in Table 11.3)			Hand Preference Class*	Possible Revised Classification		
	N	L–R Mean	SD		N	L–R Mean	SD
1	929	9.5	7.3				
2	150	9.0	7.8				
3	107	7.0	6.8	3 + ai	142	7.0	7.3
4	110	3.7	7.4				
5	63	4.2	9.4	4 + aii + biii	132	3.7	7.2
6	41	− 3.7	7.1				
7	33	− 6.8	7.8				
8	47	− 8.0	7.2				

Analysis of original class 5
a. One primary action only

i. not I	35	6.9	8.6
ii. and I	4	3.2	5.4

b. Any two primary actions

iii.	18	3.8	7.0

Note: Data for combined main samples, Annett and Kilshaw (1983).
Revised definitions:
3 + ai Right-handed writers who perform any one other primary action and/or unscrew the lid of a jar with the left hand.
4 + aii + biii Right-handed writers who perform any two primary actions and/or deal playing cards with the left hand.

little association with sinistrality, as measured by peg-moving time. Sweeping and shovelling demand gross limb movements rather than fine hand and finger control and probably involve quite different levels of neuro-muscular control from peg moving. Needle threading, however, seems to demand fine hand–eye co-ordination, which might be expected to be associated with peg-moving performance. It turned out to be a poor indicator of peg-moving asymmetry. It is conceivable that the variety of methods of needle threading led to unreliable reports of this action, though examiners were urged to record the hand "doing the guiding".

The reader will see from the above account that the co-ordination of data for preference and skill and the definition of degrees of hand preference was entirely empirical. The preference classes were defined so as to maximise L–R differences between adjacent groups. However, as the standard deviations of L–R means in Table 11.4 indicate, there is considerable overlap between groups. No absolute divisions can be drawn. This point is important in considering "misclassification" rates in the next section.

Very few research samples would be large enough to justify classifying subjects for hand preference in as many as 7 or 8 groups. I would recommend a simplified scheme, which classifies subjects first into right- or left-handed writers. Within each writing hand group a subset can be identified which has mixed right or mixed left tendencies, with a L–R means of $3.7s$ and $-3.7s$, respectively, following the criteria above (for mixed right, any two primary actions with the left hand and/or left-handed dealing of playing cards; for mixed left, any primary action performed with the right hand).

The point was made above that an apparently elusive phenomena can be pinned down if it can be approached from two independent directions (preference and skill). But having reached this empirical solution, can it be shown to have any relevance to other independent laterality data? It is shown in Chapter 12 that the preference groups identified above have significance for classifications of eye and foot preference.

Does the above demonstration of association between continua of hand preference and hand skill apply only to the particular measures used here? Peters's analysis of tapping by the index finger of each hand is mentioned in Section 11.1. When the difference between hands in tapping rate was plotted for subjects classified in 10 categories according to a laterality index, a roughly linear relationship was found, as shown in Fig. 11.9 (Peters & Durding, 1978). This demonstrates that an orderly relationship between degrees of hand preference and degrees of hand skill can be found for a task other than peg moving and for classes of preference other than the 8 identified above.

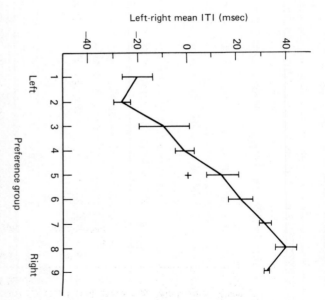

FIG. 11.9. A coordination of hand preference and tapping skill; the relation between the hand difference in mean intertap intervals (ITI) and preference group as defined by laterality quotient. Peters & Durding, 1978.

11.3. TESTS OF SKILL AS "OBJECTIVE" MEASURES OF HANDEDNESS

Table 11.5 summarises the findings for three studies that compared groups of left-handers and right-handers on tests of dexterity, strength, or speed. All found that many subjects in each preference group turned out to be no better with the preferred than the nonpreferred hand on the "objective" measure. Does this imply that there is no relationship between hand preference and hand skill (Porac & Coren, 1981; Provins & Cunliffe, 1972)?

The Crawford dexterity task used in all three studies requires the subject to pick up small pins with a tweezer, place them in holes, and then place small metal collars on the pins. Only 14% of Benton's (1962) subjects but 20% of those of Johnstone, Galin, and Herron (1979) and 33% of those of Satz, Achenbach, and Fennell (1967) were misclassified on this test. Cutting with scissors misclassified no right-handers but 30% of left-handers, as could be predicted from the preference responses in Table 10.3 (where there were 11% left writers but only 6% used scissors left-handed). Hand strength as measured by a dynamometer press gave a 23% misclassification rate. The

TABLE 11.5
Three Studies of Self-Classified Left-Handers and Right-Handers Tested for Hand Skill: Percentage Misclassified When Divided on a Criterion of R–L ≤ 0

Source/Task	Left-Handers		Right-Handers		Total
	N	Misclassified (%)	N	Misclassified (%)	Misclassified (%)
Benton (1962)					
Crawford dexterity	40	15	40	12	14
Cutting with scissors	40	30	40	0	15
Satz et al. (1967)					
Dynanometer	54	41	69	9	23
Tapping	54	35	69	13	23
Crawford dexterity	54	26	69	39	33
Questionnaire index of preference	54	13	69	1	6
Johnstone et al. (1979)					
Tapping	30	27	30	13	20
Crawford dexterity	30	30	30	10	20

smallest misclassification rate was for questionnaire responses converted to an index of preference.

How do these apparently high misclassifications arise? There are several hints in previous sections. How can we be sure the measures used are indeed objective tests of hand skill when psychologists are far from reaching agreement on what is meant by skill? How were the subjects selected? Groups of self-classified left-handers are expected to be highly variable in extent of left-hand preference (Section 10.2). If differences between the hands in skill are distributed *continuously* and not discretely, any division between right and left is arbitrary. The 39% of right-handers misclassified on the Crawford Dexterity test in the Satz *et al.* (1967) sample included 19% who showed no difference between sides. Looking at these same data another way, it can be said that about 80% or more of right-handers were at least as good with the right hand as the left. Provins and Cunliffe (1972) found only moderate correlations for measures of L–R differences between test and retest sessions; but with only 10 subjects in each handedness group and the variability within hand preference groups found above (Chapter 10), high correlations could hardly be expected.

The chief problem of these approaches to the relationship between hand preference and hand skill has been a neglect of the continuous nature of both variables. If handedness is treated as a typology, then variability appears to be noise. If it is recognised as naturally variable, more appropriate questions and research strategies will be devised.

11.4. SUMMARY

Comparisons of the hands for skilled performance, by factor analysis and by measures of speed and accuracy in aiming tasks, find no substantial differences between the hands except that one tends to be better than the other. The preferred hand is likely to do what is wanted more quickly than the nonpreferred hand. It does not move more quickly, but it has a better aim and so fewer tries are needed to reach a target. The advantage seems to be in the initial movement plan rather than in feedback control during the course of the movement.

Differences between the hands in strength (for pressing a dynamometer) and in visuo-motor speed (for peg moving) are distributed in a single, unimodal, approximately normal curve. There is no break or dip in the curve between right- and left-handers but a continuum. The L–R times of males and females are similar at the sinistral side of the distribution, but females are further to the right at the dextral side.

L–R times vary with degrees of right and left hand preference. This was demonstrated in two large samples of school-children. Patterns of hand preference were distinguished by examining the L–R times of subjects in groups suggested by the association analysis (Section 10.3.3). The relationships between hand preference and skill discovered in one large sample were replicated in a second large sample. Almost identical L–R means were found for several of the corresponding preference classes in the two samples. This demonstrated that degrees of mixed hand preference, between consistent right and consistent left, are systematically related to degrees of L–R skill. As in the association analysis, hammering was the item most discriminating for L–R skill. Through empirical study of the L–R times of subjects showing varying patterns of hand preference, it was possible to identify a subgroup of right-mixed-handers who matched a subgroup of left-mixed-handers for L–R times of opposite sign. (The right-mixed-handers were right-handed writers who used the left hand for any two of the primary actions and/or dealt playing cards with the left hand; the left-mixed-handers were left-handed writers who performed any one of the primary actions with the right hand.) Two-handed actions (sweeping, shovelling, and needle threading) were not associated with significant reductions of relative right-hand skill when compared with consistent right-hand performance.

Reports that hand preferences are unrelated to hand skill as measured by "objective tests" can be questioned on several grounds. There is no certainty that the tasks used offered valid measures of skill. Subjects were self-classified left- and right-handers who probably included some of mixed hand preferences. The continuum of differences between the hands was dichotomised at L = R, and the intrinsic variability of skill was neglected. In contrast to these former negative reports, the systematic relationships found here between hand preference and skill for peg moving and for finger tapping give reason to believe that the elusive phenomenon, "handedness", has been pinned down at last.

12

Associations between Hand Preference and other Lateral Asymmetries

The samples of school-children and undergraduates described above for hand preference and peg-moving time were assessed for several lateral asymmetries. Eye and foot preferences were always tested, but other tasks were changed from year to year in the laboratory class practicals for psychology students. For all data given below from school and university subjects, the samples can be regarded as complete for that study (i.e., not dependent on volunteers). In addition, data are cited for families (parents and children) who responded to appeals by press and radio for families with one or two left-handed parents. Families of two right-handed parents also volunteered for testing following a talk given to a women's group. The family data are not representative of the general population with respect to incidences of left-handedness, but because they include so many left-handers, questions about associations between handedness and other asymmetries can be tested more effectively than in a true population sample (where numbers of left-handers would be relatively small). Most of these data for eye, foot, and other asymmetries have not been published hitherto.

12.1. EYE PREFERENCE

If the reader points a finger to a distant object and, holding the finger steady, closes each eye in turn, it will be apparent that only one eye was lined up with the object, and information from the other eye was suppressed, without any awareness of conflict. This use of only one eye for judgements about what is straight ahead has been known for a long time, but it is a fact of which we are not spontaneously aware. Using the sight of a rifle or aiming a bow and arrow might present problems for those whose preferred eye is on the opposite side to the preferred hand, but most optical instruments such as a telescope or microscope can be used with either eye. Most people probably have no reason to discover that they have a preferred eye. It seems probable that eye preference is independent of any direct training and hence is much less influenced by social pressures than hand preference.

Each eye has a different point of view, very different for objects close to the nose but not noticeable for a distant object. Figure 2.5 shows that each eye sends information from the RVF to the left hemisphere and from the LVF to the right hemisphere. Since both eyes are connected with both hemispheres, there seems to be no intrinsic *sensory* difference to explain why one eye should be preferred. But, of course, the human visual cortex has not been studied for binocular representation experimentally in the same way as the visual cortex of the cat (Section 2.3). Perhaps when noninvasive methods of study become available, some sensory difference will be demonstrable.

Psychological studies of the sensory and perceptual efficiency of the right and left eyes have found little association between efficiency and preference (Porac & Coren, 1976, 1981). It seems intuitively reasonable to expect that the dominant eye would be the one with superior visual acuity, but this is not so, except when differences in acuity are very great. Woo and Pearson (1927) reported data for nearly 6,000 males whose visual activity had been measured along with hand strength in 1884. The acuities of the right and left eyes were about equal over the whole sample: 23% were better with the right eye, 22% better with the left eye, and in 55% there was no differences between eyes. Crovitz (1961) reported acuity dominance and sighting dominance in the same subjects and found that a majority preferred the right eye for sighting in all groups, including those with better acuity in the left eye. When there are very large differences in acuity favouring the left eye, the proportion of left-eye sighters increased, but it was still less than the increase in right sighting for subjects with a large difference favouring the right eye. In other words, there seems to be a bias to right-eyed sighting across all level of acuity difference.

Walls (1951) suggested that sighting dominance depends on asymmetries of *motor* function, and Money (1972) obtained evidence supporting this view. Without necessarily concurring with the details of Walls's theory of feedback control, it seems reasonable to accept that the control of the several pairs of muscles involved in eye movement and fixation would demand a high level of skill. If the control system for one eye is more efficient than that of the other eye, that eye is likely to be preferred for decisions about what lies straight ahead. The greater skill in controlling one eye might be analogous to the greater skill in controlling one hand.

The association between eye preference and hand preference was examined in a random sample of Glasgow school-children (Clark, 1957). About one third of the children were left-eyed and there was no significant correlation with hand preference. Porac and Coren (1976) also found no significant correlation between handedness and eyedness, but later (Porac & Coren, 1981) reported a modest but statistically significant correlation in a large sample assessed by questionnaire. Table 12.1 gives eye preference for a test of sighting in the sample of school-children (Annett & Turner, 1974) whose L–R peg-moving times were given previously (Fig. 11.4) when the *extra* left-handers are included. Table 12.1 shows that eye preference is related to hand preference, but weakly. At least one third of the total population of school-children is discordant for side of hand and eye preference. In samples representative of the general population for laterality, there are many right-handers who are discordant for eye preference and too few left-handers (18 in Clark's sample) to demonstrate that they show a similar but reversed level of discordance. This demonstration could be made here because extra left-handers were included. An association between hand and eye preference was also demonstrated by Merrell (1957), who found that 29% of 464 right-handers and 61% of 33 left-handers (for writing) were left-eyed.

Table 12.2 gives data for OU students (who tested one another) and for members of families (tested by me and assistants) for four tests of eye preference. These included sighting, viewing a distant line through a card held at arm's length, viewing a pencil through a hole in card held at half arm's length, and viewing a distant line while bringing the card up to the nose (fuller details are given in Appendix II.A.2). These data are interesting for several reasons. They confirm that only about two-thirds of right-handers are consistently right-eyed. Only about one-half of left-handers (for writing) are consistently left-eyed. The similarities between the proportions found in the two samples for both handedness groups is evidence of their reliability, increasing confidence in the students' reports of their observations. Another

TABLE 12.1

Eye and Foot Preferences in Children Classified for Hand Preference

Hand Preference	N	Left eye for Sighting (%)	Left Foot for Kicking (%)
Pure right	83	36.1	3.8
Mixed right	30	23.3	13.3
Mixed left	74	55.4	52.7
Pure left	37	67.6	83.8

Note: From Annett and Turner (1974).

TABLE 12.2

The Eye Preferences of Right-Handers and Left-Handers in the OU and Family Samples

Eye Preference	Right-Handers		Left-Handers	
	OU (N=727)	Families (N=163)	OU (N=61)	Families (N=153)
Right on all tests	62	64	20	24
Any mixture of right and left preference	20	17	29	24
Left on all tests	18	19	51	52

Note: In percentages.

feature that surprised me was the high incidence of mixed eye preferences for the four tests. My impression during family visits was that any inconsistencies of eye preference were checked and mostly resolved. As for Table 12.1, it can be concluded that the association between hand and eye preference is not close but very significant in the statistical sense. (In the OU sample, the comparison of right-, mixed-, and left-eyed individuals between right- and left-handed writers gave $\chi^2 = 48.13$, $df = 2$, $p < .001$.)

It is shown in Chapter 11 that by co-ordinating data for preference and skill it was possible to define 8 classes of hand preference, ordered fairly systematically along the continuum of difference of skill. The family data give a rare opportunity to examine relations between measures of lateral asymmetry as there were so many strong left-handers. In Fig. 12.1, the parents and children are classified for hand preference in the 8 classes defined above (but combining classes 2 and 3 as well as 4 and 5 because of relatively small numbers). The classes are compared for incidences of consistent left-eye preference and for incidences of left- and mixed-eye preference. The data are fairly orderly. They demonstrate that the degrees of hand preference, identified through an analysis of L–R peg moving, are systematically related to degrees of eye preference. Although cultural factors may influence our self-classification as right- or left-handers, they are unlikely to affect the subtleties of degrees of preference for hand or eye; the fact that these two aspects of asymmetry are related, not in an all-or-none fashion but in a fairly continuous progression, confirms that the hypothesised continua of preference and skill have some objective basis—they are not artificial constructs imposed on the data.

Merrell (1957) found an increased incidence of left-eye preference in children with parents having left-eye preference, as shown in Table 12.3,

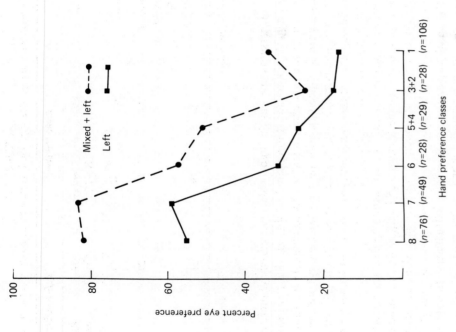

FIG. 12.1. Percentage of mixed- and left-eye preference in individuals classified for hand preference—personally tested families.

TABLE 12.3

Eye Preference in Children According to Parental Eye Preference

Parental Eye Preference	Merrell (1957)			Annett Families Visited		
	Sibships	N	Left (%)	Sibships	N	Left (%)
R × R	56	131	24	29	61	36
L × R + R × L	36	82	44	28	67	40
L × L	11	24	54	11	29	37

along with my findings for eyedness in families. Merrell's data were collected by questionnaire and by personal testing; the sampling procedure was not described but presumably depended mainly on the families of university undergraduates. Merrell did not recognise "mixed" eye preference and either omitted questionnaires giving mixed responses or retested subjects until he had determined which eye was dominant. "Mixed"-eye subjects were counted with right-eyed subjects in the data given for my sample. I found 36 to 40% left-eyed persons in all family groups. The analysis was repeated, counting mixed-eyed parents and children with the left-eyed ones. In this analysis 50 to 60% of children were mixed- or left-eyed in all family groups. There is no evidence, therefore, in my family data that parental eye preference is associated with the eye preference of children.

Some other visual asymmetries were assessed by psychology undergraduates at the University of Hull. Data for the eye closed for winking are given in Table 12.4. Most students reported they could wink with either eye. Those who could close only the left eye in winking were likely to be right-handed and right-eyed. The small number who could wink with the right eye only were more often left-handed (18%) and also more often left- and mixed-eyed (54%).

The Jasper and Raney (1937) phi-phenomenon was included in two laboratory classes at Hull but then abandoned as the findings did not justify the effort required. Jasper (1932), Raney (1935), and McFie (1952) suggested that the test might be useful for the assessment of cerebral laterality, but Carter (1953), Spreen, Miller, and Benton (1966) and Loiseau (1974) concluded that the test did not live up to its promise. The test rests on the fact that if the subject fixates a near flashing light, a second flashing light at some distance away but in line with the first light will appear as a double image; the question is whether there will be an illusion of movement between the centre light and the flashes to either side, and in which direction. The findings for 108 undergraduates are given in Table 12.5. For nearly 1 in 5 subjects no illusion appeared, and after sitting in a darkened room for 10 to 15 minutes

TABLE 12.4
Eye Closed for Winking in Relation to Hand Preference and Eye Preference

Eye Closed for Winking	N	(%)	Left-Handed in Each Group (%)	Left- + Mixed-Eyed in Each Group (%)
Both	83	71	12	51
Left only	17	15	0	18
Right only	11	9	18	54
Neither	6	5	17	33
Total	117			

TABLE 12.5

Illusions of Movement in the Jasper and Raney (1937) Phi Test in 108 Undergraduates

Direction of Illusory Movement	% of Total N	Left-Handed in Each Group %
Right only	41	2
Both	30	3
Neither	18	25
Left only	11	33

fixating flashing lights this did not seem a rewarding outcome. There was a trend for those reporting the less frequent visual experience to include more left-handers, but the test was far from diagnostic. Of the 11 left-handers in the sample, 45% experienced no illusion.

12.2.   FOOT PREFERENCE

Foot preferences were assessed in school-children, in undergraduates, and in personally visited families by asking which foot was used for kicking (as to score a goal in football), a suitable soft ball being provided when possible for demonstration. The findings for school-children are given in Table 12.1. Data for OU students and for personally visited families are given in Table 12.6. In all three sets of data only 4 to 5% of right-handers were left-footed. About two-thirds of left-handers were left-footed. The distribution of right-, either-, or left-footedness differed significantly between right- and left-handers. (For example, in the OU sample, $\chi^2 = 193.33$, $df = 2$, $p < .001$).

Figure 12.2 shows the distributions of left and either foot preference in the families when individuals were classified for hand preference, as for eye preference in Figure 12.1. Pure left-handers were 85% and pure right-handers

TABLE 12.6

Foot Preferred for Kicking in OU and Family Samples

Preferred Foot	Right-Handers		Left-Handers	
	OU (N=722)	Families (N=163)	OU (N=61)	Families (N=155)
Right	88	91	28	25
Either	7	5	13	5
Left	5	4	59	70

Note: In percentages.

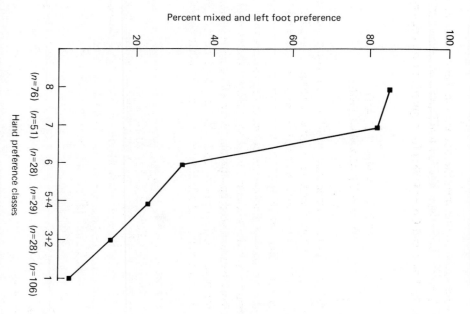

FIG. 12.2   Percentage of mixed- and left-foot preferences in individuals classified for hand preference—personally tested families.

3.8% left for kicking, incidences almost identical to those found for the school-children (Table 12.1). Intermediate hand preference classes show intermediate incidences of left-footedness. This is further strong support for the view that the distribution of lateral asymmetry is continuous. There is an orderly relationship between the series of grades of hand preference, as deduced from L–R peg-moving time and the series of incidences of left-foot preference. For both eye and foot preference, the most marked change in incidence occurred between classes 6 and 7 (left-handed writers who do or do not perform all other primary actions with the left hand). The change was much smaller between right- and left-handed writers (class 5+4 versus 6).

These data demonstrate that the association between hand and foot preference is much closer than that between hand and eye preference. This was also found by Porac and Coren (1981) for a questionnaire enquiry.

12.3. A MISCELLANY OF OTHER ASYMMETRIES

Many other variables have been examined for their association with hand preference. Although some show tendencies towards a correlation, which may be statistically significant in very large samples, none of the associations can be regarded as substantial.

Table 12.7 summarises findings for some of the asymmetries studied in undergraduate psychology classes. Numbers differ, because the tasks included differed between year groups; the large OU sample is represented here only for simultaneous drawing and writing. There were no significant differences between right- and left-handers for manner of clasping the hands,

TABLE 12.7
Miscellaneous Asymmetries Recorded in Undergraduates

	Right-Handers		Left-Handers	
	N (total observed)	%	N	%
Hand clasping Left thumb on top	284	54	34	62
Arm folding Left arm on top	283	59	34	59
Hair parting Right side	284	26	35	9*
Hair whorl Clockwise	209	65	26	62
Simultaneous drawing Preferred hand better	800	81	69	84
Simultaneous writing Mirroring by the nonpreferred hand	1008	25	94	34*
	mean	SD	mean	SD
Width of hand span R–L span in cm	−1.29	0.7	3.4	1.0
	59		9	

*Difference from right-handers statistically significant at $p < .05$.

folding the arms, or direction of hair whorl. Left-handers were reported to part their hair on the right less often than right-handers, a trend opposite to the one expected.

For simultaneous drawing, students were asked to draw a square with one hand and a circle with the other and then reverse hands drawing the square and the circle (alternating the hand drawing the square first between subjects). Class partners were asked to judge whether the square drawn by the right hand was better or equal to the one drawn by the left hand. Over 80% of subjects in both handedness groups were reported to draw a better square with the preferred hand, unlike Buffery's finding that school-children drew better with the nonpreferred hand (Buffery & Gray, 1972). Simulta-neous writing was tested in most classes by writing the numbers from 1 to 10 on a sheet of paper screened from view, listing the numbers from top to bottom (Harris, 1958). In some classes the writing was done simultaneously on either side of a vertical board at 90° to the chest (Van Riper, 1935). Left-handers were more likely to mirror-write with the nonpreferred hand than right-handers, but the difference was slight in actual percentage.

For measures of hand span, students were asked to place each hand palm down on a sheet of plain paper, spreading the fingers and thumb as wide as possible. The laboratory class partner then drew around the hand, holding the pencil perpendicularly. The distance between the further points of the thumb and little finger was measured by the students; the drawings were collected and measurements checked. For both handedness groups the span of the nonpreferred hand was a little wider than that of the preferred hand; comparison by t test found a difference significant at the 10% level. Theories associating handedness with differences in arm length (reviewed by Harris, 1980a) seem to have suggested that the preferred side was longer. The present findings suggest a slight size advantage in terms of hand span to the nonpreferred side.

Other enquiries and observations of lateral asymmetries in the psychology classes included asking the OU students at which ear they normally hold a telephone receiver when they were not writing messages at the same time. About 70% of both right-handers and left-handers reported holding the receiver in the preferred hand. This finding was repeated in a subsequent study of undergraduates at Coventry Polytechnic. Porac and Coren (1981) found 59% of their questionnaire sample right-ear preferent when asked about the ear used for listening through the earphone of a transistor radio, listening to a heartbeat, or to a conversation behind a closed door.

The suggestion that the right hemisphere of right-handers is involved more than the left hemisphere in emotional arousal (Chapter 6) might lead to an expectation that the left hand would be used more often than the right in childhood finger and thumb sucking. Just over half of 117 students recalled thumb- or finger-sucking habits in childhood. The right hand was sucked twice as often (32%) as the left (16%). There was no evidence that the nonpreferred hand was more often used for comfort sucking.

An asymmetry that should be noted, although not studied in my student samples, concerns fingerprints. Rife (1955, 1978) studied large samples of students and found slight but consistent differences between right- and left-handers. Both right- and left-handers tend to have certain patterns more often on the left than on the right palm, but this asymmetry was smaller in groups of left-handers than right-handers. Jantz, Fohl, and Zahler (1979) counted the numbers of finger ridges on each side (radial and ulnar) of all 10 fingers in right- and left-handed males and females. There were very few significant differences between handedness groups, but there were consistent trends for right-handers to have a higher and a more variable ridge count than left-handers in both sexes. Correlations between counts were higher for right-handers than left-handers, both male and female. It is not easy to interpret these findings, but Jantz and colleagues point out that they imply that handedness is influenced by prenatal developmental factors, and these could be genetic or environmental.

12.4.   SUMMARY

Associations between hand preference and other asymmetries (for eye, foot, and a miscellany of tasks tried in laboratory classes) are described for school-children, undergraduates, and personally visited families. Eye preferences are significantly associated with hand preferences but at a weak level. About one-third of the normal population is cross-lateral for hand and eye. When percentages of left- or left- plus mixed-eye preferences were compared in subjects classified for degrees of hand preference (in the classes derived in Chapter 11 from a coordination of data for preference and L–R skill), an orderly relationship was found. A similar orderly relationship was found for percentages of left foot preference in subjects classified for hand preference class. These associations between incidences of non-right-eye and foot preference with degrees of hand preference strongly support the value of the classification of hand preference reached (Chapter 11).

Merrell's finding of an association between the eye preferences of parents and children was not replicated in my family data; this could be because my families included a majority of left-handers.

Among the several asymmetries studied in undergraduate practical class-es, the majority showed no significant association with handedness. There were no associations with manner of hand clasping, arm folding, or direction of hair whorl. No evidence was found of better performance by the nonpreferred hand for simultaneous drawing of simple shapes. Winking eye, Jasper and Rayner phi-phenomena, simultaneous writing, and thumb and finger sucking were at best weakly predictive of hand preferences. There is no reason to believe that a comprehensive testing programme encompassing all such peripheral asymmetries would reveal the "essence" of human laterality. The findings for associated asymmetries support the view that the "essence" of hand preference is its intrinsic variability and that many other variable asymmetries are at best weakly associated with it. Only one of these behavioural asymmetries is strongly associated with hand preference, and this is foot preference; the concordance between hand and foot is very high but falls short of 100%.

V

THE RIGHT SHIFT THEORY

13

The Right Shift Theory of Handedness

The right-shift theory developed through a series of stages. Some of the assumptions of earlier stages were wrong from later standpoints, but they were necessary errors in the sense that movement towards the next reformulation of the problem depended upon them. The discoveries leading to each stage were experienced as surprises, in the sense that they suggested simpler ways of looking at old data and also that they led on to new discoveries. The surprises continued as the implications of the theory were examined, as will be explained. The purpose of this chapter is to outline the sequence of stages that led to the formulation of the right-shift theory (Annett, 1972). The theory has been enriched in certain ways since 1972, but there has been no change in the fundamental assumptions. The task of this chapter is to try to show why the right-shift analysis seems to me to be logically compelling (as opposed to "plucked from the air"). The key ideas have been introduced in previous chapters. Now it must be shown how they contribute to the whole.

13.1. THE CONCEPT OF MIXED-HANDEDNESS

Figure 13.1 summarises the development of my analysis of hand preference. The first main step was to distinguish mixed-handers from consistent left- and consistent right-handers. My first surprise about handedness was the large proportion of children (24%) described in a brief questionnaire to parents as changing the hand preferred between tasks (Annett, Lee, & Ounsted, 1961; see Section 5.2.2 and Appendix I.A). This suggested that

243

Hand Preferences

	Consistent Left	Mixed	Consistent Right	
1. Starting point:	Left		Right	
2. Annett et al. 1961	Consistent Left	Mixed	Consistent Right	
3. Annett 1964	ll	rl	rr	genetic model
4. Annett 1967	l^2	2rl	r^2	proportions
	4	30	66	percent human
	25	50	25	percent non-human
5. Annett 1970	8	7 6 5 4 3 2	1	preference classes (section 10.3.3)

FIG. 13.1.   Stages in the analysis of hand preferences. Based on Annett, 1976b.

many people are not consistently right- or left-handed but have mixed hand preferences. "Mixed" does not imply that both hands are equally skilful (ambidextrous) or equally clumsy (ambilevous), but rather that one hand is preferred for some tasks and the other hand is preferred for other tasks. These differing preferences are consistent for the individual (e.g., left-handed writers who are right-handed throwers, and vice versa, Section 10.3.3). A second suggestion arising from the Annett, Lee, and Ounsted (1961) findings was that mixed-handers may differ from right- and left-handers in that the pattern of cerebral specialisation may be more variable and hence more unpredictable than in consistent handers.

Previous authors had recognised that the left/right dichotomy is unsatisfactory (Section 10.3), but this uncomfortable fact was usually ignored. Humphrey's (1951) findings (Section 10.2) suggested that the majority of self-classified left-handers are in fact mixed-handers. Does this imply that *all* left-handers would be better described as "mixed", or are there some left-handers who are as consistently left-handed as most right-handers are consistently right-handed? If there are three types of handedness (left, mixed, and right), in what proportions do these variations occur in the population?

Most studies of handedness (e.g., Chapters 5 and 10) have used the right/left dichotomy, and, as said already, the inconsistency of "left"-handers continues to be rediscovered. But perhaps this inconsistency arises from a failure to differentiate consistent left- from mixed-handers. If mixed-handers are also more variable in cerebral speech lateralisation than consistent handers, the imperfect association of lateralities of hand and brain might be an artefact of inadequate classification of handedness. This idea was the chief motivator of my subsequent studies of handedness.

A widely held belief about mixed-handedness is that it results from social pressures on "natural" left-handers to adopt the right-hand habits of the majority (the "shifted sinistral" hypothesis, Section 4.2). If this were true, left-handers should prefer the left hand for actions *less* subject to social pressure and the right hand for actions *more* subject to such pressures. Gillies, MacSweeney, and Zangwill (1960) reported a study of patterns of hand preference in Cambridge undergraduates in which several individuals were found to write with the left hand but to throw a ball or to use a tennis racquet with the right hand; in some, writing was the *only* significant action performed with the left hand. The pattern was opposite to that predicted by the social-pressure theory of mixed-handedness. Gillies *et al.* (1960) wrote, "Although handedness is commonly treated in terms of a simple dichotomy, there is good reason to believe that lateral dominance is in reality a graded characteristic and that constitutional differences exist in both the strength and the consistency of lateral preference."

It seemed clear that mixed-handers exist as a natural variant of human hand preference patterns. But do consistent left-handers exist, and in what proportion of the population? These were the first research questions I tackled when I had the opportunity to collect data on large samples of undergraduates.

13.2.   THE HYPOTHESIS
THAT MIXED-HANDERS
MIGHT BE GENETIC HETEROZYGOTES

Before opportunities to study large samples of undergraduates arose, I was able to collect data on the handedness of families of children attending a speech therapy clinic (Section 5.1.1). In trying to interpret the family data in the light of Trankell's (1955) model of the inheritance of handedness (Section 3.4.1), I found that imperfect or intermediate forms of expression were less common in the recessive homozygote (Trankell's theory) than in the heterozygote (Roberts, 1959). This gave me one of those "Aha!" experiences when puzzles seem to fall into place. The heterozygote carries two different genes. If there were a gene for right-handedness and one for left-handedness, and if both genes could be expressed to varying degrees in the heterozygote, the intermediate and variable expression found in mixed-handers might be accounted for. I later found that others had suggested that heterozygotes could be left- or right-handed (Ramaley, 1913; Rife, 1950), but none had recognised a category of "mixed"-handers, and suggested that heterozygotes could be left- and right-handed.

The main attraction of this idea was a possible link with cerebral dominance for speech. The classical model of the relations between handedness and brainedness assumed that right-handers were left-brained and left-handers right-brained (Table 7.1). If handedness were genetically determined, then presumably a gene for right-handedness would be a gene for left-brainedness and a gene for left-handedness one for right-brainedness. On the heterozygote variability model there could be variability of brainedness also. If heterozygotes could be left-, right-, or bilaterally-brained as well as right-, mixed-, or left-handed, the confusion about the relations between these two sets of phenomena might be accounted for. It would be a *genuine confusion* due to natural variation. One of the main attractions of the idea of variable handedness and brainedness in heterozygotes was its potential offer of an explanation for the report that patients with left-handed relatives have a better chance of recovery from dysphasia (Section 7.1.2). Right-handers with left-handed relatives might be more likely to be heterozygotes.

The degree of expression as well as the direction of expression of handedness and brainedness in heterozygotes was expected to be variable. It was assumed (Annett, 1964) that the gene for right-handed and left-brainedness would be at least partially dominant, so that the majority of heterozygotes would be left-brained and right-handed. Direction of hand and brain asymmetry could vary independently however in heterozygotes; many were expected to be left-brained and left- (mixed)-handed; some could be right-brained and right- (mixed)-handers. Thus all combinations of handedness and brainedness were possible. "Fudge" factors in genetic theories of handedness were mentioned earlier (Section 3.4); the theory provided a magnificent "fudge" factor to account for combinations of hand and brain that were not explained by the classical model. It did make one specific prediction, however, that could be tested. If the 1964 model were taken to be as the classical genetic model (Table 3.5) but with the additional postulate of variability in heterozygotes, then all recessive homozygotes (*ll*) should be pure left-handers *and* right-brained for speech. At the time I formulated the theory I was not certain of the existence of pure left-handers. The theory predicted their existence and their right-brainedness. Thus the theory was falsifiable (Popper, 1963).

13.3.   THE BINOMIAL PROPORTIONS
OF LEFT-, MIXED-, AND RIGHT-HANDEDNESS

When opportunities arose to give handedness questionnaires to large classes of students at the universities of Aberdeen and Hull, it was found that 3 to 5% of subjects reported consistent left-hand preferences for all skilled unimanual actions. (Although 8 or 12 actions were specifically enquired about, scope was given for respondents to report on further actions they did with the "other" hand; see Fig. 10.1.) About 30% of subjects reported mixed-hand preferences. The majority of these mixed-handers were *right*-handed writers. Thus, while the majority of left-handed writers are mixed-handers (perhaps 7 out of every 10 left-handed writers) the majority of all mixed-handers are right-handers (perhaps 23 right- to 7 left-handed writers). These simple analyses of proportions of cases show how misleading it might be to regard inconsistency of preference as characteristic of "left"-handers (as shown above in the typical generalisation that right-handers tend to be consistent and left-handers inconsistent).

If the three forms of handedness (left, mixed, and right, interpreting left and right to mean consistent) are regarded as natural variants in the population, having a genetic origin, it becomes of great importance to establish the frequencies of the types in the general population. This implies that data must be collected on complete samples, free from volunteer biases. This point, which is elementary for any population genetic analysis, was not fully clear to me at first. One attempt was made to collect data on the handedness of nonpsychology students at Hull by posting questionnaires in student pigeon holes and providing special boxes for the return of the completed forms. This effort was not entirely wasted, as it led me to make further studies of handedness in mathematicians (Section 17.1.2), but for most subsequent analyses this volunteer sample was not included.

A major surprise occurred when several complete samples had been tested by questionnaire and by observation. The proportions of consistent left-, mixed-, and right-handers were as expected if *all* the mixed-handers were heterozygote (*rl* genotype), while consistent left- and consistent right-handers were of *ll* and *rr* genotypes, respectively. In Annett (1964) it was suggested that mixed-handers might be heterozygote, but it was not expected that *all* heterozygotes would manifest mixed-handedness. The observed samples were in the proportions expected if there were two genes, r and l, which combined at random in the population according to the binomial theorem $[(r + l)^2 = r^2 + 2rl + l^2$, as considered already for twin pairs in Section 3.4.4]. The proportion of consistent left- and consistent right-handers fitted expectations for l^2 and r^2. It was not anticipated that there would be such a direct relationship between the hypothesised genotype and phenotype. It was better than expected and indeed too good to be true.

Table 13.1 lists the data for seven samples available (Annett 1967) and shows that in all cases the proportions were in accord with binomial expectations. I searched the literature for other samples where the data had been reported in such a way that the mixed-handers could be separated from the pure left- and right-handers (on my criteria) and tested them for agreement with binomial proportions. Almost all the samples found were in accord with the binomial expectations (Clark, 1957; Harris, 1957; Merrell, 1957). Sutton's (1963) data for 772 Australians agreed but not that for 257 Polynesians in whom not enough mixed-handers were recorded.

It was especially surprising to find that where non-human samples could be classified as left-, mixed-, or right-handed, the proportions also agreed with binomial expectations. Data for chimpanzees (Finch, 1941), monkeys (Ettinger, 1961; Ettinger & Moffett, 1964; Warren, 1953), and cats (Cole, 1955) did not differ significantly from binomial proportions. It was this

TABLE 13.1
The Binomial Proportions of Right-, Mixed-, and Left-Handedness in 7 Samples

	Right N	Right %	Mixed N	Mixed %	Left N	Left %	Total	χ^2 1 df
A. Questionnaire 1								
1. Aberdeen First year psychology students (85% returns) No. observed	256	(71.5)	90	(25.1)	12	(3.4)	358	
No. expected*	253.0		96.0		9.0			1.400
2. Hull psychology students (96% returns) No. observed	175	(67.3)	72	(27.7)	13	(5.0)	260	
No. expected	171.2		79.7		9.16			2.436
3. Hull sample of all students (54% returns) No. observed	80	(71.4)	29	(25.9)	3	(2.7)	112	
No. expected	79.7		29.7		2.67			0.057
B. Questionnaire 2								
4. Hull first-year psychology students No. observed	99	(70.7)	36	(25.7)	5	(3.6)	140	
No. expected	97.7		38.6		3.71			0.638
5. Enlisted men No. observed	85	(63.9)	43	(32.3)	5	(3.8)	133	
No. expected	85.2		42.6		5.2			0.012
C. Demonstration								
6. School-children 5–15 years City of Hull No. observed	101	(58.4)	64	(37.0)	8	(4.6)	173	
No. expected	102.2		61.7		9.2			0.247
7. Hull honours psychology students No. observed	31	(62.0)	18	(36.0)	1	(2.0)	50	
No. expected	31.9		16.2		1.9			0.007

Note: From Annett (1967).

*Using a formula giving a correction for small numbers.

puzzle—how could binomial proportions of left-, mixed-, and right-handed-ness be found reliably in animal *and* human data when the observed proportions differ markedly (Fig. 13.1)—that provided the hinge of the right-shift theory.

If there were two genes *r* and *l*, inducing right- and left-hand preferences, with mixed expression in heterozygotes, the differences between human and nonhuman samples could conceivably be due to differences in gene frequency. However, careful studies of nonhuman samples have found no evidence for genetic influences on paw preferences in rats and mice (Section 9.2). It was also clear that the human binomial proportions could not be due to genes for *r*- and *l*-handedness. If there were a direct and simple relationship between genotype and phenotype in humans, all the children of two consistently right-handed parents (*rr* × *rr*) must be right-handed (*rr*), and all children of two consistently left-handed parents (*ll* × *ll*) must be left-handed (*ll*). To identify parents who were consistently right-handed, students were asked to take home sets of questionnaires during vacation so that parents and siblings could each answer for themselves. (Sampling biases are not important here, as a question was being asked about relationships *within* families.)

Families of left-handed parents were sought through the press and radio, and sets of questionnaires were sent to those responding who had children old enough to complete their own questionnaire (or at least try out most of the actions for parents to report upon). The questionnaires returned from families made it evident that separating consistent left- and right-handers from mixed-handers did not make it easier to predict children's handedness than did the earlier classifications based on the right–left dichotomy (Table 3.6).

A further test of the model could be made for brainedness. As explained above, the 1964 model predicted that the *ll* genotype would be associated with consistent sinistrality and right-brainedness for speech. If pure left-handers could be found whose speech hemisphere was known to be the left and not the right, the model would be falsified. Letters were sent to neurologists and neurosurgeons throughout the U.K. explaining the need for information on the speech hemisphere of very strong left-handers. Very few such cases would be expected in the experience of any one specialist, but I needed only one clear case to disprove the theory, and such a case was reported to me.

Thus it seemed that the 1964 model had led to a very interesting discovery above the binomial proportions of left-, mixed-, and right-handers, but the model itself was not tenable. It could not predict the speech hemisphere of strong left-handers, nor could it predict handedness in families (if phenotypes were considered to be related to genotypes more directly than postulated in 1964 but as suggested by the binomial proportions in 1967, Table 3.5C2). How could the binomial proportions be explained?

13.4.   THE   COORDINATION
OF THE DISTRIBUTIONS
OF HAND PREFERENCE AND SKILL;
THE DISCOVERY OF THE RIGHT SHIFT

A referee of the binomial distributions paper (Annett, 1967) asked how this data might relate to the finding of Woo and Pearson (1927) that differences between the hands in strength take the form of a single unimodal normal curve. Of course I had no idea, and I believe I admitted this. By 1970 I was convinced that the distribution of hand preference should be thought of as continuous (Section 10.3.3), rather than as falling into two or three categories. The last line of Fig. 13.1 shows that through a co-ordination of data for preference and skill I distinguished eight classes of hand preference (Section 11.2). These were regarded as ordered along the preference continuum, but with all divisions of the continuum as essentially arbitrary.

'There were several outstanding questions posed by my research efforts of the 1960s.

1.   How can the distributions of hand preference and hand skill be co-ordinated when they take the form of a J for preference and a normal curve for skill (Figs. 10.2 and 11.3)?

2.   How can the proportions of left-, mixed-, and right-handed humans, *and* left-, mixed-, and right-handed nonhumans both agree with the expectations of the binomial theorem, when the incidences are about 4, 30, 66, and about 25, 50, 25, respectively?

3.   How can the considerable quantity of data on handedness in families, collected by student report and also by the personal report of parents and siblings, be accounted for when it clearly does not fit the classic Mendelian gene pair model, nor the heterozygote variability modification of the classic model (Table 3.5)?

The geneticists I consulted about this last problem were unwilling to speculate about gene pair models but talked enthusiastically about models of polygenic inheritance, as applied, for example, by Carter (1961) to the problem of pyloric stenosis and formalised by Falconer (1965) for the estimation of the heritability of such diseases. Figure 13.2 reproduces Carter's (1961) illustration of the distributions hypothesised to underlie the expression of pyloric stenosis. This is a disorder of infancy and childhood in which hypertrophy of the muscles of the pylorus prevents the passage of food from the stomach to the duodenum. It occurs more often in males than in females. The incidence of disorder is higher in the relatives of affected cases than in the general population. It is higher in the relatives of affected females

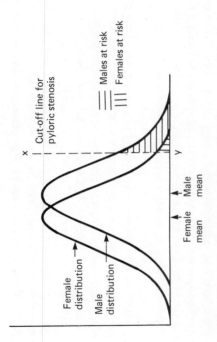

FIG. 13.2.   Hypothetical distribution of multifactorial genotypes contributing to pyloric stenosis in males and females. Carter, 1961.

than of affected males. The main features of the polygenic hypothesis represented in Fig. 13.2 are as follows:

1. The factors contributing to the disease can be thought of as varying along a continuous scale. The risk of developing the disorder is greater for those who are higher on the scale (to the right of Fig. 13.2).

2. The distribution of risk factors in the population takes the form of a normal curve; only those at the extreme right are likely to develop a clinically recognised disorder.

3. There is no absolute division between those who develop the disease and those who are free of symptoms. Some may have symptoms such as chronic indigestion, which may be a subclinical expression of pyloric stenosis.

It is convenient to think of the proportion of the population identified as suffering the disorder as separated from the rest by a threshold, the line X–Y. The threshold is an abstraction in the sense that there is no absolute point along the risk continuum at which breakdown is certain; in the analogy of straws being placed on camels' backs (Section 3.4.3), perhaps a smaller but especially tough camel does not break down before another slightly larger but less fortunate camel. The threshold is defined empirically in terms of the *proportion of the population identified* above (or below) it. The threshold is also movable, in the sense that the chances of being identified as having a disease depends on the thoroughness of the medical examination. In this sense the threshold is a function of the methods of enquiry and the criteria adopted by the investigator.

4. There can be differences between the sexes (or other subgroups of the total population) in liability to the disorder. Assuming a similar scale of risk in both sexes and a common threshold for clinical symptoms, females as a group may be less likely to breakdown than males. Perhaps they are protected by other factors associated with their sex. Females who are affected, however, can be assumed to be carrying a very high proportion of risk factors. In so far as the risk factors are genetic, the relatives of affected females will be at greater risk than the relatives of affected males.

There were some immediately obvious parallels between this model of polygenic inheritance and handedness. There is a continuous scale of difference between the hands in skill. The distribution of L–R skill takes the form of a normal curve. The division between left- and right-handers depends on methods of enquiry and criteria that vary between investigators. The threshold concept was especially attractive, as the association analysis had found no evidence of a natural break in the scale of preference, and there is no dip in the distribution of L–R skill. The eight preference classes suggested that the continuum of preference could be divided equally well at any of seven points; acknowledging that the classes themselves are arbitrary, the division could be made at other points also. If the threshold of left-handedness could be drawn anywhere between consistent left- and consistent right-handedness, the large range of incidences reported in the literature (Table 10.1) can be accounted for. Sex differences in hand preference, though small, are well established (Table 4.4), and females were more biased to the right in L–R skill than males (confirmed in Fig. 11.3). There seemed to be evidence that the association between relatives for handedness is higher for females than for males (Tables 4.5 and 15.1).

But what could this model suggest about the binomial proportions of left-, mixed-, and right-handedness in man and in other species? The chief discovery on which the right-shift theory depends came from looking at the table of the normal distribution function to ascertain where the thresholds would need to be drawn to represent the data for hand preference. Table 13.2 shows the locations of the required thresholds.

The key question is *what distance between these thresholds would be needed to represent the mixed handers?* The distance, or the difference between the two sets of thresholds, turned out to be more or less identical for human and nonhuman data. We can think of mixed-handed humans and mixed-handed nonhumans as depending on a similar range of differences between the hands in skill. The difference in proportions is simply a function of the location of the thresholds along the *x*-axis and hence of the areas under the normal curve. Figure 13.3 shows how the apparently different distributions of hand preference in man and other species could be similar in all respects except that the human distribution is *shifted to the right* in comparison with the

TABLE 13.2

The Thresholds of the Normal Distribution Required to Represent Observed Incidences of Left-, Mixed-, and Right-Handedness in Human and Nonhuman Samples

	Consistent Left (%)	Location of Threshold*	Left and Mixed (%)	Location of Threshold	Difference Between Thresholds
Human	4	−1.75	34	−0.41	1.34
Nonhuman	25	−0.67	75	+0.67	1.34

*Distances from mean in standard deviation units.

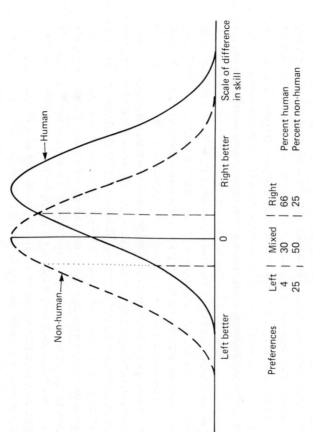

FIG. 13.3. Probable relations between differences in manual skill and hand preference. Annett, 1976b.

nonhuman distribution. The distribution of hand preferences in other species is just as expected if preferences depended on a normal distribution of differences between the sides in skill with a mean difference of 0, or L = R. The distribution of preference in man is as expected if preferences depended on a normal distribution of differences between the sides in skill but with a mean to the right of 0. There is no other substantial difference between the human and nonhuman samples except the location of the mean.

The fact that there are about 25, 50, 25% consistent left-, mixed-, and consistent right-preferent individuals in other species is an accident of the criteria of mixed versus consistent handedness adopted. Given that there is no systematic bias to right- or to left-handedness in nonhuman species, some variable proportion could be called mixed; if this proportion is centered on the mean of a normal distribution, a substantial proportion of animals are likely to be called mixed. The fact that human samples are also in binomial proportion is due to the fact that as a normal curve is shifted a short distance to either side, retaining thresholds at the same position along the x-axis as required to give binomial distributions in the unbiased curve (25, 50, 25), the areas under the normal curve remain roughly binomial. This property of the normal curve was a surprise to a statistician I consulted about this phenomenon.

Thus the heterozygote variability hypothesis was inadequate as a genetic model, but it led to the discovery that both human and nonhuman samples classified for left-, mixed-, and right-handedness are in binomial proportions. The binomial proportions are unimportant in themselves, but without them the remarkable consistency of animal and human data would not have been discovered. This consistency depends on the region of the scale of differences between the sides in skill in which mixed hand preferences are likely to be observed. Within this "mixed" region various degrees of relative left- and right-hand preferences may occur. Beyond this region, humans and other animals are likely to show consistent right-hand or left-hand preferences.

How does the normal distribution of L–R skill fit the J-shaped distribution of preference in man and the U-shaped distribution of preference in other species? Figures 13.4A and 13.4B illustrate the relationships. The 4% consistent-left and 66% consistent-right humans and the 25% consistent-left and 25% consistent-right nonhumans show no variability of preference, and are fully sinistral or dextral on the preference scale. All the variability is due to the mixed-handers, such that 30% of humans and 50% of nonhumans are mixed-handers who fall between the two thresholds that define mixed-handedness. These relationships are not easy to draw to scale when the preference and skill distributions are represented in the same diagram, but it is essential to recognise that proportions of the population represented as areas of the normal curve outside the "mixed" thresholds are fully right- or left-handed on the preference continuum. The underlying distribution of skill is unimodal, and the apparent bimodality of preference is an artefact of the consistency of preference beyond the thresholds. To represent the consistency in Figs. 13.4A and B, the straight arms of the J and the U must coincide with the thresholds (cf. Porac & Coren, 1981, Fig. 2.1, which does not represent these relationships as given in Annett, 1972).

The co-ordination of the scales of preference and skill assumed in Fig. 13.4 were discovered empirically for human samples but were inferred for

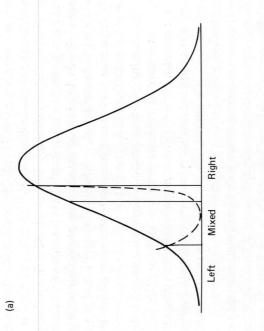

(a)

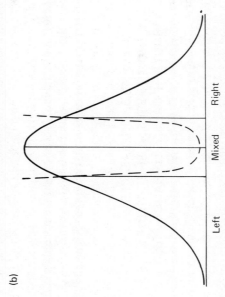

(b)

FIG. 13.4.   (a) The probable relationship between asymmetry of skill and the J-shaped preference distribution in man. (b) The probable relation between asymmetry of skill and the U-shaped preference distribution in non-human mammals.

nonhuman ones. Collins (1970) measured the grip strength of each front paw in mice and showed that the mean strength of the preferred paw was significantly greater than of the nonpreferred paw. Thus it is a reasonable inference that paw preference in nonhuman species depends on an underlying continuously distributed asymmetry.

Figure 13.3 encapsulates all the main features of the analysis made so far of hand preference and skill. To summarise:

1. There is a continuous scale of difference between the sides in skill in all species having hand or paw preferences.

2. The likelihood of manifesting mixed as opposed to consistent left or right preferences depends on a region of the continuum of L–R skill to either side of 0 or L = R. The extent of this region is about the same in all species so far classified for handedness.

3. L–R differences in man and other species are distributed in a single unimodal approximately normal curve.

4. The mean of the L–R distribution in nonhumans is at L = R, and the mean for humans is to the right of L = R.

5. The distribution of left/right, or left/mixed/right preferences differs between man and other species but in proportions that are directly predictable from areas under the normal curve and the relatively fixed thresholds of mixed handedness.

6. There is no fundamental difference between the human and nonhuman distributions, except that the human distribution is shifted towards dextrality, whereas the nonhuman one is symmetrical about L = R and hence unbiased to either side.

This way of looking at laterality suggests that there is only one fundamental characteristic that is special to human lateral asymmetry—the shift to the right. Hence this analysis has come to be called the "Right-Shift Theory".

13.5.   INFERENCES
FROM THE RIGHT SHIFT THEORY
ABOUT THE CAUSES OF HANDEDNESS

When handedness is interpreted in terms of the distributions represented in Fig. 13.3, certain old problems are resolved, but new ones arise. The distributions suggest that there are two fundamental features to be explained. First there is the normal distribution of differences between the sides in skill, common to man and other species. Second, there is the human shift to dextrality. Normal distributions are usually the product of several factors, each having small effects and combining at random. There could be genetic, nongenetic, or some combination of both types of influence. A genetic contribution to the distribution of L–R paw preferences of mice and rats has been ruled out by studies of the effects of selective breeding (Section 9.2). If the normal distribution of L–R differences in nonhuman species can be produced *without* genetic influence, there is no need to postulate a genetic mechanism for the human normal distribution. Of course this does not mean that polygenic inheritance of L–R skill in man is definitely disproved—but it would be unparsimonious to suggest that such a mechanism is needed in man when it is not needed in other species. The findings for other species suggest that the normal distribution of L–R skill is a product of numerous small accidental influences on the development of the two sides of the body. Given the *same* genetic instructions for building the two sides of the body, it is not unlikely that there are many small differences between the sides in the efficiency with which these instructions are put into effect; one side could have slightly larger muscles, more efficient neuromuscular co-ordination, more neural connections to the motor cortex of the brain, or a richer supply of neurotransmitters. Slight differences of these kinds would be sufficient to give an "edge" to one side, though the majority of animals would be fairly well balanced on both sides and hence not strongly inclined to favour one side or the other. These slight constitutional biases most probably occur in the course of embryonic and fetal growth, though it is possible that accidental influences on postnatal growth continue to affect lateral asymmetry. Collins's (1975) experiments on the effects of rearing mice in biased R or L worlds and changing animals from one biased world to the other (Section 9.2) suggested that the major determinants of lateral preference were probably congenital. In studies of the implications of the right-shift theory (below) I have found no reason to change this fundamental assumption about the congenital and nongenetic origin of the distribution of L–R differences.

The second factor to be explained is the shift of the human distribution to the right. If the shift to the right occurs in all human societies (and none have been found biased to the left), the influence must be systematic and not accidental. Why always to the right? In principle, it could be argued that the bias to the right is due to cultural transmission from our earliest cultural antecedents. But this argument would entail the assumption that the bias to the right hand is learned, and that humans become more right-handed with age. There is no substantial support for this view (Sections 4.2 and 20.1). The main alternative is that the bias of the distribution to the right has a genetic foundation. By distinguishing the two features of the distribution, its shape and its location on the scale of the L–R skill, we can see how the first, the shape, may arise from nongenetic factors in all species showing lateral differences, while the second, the human shift to the right, could be genetic. It would depend on one or more genes that are specifically human, and thus explain why the search for genetic determinants of paw preferences in rats and mice was negative while in humans there is some definite but small evidence of genetic influence.

Cultural influences undoubtedly raise or lower the observed incidence of left-handedness for socially significant actions such as writing or eating. This is probably best thought of as a change in the threshold of expression of left-handedness. The proportion of the population recognised as manifesting sinistrality is lowered or raised as the threshold is moved to the left or the right along the scale of differences between the hands in skill. When pressures against left-hand use are great, as in Japan (Komai & Fukuoka, 1934) or Taiwan (Teng, Lee, Yang, & Chang, 1976), less than 1% may use the left hand for writing, although incidences for other actions such as using scissors or throwing balls may be similar to those of Western samples. There is no reason to believe, on present evidence, that the distribution of L–R skill differs between Oriental and Western samples (Ashton, 1982), or that there are differences in extent of right shift (but see Section 20.1).

The possibility that all of the nonhuman and most of the human variation in L–R skill is accidental leads on to several further hypotheses. It suggests that in humans there could be a systematic bias towards right-handedness but no systematic bias towards left-handedness. If left-handedness arises in other species accidentally, why not in man also? That is, there may be a gene that makes its possessor more likely to develop right-handedness but no gene giving the contrary bias. Thus the difficult problem of how genes could be programmed to recognise *R or L* is avoided (Section 3.2), although some mechanism has still to be found for giving a boost to the skill of the right hand. There can be no *absolute* determination of right-handedness, since all effects occur against the background of accidental determinants of the normal distribution of L–R skill. Given a set of accidentally determined chances of becoming right- or left-handed, the chances are weighted in humans by some bias to the right that may or may not be sufficient to outweigh the accidental bias to the left.

If the right biasing factor should be absent in some individuals, the chances of left-handedness would depend entirely on the accidental normal distribution. There would be approximately 25% right-handers, 50% mixed-handers, and 25% right-handers, as in nonhuman species. At the time the right-shift theory was formulated (Annett, 1972) I had questionnaire data on 47 children of two left-handed parents. *If all* the left-handed parents lacked the genes giving the shift to the right, the hand preferences of their children should be as in other species. The proportions observed were 23% pure left, 28% mixed, 49% pure right; 40% were left-handed writers. The proportions were not far from those predicted for a chance distribution, but there were more pure right-handers than expected. From the first formulation of the theory, however, it was never suggested that all left-handers would lack the genetic bias to the right, since observed handedness is a product of accidental and genetic factors. Thus some left-handed parents might carry the genetic bias to the right, and there would be slightly more right- and left-handers among their children. Subsequent studies based on visits to families of L × L parents to measure L–R skill confirm this view (Section 15.1.2). What is clear from the right-shift theory and from the questionnaire data is that there is no reason to postulate a systematic bias to the right that may or may not be present or absent is sufficient to account for the evidence.

The final question (in Annett, 1972) concerned the nature of the factor inducing the right shift for handedness. It is a factor with the following qualities:

1. It is present in humans but no other primate (as far as we know).
2. It has a slightly greater effect in females than males.
3. It increases the strength/skill of the right side of the body.

The hypothesis that must immediately leap to mind is that it is something to do with the human tendency to develop speech in the left cerebral hemisphere. No other primate is capable of speech in the full sense of human vocalisation of meaningful sounds. Females have a slight advantage over males in the rate of speech acquisition, and they are much less likely to suffer delays and handicaps in the acquisition of speech and reading. Some boost to the left hemisphere's growth or organisation, which made it readier to serve speech, might incidentally increase the skill of the right side of the body in motor functions. The fact that some people are right-brained or bilateral for speech could arise in just the way suggested for handedness—accidental variation in the absence of the factor inducing left-brainedness. There must be some genes that man does not share with the rest of the animal kingdom, and what could be more probable than that they have a role in human speech?

Since 1972, I have tried to work out the implications of the theory and to test them. The following chapters report this process and show ways in which the theory has been strengthened and led to new hypotheses. None of the fundamental assumptions has been changed.

13.6.   SUMMARY OF ASSUMPTIONS OF THE RIGHT SHIFT THEORY

1. Hand preferences depend on continuously distributed differences between the hands in skill. Differing assessments of incidence depend on arbitrary divisions of the continuum.

2. L–R skill is distributed in a unimodal, approximately normal manner in man and in other mammals showing lateral preferences.

3. The distribution of L–R skill is a product of accidental influences on early development that affect the efficiency of sensorimotor control on the two sides of the body. These accidental influences are equally probable on both sides of the body, so that the mean of the distribution of L–R differences is L = R or 0 (no difference).

4. The human distribution resembles that of other mammals in all

essential respects (including shape, origin, and the range of L–R differences likely to give mixed preferences), except that the human distribution is shifted to the right of the nonhuman distribution.

5. The right shift of the human distribution is a by-product of a factor that induces speech representation in the left cerebral hemisphere.

6. The left-hemisphere speech-inducing factor is probably genetic. The gene(s) involved are specific for left-hemisphere speech. There are no genes inducing speech representation in the right hemisphere or giving a specific boost to left-hand skill.

I talked about heterozygote variability as a "fudge" factor—a factor that makes it impossible to formulate and test precise predictions. I have also talked about the search for the elusive "essence" of laterality. The right-shift theory turns this whole approach on its head by asserting that the chief fact about laterality is its variability—a variability that arises afresh in each individual. The variability is not a "fudge" factor but rather a constant background against which the small specific trends associated with the human shift to the right have to be detected. This theory certainly makes it more difficult to test predictions about laterality, as all the predictions have to be formulated in terms of probabilities. There can be no absolute assertions such as "all right-handers are . . ." or "no left-handers are . . .". The task of working out the implications of the right-shift theory involves trying to work out just what proportions of so-called right- and left-handers should be left- and right-brained, have right- or left-handed children, or suffer advantages and disadvantages of intellectual growth. The variability or unpredictability is the "essence" that has to be analysed.

14

Cerebral Speech Laterality and Handedness

The analyses that led to the RS theory, reviewed in Chapters 10 to 13, were focussed on asymmetries of handedness. The analyses led to the conclusion that human handedness resembles that of other primates in all essential respects except that the human distribution is shifted to the right. The inference that the right shift is a by-product of a factor that induces the development of speech in the left hemisphere of the human brain seemed compelling at an intuitive level, but there was nothing in the material reviewed in chapters 10 to 12 to give substantial support to this inference. The task of the present chapter is to examine the implications of this inference for questions about cerebral speech and handedness. It is hoped to demonstrate that the RS theory is extremely powerful in its ability to predict apparently paradoxical phenomena. It offers an incisive analysis of the relations between the lateralities of hand and brain and shows how several of the apparent puzzles were products of previous methods of approach.

14.1. PREDICTIONS OF THE RIGHT SHIFT THEORY FOR CEREBRAL SPEECH LATERALITY

The RS analysis (Chapter 13) found it necessary to postulate only one systematic influence on handedness. All the rest could be attributed to chance. This one systematic influence was hypothesised to be a factor (RS+) that induces the left cerebral hemisphere to serve speech. If this factor were universal in humans, there would be no instances of right-hemisphere speech except in cases of pathology. The observation of speech loss following unilateral right-hemisphere war wounds in young and otherwise healthy adult brains suggests that right-hemisphere speech does occur as a natural variant. This implies that in some people the **RS+** factor is absent (**RS−**). (In Chapter 15 the factors are attributed to $rs+$ and $rs−$ genes that occur in $rs+ +$, $rs+ −$ and $rs− −$ genotypes, but for the present purpose it is convenient to use **RS+** for $rs+ +$ and $rs+ −$, assuming the $rs+$ gene is dominant for left-hemisphere speech, and **RS−** for $rs− −$.)

The theory suggests that the **RS+** enjoy some advantage in the growth of the left hemisphere, which induces speech development on that side. A slight bias towards the right hand is conferred as a by-product of the left-hemisphere advantage. This is sufficient to shift the distribution of L–R hand differences towards the right, but the main agent of L–R variation is accidental, as in other species. The **RS+** factor is not sufficient to ensure right-handedness in every case. In the **RS−** there is no reason to postulate systematic biases to either hemisphere or either hand. Unless grounds are found for modifying this assumption, it is necessary for us to examine the implications of the simplest possible set of postulates. The simplest assumption is that in the **RS−** the lateralities of hand and brain are determined by chance, and by chance that are independent of each other. That is, about 50% of the **RS−** are right-brained and about 50% are left-brained; some unknown proportion could be unbiased to either side and develop bilateral braineness.

The starting point for an analysis of the implications of the RS model for cerebral speech as used in Annett (1975) is given in Fig. 14.1. The main features are a continuum of differences between the hands in skill, a larger distribution (**RS+**) with mean to the right of L=R, and a smaller distribution (**RS−**) with mean at L=R. The sum of these two distributions, shown by the dashed line, gives the L–R differences observed in the total population. This is roughly normal, but with a slight negative skew (as observed by Hoadley and Pearson, 1929, Fig. 3.1). The vertical lines show the point of no difference between the hands or L=R, and also a possible threshold of left-handedness marked X. The interesting properties of the model depend on where the threshold (X) is drawn. Divisions between left and right are arbitrary (Chapters 11 and 13) but they are also critical for the proportions of left- and right-handers who are predicted to be left- and right-brained for speech.

The predictions of the model depend on the relative areas of the normal curves, **RS+** and **RS−**, included in the various possible divisions. It is important to notice that these areas must be calculated systematically, using tables of the normal curve. I have seen many cursory references to the RS theory, and also to alternative suggestions as to possible distributions, where the curves were clearly drawn "ex imagination". Without wishing to be

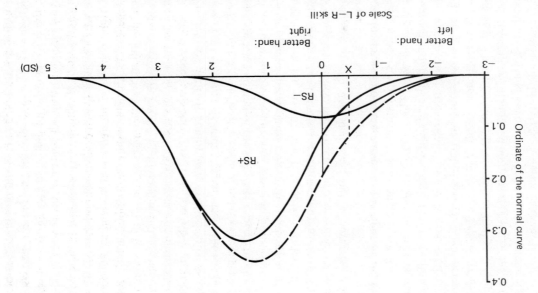

Ordinate of the normal curve

Scale of L–R skill

Better hand: left

Better hand: right

FIG. 14.1. The hypothesised distribution of L–R skill in the population. The rs+ proportion is 0.8 and the rs+ mean is 1.5 SD to the right of the rs– mean. Variances of rs+ and rs– are equal. X is a possible threshold for sinistrality. Annett, 1975.

pedantic, I must assure the reader that the development of the RS theory and the analysis of its implications depends closely upon the table of the normal curve and calculations of areas under curves of varying sizes and varying distances between the means.

The distributions in Fig. 14.1 are drawn in the proportions required if 80% of the population were RS+ and 20% RS−. They are also drawn to show the mean of the RS+ distribution falling at $1.5z$ (where z stands for units of the standard deviation) from the mean of the RS− distribution. These proportions and extent of shift were preliminary guesses, before methods of estimating these parameters of the model became clear to me. Estimates derived from data for patients with unilateral lesions and dysphasia are considered in Section 14.4 and estimates derived from the normal samples tested for L−R skill in Section 16.2.

The distributions represented in Fig. 14.1, although based on guesses as to parameters, make some interesting suggestions about the distribution of handedness and cerebral speech. Notice first that the RS+ distribution extends well into regions of the L−R continuum expected to be associated with left-handedness. That is, the areas under the curves to the left of the X are almost as large for the RS+ as the RS−. All of the RS+ are expected to have left-hemisphere speech, and half of the RS− are expected to have left-hemisphere speech. It is immediately obvious that the proportion of left-handers with left-hemisphere speech must exceed the proportion of those having right-hemisphere speech. As the line X is moved to the left, with stricter classifications of left-handedness, the relative proportion of RS− to RS+ left-handers increases. Hence, the expected proportion of left-handers having right-hemisphere speech also increases, but it never exceeds the theoretical maximum of 50%.

Considering now the areas under the curves to the right of the line X, which represent right-handers, it is evident that the majority of RS− in the total population are *right-handed*. This implies that the majority of cases of right-hemisphere speech should also be right-handed. This prediction of the model looks at first sight highly paradoxical. It is widely believed that right-hemisphere speech is extremely rare in right-handers. *Right-hemisphere speech would be rare in right-handers only if a very generous criterion of sinistrality were adopted*. That is, if line X were moved well to the right of L=R, to include all those mixed-handers who have very minor inclinations to use the left hand, then we would have reclassified all of these right-handers as left-handers. The analysis of the dysphasic series below will suggest that this is precisely what happened in some of the most influential clinical series.

Table 14.1 gives the calculations (Annett, 1975) of the percentages of cases of right-hemisphere speech expected in sinistrals and dextrals if the line X is drawn to give various possible thresholds of left-handedness. The proportion of right-hemisphere speakers is highest at the most severe criteria of

TABLE 14.1

The Incidence of Right- and Left-Hemisphere Speech in Right- and Left-Handers as a Function of the Criterion of Left-Handedness

Location of the threshold of left-handedness	Incidence of left-handedness in the population	Percent Right-Hemisphere Speech	
		In Left-handers	In Right-handers
-1.0z	3.7	43	9
-0.5z	8.0	36	7
0.0	15.3	33	6
+0.5z	26.5	26	4
+1.0z	41.5	20	3

Note: Based on Annett (1975).

sinistrality in *both* handedness groups and falls in both groups as the criteria becomes more generous. This also looks paradoxical at first sight, but a brief study of the areas of the RS+ and RS− distributions included at each division will show that this fall in proportion within both handedness groups with more generous criteria of left-handedness is, indeed, predicted by the model.

At the time I was beginning to work out the implications of the model for cerebral speech laterality, I had data on the handedness of children of two left-handed parents, by questionnaire as mentioned above, and also from personal visits to L × L families. In both sets of data 40% of the children were left-handed writers. Assuming for the moment that the majority of the left-handed parents were RS−, then the majority of their children should be RS− and have a distribution of L–R differences between the hands for peg-moving times approximately as represented for the RS− distribution in Fig. 14.1. This was found (as described in Section 15.1.2). The 40% sinistral writers gave an indication (perhaps a rough one, but the best available at that time) of the proportion of left-handed writers to be expected among a population sample of right-hemisphere speakers. Where would such a sample be found to test this prediction?

Newcombe and Ratcliff (1973) published a reanalysis of the British World War II Head Injury series. They reported on 27 cases of dysphasia associated with unilateral right-hemisphere lesions. Of the 27, 8 (30%) were left-handed. As the RS theory predicted, there were more right-handers than left-handers with right-hemisphere speech. Looking at the German World War II head injury data (Conrad, 1949), there were 18 cases of right-lesion dysphasia, of whom 7 (39%) were left-handed. Among series of patients reported from neurological clinics, the findings were quite different. Hécaen and Ajuriaguerra (1964) classified 100% of their 22 right-lesion dysphasics as left-handed. It seemed evident that a detailed comparison was required of the data for dysphasia, lesion side, and handedness in consecutive series of patients.

14.2. COMPARISON OF THE CONSECUTIVE SERIES STUDIED FOR DYSPHASIA AND LATERALITY

The predictions of the RS theory as represented in Fig. 14.1 concern proportions of left- and right-handers with right- and left-hemisphere speech in the population. Only samples that have included patients consecutively, without prior selection for handedness or lesion laterality, can be used to answer questions about possible distributions in the general population. (The patients whose speech hemisphere was assessed by the Wada technique were selected because atypical laterality was suspected; this series cannot be used to answer population questions, but it can be used to answer questions about distributions *within* groups of patients of known hemisphere speech—see Section 14.5.1).

There were five series in the literature identified by Zangwill (1967) as drawn from the population without selection for lesion laterality or handedness. Zangwill's summaries of these five series were used, as listed in Table 14.2, except that the later report of the British War Wound series by Newcombe and Ratcliff (1973) was substituted for the earlier report by Russell and Espir (1961). There is a further series (Gloning & Quatember, 1966), which did not give sufficient information on right-handers for

TABLE 14.2
Incidences of Dysphasia in Five Series of Patients with Unilateral Cerebral Lesions, Analysed for Lesion Laterality and Handedness

		Left		Right	
Handedness	Lesion	Left	Right	Left	Right
Conrad (1949)	N	19	18	338	249
	Dysphasic	10 (52.6%)	7 (38.9%)	175 (51.8%)	11 (4.4%)
Newcombe and Ratcliffe (1973)	N	30	33	338	216
	Dysphasic	11 (36.7%)	8 (24.8%)	218 (56.2%)	19 (6.0%)
Penfield and Roberts (1959)	N	18	15	157	196
	Dysphasic	13 (72.2%)	1 (6.7%)	115 (73.2%)	1 (0.5%)
Bingley (1958)	N	4	10	101	99
	Dysphasic	2 (50.0%)	3 (30.0%)	68 (67.3%)	1 (1.0%)
Hécaen and Ajuriaguerra (1964)	N	37	22	163	130
	Dysphasic	22 (59.5%)	11 (50.0%)	81 (49.7%)	0 (0.0%)

Note: Adapted from Zangwill (1967) by Annett (1975).

inclusion in Table 14.2, but aspects of the findings for this series will be considered below.

The first two series listed in Table 14.2 were of servicemen with war wounds, as already mentioned. Penfield and Roberts (1959) reported a series of patients having brain operations for the treatment of focal cerebral seizures. Cases with evidence of brain injury before the age of two years are excluded. Bingley's (1958) series was of patients operated for temporal lobe gliomas. Hécaen and Ajuriaguerra (1964) reported a series of neurological clinic patients with various unilateral cerebral lesions.

The percentages in Table 14.2 refer to the proportions of patients recorded as having disorders of speech—dysphasias—within each lesion and handed-ness group. The most striking feature of the table is the apparent variability between series. In order to identify the source of the differences, the series were compared for each of several characteristics, as shown in Table 14.3. Incidences of dysphasia were highly similar, ranging between 32.4 and 34.6%. The series by Penfield and Roberts (1959) differed from the others in having a slightly smaller proportion of cases with left-hemisphere lesions, and also a smaller proportion suffering dysphasias associated with right-hemisphere lesions. The only other differences concerned incidences of left-handedness, Conrad recording slightly fewer and Hécaen and Ajuriaguerra considerably more left-handers than other series. Hécaen and Ajuriaguerra noted that their left-handers included patients of mixed manual preference. On the RS theory, this difference of criterion is expected to make a considerable difference to the proportion of right-handers recorded as dysphasic following right-hemisphere lesions, as explained earlier.

Table 14.4 shows the effect of analysing the series again for dysphasic patients only. This analysis has the advantage that all cases are known to have a lesion that affected the speech areas. (The Ns in Table 14.2 included

TABLE 14.3

Comparison of the Five Series for Incidences of Several Variables

	Total N	Dysphasic	Left-Handed	Lesion Side Left	Dysphasia and Right-Sided Lesion
Conrad (1949)	624	32.5	5.9*	57.2	2.9
Newcombe and Ratcliff (1973)	767	33.4	8.2	54.5	3.5
Penfield and Roberts (1959)	386	33.7	8.5	45.3*	0.5*
Bingley (1958)	214	34.6	6.5	49.1	1.9
Hécaen and Ajuriaguerra (1964)	352	32.4	16.8*	56.8	3.1

* $p < .05$ or less by χ^2.

TABLE 14.4
Comparison of the Five Series: Data for Dysphasics Only

Series	Dysphasics N	Left-Handed		Right Lesion		Right-Handers Among Dysphasics With Right-Sided Lesion	
		N	%	N	%	N	%
Conrad (1949)	203	17	8.4	18	8.9	11	61.1
Newcombe and Ratcliff (1973)	256	19	7.4	27	10.5	19	70.4
Penfield and Roberts (1959)	130	14	10.8	2	1.5*	1	50.0
Bingley (1958)	74	5	6.8	4	5.4	1	25.0
Hécaen and Ajuriaguerra (1964)	114	33	28.9*	11	9.6	0	0.0

*indicates $p < .01$ by Chi².

patients who suffered *any* unilateral cerebral lesions, and in about two-thirds speech was not affected. Inferences about the lateralisation of speech in the total sample would have to include *negative* cases—those with lesions of speech areas of the left hemisphere that did *not* cause loss of speech, as well as patients with lesions of corresponding areas of the right hemisphere that did *not* cause loss of speech. By examining dysphasics only, we have a complete set of patients with lesions of the speech areas on *either* side.) Assuming that unilateral lesions of the speech areas are equally probable on either side of the brain, the proportion of patients suffering dysphasias associated with right-sided lesions gives an estimate of the proportion of right-brained speakers in the population.

Table 14.4 reveals several interesting features of the data. First, with regard to handedness, the sample of Hécaen and Ajuriaguerra (1964) is outstanding in that 29% of the dysphasics were recorded as left- or mixed-handed. It is shown in Chapter 10 that over 30% of normal samples are classifiable as left- or mixed-handed. It is not the incidence in itself that is surprising, but it is evident that the criterion of sinistrality in this series is very different from that of the other series. As shown in Table 14.1, the RS theory predicts that the proportion of right-handers with right-hemisphere speech should be high when the criterion of left-handedness is strict and low when the criterion is generous. The last column in Table 14.4 shows that this is indeed the case. Hécaen and Ajuriaguerra found no instance of right-handers with dysphasia and right-hemisphere lesion. Comparison of the 29% incidence of left- and mixed-handers among dysphasics and the 17% incidence in the total sample (Hécaen and Ajuriaguerra) in Table 14.3 suggests that the criterion of sinistrality *changed within the sample*. For nondysphasics the incidence was 11%, and for dysphasias 29%. It is easy to see how this change in criterion could arise, as fuller enquiries are made of dysphasic patients (Section 7.1.3). In all series, including the war-wound cases, incidences of left-handedness were a little higher in cases recorded as dysphasic than those recorded as nondysphasic, suggesting that more attention was paid to questions of handedness in the former. The difference in incidence was greatest for the series by Hécaen and Ajuriaguerra. This analysis leads to the very important conclusion that the chief differences between the series are due to differing criteria of sinistrality. The view that right-handers are not likely to have dysphasias associated with right-hemisphere lesions is a function of the very generous criteria of left-handedness adopted for one of the most influential series. With a reasonably strict criterion of handedness (such as writing hand), the majority of right-hemisphere lesion dysphasias are *right-handed*, as expected by the RS theory.

What proportions of the samples suffered dysphasias in association with right-hemisphere lesions? Table 14.4 shows that Hécaen and Ajuriaguerra's series resembled those of Conrad and of Newcombe and Ratcliff in finding about 9 to 10% of dysphasias associated with right-sided lesions. The series out of line here is that by Penfield and Roberts, who observed only 2 cases of dysphasia following right-hemisphere lesion; it should be noted that Penfield and Roberts omitted cases of speech disorder that seemed to affect "articulation" only. There is reason to believe that disorders of speech following right-sided lesions include a relatively high proportion with transitory problems, as discussed later. Hence, in calculating the incidence of right-hemisphere speech in the population, Penfield and Roberts's series will be omitted.

The series of Gloning and Quatember (1966) offers an excellent replication of the analysis just made for the data of Hécaen and Ajuriaguerra. Was their finding that all right-brained speakers ($N=20$) were non-right-handed also a function of a generous criterion of sinistrality? In the total series there were 8%, but among dysphasics 17% were recorded as non-right-handers; this implies that 2% of nondysphasics were so recorded. Clearly, there was a massive shift in criteria of non-right-handedness between dysphasics and nondysphasics in this series. As for Hécaen and Ajuriaguerra, it can be inferred that the absence of right-handers with right-hemisphere lesions and dysphasia was due to a very generous criterion of left-handedness in dysphasics.

14.3. THE BILATERAL SPEECH IN LEFT-HANDERS HYPOTHESIS

The foregoing analysis has implications for the question of bilateral speech. It was reported that left-handers suffered dysphasias in more than 50% of cases, whether the brain lesion was right- or left-sided (Hécaen & Piercy, 1956). This observation led to the suggestion that speech lateralisation may more often be diffuse or bilateral in left-handers than in right-handers. It has been widely accepted that left-handers are typically bilateral for cerebral speech (Sections 3.3.1 and 7.1.1).

The present analysis suggests that instead of an excess of dysphasics among left-handers, there has been an excess of left-handers among dysphasics. That is, dysphasics were more likely to be recorded as left-handers than nondysphasics. Table 14.5 gives Hécaen and Piercy's data for dysphasia experienced as part of an epileptic aura. The percentage of left-handers in the total series was high (23%), but in the group of paroxysmal dysphasics it was nearly twice as high (42%). Clearly the criteria of left-handedness were generous, and especially generous for dysphasics.

Of 64 men reporting dysphasic aura in the British War Head Injury series (Russell & Espir, 1961, Table 18), 14% were left-handed, in contrast to about 8% in the total series. There may be some slightly greater risk of epilepsy in left- and mixed-handers than in right-handers (Section 4.3.1), but this could not account for an incidence of 42% in paroxysmal dysphasics. It seems likely that the cerebral bilaterality in left-handers has been over-estimated.

On the RS theory, speech laterality depends on chance factors in the RS−; it may be left, right, or bilateral. In what proportion these three forms of speech laterality occur in the population is at present unknown. Evidence from amytal testing (Table 3.2) and the dichotic monitoring test (Figure 7.1) suggest that bilateral speech is a natural variant of hemisphere organisation. It can occur in left- or right-handers who are RS−, but it is not the predominant form of speech laterality in any group. A possible indication of the proportion of bilateral speakers is offered by the incidence of transitory

TABLE 14.5
Handedness and Lesion Laterality in Cases Experiencing Dysphasia as an Epileptic Aura

Handedness	Side of Unilateral Lesion Associated With Any Epileptic Aura			
	Left		Right	
	Left	Right	Left	Right
Total aura cases N=126	18	11	63	34
Dysphasic aura N=62	17	9	32	4

Note: Based on Hécaen and Piercy (1956).
Left-handers as a percentage of all cases = 23%.
Left-handers as a percentage of cases of dysphasic aura = 42%.

dysphasia (Section 7.1.2), but bilaterality is only one of the factors that may contribute to rapid recovery from speech disorders.

14.4. ESTIMATING THE PARAMETERS OF THE RIGHT SHIFT MODEL FROM THE DYSPHASIA SERIES

14.4.1. The RS− Proportion as Twice That of Right-Brained Speakers

If right-brainedness arises, in most cases, as a natural variant in those who lack the right-shift factor, and if in such cases each hemisphere is equally likely to serve speech, the size of the RS− proportion of the population can be inferred to be twice the proportion of right-hemisphere speakers. An estimate of this proportion is offered by the data in Table 14.4 for incidences of right-hemisphere lesion. Omitting the data of Penfield and Roberts for the reasons explained, there is a total of 647 dysphasics, of whom 9.27% suffered unilateral right-hemisphere lesions. This suggests that 18.54% of the population are RS−, and this estimate is used to infer the frequency of the rs− gene in Chapter 15. It is important to ask how much confidence can be placed in this estimate of right-brainedness.

Previous discussions of right-brainedness have asked about incidences among right-handers or among left-handers. In this form, the questions are thoroughly misleading, because, as we have seen, the incidence depends on the criterion of left-handedness. The question that must be asked first is *what proportion of the total population has right-hemisphere speech?* The proportion estimated above (9.27%) implies that about 1 in 11 of the general population have right-hemisphere speech laterality. This estimate seems surprisingly high, in the experience of neurologists (Geshwind, personal communication). What further evidence can be found to assess the reliability of this estimate?

Table 14.6 lists three incidences of right-hemisphere cases among dysphasics with unilateral cerebral lesions. The first is the estimate from the four series above, which included Newcombe and Ratcliff's report of the British War Head Injury Series. Two other estimates have been derived from this last series. One is from the 64 cases in which dysphasia was experienced as an epileptic aura; in 6 (9.37%) the lesion was right-sided (Russell and Espir, 1961, Table 18). The other estimate is derived from a personal re-examination of the case records for this series.

The purpose of this re-examination was to assess (1) the incidence of dysphasia associated with right-hemisphere lesions and (2) the duration of dysphasias associated with unilateral lesion of each side. My procedure was to list all cases coded on the data card summaries for presence of dysphasic

TABLE 14.6

Estimates of the Incidence of Right-Hemisphere Speech in the Population (Irrespective of Handedness)

	Total Cases of Dysphasia	Right-Sided Lesions	%
A. In 4 series combined	647	60	9.27
B. Personal assessment of British War Wound series	217	20	9.22
C. Aphasia as epileptic aura (Russell and Espir, 1961, Table 18)	64	6	9.37

symptoms on admission or discharge, noting the side of lesion, handedness (where known), and the record of the missile track (whether absent, to the right, or to the left). The individual case records were then inspected for every case where the track was absent, or to the same side as the lesion; cases with track to the opposite side were at greater risk of bilateral damage, and these were omitted, together with all other cases with possibly bilateral or midline lesions. Of course, the reader may not be surprised that my final estimate of the proportion of right-lesion cases among the dysphasias (9.22%) was very close to the estimate it was designed to check (9.27%); questions about possible experimenter bias spring to mind. However, the closeness of this estimate was a great surprise to me. It may be pointed out that my criteria for inclusion of cases differed from those of Russell and Espir (1961) and Newcombe and Ratcliff (1973). I included men of mixed and ambidextrous handedness (omitted by Newcombe and Ratcliff) and also men of *unknown* handedness. As explained above, it is the total incidence of right-hemisphere speech in the population, irrespective of handedness, that is required.

Were dysphasias in cases of right-hemisphere lesion more likely to be transitory than those associated with left-hemisphere lesion? Table 14.7A gives the analysis in handedness groups (unknowns of course now omitted), and Table 14.7B gives the analysis for side of cerebral lesion. (Two of the original N could not be assessed for duration of dysphasia from the case records.) There is a trend for left- and mixed-handers to be a little more likely than right-handers to have transitory dysphasias, but the second analysis shows that the critical variable is laterality of lesion. Disorders of speech that recovered in hours or days were noted for 35% of right-lesion and 14% of left-lesion cases. (Of course in absolute *number* they are more frequent among left-lesion cases.) Disorders of speech lasting for years were recorded for 40% of right- and 56% of left-lesion cases. The χ^2 test finds a significant difference between the right- and left-lesion cases in the duration of dysphasia. This suggests that one reason that dysphasias associated with right-

TABLE 14.7

Duration of Dysphasia in Relation to (a) Handedness, and (b) Side of Cerebral Lesion

A.

	Handedness	
Duration of dysphasia	Left + Mixed (N=24) (%)	Right (N=182) (%)
Hours or days	21	16
Weeks	29	27
Years	50	57
		χ^2 NS

B.

	Side of Cerebral Lesion	
	Right (N=20) (%)	Left (N=195) (%)
Hours or days	35	14
Weeks	25	30
Years	40	56
		$\chi^2=6.16$
		$df=2, p<.05$

hemisphere lesions seem relatively rare in the experience of neurologists is that these dysphasias are more often transitory. This difference must not be exaggerated, however, since follow-up examinations of these cases 20 or more years after injury have confirmed that some right-hemisphere lesion dysphasias can be as dense and persistent as those associated with left-hemisphere lesions (Newcombe—personal communication).

If the cases of persistent dysphasia (weeks or years) are taken as the basis for the estimate of right-hemisphere speech, there were 181 cases, of whom 13 (7.2%) suffered right-sided lesions. This percentage offers a minimal estimate of the incidence of right-hemisphere speech, and it presumably excludes cases of bilateral speech. The proportion of cases of right-sided unilateral lesion in the series of Gloning and Quatember (1966) was also 7.2% (20 out of 279 cases). Hence it seems probable that the incidence of right-hemisphere speech in the population is of the order of 7.2 to 9.3%. The lower figure could represent cases of right-hemisphere speech, and the upper figure could represent right hemisphere + bilateral speech. Since right-sided and bilateral speech are expected only in the RS−, there is no reason to change the assumption with which this section began, that about 18% of the population are RS− and about 82% RS+.

14.4.2. The Extent of Right Shift of the RS+

The extent of shift of the RS+ distribution with respect to the mean of the RS− distribution cannot be known directly, but it can be estimated theoretically. The estimate depends on the assumption that the threshold for left-handedness remains at the same point along the scale of L–R skill in the RS− and RS+ subgroups of the population (as in Fig. 14.1).

If the incidence of left-handedness is known in the total population and also in the RS− subgroup, the incidence of left-handedness in the RS+ subgroup can be derived by subtraction. The incidence of left-handedness in each subgroup can then be looked up in the table of the normal curve to discover where the threshold of left-handedness must be in each distribution. Assuming that the actual thresholds stay constant in both distributions, the difference between the estimates tells us how far the mean of the RS+ distribution is shifted in comparison with the mean of the RS− distribution.

TABLE 14.8
Deducing the Extent of Right Shift for the RS+
Observed Distribution of Dysphasics for Cerebral Lesion and Handedness

a. Side of Cerebral Lesion

	Handedness	
	Left	Right
Left	4.3	86.5
Right	3.4	5.8

b. Inferred Distribution of Handedness in RS− and RS+ (if Right Lesion Dysphasics are 50% of RS−)

	Handedness		
	Left	Right	Total
RS+	4.3 − 3.4 = 0.9	86.5 − 5.8 = 80.7	81.6
RS−	3.4 × 2 = 6.8	5.8 × 2 = 11.6	18.4

c. Location of the Threshold of Left-Handedness in the RS+ and RS−

	% Left-Handed	Z Under Normal Curve
RS+	1000.9/81.6) = 1.14*	−2.276z
RS−	1006.8/18.4) = 36.73*	−0.339z

d. Extent of Right Shift

$$-2.276 - (-0.339) = 1.937z$$

Note: N = 533.
*Using more decimals than given.

This calculation was made (Annett, 1975, Table 6) for the combined data of the three dysphasic series that did not differ significantly for any major variable (Conrad, Newcombe, & Ratcliff, and Bingley). The calculations are set out more fully in Table 14.8. It is assumed that patients with dysphasia and right-hemisphere lesions are 50% of dysphasics who are RS−; the other 50% have left-hemisphere lesions. It is also assumed that the handedness of the RS− dysphasics with left-hemisphere lesions are in the same proportion as for right-lesion dysphasics. Hence the "hidden" RS− are subtracted from left-lesion cases. On the data used in Table 14.8 it is inferred that 1.14% of the RS+ are left-handed and that the threshold of left-handedness must be 2.276z (according to the normal curve table) below the mean. Among the RS−, 36.73% are expected to be left-handed, and this threshold is .339z below the mean. Since the mean of the RS− is at 0, (by definition) the extent of Right-Shift of the RS+ (assuming common thresholds) is 1.937z. This estimate was found to serve very well in later genetic calculations—but further attempts to derive improved estimates of shift are described in Section 16.2.

14.5. FURTHER SUPPORT FOR THE RIGHT SHIFT THEORY

14.5.1. An Independent Test in Patients of Known Speech Hemisphere

In the data considered so far, the laterality of cerebral speech was inferred from the symptom of loss of speech. Patients of known speech hemisphere (by the Wada technique) were examined by Ratcliff, Dila, Taylor, and Milner (1980) for the asymmetry of the angles formed by the posterior branches of the middle cerebral artery in the region of the Sylvian fissure. It was shown (Table 3.3) that two-thirds of right-handers have a narrower angle on the left, but only one-fifth of left-handers. Patients at the Montreal neurological clinic undergoing amytal tests for the laterality of cerebral speech are normally given a carotid arteriogram before each test. By going through patients' records, it was possible to examine the relation between this asymmetry of cerebral structure and the identified speech hemisphere, as well as handedness.

Figure 14.2 shows the distribution of patients for the difference between the angle of the carotid arteries of the left and right hemispheres. Patients with right-sided and bilateral speech are graphed separately from those with left-hemisphere speech. Both distributions are continuous and roughly normal. The upper distribution has a mean to the right of L = R, and 67%

(a)

(b)

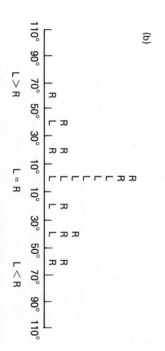

L > R   L = R   L < R

110° 90° 70° 50° 30° 10° 10° 30° 50° 70° 90° 110°

FIG. 14.2.   Distribution of sylvian arch asymmetry in right-handed (R) and left-handed (L) patients with (a) left and (b) right or bilateral speech representation. Redrawn from Ratcliff et al., 1980.

have the typical L < R bias. The proportion of left-handers in the upper distribution (28%) is relatively high, but as said earlier (Chapter 2), this was not a random population sample but included an excess of left-handers. The lower distribution is centered on L = R, and 35% are biased to L < R. The proportion of left-handers in the lower distribution was 45%. This finding agrees with the expectation of the RS theory that among those of atypical cerebral speech there would be more right- than left-handers. The distributions of Fig. 14.2 are as expected from Fig. 14.1, one distribution unbiased to either side and a second distribution with a bias to the right. No theory of hand and speech laterality other than the RS theory would have predicted that among cases of known right-hemisphere and bilateral speech there would be an absence of bias to either side for structural brain asymmetry and handedness.

14.5.2. Asymmetries of Structure and Function Considered in the Light of the RS Theory

The distributions of structural asymmetries, see Table 3.3. and 3.4. are as expected for proportions under the normal curve. In Geschwind and Levitsky's

(1968) data for asymmetries of the planum temporale, the proportions of brains with left-larger, no difference, or right-larger planum (65, 24, 11, respectively) are similar though not identical, to the proportion found for right-, mixed-, and left-handedness (66, 30, 4). The proportions depend, of course, on the criterion of L=R for both brain and hand asymmetries, and the proportion in the middle group can be reduced or increased by changes in criterion. The distributions of anatomical asymmetries in right- and left-handers are fully compatible with the hypothesis that in right-handers the normal distribution of differences is shifted to give a mean difference to one side of L=R, whereas in left-handers the mean is much closer to L=R. When any bias is detected in left-handers, it is always in the same direction as in right-handers, never in the opposite direction. This is as expected on the RS theory, since there is only one systematic factor biasing the distribution; the factor is more often absent in left-handers than in right-handers, but in those left-handers in whom the factor is present, the bias to the left brain is probably as strong as in right-handers having the factor.

It is not often that data on lateral asymmetries of perception are reported in such a way that the nature of the distribution can be inspected, but whenever distributions are plotted they turn out to be continuous. Shankweiler and Studdert-Kennedy (1975) confirmed earlier findings of Orlando (1972), that asymmetries of dichotic speech perception should be regarded as continuous and associated with the continuum of asymmetry of manual skill. The continuity of the distribution of dichotic ear asymmetry is evident in Fig. 7.1. It is also clear in the distributions obtained by Wexler and Halwes (1983) for 194 right-handers and 175 left-handers given a dichotic fused rhymes test (Fig. 14.3). They report that 12% of right-handers and 29% of left-handers had LEAs. Similar proportions were found by Satz, Achenbach, and Fennell (1967) for self-classified left- and right-handers, as shown in Table 14.9A. The data in Table 14.9B show the effect of a more stringent criterion of left-handedness on the percentage LEA. As predicted in Table 14.1, the proportion of sinistrals having atypical laterality increases as the criteria of sinistrality are moved to the left (of the L–R continuum of skill). The proportion of LEA's observed (45%) is about as high as can be expected.

One of the most important supports of the RS theory lies in the fact that no convincing evidence of a significant group bias to the left hand or to the right hemisphere has been found, in all the years of intensive research on lateral asymmetries. Whenever significant biases are found for the majority of the population, the special groups that might have been expected to show the opposite asymmetry show rather a reduction of the typical bias, or no bias to either side. There is no evidence of factors giving significant biases in the atypical direction. All claims to have found evidence of group biases in the atypical direction are based on small numbers of cases. When groups of atypical laterality have an N of 12 or less (as for Bryden, 1965; Davidoff, 1975; Haun, 1978; Herron, 1980), the proportion of cases with atypical bias

(a) Right handed subjects (n=194)

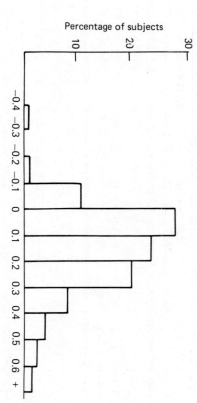

Percentage of subjects

30

2J

10

−0.4 −0.3 −0.2 −0.1   0   0.1 0.2 0.3 0.4 0.5 0.6 +

(b) Left handed subjects (n=175)

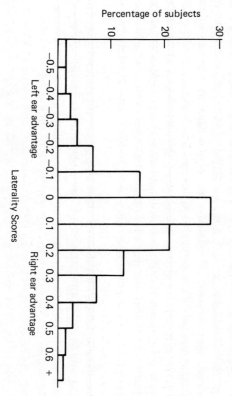

Percentage of subjects

30

20

10

−0.5 −0.4 −0.3 −0.2 −0.1 0 0.1 0.2 0.3 0.4 0.5 0.6 +

Left ear advantage   Right ear advantage

Laterality Scores

FIG. 14.3.   Distributions of laterality scores for dichotic listening. Adapted from Wexler & Halwes, 1983.

could easily depart from the 50% predicted by the RS theory. To give a serious challenge to the RS theory, groups claimed to show atypical bias must be large enough to make chance differences from 50% unlikely.

The distributions found for dichotic listening asymmetries are surprisingly close to those expected by the RS theory. The analyses of handedness described in Chapters 10 to 12 led to the view that lateral asymmetries must

TABLE 14.9
Distribution of Dichotic Listening Asymmetries With Handedness

A. Self-classified hand preference

	Left (N=54)		Right (N=69)	
	Right	Left or Equal	Right	Left or Equal
Ear with advantage on dichotic listening test	37	17	61	8
% Left ear advantage		31		12

B. More stringent handedness classification based on tests of skill

	Left (N=33)		Right (N=90)	
	Right	Left or Equal	Right	Left or Equal
Ear with advantage on dichotic listening test	18	15	80	10
% Left ear advantage		45		11

Note: Based on Satz, Achenbach, and Fennell (1967).

be thought of as continuously distributed. This chapter has shown that data for speech loss in association with right and left cerebral lesions in left- and right-handers makes sense if it is interpreted in terms of continuous and normal distributions. The studies of asymmetries in normal subjects (Chapters 6 and 7) have struggled to describe their continuously distributed data in terms of the discrete categories of the neurological literature but never quite succeeded because of the contradictions arising from shifting criteria within that literature. It is time to face up to the fact that lateral asymmetries are manifested as continuous and not discrete variables. Convincing tests of the RS theory (and any alternatives) will come when reliable, noninvasive methods are discovered for assessing cerebral speech in population samples of normal subjects. In my view, the perceptual asymmetries studied so far are not sufficiently convincing to offer a full test, but, for what they are worth, they offer no contrary evidence.

14.6.   SUMMARY

The inference that the right shift of the human handedness distribution is a by-product of a factor inducing left cerebral speech is examined through analyses of data for incidences of dysphasia in consecutive series of patients with unilateral cerebral lesions studied for lesion side and handedness. The evidence for right-hemisphere speech in young men suffering from war wounds suggests that in some people the RS factor is absent (RS+ present and RS− absent). If there are no systematic influences on human laterality except for RS+, all asymmetries in those who are RS− are due to chance, and asymmetries of hand and brain each occur with independent 50% probabilities. Because most of those who are evenly balanced for skill are induced by cultural pressures to use the right hand, a majority of the RS− and a majority of cases of right-hemisphere speech are expected to be *right-handed*. This apparently paradoxical prediction of the theory is strongly supported by the evidence. Series that do not find a majority of right-handers among those with right-hemisphere speech have very high incidences of left-handedness. It can be inferred that very generous criteria of sinistrality were adopted for dysphasics, and especially for dysphasics with right-sided lesions. The widely held belief that right-hemisphere speech is rare in right-handers is a consequence of this re-definition of right-handers on account of probably trivial sinistral preferences.

Questions concerning the cerebral speech of left-handers cannot be answered without reference to the criteria of left-handedness in the population; the expected incidences vary systematically in right-handers and in left-handers, according to the location of the threshold that represents the incidence of left-handedness (as can be seen from Fig. 14.1 and Table 14.1).

The argument that bilateral speech is characteristic of left-handers depended on series using very generous criteria of sinistrality. Whereas there was thought to be an excess of dysphasics in left-handers, there was in fact an excess of left-handers in dysphasics. Some small proportion of the RS− may have bilateral speech, but there is no reason to believe that this is characteristic of any group.

The incidence of right-hemisphere speech in the general population is of interest as a means of estimating the proportion of the population who are RS−. An incidence of 9.27% right-hemisphere speakers was deduced from the consecutive series of dysphasics. This estimate, which seems high in comparison with usual beliefs about hemisphere speech, was checked in two further analyses and upheld.

The duration of dysphasias was analysed in relation to lesion side and to handedness. Dysphasias associated with lesions on either side varied in duration from hours to decades, but there was a significant tendency towards faster recovery for right- than left-sided cases. When the relationships were examined for handedness, there were nonsignificant trends to faster recovery in left-handers. It seems probable that the significant variable is RS+ or RS−, not handedness.

An estimate of the extent of shift of the RS+ distribution in comparison with the RS− distribution was based on a comparison of incidences of left-handedness in right- and left-lesion dysphasics. The shift was estimated to be just under two standard deviations (1.937z).

Further support for the RS analysis of relationships between handedness and brainedness is to be found in a comparison of physical asymmetries of the hemispheres and handedness in patients of known cerebral speech. Patients with right-sided and bilateral speech showed a normal distribution of asymmetries but no systematic bias to either side; 45% were left-handed. The evidence for structural brain asymmetries (Chapter 3) and for perceptual asymmetries in normal right- and left-handers (Chapter 7) is in accord with the assumption that most of the latter lack systematic biases to either side; when asymmetries are found, they are always in the same direction as in right-handers and usually in subjects who have been classified as sinistral on generous criteria.

15 The Genetic Hypothesis

The evidence for a genetic influence on human handedness, but not on the paw preferences of other species, was considered in Section 3.4. The RS theory suggests that two features of the human laterality distribution must be distinguished, first, the *variability*, and, second, the *shift to the right*. It suggests that the variability is not genetic, but depends on chance developmental differences between the sides in all species, including man. The shift to the right could be inherited. It could be inherited in the sense of a universal human species characteristic, but the analysis of speech disorders associated with right-hemisphere lesions (Chapter 14) suggests that left-hemisphere speech laterality varies between people in the normal population. The observation of right-hemisphere speakers in the general population implies that some people inherit the factor (RS+) and other do not (RS−). The RS− are without systematic bias to either side. On an unbiased measure of hand skill, the RS− should be evenly divided between those with greater right-hand and those with greater left-hand skill. Cultural pressures towards dextrality induce more than 50% to be right-handed for writing and for other socially significant actions. Some RS+ are expected to be left-handed, since accidental biases towards the left hand will not always be compensated by the advantage to the right hand conferred by the RS factor. Among groups of left-handers, however, an unknown but substantial proportion are expected to be RS−. The children of two left-handed parents (L × L families) should show a marked reduction of the typical bias to the right hand, but no systematic bias to the left hand. That is, a genetic influence on handedness might be demonstrable if it could be shown that the children of two left-handed parents have an absence of bias to the right. The success of this prediction was one of the first supports of the RS theory. It was consistent with the assumption of a genetic influence, in the sense that an absence of bias could be transmitted from one generation to the next.

As for other aspects of the RS theory, ideas about possible genetic mechanisms developed in stages. From first formulating the RS theory, I thought that the normal distribution of L–R differences depended on chance and not on multigene inheritance. However, I used the methods of estimating heritability appropriate to multigene theories (Annett, 1973a, 1978a, 1979) because they were the methods developed to deal with threshold models for continuously varying characters. The estimates of heritability showed some striking sex differences in the association of left-hand preference in relatives, which are considered in the next section.

This chapter considers the genetics of the RS in three sections addressed to two main questions, as follows:

1. What is the evidence for a genetic influence on human handedness? This will be considered in relation to estimates of heritability, as derived from the association between relatives, and also in relation to evidence from L × L families.

2. Can the RS be attributed to a single allele, $rs+$? Evidence for this assumption, when the parameters of the RS model are as derived from the dysphasia series in Chapter 14, is presented for family data, without reference to sex. Sex differences and twinning are considered in Chapter 16.

15.1   EVIDENCE THAT THE RIGHT SHIFT HAS A GENETIC BASIS

15.1.1. The Association Between Relatives for Left-Handedness in Normal Samples

The handedness questionnaire (Fig. 10.1) was usually given along with an enquiry about the respondent's relatives. This took the form of a family tree, with boxes labelled for father, mother, brothers, sisters, parents' parents, and parents' siblings. Respondents were asked to record the handedness of as many of these relatives as known, recording U (unknown) where necessary, and noting any relatives who were of twin birth. All families in which a parent was unknown or a twin were omitted from further analyses of family data. The data for students at the Universities of Aberdeen and Hull and for service recruits were described for association between relatives for left-handedness (Annett, 1973a). The criterion of sinistrality was the writing hand of respondents completing the questionnaire personally (all of the filial generation and a subset of the parental generation) or a report of left-handedness in relatives. (The Hull sample in Appendix I.B.6.a). The subset of families where parents and students personally completed a questionnaire was described later for the generous criterion of any left-hand preference for the 12 items (Annett, 1978a; the generous criterion sample of Appendix I.B.6.b). Analyses of association between relatives, using the same methods of estimating heritability, were also made for the data of Chamberlain (1928), Rife (1940), and for samples of Open University students (Annett, 1978a). (The reconstruction of Chamberlain's sample is considered in Section 3.4.2.)

Tables 15.1A and B summarise the findings for these several sets of data for males and females, respectively. The table gives the numbers of left-handers (probands) in each sample and the incidences of left-handedness in the samples from which they were drawn; the estimates of heritability (h^2) are then given, and the standard error of the estimate (SE) for first-degree relatives. The estimate depends on comparing, for example, the incidence of left-handedness in the mothers of left-handers with that in all mothers in the sample (see Falconer, 1965). Among the Hull sample respondents, there were

TABLE 15.1a

Heritability Estimates for Relatives of Male Left-Handers

Source	Number of Male Left-Handers (Probands)	Incidence of Left-handedness in the Proband Sample	Fathers h^2	Fathers SE	Mothers h^2	Mothers SI
Chamberlain (1928)	267	5.3	40.4*	11.5	49.2*	12.1
Annett (1978a) OU males	26	6.8	—	—	79.1*	30.4
Rife (1940)	123	9.6	35.0	19.6	20.6	21.1
Annett (1973a) Main sample	253	11.8	17.4	15.6	56.6*	13.8
Annett (1978a) Hull: generous criterion	236	39.5	16.8	20.1	42.3*	20.4

Source	Number of Male Left-Handers (Probands)	Incidence of Left-handedness in the Proband Sample	Brothers h^2	Brothers SE	Sisters h^2	Sisters SE
Annett (1973a) Main sample	253	11.8	20.0	16.6	20.5	17.8
Annett (1978a) OU males	26	6.8	—	—	—	—

*indicates $p < .05$ or less.

TABLE 15.1b

Heritability Estimates for Relatives of Female Left-Handers

Source	Number of Female Left-Handers (Probands)	Incidence of Left-Handedness in the Proband Sample	Fathers		Mothers		Brothers		Sisters	
			h^2	SE	h^2	SE	h^2	SE	h^2	SE
Chamberlain (1928)	101	3.8	29.3	17.3	65.1*	15.1				
Rife (1940)	68	7.6	72.2*	20.7	81.1*	20.5				
Annett (1978a) OU females	35	8.6	—	—	46.5	31.1				
Annett (1973a) main sample	171	11.4	3.5	20.0	51.1*	16.7				
Annett (1978a) Hull: generous criterion	176	39.7	21.9	24.1	58.3*	23.6				
Annett (1973a) main sample	171	11.4					15.6	22.1	43.8*	23.0
Annett (1978a) OU females	35	8.6					58.5	32.1	74.3*	30.8

*indicates $p < .05$ or less.

2,151 males, of whom 253 (11.8%) were left-handed; the incidence of left-handedness in the mothers of these left-handers was 9.5%, in comparison with 3.7% for the mothers of all respondents. This comparison gives a statistically significant estimate of h^2 (56.5+13.8).

Table 15.1A shows that for male respondents, 4 out of 5 estimates were significant for mothers but only 1 for fathers and none for siblings. Table 15.1B shows that for female respondents, h^2 was substantial for all female relatives. The lack of significance in one case was mainly due to the small N. There was only one significant estimate for fathers of females (in Rife's data). Comparison of Tables 15.1A and 15.1B shows that the estimates of h^2 were larger for female relatives of female respondents than the corresponding estimates for female relatives of male respondents in all except one case. These findings suggest that the association between relatives for left-handedness is stronger for females than for males. The interpretation of this finding, and the question whether there is a true excess of left-handers born to left-handed mothers in comparison with left-handed fathers, is considered further in Section 16.3.

Significant associations between relatives do not prove that the basis of the association is genetic. Before the genetic hypothesis can be regarded as probable, it must be shown that the association is not a result of the experience of living with a left-handed relative. The usual way of tackling this problem is through studies of adoptive families. As adoptions are treated as confidential in Britain, it is not easy to collect data on the children of left-handed adoptive parents; my collection of such families is small and relies entirely on volunteers. Carter-Saltzman (1980) was able to collect information on a substantial number of adoptive families in the United States and found that the incidence of left-handedness in the children was not higher when the adoptive parents were left-handed than when they were right-handed (Table 3.9). This finding suggests that the association between biological relatives could have a genetic basis.

15.1.2. Children of Two Left-Handed Parents

The findings for a first sample of L × L families (Annett, 1974) were considered important enough to need checking in a second sample (Annett, 1983). The findings it was wished to confirm were as follows:

1. There is no evidence of systematic bias to the left side for hand preference or hand skill.
2. As a group, the children show an *absence* of bias; they have a mean L–R difference close to 0 (L = R).
3. In families where the parental sinistrality may be pathological, the children are biased to the right hand, despite being reared in a L × L family.

Point 3 complements the adoptive studies. If the children of left-handed parents who are likely to be carrying the $rs+$ gene are as biased to the right as children reared in R × R families, a genetic basis for the human species bias to the right will be more probable. In the first sample of L × L families, there were 8 children with a parent whose left-handedness was judged possibly pathological. These children were as biased to the right hand, as school-children controls. Additional L × L families were sought to confirm this finding. Points 1 and 2 depend, of course, on basic postulates of the RS theory.

Comparison of the first sample (60 children in 28 families) and the second sample (55 children in 27 families) found no significant differences for measures of laterality, and the data are described here as a single sample of

115 children. The data are given first for all children of 5 years or more (except for two boys with abnormal hand movements on the peg-moving task, whose mothers reported suspected brain damage). Subgroups in the sample will then be examined for the effects of possible pathological sinistrality in parents and for the effect of presence of left-handed relatives of the parents.

Table 15.2 describes the findings for preferences of hand, eye, and foot, and Table 15.3 gives the L–R peg-moving times. In both tables there is a striking *absence* of sex differences. About 34% of the children are left-handed writers, and just over 50% show some mixed- or left-eye preference. The L–R means are given for two samples of controls (the birthday samples and the combined main samples, Appendix I.B.9 and 10). Both control samples show highly significant sex differences, with females more biased to the right hand than males. Table 15.3 also gives the L–R means for all left-handed writers in the combined main sample controls, for comparison with the means of the left-handed parents. It is clear that the parents in the L × L samples resemble the left-handed controls and can therefore be presumed to be representative of left-handers in the population. The children of L × L families show slight and nonsignificant biases to the right hand. The absence of sex differences in the left-handed controls, left-handed parents, and the children of L × L families will be considered in Chapter 16.

Figure 15.1 shows the distribution of L–R times in the 115 children. The hatched distribution shows the times of 20 children with one or more parent

TABLE 15.2
Preferences for Hand, Eye, and Foot in Children of L × L families

Preferences	Males (N = 58)	Females (N = 57)	Total (N = 115)
Hand			
Right consistent	38	42	40
Right writing but some left preferences	28	25	26
Left-handed writing	34	33	34
Eye			
Right consistent	48	47	48
Mixed	21	25	23
Left consistent	31	28	29
Foot			
Left or either for kicking	22	35	29

Note: Revised from Annett (1983a). In percentages.

TABLE 15.3

L–R Hand Peg-Moving Times in Parents and Children of L × L Families and in Two Control Samples

Controls	Males			Females			
	N	Mean	SD	N	Mean	SD	t
Birthday samples (6–15 yrs)	122	7.1	13.1	156	12.0	12.7	3.148*
Combined main samples (12–63 yrs)	617	6.4	8.4	863	8.0	8.8	3.395**
Left-handed writers in combined main samples	46	−6.4	7.9	75	−6.0	7.3	NS
L × L Families							
Parents	55	−6.2	7.0	55	−7.6	7.9	NS
Children	58	2.5	15.1	57	2.8	13.4	NS

Note: Revised from Annett (1983a).
*indicates $p < .002$, **indicates $p < .001$.

whose left-handedness was judged possibly pathological (based on a clear history of personal birth complications or abnormally slow right-hand time on the peg-moving task, and the absence of a close left-handed relative). Table 15.3 gives the L–R mean and also the percentage of children with a bias to the left hand for peg moving, in children with and without a pathologically sinistral parent. The former were as biased to the right hand as the controls in Table 15.3. The 95 children whose parents did not fulfil any of the criteria of pathological sinistrality above were not significantly biased to the right hand, and 42% showed a left-hand advantage for peg moving.

Another analysis for evidence of genetic influence was possible in the combined L × L samples. This was an examination of the effect of presence of left-handers among the parents and siblings of the left-handed parents. Parents with a close left-handed relative would be more likely to be RS – than parents without such a relative. Table 15.4 gives the L–R means of children classified for presence or absence of left-handed relatives of the parents. The 33 children of families where neither parent had a close sinistral relative were significantly biased to the right hand, and only 30% showed a personal bias to the left hand. None of the other groups were significantly biased to the right hand, and 39 to 50% were personally biased to the left hand. This analysis demonstrates that the bias to the right hand in the children differs according to the handedness of the parents' relatives,

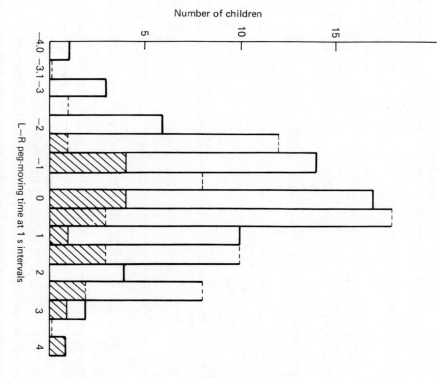

FIG. 15.1.　Distribution of L–R peg-moving times in 115 children in L × L families. Numbers of males (——) and females (– – –) grouped for L–R time on the peg-moving task, for the total sample of children ($n = 115$) and for the children with a possible "pathologically" sinistral parent ($n = 20$, hatched). Annett, 1983a.

although all the parents were phenotypically left-handed and all the children had the experience of being reared in a L × L family.

The increased proportion of left-handed children in L × L families cannot be due only to the experience of being reared in such a family, as there are marked differences *within* L × L families when parents are classified for possible pathology or for the presence or absence of left-handed relatives. The extent of right shift in the two groups with significant shifts suggests, on the contrary, that the RS factor is expressed about as strongly in children who inherit it in L × L as in R × R families. These findings offer strong support for the hypothesis that the shift to the right is genetic and that the

TABLE 15.4

L–R Peg-Moving Times of Children in L × L Families Classified for (a) Presence of a Possible Pathologically Left-Handed Parent and (b) Presence of Left-Handed Relatives of Parents

| | N | L–R | | L–R<0 |
		Mean	SE	%
"Pathologically" left-handed parent				
Present	20	8.0	2.9	25
Absent	95	1.5	1.5	42
Left-handed parents with a sinistral parent or sibling				
i. Neither parent	33	5.3	2.4	30
ii. Father only	24	−0.4	2.4	50
iii. Mother only	38	2.0	2.3	39
iv. Both parents	20	3.0	3.8	40

Note: Revised from Annett (1983a).

gene(s) responsible for the RS are absent in the majority of children in L × L families.

15.2. A SINGLE-ALLELE MODEL OF THE RIGHT SHIFT

The review of the characteristics of the RS factor (Chapter 13) suggests that it is something that distinguishes man from his nearest primate relations. The tendency to develop hand preferences is present in primates, but there is no evidence of species bias to one side except in man. If the RS factor is responsible for the bias to the left hemisphere for speech, as argued in Chapter 14, it clearly does not *cause* human speech but merely increases the chances that speech will depend on the left hemisphere. The shortness of the evolutionary time scale, the relative paucity of genetic differences between man and chimpanzee (Chapter 1), and the limited role of the RS factor all argue for some very simple agent for the RS. Parsimony alone should urge us to look for a simple mechanism. Very small changes in genotype can have major consequences for individuals. Changes that seem to be of great evolutionary significance from the human viewpoint could well depend on very small modifications of the genetic code. This section argues that the RS could depend on a single change at one gene locus (a single allele). It is hypothesised that when this allele is present on one or both chromosomes, some advantage is likely to be conferred on the left cerebral hemisphere, which tends to induce speech on that side and incidentally increases the skill of the right hand in comparison with the left hand. When the right shift allele ($rs+$) is absent on both chromosomes, the alternate allele(s) at that locus ($rs-$) are indifferent or neutral for speech and handedness.

There were several years between the formulation of the RS model (Annett, 1972) and the demonstration that a single allele would be sufficient (Annett, 1978b). The analysis depends on the assumptions that are outlined in Fig. 14.1. These are as follows:

1. Handedness depends on a continuous normal distribution of L–R skill.
2. In those who lack the gene on both chromosomes ($rs--$) the mean of the distribution of L–R skill is 0. In those in whom the gene is present ($rs+-$ and $rs++$), the mean of L–R skill is to the right of 0.
3. The expression of left- or right-handedness depends on a threshold that can move to the left or the right along the scale of L–R skill to give large or small incidences of left-handedness.
4. The threshold is at the same position on the L–R scale for all genotypes. That is, whatever pressures make people able or unable to express their sinistral tendencies apply equally to both of the main subgroups, for any given level of L–R skill, so that only one threshold is necessary, as in Fig. 14.1.
5. The variance of the two subdistributions is equal. This implies that the distance along the L–R scale that represents a standard deviation under the normal curve is the same for both distributions.

The main unknown parameters of the model are:

1. The proportion of the population who are $rs--$, and hence the relative size of the two distributions.
2. The extent of right shift; that is, the distance between the means of the $rs--$ and $rs+-$, $++$ subgroups.

If these two parameters were known, it would be possible to say, for any given incidence of left-handedness, what proportion of left-handers in the population belongs to each subdistribution, or, in terms of Fig. 14.1, how many right-handers and left-handers on either side of the threshold are of each genotype. The best possible guesses as to the values of the two unknown parameters were based on the data for patients with loss of speech following right- and left-sided unilateral lesions (as deduced in Section 14.4). Patients with dysphasia following right unilateral lesions must be $rs--$. Provided the sample of patients is drawn from the general population without bias as to handedness or lesion laterality, the proportion with right-hemisphere speech represents 50% of the $rs--$. The combined data for four samples gave an estimate of 9.27% with right-hemisphere speech; two further analyses found similar percentages (Table 14.6). On this estimate, the $rs--$ subgroup is 18.54%, and the $rs+-$, $rs++$ subgroup is therefore 81.46% of the population.

This estimate of the relative sizes of the distributions can be used to deduce the frequencies of the $rs-$ and $rs+$ genes. If the genes are distributed at random in the population and the combinations of genes in pairs (genotypes) have reached stable equilibrium through many generations of random mating (Hardy-Weinberg equilibrium, see Chapter 1), then the gene pairs must be distributed in the population in binomial proportions (Section 3.4.4). It is usual to describe genetic quantities as proportions of 1, such that

$$rs+ \ + \ rs-\ = 1.$$

The three possible genotypes must be in the proportions given by,

$$(rs+ \ + \ rs-)^2 = rs+^2 \ + 2rs+- \ + \ rs-^2 = 1.$$

If we know the proportion of $rs--$, estimated above to be .1854, then the frequency of the $rs-$ gene is given by the square root of this quantity:

$$rs- = \sqrt{.1854} = .43;\ rs+ = 1 - .43 = .57.$$

Table 15.5 illustrates that if the $rs+$ and $rs-$ genes occur in these proportions in the gametes (ova and sperm), then the genotypes of offspring will be in the proportions,

$$rs++ \ = .3242, rs+- = .4904, rs-- = .1854.$$

The second unknown parameter of the RS model, the extent of right shift, was also deduced from the findings for dysphasics, as shown in Table 14.8, where the distance between the means of the RS+ and RS- distributions was inferred to be 1.937z. The reader will appreciate that this calculation depends on the reported handedness of patients with left- and right-sided

TABLE 15.5

The Proportion of $rs++$, $rs+-$ and $rs--$ Genotypes in the Population for the Estimated Gene Frequencies

Gene	Proportions	Father's gametes	
		$rs+$ .5694	$rs-$ .4306
Mother's gametes $rs+$	.5694	.3242	.2452
$rs-$	.4306	.2452	.1854

Note: Population genotypes: $rs++ = .3242, rs+- = .4904, rs-- = .1854.$

brain lesions. Even in the combined series of 533 cases, the *number* of RS+ inferred to be left-handed was very small. Thus there is considerable scope for error in the estimate. The inference also depends on treating the RS+ as a single group and ignoring possible differences between the $rs+-$ and $rs++$ genotypes. That is, it treats the $rs+$ gene as fully dominant. The estimate of extent of shift is expressed in terms of the standard deviation units of the theoretical distribution of L–R skill, not in terms of measured units in an actual test of skill. Thus, there are several aspects of the calculations that can be reconsidered in later sections, such as additive versus dominant versions of the model and empirical versus theoretical distributions of skill, as well as the fit of the genetic calculations to observed family data. However, all these possible refinements of the model are worthwhile only if the broad general approach can be shown to be useful. The aim of this section is to show how the initial calculations, as described above, were used to predict data already available for handedness in families. The stages of calculation are as follows:

1. *Calculate the Proportions of Right- and Left-Handers of Each Genotype in the Parents.* If the relative sizes of the two subgroups of the population are as estimated above ($rs--=.1854$ and $rs+-,++=.8146$) and the distance between the means of these two groups is 1.937z, then for any incidence of left-handedness it can be worked out, from the table of proportions under the normal curve, what proportions of each subgroup are called left-handed and right-handed. This can be done by trial and error, given the normal curve table and a desk calculator, but more efficiently, of course, by computer program. Table 15.6 sets out the main steps of the analysis, using the data of Chamberlain as an example.

Ignoring sex differences, the incidence of left-handedness in parents was recorded as .0356. The location of the threshold required to give this incidence is $-.907z$ for the $rs--$ distribution and $-2.844z$ for the $rs+-,++$ distribution ($-2.844--.907=1.937z$. For this very severe threshold of left-handedness, 82% of $rs--$ are called right-handed, and 18% are called left-handed. Of the $rs+-,++$ only .2% are called left-handed. (The proportions must be calculated to several decimal places.) In the parental generation, the genotypes of the total population are divided into dextrals (summing to .9644) and sinistrals (summing to .0356), as shown in Table 15.6.A.1).

2. *Calculate the Genotypes of Offspring of R × R, L × R and L × L Matings.* Given the above genotype frequencies of parents and assuming random mating (that is, that handedness is not likely to affect the choice of mate or the number of children in mating groups—these are possible, of course, but must be ignored for the calculations), the genotypes of children

having $R \times R$, $L \times R$, and $L \times L$ parents can be worked out. The calculations follow the basic Mendelian laws of the assortment of genes in pairs, as shown in Table 1.1 and Appendix IV. Notice that the proportion of offspring of $L \times R$ matings must be doubled, as it includes $L \times R$ and $R \times L$ (left-handed fathers, and left-handed mothers, respectively) which are not being distinguished here.

There are two possible methods for expressing the proportion of children within each mating type. The proportions can be expressed either as percentages of the total population (summing to 1 over the whole table, which must be tested as a check on the arithmetic), or as percentages within each mating type (summing to 1 for each mating). The latter method is used in Table 15.6 and Appendix IV, and the former is used in Chapter 16, for reasons explained there.

Table 15.6.A.2 shows the genotype distribution within the three family types. For a very strict criterion of left-handedness, as in the parents of Chamberlain's sample, the genotype distribution of children of $R \times R$ parents is very like that of the population as a whole. When one parent is left-handed, the proportion of $rs--$ is increased, but the most frequent genotype remains the $rs+-$. When both parents are left-handed, the majority of children are $rs--$, very few are $rs++$ (about .1%), but some are $rs+-$ (about 7%). With a more generous threshold of left-handedness in parents, the proportion of children of $L \times L$ parents carrying the $rs+$ gene is raised.

3. *Calculate the Proportion of Right- and Left-Handers of Each Genotype in the Offspring.* In all studies of handedness in families, the incidence in children is higher than in parents. It is necessary to return to the normal distribution table and trial and error to find the location of the threshold to fit the observed incidence in children. From this is found the proportion of children of each genotype expected to manifest right- and left-handedness, as shown in Table 15.6.A.3. For the filial incidence of .0477 found in Chamberlain's sample, the thresholds must be at $-.7$ and -2.6 of the $rs--$ and $rs+-$, $++$ distributions, respectively. About 24% of the $rs--$ and about .4% of the $rs+-$, $++$ are called left-handed. These values are then used to translate the genotype distributions of Table 15.6.A.2 into the expected proportions of right- and left-handers in each family type, as shown in Table 15.6.A.4. It was predicted that 7,225 children of $R \times R$ parents in Chamberlain's data, 316 would be left-handed, and 308 were recorded. Test by χ^2 over all three mating types found no significant difference between the predicted and observed distribution.

These calculations were repeated to fit the observed incidences of parental and filial handedness of all series available to me in 1977–78, as shown in Table 15.6B–G, which summarise the main values. The only statistically

TABLE 15.6
Predicting the Distribution of Left-Handedness in Families in 7 Series: Distance Between RS+ and RS− Means is 1.937z

A. Chamberlain

1. Parental genotype frequencies in right- and left-handers

Parent incidence	Threshold: SD from mean	Dextral proportion	Sinistral proportion	Popul. genotypes	Genotype frequencies Dextral	Sinistral
0.0356	RS++ −2.844	0.99777	0.00223	0.3242	0.3235	0.0007
	RS+− −2.844	0.99777	0.00223	0.4904	0.4893	0.0011
	RS−− −0.907	0.8178	0.1822	0.1854	0.1516	0.0338
						0.0356

2. Genotype distribution of offspring in family types

Mating	RS++	+−	−−
Right × Right	0.3470	0.4841	0.1688
Left × Right	0.0210	0.5827	0.3962
Left × Left	0.0013	0.0688	0.9299

3. Proportion of sinistrals in each genotype in the filial generation

Filial incidence	Threshold	Sinistral proportion
0.0477	RS++ −2.6455	0.00408
	RS+− −2.6455	0.00408
	RS−− −0.7085	0.2394

4. Predicting the numbers of left-handers in family types

Mating		No. children	Obs. No.	χ^2
Right × Right	0.00408 (1−0.1688)+0.2394 (0.1688)×	7225 = 316	308	0.2302
Left × Right	0.00408 (1−0.3962)+0.2394 (0.3962)×	464 = 45	53	1.3617
Left × Left	0.00408 (1−0.9299)+0.2394 (0.9299)×	25 = 6	7	0.3655
				1.9574
				2 df

TABLE 15.8 — continued

	Sinistral incidence	Threshold RS--	Sinistral prop. in genotypes		Mating	RS-- prop.	Total No. children	Exp. No. sinist.	Obs. No. sinist.	Chi square		Sum χ^2
			++,+-	--								
B. Annett												
Parents	0.0405	−0.822	0.0029	0.2056	R × R	0.1667	6875	673	669	0.0247		
Children	0.1063	−0.065	0.0226	0.4741	L × R	0.3916	596	119	125	0.3158	0.2066	
					L × L	0.9201	5	2	1			
												0.2313 1 df
C. Rife												
Parents	0.0524	−0.64	0.0050	0.2611	R × R	0.1617	1993	156	151	0.1670		
Children	0.0877	−0.235	0.0149	0.4071	L × R	0.3803	174	29	34	1.0400		
					L × L	0.8948	11	4	6	0.9628		
												2.1698 2 df
D. OU												
Parents	0.0547	−0.61	0.00544	0.2709	R × R	0.1608	1786	135	130	0.1800		
Children	0.0850	−0.261	0.01397	0.3970	L × R	0.3782	210	33	40	1.3228 ⎫	0.7837	
					L × L	0.8899	4	1	0	⎬		
												0.9637 1 df
E. OU (generous criterion)												
Parents	0.0547	−0.61	0.00544	0.2709	R × R	0.1608	657	229	229	0.0006		
Children	0.3640	+1.242	0.2436	0.8929	L × R	0.3782	92	45	43	0.0889 ⎫	0.0724	
					L × L	0.8899	1	1	1	⎬		
												0.0730 1 df
F. Ramaley												
Parents	0.0803	−0.3085	0.0124	0.3789	R × R	0.1510	953	131	116	1.6355		
Children	0.1566	+0.304	0.0513	0.6194	L × R	0.3544	170	43	55	3.3828		
					L × L	0.8320	7	4	6	1.4832		
												6.5016 2 df *p < .05 > .025*
G. Annett (generous criterion)												
Parents	0.2371	+0.74	0.1157	0.7704	R × R	0.1156	623	219	214	0.1322		
Children	0.3961	+1.351	0.2790	0.9117	L × R	0.2455	341	148	153	0.1613		
					L × L	0.5215	76	46	45	0.0353		
												0.3288 2 df

Note: From Annett (1978b).

significant difference between prediction and observation occurred for Ramaley's sample (at the 5% level). He reported more left-handers in L × R families and fewer in R × R families than expected, but the misfit was not gross. In all other series, the fits were good. These include the data of Rife (1940), Annett (1973a), and the OU sample (Annett, 1978a). The OU sample was analysed at two levels of criterion for the filial generation, either left-handed writing (Table 15.6D) or left preference for any 1 of 12 actions (Table 15.6E). A subset of the Hull data could be analysed at the more generous criterion for both parents and children (Table 15.6.G). This last analysis classified a large number of families as L × L (strictly non-right × non-right) and included 76 children classified in this mating type. The fit of observed to predicted numbers of children classified as non-right on this generous criterion was excellent (45 to 46, respectively).

Thus, the numbers of children of each handedness type, in families of 0, 1, or 2 left-handed parents, are predictable on a single allele interpretation of the RS theory, for several series that differ in the incidences of left-handedness recorded for the parents and for the children. They are also predictable within the *same* series when different thresholds are used to classify one or both generations. That the theory should be equally successful for incidences of 4 to 24% in parents and 11 to 40% in children seems most unlikely unless there are stable underlying distributions of the kind postulated.

Several variations of gene frequency and shift were tried on the various sets of data in 1977–78, but this could not be done systematically as I did not have a computer program at that time for the calculations. It was clear that an additive version of the model could be used equally successfully (as pointed out in Annett, 1978b), but the slightly simpler calculations of the dominant model were published. It was also discovered that small changes of gene frequency or shift would permit reasonable predictions to be made, but there were no clear grounds for changing the values derived from the dysphasia series as used in Table 15.6. The predictions of the model for handedness in twin pairs were given in Annett (1978b), and the effect of distinguishing sex of parents and offspring in the family calculations was described in Annett (1979). The effects of sex and twinning and data for new family series is considered in Chapter 16.

This chapter has demonstrated that it is possible to predict the distribution of left-handedness in families in *all* the sets of family data available in 1977. The predictions were based on the RS model, using estimates of parameters of the model derived from the entirely independent data of the dysphasia series. It is especially important to notice that the gene frequencies were not derived from the family data (as is usual in genetic calculations) but from the incidence of right-hemisphere speech. This concordance between two independent sets of data, when interpreted in the light of the RS model, gives powerful support to the model.

15.3.   SUMMARY

Increased incidences of left-handedness are found in the relatives of left-handers, and associations between relatives are stronger for females than males. Evidence that these associations have a genetic foundation comes from two main sources: first, comparison of adoptive and biological families (Carter-Saltzman, 1890) and, second, study of the families of two left-handed parents (L × L). Children in L × L families where neither parent is suspected of pathological sinistrality and children in families where the left-handed parents have close left-handed relatives show an absence of significant bias to the right hand. Children in L × L families where a parent is probably pathologically sinistral and in families where neither parent has a left-handed relative are significantly biased to the right hand. These comparisons show that within families where both parents use the left hand for writing, children are more often biased towards the right hand when the parent is more likely to be carrying a genetic bias to the right (even though not expressed in parental handedness). One of the striking findings for children and parents in L × L families is an *absence* of sex differences in hand preference and L–R skill.

A genetic model is proposed in which there is a single allele ($rs+$) at one locus, which induces RS; the alternative allele(s) at that locus are neutral or indifferent to laterality ($rs-$). It is assumed that $rs+$ is dominant in the sense that left-hemisphere speech is likely to be induced when the gene is present on one or both chromosomes. Right-hemisphere and bilateral speech in the general population is assumed to occur only in the $rs--$. The frequency of the $rs-$ gene can be inferred from the incidence of right-hemisphere speech (Section 14.4.1). The effectiveness of the gene, in the sense of the mean shift of the L–R distribution in the $rs-$ and $rs++$ genotypes, is taken to be as deduced in Section 14.4.2. Using these parameters of the model and deducing the threshold of left-handedness from the incidences observed in each generation and each sample it was possible to predict the numbers of left-handed children born to R × R, L × R and L × L parents in the samples described by Chamberlain (1928), Rife (1940), Annett (1973a), and Annett (1978a). The last two samples were examined for generous as well as strict criteria of sinistrality. The sample of Ramaley (1913) was the only one to depart significantly from expectations, and only at the 5% level of significance. A worked example of the genetic calculations is given in Appendix IV.

16

Variable Gene Expression with Sex and Twinning

16.1. THE HYPOTHESIS
OF VARIABLE EXPRESSION
OF THE *rs*+ GENE

Sex differences may have a genetic basis either in the sense that the genes concerned are carried on the sex chromosomes (such as for haemophilia and certain forms of colour blindness) or in the sense that the expression of autosomal genes differs between the sexes (such as for height, baldness, liability to diseases including pyloric stenosis—see Fig. 13.2 and Section 1.4). This chapter considers evidence for the hypothesis that sex differences in handedness (and by implication braineness) result from sex modification of the expression of the *rs*+ gene. The mechanisms producing the variability between the sexes are hypothesised to affect the expression of the *rs*+ gene in twins also.

Questions about sex differences for handedness are usually asked in terms of whether males are more likely to be left-handed. Table 4.4 shows that there are small but consistent trends in this direction. Figure 11.3 shows, however, that for L–R skill there is a clear sex difference in that the female distribution is more strongly biased to the right hand than the male distribution. It is of the greatest importance to notice that the sex difference is clear at the dextral side of the distribution but *absent at the sinistral side*. There are no sex differences in the L–R times of those with biases to the left hand. It is seen in Table 15.3 that control left-handers, left-handed parents, and the children of L × L families do not differ between the sexes for L–R time. Table 16.1 gives the L–R means of males and females in the combined main samples

TABLE 16.1

Sex Differences in L–R Peg-Moving Time for Subjects Grouped in Preference Classes (1/10 s)

Hand Preference Class	Males			Females			t
	N	Mean	SD	N	Mean	SD	
1	399	8.3	7.0	530	10.4	7.4	4.287**
2	40	8.2	7.0	110	9.3	8.1	0.715
3	47	6.9	6.3	60	7.0	7.3	0.172
4	60	3.0	8.0	50	4.7	6.5	1.179
5	25	4.2	11.7	38	4.2	7.7	0.024
6	15	-4.9	7.1	26	-3.0	7.2	
7	15	-9.1	8.3	18	-4.8	6.9	0.255
8	16	-5.3	8.1	31	-9.4	6.3	
Total	617	6.4	8.4	863	8.0	8.8	3.395**
Birthday samples	122	7.1	13.1	156	12.0	12.7	3.148*

Note: Annett and Kilshaw (1983).
* $p < .002$.
** $p < .001$.

(Appendix I) when subjects are classified for hand preference in the ten preference classes (Table 11.3). The combined sample and the birthday sample show highly significant sex differences over-all, but when analysed by preference class, significant differences were found only for class 1 (consistent right-handers). There are nonsignificant trends to greater dextrality in females than males in classes 2 to 4.

All of these observations point to the hypothesis that sex differences for handedness occur in those likely to carry the rs+ gene but are absent in those of rs− genotype. That is, sex differences are a function of the gene but are absent in those of rs− genotype. That is, sex differences are a function of the gene when it is present but absent when the gene is absent. The absence of sex difference is not just a function of left-handedness; the children of L × L parents included more right- than left-handers but still showed a lack of sex differences. On the RS theory, the right-handedness of many of these children depended on chance in those of rs− genotype.

The possibility that sex differences in handedness are due to stronger expression of the right shift gene in females was suggested by Annett (1973a), and the implications for handedness in families were examined by Annett (1979). If the rs+ gene is more effective in females than in males, the proportion of left-handers carrying the gene will be smaller in females than males. This would imply that left-handed mothers would be a little more likely to have left-handed children than left-handed fathers. With regard to the L–R distributions, the means would be the same for $rs--$ genotypes of both sexes but further to the right for females than for males who carry the gene. The estimates of shift in each sex used in the genetic calculations (Annett, 1979) were guesses based on the common mean of $1.9z$ ($1.6z$ for males and $2.2z$ for females). Improved estimates of shift for each sex will be derived below and used to re-examine all available family data, taking sex into account.

The idea that twins differ from the singleborn in having a smaller shift to the right was prompted by the discovery that the distribution of handedness in twin pairs can be predicted keeping all values of the model the same as used in the genetic calculations in Chapter 15, except that the mean shift must be reduced (Annett, 1978b). If the mean shift were taken to be $1.0z$ instead of the $1.9z$ used above, the predicted distributions of handedness in pairs of twins were in close accord with those observed in the very large data compiled by Zazzo (1960) ($\chi^2 = .0045$ for 1210 MZ twin pairs and $\chi^2 = .1049$ for 1145 DZ twin pairs, $df=1$ for both calculations). It is worth noting that the same reduction of shift was required for both MZ and DZ pairs, suggesting that the reduction is a function of twinning and independent of zygosity.

When it was first discovered that the shift for twins must be smaller than for the singleborn, it seemed an unwelcome complication of the model. It has been suggested that as the RS model cannot account for handedness in twins without a change in the parameters used for singletons, the model is put in doubt (Boklage, 1981; McManus, 1980a). There are reasons for believing, however, that this change in parameters is consistent with other facts about twins.

First, the $rs+$ gene is hypothesised to facilitate *language* development. One of the best-established findings of twin research is that twins may be slow to talk and suffer delays in the growth of other language skills (Mittler, 1971). The widely proffered explanation that twins do not need to talk because they develop special methods of communication with their co-twin may be true but only part of the story. Perhaps twins develop special methods of communication *because* the development of speech is delayed. On the RS theory, the observation that twins are slower to talk than the singleborn and that males are slower to talk than females would have a single consistent explanation in terms of the relative expression of the $rs+$ gene.

A second characteristic that varies with sex and twinning is relative maturity in the neonatal period. Singleborn females tend to be more mature than singleborn males at birth and up to adolescence. The rate of growth of twins is slowed in later fetal life, in order to accommodate two fetuses in the womb (Tanner, 1978). This physical constraint applies to both MZ and DZ twins; as noted above, the same level of reduction of shift is needed to account for the distribution of handedness in both types of twin pair. The mechanism of operation of the $rs+$ gene is unknown, but it may depend on the relative rates of maturation of the right and left cerebral hemispheres. If development were slower (in twins or in males), differences between the hemispheres might be reduced. Chi, Dooling, and Gilles (1977) found, in a study of fetal brain growth, that twins were delayed by two or three weeks in the appearance of cerebral convolutions in comparison with nontwins. No differences were observed in this study between the sexes. However, the difference expected between the sexes in expression of the $rs+$ gene is smaller than the difference expected between twins and the singleborn, and would be correspondingly more difficult to detect (Table 16.11A).

Weaker expression of the $rs+$ gene in twins implies that incidences of left-handedness should be a little higher in twins than the singleborn. As discussed in Chapter 3, evidence for this possibility was unclear, since twin studies have not assessed controls for handedness, using the same procedures and criteria as for the twins. As shown in Fig. 10.1, my handedness questionnaire began with an enquiry about twin birth so that twins could be excluded from genetic calculations, in case twinning should prove to be a relevant variable. A count of the excluded twins in the late 1960s (unpublished) found 13.6% left-handed writers in 103 twins, in contrast to 11.0% in 2,196 singleborn. The difference was not statistically significant and for many years I believed that the supposed excess of left-handers in twins had probably been exaggerated. However, the expectation of the RS theory that the incidence of left-handedness should be a little higher in twins led me to look for more evidence. Table 16.2 gives the incidences of Rife (1940, 1950) for singleborn students and for twins who were assessed by the same criteria.

TABLE 16.2
Twins and Non-Twins Compared for Incidences of Left-Handedness

	Non-Twin		Twin			
	N	%L	N	%L	χ^2	1 df
Rife (1940, 1950)						
Both sexes	2178	8.77	MZ 686	12.83	10.56*	
			DZ 422	11.61		
Annett (1973a)						
Males	2151	11.76	50	14.00	0.50	
Females	1493	11.45	35	14.29		
Fathers	1040	4.52	20	10.00	7.06*	
Mothers	1040	3.56	32	12.50		

*$p > .01$.

(The bulk of Rife's twin data was described in the 1940 paper, along with that of the singleborn, but additional pairs were included in the 1950 paper.) Rife was able to assess zygosity. Table 16.2 also gives my findings for question-naires in the Hull samples (Appendix I), where students, recruits, and parents made personal returns (that is, reports of relatives' handedness are not included). Zygosity information was not sought in the questionnaire and is not important if, as said above, the reduction of shift is a function of the slowing of fetal growth experienced by twins of both types. For all six sets of twins in Table 16.2, incidences are higher than for the corresponding samples of singletons. The difference for students continues to be statistically insignificant, but the differences for parents and for Rife's samples are highly significant. Further data on the handedness of twins and singletons, collected as part of a large population survey of hearing difficulties, has found incidences of left-handedness higher in twins in all of 6 comparisons of males and of females in three age bands (Davis—personal communication). Together with the 6 sets of twins in Table 16.2, this new data gives 12 comparisons, in all of which the incidence is higher in twins than in the singleborn ($p < .001$ on binomial test). It seems clear that twins are more likely to be left-handed than the singleborn, as required to fit the RS model.

It may be concluded that twinning and sex are associated with differences in neonatal maturity, in rate of language acquisition, and in incidences of right-handedness. All of these differences are consistently in the direction expected if the expression of the $rs+$ gene is correlated with neonatal maturity; that is, greater in females than males and greater in the singleborn than in twins. The postulate that twins have a reduced right shift now seems an essential part of the RS theory and not at all "ad hoc".

16.2. THE EXTENTS OF RIGHT SHIFT IN NORMAL MALES AND FEMALES

16.2.1. The Distributions of L–R Peg-Moving Times of Males and Females in Normal Samples

The observation that differences between the hands in skill are distributed in an approximately normal fashion led to the right-shift theory. The analyses in Chapters 14 and 15 have depended on the assumption that the total distribution is *not* a single normal curve, but rather that it is made up of subdistributions, as represented in Fig. 14.1. It is now proposed to ask whether real L–R times, as measured by peg-moving in normal samples, are consistent with the assumptions in Fig. 14.1, and whether this real data can be used to deduce the relative extents of shift of males and females. Two possible modifications of Fig. 14.1 must be explored. First, would an additive version of the genetic model (in which the right shift of the $rs++$ genotype is greater than that of the $rs+-$ genotype) be more appropriate than the dominant model (which assumes the same shift for both of these genotypes, as in Fig. 14.1). Second, is the shift to the right greater in males than females.

Figure 16.1 illustrates a possible distribution for the total population if the $rs+$ gene were fully additive, which would imply that the $rs++$ are shifted twice as far to the right as the $rs+-$. The proportions of each genotype are as deduced in Section 15.2. No attempt has been made to represent the effect of sex differences, as this would complicate the diagram, but the reader is asked to imagine that for females the $rs+-$ distribution is a little further to the right than that of males; the female $rs++$ distribution should then be twice as far to the right as the female $rs+-$ distribution, making the sex difference greater for the $rs++$ than for the $rs+-$. Starting from these imagined distributions, it is now asked whether the real L–R data can give substance to them.

To make inferences about L–R distributions in the general population, samples should be drawn from the population without bias as to handedness. Unfortunately, no opportunity arose to collect such an ideal sample, but data has been collected on the peg-moving times of school-children drawn from their classes according to birth date, and of whole class groups of students and school-children. These several samples (Appendix I) cannot necessarily be regarded as representative of the general population, especially as the majority of subjects were students (see Section 19.2), but they offer the best data available. Annett and Kilshaw (1983) compared the several samples for consistency and combined them as far as possible to give large samples with which to examine the L–R distribution. More is said about this analysis of samples for the effects of age and for actual hand skill (Kilshaw & Annett, 1983) in Chapter 17. In the analysis for L–R skill, all subjects in complete samples aged 6 years or older who were observed for hand preference and measured for peg-moving time by each hand were included. The samples are described in Appendix 1, 9 and 10 and notes on methods of assessment are given in Appendix II.

Table 16.3 describes the samples for hand preference, and Table 16.4 describes them for L–R peg-moving time. Open University students who reported having been forced to write with the right hand are here counted as left-handers (whereas in Table 16.1 the analysis was based on actual hand used for writing). Methods of assessment of hand preference differed between the main samples and birthday samples (Appendix 2), and there were differences between the main and birthday samples for aspects of L–R time. The birthday samples were more variable and females more shifted to the right than in the main samples. These differences require that the two groups of samples be analysed separately, and close comparisons are inappropriate. It is useful, however, to refer to the birthday sample findings as checks on

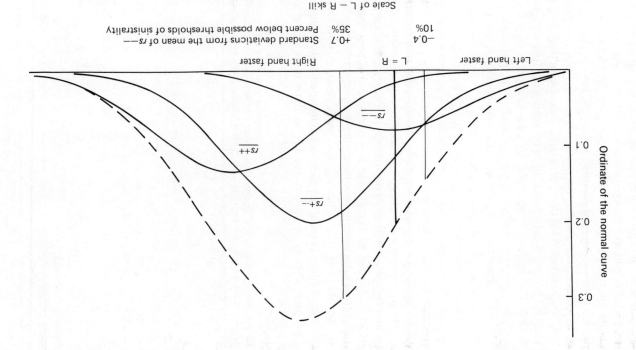

Ordinate of the normal curve

| 0.1 | 0.2 | 0.3 |

Left hand faster   L = R   Right hand faster

Right hand faster   L = R   Left hand faster

| —0.4 | +0.7 | Standard deviations from the mean of *rs*— |
| 10% | 35% | Percent below possible thresholds of sinistrality |

Scale of L — R skill

FIG. 16.1.   Distributions of L–R skill assumed for the additive version of the right shift model.
Annett & Kilshaw, 1982.

307

LRHB-K

TABLE 16.3

Hand Preference: Percentages of Males and Females in Three Preference Groups in Each Sample

Hand preference	Males					Females			
	Class N	Left writing 6-8	Right mixed 2-5	Right consistent 1	N	Left writing 6-8	Right mixed 2-5	Right consistent 1	N
Main Samples									
LS	79	6.3	30.4	63.3	86	7.0	29.1	63.9	
HL	140	13.6	28.6	57.8	213	10.3	23.5	66.2	
OU	398	6.5	26.4	67.1	406	10.3	29.8	59.9	
DA					158	8.9	34.2	56.9	
Total	617	8.1	27.4	64.5	863	9.7	29.0	61.3	
Birthday Samples	122	20.5	20.5	59.0	156	11.5	18.6	69.9	

Note: LS = comprehensive school children, about 12 years; HL = University and polytechnic students; OU = Open University students; DA = sixth form schoolgirls, 16–18 years; Birthday samples = schoolchildren 6–15 years. See Appendix I.B.9 and 10 for further details.

some features of the main samples. The five samples of females were fairly consistent for hand preferences, incidences of left-handed writing (drawing for the birthday samples) ranging between 7.0 and 11.5%. The four samples of males were more variable for left-handedness, ranging between 6.3 and 20.5%, but they were more similar for percentages of consistent right-handers. The very high incidence of left-handed males in the birthday sample is probably due to inadequacies of sampling (Kilshaw & Annett, 1983).

With regard to L–R time (Table 16.4), the main sample females were remarkably consistent, but the main sample males were relatively inconsistent. The H.L. males were less dextral than others in L–R mean, and they included 30% biased to the left hand in skill. The OU males were more dextral in L–R skill; as shown in Table 16.3, they included relatively few left-handers (6.5%); this was especially surprising as OU females included 10.3% left-handers. However, the L–R mean of male OU students was smaller than that of OU females, in keeping with the hypothesis that the $rs+$ gene is expressed more strongly in females than in males. Inspection of the L–R means shows that the female means were larger than the corresponding male means in every case, and there was no overlap between the range of male means (4.0–7.2) and the range of female means (7.6–12.0).

The question whether the L–R distribution could be adequately represented by a single normal curve can be answered with a definite negative for both sexes. All four totals show a significant kurtosis—that is, they are more peaked than expected of a true normal curve. Three of the four totals show a

TABLE 16.4

Hand Skill: L–R Peg-Moving Time for Each Sample and Sex (1/10s)

Main Samples	Males						Females					
	N	L–R < 0 (%)	Mean	SD	Skew	Kurtosis	N	L–R < 0 (%)	Mean	SD	Skew	Kurtosis
LS	79	15.2	6.8	10.8	−1.16**	5.69**	96	15.1	7.8	9.4	−0.14	3.38
HL	140	29.6	4.0	7.2	−0.50	3.16	213	14.5	7.6	8.5	−0.46**	3.72*
OU	398	13.1	7.2	8.1	−0.26*	4.55**	406	13.8	7.9	8.8	−0.23*	3.19
DA							158	11.4	8.7	8.7	−0.40*	4.06*
Total	617	15.6	6.4	8.4	−0.49**	4.97**	863	13.7	7.9	8.8	−0.30**	4.49**
Birthday samples	122	24.6	7.1	13.1	−0.06	3.98*	156	14.1	12.0	12.7	−0.76**	5.28**

Note: Annett and Kilshaw (1983).
*indicates $p < .05$, ** indicates $p < .01$.

significant negative skew—that is, the left-hand tail of the distribution extends further than the right-hand tail. These features are evident in Fig. 11.3, which represents the combined main samples. Can the observed distributions be shown to be compatible with the sum of two or three normal subdistributions, as represented in Figures 14.1 or 16.1?

To attempt to answer this question, a computer program was written that would predict the shape of the total distribution as the sum of three normal curves. The program asked for the values of the proportions, means, and standard deviations to be used for each subdistribution on each trial. It plotted a graph of the actual data and then superimposed a graph of the predicted curve, so that the adequacy of fit was visible, as well as being calculated statistically, as shown in Figure 16.2A and B for the main sample males and females, respectively. The Kolmogorov–Smirnov (K–S) statistic depends on the largest difference between the observed and predicted distributions to be found at any point measured, in the cumulative proportion of cases. As there were more than 80 data points (L–R times in 1/10 s) and large Ns for each sex in the combined main samples, the test was believed to be highly sensitive to differences between the observed and predicted distributions.

Before testing the distributions for compatibility with those of the RS model, the K–S program was used to confirm that they were not compatible with (1) a single normal curve and (2) the sum of two distributions representing right-handers and left-handers, when the proportion of left-handers is taken to be 8.2%, as observed in Table 16.1 for the main samples, not distinguishing for sex. Table 16.5.A.1 shows that the hypothesis of a single normal curve could be rejected at the 5% level of confidence for males and the 20% level of confidence for females. The right-handers plus left-handers hypothesis could be rejected at the 1% level of confidence for both sexes, as shown in Table 16.5.A.2.

The main question being asked in the K–S analyses is whether the empirical L–R data are compatible with the assumptions of the model, as derived from data for dysphasics in Chapter 14 and applied successfully to the problem of handedness in families in Chapter 15. Of course, the data could be compatible with a large number of possible models. Since the main purpose was to ask whether the observed distributions were consistent with the assumptions used in the prior analyses of Chapters 14 and 15, the values of proportions and $rs--$ mean used there were retained as constants on every trial. These were as follows:

1. The proportions of the three distributions are as deduced for the genotype frequencies: $rs--=.1854$, $rs+-=.4902$, $rs++=.3242$. (For the dominant version of the model, the same means and standard deviations were used, of course, for $rs+-$ and $rs++$.)

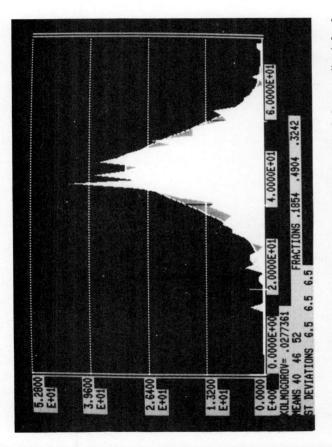

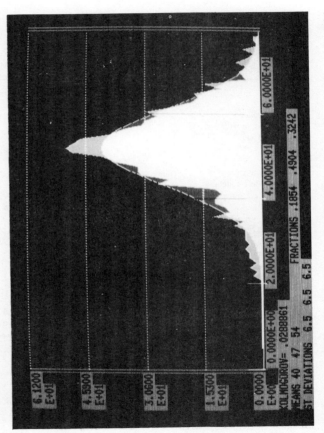

FIG. 16.2. Computer graphic displays: L–R times observed, and those predicted for 3 subdistributions with values of parameters taken from Table 16.5.A.4. Males (top) and females (bottom) in combined samples (Appendix IB10). *Notes:* Kolmogorov = D statistic L-R = 0 set at 40 to avoid negative scores.

TABLE 16.5

Kolmogorov–Smirnov Tests of the L–R Distributions: *D* Values for Tests of Several Hypotheses and the Derived Means, Standard Deviations and *z* Values: (*z* for the *rs* + − Genotype of the Additive Model and for the *rs* + −, *rs* + + Genotypes of the Dominant Model)

		Males						Females				
A. Main Samples		$N = 617$				*D*		$N = 863$				*D*
1. 1 distribution with mean and SD observed						0.0557**						0.0404*
2. 2 distributions: right and left writers						0.0701***						0.0608***
3. 2 distributions:		Means		SD	*z*			Means		SD	*z*	
dominant version of	*rs* − −	*rs* + −	*rs* + +				*rs* − −	*rs* + −	*rs* + +			
RS theory (see text)	0	8	8	6.5	1.23	0.0257	0	10	10	7.0	1.43	0.0247
4. 3 distributions: additive version of RS theory	0	6	12	6.5	0.92	0.0277	0	7	14	6.5	1.08	0.0289
B. Birthday Samples		$N = 122$						$N = 156$				
as 3. above	0	8.5	8.5	11.0	0.77	0.0341	0	15	15	9.0	1.67	0.0435
as 4. above	0	6.5	13	11.0	0.59	0.0339	0	11	22	7.0	1.57	0.0473

Values of $D = .20$
for hypothesis rejection: Rejection levels
N 122   .0969   *$p < .20$
    156   .0857   **$p < .05$
    617   .0431   ***$p < .01$
    863   .0364

Note: Revised from Annett and Kilshaw (1983).

2. All three distributions have the same standard deviation.

3. The mean of $rs-- = 0$.

4. The means of $rs+-$ and $rs++$ are either the same—as required for full dominance—or $rs++ = 2(rs+-)$—as required for full additivity effect of the $rs+$ gene.

Some of these assumptions may be shown, in future research, to have been unduly restrictive. Perhaps the estimates of genotype frequency will be improved. Perhaps the $rs+$ gene is of intermediate dominance. The genotypes may differ in standard deviation; it has been discovered that better fits can be obtained if the standard deviation of $rs--$ genotypes is allowed to be a little larger than for other genotypes, but as there was no clear prior theoretical justification for this difference in variance, it has not been used in the following calculations.

If the empirical L–R data should be demonstrated to be compatible with the model as used in Chapters 14 and 15, a second purpose of the K–S analysis was to estimate the means and standard deviations of the $rs+-$ and $rs++$ sub-distributions in males and females separately. The procedure adopted was to vary, first, the mean and, second, the standard deviation, to find the smallest D value for each sex and sample. This procedure was used for both the dominant and additive versions of the model. Table 16.5 gives the means, standard deviations, and the D values obtained. The value of D that could be rejected at the 20% level of confidence is given for each N. In all cases, the obtained D values are well within the limits required for this test. There are some important points that can be made about the values of means and standard deviations given in Table 16.5:

1. The observed distributions of L–R times are compatible with those predicted as the sum of 2 or 3 normal subdistributions, as represented in Figs. 14.1 or 16.1. That is, they are compatible with the assumptions of the RS theory as developed above.

2. The D values obtained for the dominant and additive versions of the model are similar, and there are no clear grounds here for preferring one version more than the other.

3. The means derived for males are similar for the main and birthday samples.

4. The means derived for females are shifted further to the right than those of males in all cases. This was expected, of course, in the light of the sex differences in sample means discussed earlier. The means for main sample females were only a little further to the right than those of males, but for birthday-sample females the mean was considerably further to the right than that of males. Apart from the birthday sample females, all the derived means can be regarded as highly consistent.

5. The standard deviations in all combined sample analyses were in the

range between 6.5 and 7.0. Larger SDs occurred in three of the four birthdays sample analyses.

6. The means of $rs+-$ are expressed for the combined main samples as a proportion of the standard deviation, to give an estimate of the extent of shift. (For the dominant model this value applies to the $rs++$ genotype also.) The estimates for the dominant model this value applies to the $rs++$ genotype females, respectively, are smaller than the $1.9z$ used in the genetic calculations in Chapter 15. On the additive model, the estimates are about $.9z$ for males and $1.1z$ for females for $rs+-$, and twice these values for the $rs++$ genotypes. (The corresponding estimates for the birthday samples range from $.6z$ to $1.7z$; these estimates are of less value than those of the combined samples, in view of the smaller Ns and more variable SDs.)

It may be concluded from these analyses of observed L–R times in normal samples that the distributions could be a product of two or three normal subdistributions, in the proportions representing the genotypes (in Chapter 15), and with an $rs--$ mean at 0. An unexpected feature of the analysis was that the extent of shift was smaller than that estimated from data for dysphasics on the dominant version of the model. The question whether the extents of shift found here can predict the distribution of handedness in families as efficiently, or more efficiently, than the values used above, is examined in Section 16.3. First, another important clue as to the relative extents of shift in males and females must be presented (Section 16.2.2).

McManus (1985) has criticised the above approach on the grounds that inappropriate algorithms were used to deduce the parameters of the model. Using algorithmic procedures, the best description of the L–R data was found to be in terms of two subdistributions, a major one with mean to the right of 0 and a minor one with mean to the left of 0. Among several reasons for rejecting McManus's approach (Annett, 1985) perhaps the most important is that algorithmic solutions could be searched for only if we had a perfect model and perfect data. Neither of these is being claimed. The procedure adopted here (Chapter 13 onwards) is heuristic. An example of the benefits of this approach is to be seen at this point in the analysis. Measures of right shift derived in Table 16.5 differ from those derived previously (as shown in Table 14.8). In testing the application of these new measures to family handedness data, an even more promising lead as to relative shifts of males and females was discovered, as explained in Section 16.2.2.

16.2.2. The Threshold Required to Represent the Incidences of Left-Handedness in Paired Samples of Males and Females

When handedness is assessed by the same methods in males and females drawn at random from the same population, the incidence of left-handedness is expected to be slightly smaller in females than males, due to the stronger expression of the $rs+$ gene in females. If the relative extents of shift were known for the sexes and differences between the sexes were due only to the differing extents of shift, then thresholds calculated from the incidences of males and females in paired samples should match. If values of the parameters of the model giving matching thresholds for incidences of males and females drawn from the same sample could be found, confidence in these values would be increased. It would not be expected that thresholds would match in every case, as there are many sources of error in the assessments of incidence of any one sample. Some of the major sources of doubt about the majority of published samples are, first, that they depend on students who are not necessarily representative of the general population for handedness, and, second, that assessments of handedness of relatives usually depend on the students' report, not on self-report. Although it seemed desirable to find matching thresholds, there seemed insufficient good evidence available to make this a strong requirement of the model. When values of shift that did give matching thresholds for males and females were discovered in a large sample not subject to the above limitations, they were given careful attention.

Ashton (1982) published the findings of the Hawaii Family Study of Cognition (HFSC) for handedness in families. This very large sample was drawn from several ethnic groups in Hawaii. It does not depend on students, and all parents and children answered the two questionnaire items on handedness personally. These questions were:

1. What hand do you write with? (right, left)
2. Which hand do you use most? (right, left, use equally)

The data were analysed for the strict criterion of left-handed writing and also for the more generous criterion of left+use equally, for both generations. (Differences due to ethnic origin, considered in Section 4.2, do not affect the present analyses, as the sex groups must have been fairly well matched for ethnic composition.)

Table 16.6 gives the incidences of left-handed writing and of left-hand use in both sexes for both generations, with the thresholds corresponding to these incidences, if the means of the three genotype distributions (as of Figure 16.1) are at $.0z$, $1.0z$, $2.0z$ for males and at $.0z$, $1.2z$ and $2.4z$ for females, respectively. The matching thresholds for males and females were noticed, then values of shift close to those deduced in Table 16.5 were being tested for their ability to predict the family distributions (described in Section 16.3). In three out of four comparisons, matching thresholds were found between corresponding samples of males and females. The exception occurred for writing hand of parents, where there were slightly more left-handed mothers than fathers, contrary to the usual trend.

Having found these identical thresholds between the sexes in Ashton's sample, all the major samples in the literature and some new ones of my own

TABLE 16.6

Incidences of Left-Handedness and the Thresholds Required to Represent Them in Matched Samples of Males and Females, for the Additive Version of the RS Model When the Means are 0, 1.0, 2.0 for Males and 0, 1.2, 2.4 for Females, for the $rs--$, $rs+-$ and $rs++$ Genotypes, Respectively

Sample*	Criterion	Males			Females		
		N	Incidence	Threshold	N	Incidence	Threshold
Parents (Table 1)	left-hand writing	1813	5.29	−.84	1812	5.46	−.74
Parents (Table 1)	use of left hand	1813	8.93	−.51	1812	7.73	−.51
Children (Table 2)	left-hand writing	1435	11.57	−.33	1491	9.93	−.33
Children (Table 3)	left plus ambidextrous	1435	16.65	−.04	1491	14.29	−.04

Note: Data from Ashton (1982).
*Table numbers refer to Ashton.

were examined for the comparability of the thresholds in pairs of samples of males and females, for the same levels of shift as used in Table 16.6. The findings are shown in Fig. 16.3. The axes gives the thresholds and the incidences to which they correspond for each sex. The letters indicate the samples from which the matched sets of males and females were drawn. Where two data points are indicated, the higher represents the filial generation and the lower incidence the parental generation. For the Hull, OU, and Lanchester samples there are more than two data points, because the samples were examined for more than one level of criterion or because there were more than two generations. These details are not important for the present purpose, which is to show the close association between the thresholds representing male and female incidences for corresponding samples ($r = .973 + .14$; the intercept of the regression line is −.01). There are several points that fall on the diagonal line, which represents matching thresholds, and about as many above as below the line, as expected if mismatches depend on random errors in the determination of incidences. For the lowest incidences, however, there is a cluster of points below the line. These are for the parents in Chamberlain's (1928) sample, the parents in the Annett (1973) sample, and for the grandparents of Lanchester students, whose handedness was reported in questionnaires completed by the parents (Appendix I.B.6.d). The location of this cluster suggests that the handedness of mothers may have been underestimated in comparison with that of fathers when assessment depended on indirect report and the level of ascertainment was low (see Section 10.1).

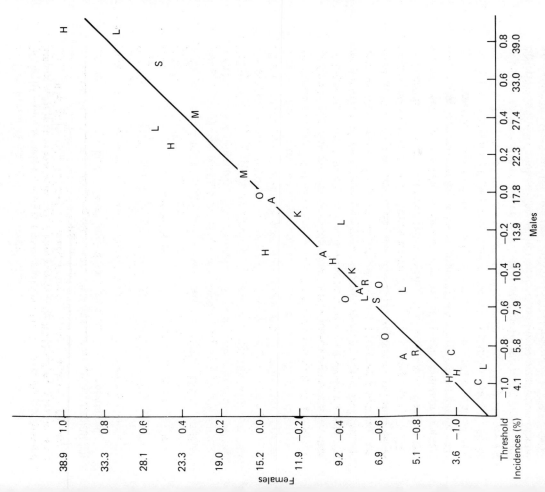

FIG. 16.3. Incidences of left-handedness at corresponding thresholds for paired samples of males and females if the means of the L–R distributions for the rs− −, rs+ − and rs+ + genotypes are 0.0, 1.0z, 2.0z for males and 0.0, 1.2z and 2.4z for females respectively. A = Ashton, 1982; C = Chamberlain, 1928; H = Hull (Annett, 1973a, 1978a); K = Speigler & Yeni-Komishan (1983); L = Lanchester (Appendix I B6d); M = McGee & Cozad (1980); O = Open University (Annett, 1979); R = Rife, 1940; S = Carter-Saltzman (1980, all parents at two levels of criterion).

The threshold required to represent incidences in corresponding samples of males and females can be discovered for the shifts deduced for the dominant model ($1.23z$ for males and $1.43z$ for females in Table 16.5). The agreement between the thresholds of paired samples of males and females is good for these values also ($r = .971 + .13$). Once again, there is no ground for selection between the dominant and the additive versions of the model.

16.3. PREDICTING HANDEDNESS IN FAMILIES, TAKING SEX INTO ACCOUNT

This section examines the genetic predictions for handedness in families, using the estimates of shift discovered in Section 16.2, for males and females. If there are sex differences in the family data (between left-handed fathers and left-handed mothers, or between sons and daughters within family types), can these differences be accounted for on the hypothesis of more effective expression of the $rs+$ gene in females? Are there any grounds for choosing between the dominant and additive versions of the model, in the prediction of family distributions?

The calculations required to predict the handedness of children in families, when sex is taken into account in both generations and when the additive version of the model is used, are similar to those used in Section 15.2, but the genotype distributions of males and females must be distinguished, and the predictions differ between $L \times R$ and $R \times L$ (father $\times$ mother) families. A worked example is given in Appendix V.

There is a further difference between the calculations to be used in this section and those used above. The numbers of left-handed children expected in each family type can be deduced either (1) as a proportion within each family type, or (2) as a proportion of genotypes over the population as a whole (Section 15.2). The first method was used above, and the second will be used here. The first method asks, for example, what proportion of sons are expected to be left-handed in $L \times R$ families, given the number of sons observed in $L \times R$ families. The second method asks what proportion of sons are expected to report that they are left-handed *and* belong to $L \times R$ families, in the context of the sample as a whole. The two methods should give equally good predictions if families are drawn at random from the population, but if there are distortions in the representation of certain family types or if there are inaccuracies in the ascertainment of parental handedness, there could be advantages in using one or other method of calculation. The fit between predicted and observed family data can be improved by assuming that parental incidences of left-handedness are slightly misrepresented when the data depends on indirect report, rather than self-report, as will be demonstrated later.

Table 16.7 summarises the predicted and observed numbers of left-handers in the four family types, including all studies considered in Table 15.6 and more recent ones (Ashton, 1982; McGee & Cozad, 1980; Spiegler & Yeni-Komshian, 1983; a new sample of Polytechnic students and their parents, described in Appendix I.B.6.d). Table 16.7A lists studies in which ascertainment of handedness was by self-report in both generations, and Table 16.7B lists studies relying on mixed report, self-report in the filial generation, and filial report of parental handedness. The only study not relying on students (Ashton, 1982) is given first. The studies are also ordered for the incidence of left-handedness in fathers, from high to low (with the exception that where the same study is analysed at two levels of incidence, the two analyses are adjacent). Chi squares comparing the observed and predicted numbers are summed over the four family types for each sex separately. (Three degrees of freedom are assumed, as the gene frequencies are not deduced from the family data but from independent evidence. When $df=3$, for $p=.05$, $\chi^2=7.81$ and for $p=.01$, $\chi^2=11.34$.)

There are several points to be made about the findings in Table 16.7.

1. There is excellent agreement between the observed and predicted numbers for both sexes in all samples that use self-report in both generations. The agreement is equally good when the samples are drawn from nonstudent and student populations. In the three samples that could be analysed at two levels of criterion, agreement is good at both levels.

2. In samples relying on mixed report, there are good fits for males, except for the two samples with the lowest incidences of parental sinistrality (Annett, 1973a; Chamberlain, 1928).

3. For females, in samples relying on mixed report, the majority (6 out of 8) gave significant chi squares. In 7 of these 8 samples, more left-handed daughters were reported in R × L than L × R families, whereas this pattern was predicted only once.

The samples listed in Table 16.7 were also tested against the dominant version of the model, using the shifts $1.23z$ for males and $1.43z$ for females. Table 16.8 gives the chi square values obtained, together with the corresponding chi squares found for the additive model, as listed in Table 16.7. The findings are substantially similar for both versions of the model. There are good fits for both sexes when information depends on self-report in both generations, good fits for males on mixed report except when parental incidences are low, and poor fits for females on mixed report in most samples. Summing the chi squares finds slightly higher totals for the dominant than for the additive version of the model in all four comparisons, but there are no strong grounds for rejecting either version of the model.

If there are excellent fits between the predictions of the RS model for many

TABLE 16.7
Predicted and Observed Numbers of Left-Handers in Family Types

Source	Criterion	Incidences of Left-Handedness in Total Sample	Family types (Father × Mother)	Sons No. left-handers			Daughters No. left-handers		
				Exp.	Obs.	Sum χ^2	Exp.	Obs.	Sum χ^2
A. Self-report by all individuals									
Non-student				Total $N=1435$			Total $N=1491$		
1. Ashton	use of left	fathers	8.97	R × R	185	191		161	161
(1982)	hand	mothers	7.64	L × R	28	27		26	21
		sons	16.65	R × L	25	17		23	29
		daughters	14.35	L × L	4	4		4	3
						2.85			2.58
2. Ashton	left-hand	fathers	5.26	R × R	138	143		122	123
(1982)	writing	mothers	5.37	L × R	13	10		12	10
		sons	11.57	R × L	14	12		13	14
		daughters	9.93	L × L	1	1		1	1
						0.96			0.50
Student				Total $N=357$			Total $N=390$		
3. Annett:	any 1/12	fathers	25.23	R × R	65	68		52	61
Lanchester	actions	mothers	26.17	L × R	30	28		26	22
(new data)	left-handed	sons	39.50	R × L	32	30		28	22
		daughters	30.51	L × L	14	15		13	14
						0.51			3.78

4. Lanchester (new data)	left-hand writing	fathers	9.03	R × R	42	50		26	26	
		mothers	5.61	L × R	7	2		5	6	
		sons	14.85	R × L	4	7		3	2	
		daughters	8.72	L × L	1	1		0	0	
							6.95			1.23
					Total $N = 597$			Total $N = 443$		
5. Annett (1978a): Hull subgroup	any 1/12 actions left-handed	fathers	22.88	R × R	116	127		85	87	
		mothers	24.52	L × R	47	35		36	29	
		sons	39.53	R × L	53	49		40	40	
		daughters	39.73	L × R	20	25		16	20	
							5.64			2.56
6. Hull subgroup	left-hand writing	fathers	4.52	R × R	63	62		57	59	
		mothers	3.56	L × R	5	6		5	3	
		sons	12.06	R × L	4	4		4	3	
		daughters	14.67	L × L	0	0		0	0	
							0.55			1.05
					Total $N = 737$			Total $N = 849$		
7. McGee and Cozad (1980)	any 1/10 actions left-handed	fathers	19.64	R × R	115	112		99	99	
		mothers	16.72	L × R	41	39		38	38	
		sons	27.27	R × L	35	38		33	35	
		daughters	21.44	L × L	12	12		12	10	
							0.39			0.50

See *Note* page 323.

TABLE 16.7—*continued*

Source	Criterion	Incidences of Left-Handedness in Total Sample	Family types (Father × Mother)	Sons No. left-handers			Daughters No. left-handers		
				Exp.	Obs.	Sum χ²	Exp.	Obs.	Sum χ²

B. Mixed report (usually self-report for students and student's report of parents and siblings)

Student

Source	Criterion	Incidences	Family types	Exp.	Obs.	Sum χ²	Exp.	Obs.	Sum χ²
				Total N=3196			Total N=3413		
1. Spiegler and	left or either	fathers 10.19	R × R	361	372		299	330	
Yeni-Komshian	hand for	mothers 8.20	L × R	64	58		57	37	
(1983)	writing	sons 15.24	R × L	53	49		48	42	
		daughters 12.07	L × L	9	8		9	3	
						1.50			15.09**
				Total N=414			Total N=404		
2. Annett	left-hand	fathers 9.32	R × R	63	61		47	44	
(1979):	writing	mothers 6.71	L × R	10	12		8	6	
OU students	including	sons 19.56	R × L	7	7		6	11	
as parents	"mixed" for	daughters 15.10	L × L	1	1		1	0	
	relatives					0.51			6.13
				Total N=366			Total N=384		
3. Annett (1979):	any 1/12	fathers 6.27	R × R	101	105		127	124	
OU students	actions	mothers 6.27	L × R	10	5		12	13	
as filial	left-handed	sons 33.06	R × L	10	10		13	15	
generation		daughters 39.58	L × L	1	1		1	0	
						2.39			1.71
				Total N=1041			Total N=959		
4. Annett	left-hand	fathers 6.27	R × R	71	65		65	61	
(1979):	writing	mothers 6.27	L × R	8	8		8	5	
OU students	including	sons 8.45	R × L	8	15		8	16	
and sibs as	"mixed" for	daughters 8.55	L × L	1	0		1	0	
filial	relatives					6.59			9.72*
generation									

					Total N=1282		Total N=896		
5. Rife (1940)	any 1/10 actions left-handed	fathers	5.38	R × R	103	105	56	46	
		mothers	5.09	L × R	10	9	6	9	
		sons	9.59	R × L	10	6	6	10	
		daughters	7.59	L × L	1	3	1	3	
						6.37			17.01**
					Total N=1226		Total N=1201		
6. Annett: Lanchester (new data) parents and sibs as filial generation	left-hand writing including "mixed" for relatives	fathers	4.75	R × R	95	100	80	72	
		mothers	2.72	L × R	8	6	7	14	
		sons	8.78	R × L	5	5	4	9	
		daughters	7.65	L × L	0	1	0	1	
						1.69			13.15**
					Total N=4194		Total N=3282		
7. Annett (1973a): Hull total	left-hand writing including "mixed" for relatives	fathers	4.39	R × R	417	402	279	267	
		mothers	3.71	L × R	32	28	22	15	
		sons	11.30	R × L	28	43	20	39	
		daughters	9.78	L × L	2	1	2	0	
						9.41*			22.43**
					Total N=5032		Total N=2682		
8. Chamberlain (1928)	left-hand writing	fathers	4.18	R × R	236	224	88	84	
		mothers	2.94	L × R	18	21	7	5	
		sons	5.31	R × L	13	18	5	9	
		daughters	3.76	L × L	1	4	0	3	
						11.92**			18.86**

Note: Predictions are based on the additive version of the RS model with means of 0, 1.0, 2.0 for males and 0, 1.2, 2.4 for females, in z units, for the $rs--$, $rs+-$ and $rs++$ genotypes, respectively.

*indicates $p < .05$, **indicates $p < .01$, $df = 3$, chi².

TABLE 16.8

Comparison of the Dominant and Additive Versions of the RS Model for Sums of Chi Square for Family Predictions

Source	Criterion	Males		Females	
		Dominant	Additive	Dominant	Additive
A. *Full self-report*					
Ashton (1982)	generous	1.52	2.85	3.60	2.58
Ashton (1982)	strict	0.19	0.96	0.57	0.50
Annett:					
Lanchester	generous	1.36	0.51	1.59	3.78
Lanchester	strict	6.82	6.95	1.68	1.23
Annett (1978a)	generous	5.59	5.64	5.64	2.56
Annett (1978a)	strict	0.98	0.55	0.58	1.05
McGee and Cozad (1980)	generous	3.95	0.39	2.88	0.50
Total		20.41	17.85	16.54	12.20
B. *Mixed report*					
Spiegler and Yeni-Komshian (1983)		0.07	1.50	8.16	15.09
Annett (1979): OU students					
as parents		1.50	0.51	7.79	6.13
as filial g.		1.64	2.39	3.48	1.71
and sibs as filial g.		8.84	6.59	11.62	9.72
Rife (1940)		6.73	6.37	21.05	17.01
Annett:					
Lanchester		0.78	1.69	17.00	13.15
Annett (1973a)		13.97	9.41	27.20	22.43
Chamberlain (1928)		14.10	11.92	19.68	18.86
Total		47.63	40.38	115.98	104.10

Note: Full dominance or additivity assumed; for parameters see text.

samples, including all those that depend on self-report, what can the poor fits be due to? It is possible, of course, that some adjustment of the model will lead to the discovery of a set of parameters that will predict *all* the available data, but since the model already gives excellent predictions for the data in which we can have most confidence (the self-report samples and especially that of Ashton), it seems possible that the fault may lie in some of the data rather than in the model.

The data need to be examined further from two points of view: first, for the incidences of parental left-handedness and, second, for a comparison of L × R and R × L families. Is it possible that the poor fit of the Annett (1973) and Chamberlain (1973) males is due to under-reporting of parental left-handedness? If parental left-handedness is under-reported, is this more marked for mothers than for fathers, as suggested by Fig. 16.2? Is there a genuine excess of left-handers born to left-handed mothers in comparison with left-handed fathers, or could this apparent effect be linked with under-reporting of maternal left-handedness?

Table 16.9 gives the numbers of left-handed children reported in L × R and R × L families in all the available studies, grouped for self-report and mixed-report as before (but taking only one level of criterion, the more generous, where two levels were used in Table 16.5). In the self-report studies there are almost identical numbers of left-handers reported in L × R and R × L families. In the mixed-report studies, the numbers of males in the two types of family are about the same; for females, there is a significant excess of left-handers in families where the mother is left-handed, in comparison with families in which the father is left-handed ($\chi^2 = 8.92$, $df = 1$, $p < .005$). (Alternatively, it could be said that there is a deficit of left-handed daughters of left-handed fathers.) The trend is evident in 6 out of 7 studies for daughters, using mixed report. It is most marked in my samples (for OU students when their children are the filial generation, OU students when they and their siblings are the filial generation, and especially for the 1973a Hull sample). Omitting my samples and considering the data for the other three studies alone (Spiegler & Yeni-Komshian, 1983; Rife, 1940; Chamberlain, 1928), there are trends towards more daughters in R × L than L × R families, but the trend is far from significant statistically.

The question whether the marked excess of daughters reported for R × L families in the Hull sample could be due to some subset of the data prompted me to re-examine the original data counts. The Hull data included four student subsamples. One of these depended on self-report in both generations and is listed separately at the generous criterion in Table 16.7. The other three samples included male and female students, each reporting on the handedness of themselves and their brothers and sisters, giving 18 sets of data in which the numbers of left-handers in L × R and R × L families could be compared. In 14 of the 18 counts, more left-handers were reported in R × L than L × R families. Clearly, this was a highly consistent trend in my samples.

The question what kind of reporting biases might affect mixed-report data can be approached through the evidence reviewed in Section 10.1. It was found that children tend to underestimate the left-handedness of their parents, but that left-handers are more likely to be aware of handedness as a personal trait than are right-handers. These observations suggest that the most probable source of error in samples relying on mixed-report is the under-reporting of left-handed parents by right-handed students. This would

TABLE 16.9

Comparison of L×R* and R×L Families for the Numbers of Left-Handers Reported

Source	Sons		Daughters		Both sexes	
	L×R	R×L	L×R	R×L	L×R	R×L
A. Self-report by all individuals						
Ashton (1982): use of left hand	27	17	21	29		
Annett: Lanchester new data	28	30	22	22		
Annett (1978a): Hull subgroup	35	49	29	40		
McGee and Cozad (1980)	39	38	38	35		
Carter-Saltzman (1980)					55	35
Total	129	134	110	126	294	295
B. Mixed report						
Spiegler and Yeni-Komshian (1983)	58	49	37	42		
Annett (1979): OU students: Their children	12	7	6	11		
Annett: Lanchester new data. Parents and sibs as filial generation						
OU students and sibs. as filial generation	8	15	5	16		
Rife (1940)	6	5	14	9		
Annett (1973a): total	9	6	9	10		
Chamberlain (1928)	28	43	15	39		
Leiber and Axelrod (1981a)					34	29
Total	142	143	91	136	267	308
					χ^2 8.921, $df = 1$	

* Fathers × mothers.

imply that more confidence can be placed in the reports of left-handers than of right-handers. Thus, the reports of left-handers that they belong to the various family types are likely to be accurate over the sample as a whole. The main errors probably concern the number of right-handers in $L \times R$ and $R \times L$ sibships. If this is true, calculations based on the percentages of left-handers within these sibships are likely to be less accurate than proportions of left-handers within the sibships over the total population, provided some adjustment can be made for parental incidences. If this line of reasoning is correct, the underestimation of parental sinistrality can be simply corrected by raising the parental incidences (thus increasing the numbers of $L \times R$, $R \times L$ and $L \times L$ sibships) and calculating predictions for left-handers in these sibships in the total population.

Table 16.10 shows the effect of repeating those calculations in Table 16.7 that gave significant chi squares, but with small changes in the parental incidences. In all six samples, a change of about 2% in one or both of the parental incidences is sufficient to give a marked improvement of the fit between observed and predicted numbers. For five of the six samples, the parental incidences needed to be raised slightly. In one sample (Spiegler & Yeni-Komshian, 1983), where the students reported relatively high incidences of parental sinistrality, small reductions of parental incidence were necessary.

With regard to the prediction of more left-handed children born in $R \times L$ than $L \times R$ families, the RS model does predict a slight excess in the former, on the values of parameters used here, provided there are *more left-handed mothers* than expected for the corresponding incidences for fathers (in Fig. 16.3). That is, if the incidences of left-handedness in fathers and mothers are the *same* (as for the parents of OU students, or for the "corrected" parental incidences for Chamberlain) or higher (as for Ashton's parental writing hand, and several other observed and "corrected" incidences) then more left-handed children are predicted in $R \times L$ than $L \times R$ families. The "corrected" incidences in Table 16.10 do not fully meet the observed differences, especially in my OU and Hull samples. It would be possible, of course, to increase further the maternal incidence, but this approach is arbitrary unless it can be shown that students (and perhaps especially female students?) tend to have more left-handed mothers than expected in the general population. This is a problem for further research.

What other explanations might there be for the dramatic differences between $L \times R$ and $R \times L$ families in my Hull sample? It has been shown above that the trend was observed in most of the data subsets when students were reporting the handedness of themselves and their siblings. Could there be some distortion in the report of sibling handedness, perhaps because students were more aware of left-handedness in siblings (especially sisters) when there was a left-handed parent? If the Hull 1973 analysis is restricted to

TABLE 16.10

The Effect of Changing the Incidences of Left-Handedness in One or Both Parents, on the Prediction of Left-Handedness in Family Types

Source	Incidences of Left-Handedness in the Total Sample			Family types (Father × mother)	Sons			Daughters		
	Observed		Revised		Exp.	Obs.	Sum χ²	Exp.	Obs.	Sum χ²
1. Spiegler and					Total N = 3196			Total N = 3413		
Yeni-Komshian	fathers	10.19	8.0	R × R	381	372		317	330	
(1983)	mothers	8.20	7.0	L × R	53	58		47	37	
	sons	15.24	—	R × L	47	49		43	42	
	daughters	12.07	—	L × L	6	8		6	3	
							1.20			4.40
					Total N = 1041			Total N = 959		
2. Annett	fathers	6.27	8.0	R × R	66	65		61	61	
(1979):	mothers	6.27	8.5	L × R	10	8		9	5	
OU students	sons	8.45	—	R × L	11	15		10	16	
and sibs as	daughters	8.55	—	L × L	1	0		2	0	
filial							3.46			6.47
generation										
					Total N = 1282			Total N = 896		
3. Rife	fathers	5.38	6.5	R × R	98	105		53	46	
(1940)	mothers	5.09	7.0	L × R	11	9		7	9	
	sons	9.59	—	R × L	13	6		7	10	
	daughters	7.59	—	L × L	1	3		1	3	
							6.28			7.27

					Total N=1226			Total N=1201	
4. Annett:	fathers	4.75	5.0	R × R	92	100		77	72
Lanchester	mothers	2.72	4.5	L × R	8	6		7	14
(new data)	sons	8.78	—	R × L	8	5		7	9
parents	daughters	7.65	—	L × L	1	1		1	1
and sibs as							2.41			7.22
filial									
generation									
					Total N=4194			Total N=3282	
5. Annett	fathers	4.39	—	R × R	405	402		270	267
(1973a):	mothers	3.71	5.5	L × R	31	28		22	15
Hull	sons	11.30	—	R × L	40	43		29	39
total	daughters	9.78	—	L × L	3	1		2	0
							1.78			8.12
					Total N=5032			Total N=2682	
6. Chamberlain	fathers	4.75	5.0	R × R	224	224		83	84
(1928)	mothers	2.72	5.0	L × R	21	21		8	5
	sons	5.31	—	R × L	22	18		9	9
	daughters	3.76	—	L × L	2	4		1	3
							2.66			6.76

Note: Parameters of the RS model as in Table 16.7.

the respondents themselves (omitting siblings), acceptable chi squares are found for both sexes (3.27 for males and 2.84 for females).

In conclusion, questions remain about the prediction of left-handedness in L × R and R × L families in studies that rely on mixed report. Is the increased number (proportion in some studies) of left-handers in R × L families a true finding, or is it an artefact of under-reporting of left-handedness in parents and siblings? Could there be a true excess of left-handed mothers in students (albeit one of which most students are unaware)? The possibility that the fault lies with the model rather than the data seems unlikely, since the model predicts the distribution of handedness in families very well in all samples that have ascertained handedness by self-report.

16.4. TWINS

It was said in Section 16.1 that the distribution of handedness in twin pairs can be predicted on the dominant version of the model, given a shift of about 1.0z in twins. In Section 16.2, new estimates of shift were derived from data for normal samples, for the additive and dominant versions of the model and distinguishing sex. What would be the implications of these revised estimates for twins?

As found for the earlier analyses, when the same levels of shift were assumed for twins as for non-twin samples, more concordant and fewer discordant pairs were predicted than observed. When a smaller shift was assumed for twins, good fits were found for all samples tested.

Table 16.11 shows the expectations of the model if the extent of shift is hypothesised to be smaller in twins than the singleborn by 33%. Table 16.11A shows the shifts assumed for each genotype in male and female and Table 6.11B shows the incidences of left-handedness expected in the singleborn and twins at three levels of threshold. When criteria of left-handedness are such as to identify about 9% of the general population as sinistral, about 13% of twins are expected to be so identified (Table 16.11B; compare the incidences in Table 16.2). When criteria of left-handedness are more generous, the corresponding incidences for the singleborn and twins are expected to be 11% and 16% (Table 16.11C) and 16% and 23% (Table 16.11D), respectively. Expectations for incidences differ slightly between the sexes.

In calculating the distributions of RR, RL, and LL pairs, it has been assumed throughout that the reduction of shift is the same for MZ and DZ twins. MZ and DZ pairs differ, of course, in the calculations required to estimate the proportions of RR, RL, and LL pairs, as MZ pairs have the same genotypes, and DZ pairs are expected to be as similar as any other pair of siblings. Table 16.11 shows that slightly more concordant RR pairs are expected for females than males and for MZ than DZ twins in each set of

TABLE 16.11

Examples of Predictions for MZ and DZ Twins and Tests Against Published Data for Corresponding Levels of Incidences of Left-Handedness

A. Shifts Assumed (z Value of Means of Each Genotype)

	Genotype		
	− −,	+ −,	+ +
Singleborn males	0.0	1.0	2.0
Twin males	0.0	.66	1.33
Singleborn females	0.0	1.20	2.40
Twin females	0.0	.80	1.10

B. Threshold for sinistrality at −.45z of rs− − distribution

	Incidences of left-handedness			*Expected Proportions in Twin Pairs*							
				MZ				*DZ*			
	Singleborn	*Twin*	*No. pairs*	*RR*	*RL*	*LL*	χ^2	*RR*	*RL*	*LL*	χ^2
Male	9.9	13.8		75.3	21.8	2.9		74.8	22.8	2.4	
Female	8.6	11.9		78.8	18.7	2.5		78.2	19.8	1.9	
Sexes combined	9.2	12.8		77.0	20.3	2.7		76.5	21.3	2.2	

TABLE 16.11—*continued*

Examples of Predictions for MZ and DZ Twins and Tests Against Published Data for Corresponding Levels of Incidences of Left-Handedness

Tests against observed data

		Twin	No. pairs	MZ RR	MZ RL	MZ LL	MZ χ²	DZ RR	DZ RL	DZ LL	DZ χ²
Loehlin and Nichols (1976)	MZ males	13.8	217	exp. 163	47	6					
				obs. 162	50	5	0.414				
	DZ males	12.1	136					exp. 102	31	3	
								obs. 104	31	1	1.611
	DZ females	10.4	197					exp. 154	39	4	
								obs. 157	39	1	2.140
Rife (1950)	MZ both sexes	12.8	343	exp. 264	69	9					
				obs. 261	76	6	1.796				
	DZ both sexes	11.6	211					exp. 161	45	5	
								obs. 164	45	2	1.486
Zazzo (1960)	DZ both sexes	12.9	1145					exp. 876	224	25	
								obs. 871	253	21	.928

C. Threshold for sinistrality at − .30z of the rs− − *distribution*

	Incidences of left-handedness			Expected Proportions in Twin Pairs							
				MZ				DZ			
	Singleborn	Twin	No. pairs	RR	RL	LL	χ²	RR	RL	LL	χ²
Male	12.2	17.0		70.2	25.7	4.2		69.5	27.0	3.5	
Female	10.5	14.7		74.3	22.1	3.6		73.4	23.6	2.8	
Sexes combined	11.3	15.8		72.2	23.9	3.9		71.5	25.3	3.2	
Tests against observed data											
Zazzo (1960)	MZ both sexes	16.2	1210	exp. 874	289	47					
				obs. 867	295	48	0.202				
Loehlin and Nichols (1976)	MZ females	14.3	297	exp. 221	66	11					
				obs. 218	73	6	2.917				

Kasriel (1977)*	MZ males	15.5	194	exp. 136	50	8					
				obs. 138	52	4	2.228				
	MZ females	14.4	430	exp. 319	95	15					
				obs. 318	100	12	1.049				
	DZ females	15.6	278					exp. 204	66	8	
								obs. 201	67	10	0.636

D. Threshold for sinistrality at 0_z of the rs$--$ distribution

	Incidences of left-handedness			Expected Proportions in Twin Pairs							
				MZ				DZ			
	Singleborn	Twin	No. pairs	RR	RL	LL	χ^2	RR	RL	LL	χ^2
Male	17.8	24.7		58.6	33.3	8.1		57.7	35.2	7.1	
Female	15.2	21.4		64.1	29.0	6.9		62.9	31.3	5.7	
Sexes combined	16.5	23.1		61.3	31.1	7.5		60.3	33.3	6.4	
Test against observed data											
Newman et al.;+	MZ both	21.1	327	exp. 200	102	25					
Verschur;+	sexes			obs. 205	106	16	3.249				
Dechaume											
(in Zazzo 1960)											
Siemens+	DZ both	23.4	64					exp. 39	21	4	
Dechaume	sexes							obs. 37	24	3	0.698
(in Zazzo 1960)											

Note: Predictions are for the additive model, assuming shift for the general population as in Table 16.7 and assuming that shifts in twins are reduced by 33%.

*Personal communication from the Institute of Psychiatry, London.

calculations, but the differences are so small as to be untestable except in very large data sets.

Tests of the predicted proportions are made against reports in the literature where incidences approximate those calculated here for sinistrality in twins. The observed and predicted distributions agree well at each level of incidence. This is true for the very large collection of combined samples described by Zazzo (1960) for MZ (Table 16.11C) and DZ (Table 16.11B) twins. The data for some of the samples included by Zazzo are examined separately in Table 16.11D to show that predictions are in accord with observations when incidences of left-handedness are about 23% as well as when they are about 13%.

These calculations are based on a guesstimate that the reduction of shift in twins is about 33%. Further research may show that a slightly larger reduction is required if more concordant LL pairs are predicted than observed (the trend in Table 16.11). A possible need for fine tuning of the values of parameters of the model does not invalidate the general demonstration that the model is able to account for the findings for MZ and DZ twins over a wide range of incidences of left-handedness.

16.5. SUMMARY

The expression of the $rs+$ gene is hypothesised to be stronger in females than males and stronger in the singleborn than in twins. Evidence for the hypothesis of variable gene expression is to be found in the increased proportions of left-handers in males than females and in twins than non-twins. Sex differences in L–R time are clear at the dextral side of the distribution, but absent at the sinistral side where the $rs+$ gene is expected to be absent; they are also absent in left-handers and in the children of L × L parents. Variable gene expression would account for observed differences in speech acquisition between the sexes and between twins and singleborn. If gene expression depends on rates of cerebral hemisphere growth in late fetal life, the observed differences in handedness and in language development would correlate with relative maturity at birth.

The question whether the relative extents of right shift in males and females can be deduced for normal samples was explored in two ways. One was to analyse the observed L–R times of large samples of males and females to test their compatibility with subdistributions expected for the RS model. The total distributions were not normal but were peaked and negatively skewed. They could consist of two or three normal subdistributions, as represented in Figs. 14.1 and 16.1. The means and standard deviations obtained for these subdistributions, by minimising the D value of the K–S statistic, were remarkably consistent for the combined main samples. The means for females were slightly further to the right than those of males, as expected.

A second source of evidence as to the difference in extent of shift between the sexes was available in the incidences of left-handedness in paired samples of males and females. It was discovered that when the means of the $rs--$, $rs+-$, and $rs++$ distributions were taken to be 0.0, 1.0z, and 2.0z for males, and 0.0, 1.2z, and 2.4z for females, respectively (on the fully additive model), the thresholds required to represent incidences in corresponding samples of males and females often matched.

These values of shift were used in further analyses of the distribution of handedness in families, taking sex into account in both generations. Several newly published samples and further unpublished samples were added to those used in Section 15.2. Excellent fits were found between expected and observed numbers for all samples where information was gathered by self-report in both generations. Good fits were also found for most samples of males where information was by mixed report (reports by students of the handedness of themselves and their relatives), except where parental incidences were very low. Most mixed-report data for females gave poor fits between observed and predicted numbers of left-handers in families.

Mismatches between observed and predicted numbers of females were largely due to greater numbers of left-handed females in the families of left-handed mothers than expected. The question whether there is a true excess of left-handed children of left-handed mothers, and whether this applies especially to daughters, was explored. There was no clear evidence for this excess when data depended on self-report. It is possible that the apparent excess in mixed-report data is due to under-reporting of the true incidence of maternal left-handedness. When incidences of parental handedness were "corrected" by small adjustments of percentages (up to 3%), substantial improvements of fit were obtained.

Predictions of the RS model for MZ and DZ twin pairs are given for the assumption that the extent of right shift is reduced in twins of both types by about one third. It is shown that incidences of left-handedness would be a little larger in twins than in the singleborn, on the same criteria. Distributions of pairs observed at each level of incidence are close to those expected.

17 A Balanced Polymorphism Hypothesis for the rs+ Gene: Hand Speed and Mathematical Ability

The hypothesis that there is a balanced polymorphism for the $rs+$ gene has led to the most recent surprises of the RS theory. Faster hand speeds in left-handers were first noticed by Diana Kilshaw, herself a strong left-hander. The surprise about mathematical ability was that the data almost, but not quite, matched my expectations; the mismatch led me to see that the data supported the balanced polymorphism hypothesis more strongly than I had anticipated. Similarly, with regard to a study of pupils attending a dyslexia clinic (Chapter 18), there was a partial mismatch between expectations and findings that required a reformulation in the light of the balanced polymorphism hypothesis. I believe that the findings from these several sources, a re-analysis of vocabulary scores in normal school-children (Chapter 19), and a cross-cultural replication of some findings (Chapter 20) all tell a consistent story. They imply that the effects of the $rs+$ gene are advantageous in a small dose but disadvantageous in a large dose. That is, the heterozygote ($rs+-$) is the most advantageous genotype and both homozygotes ($rs--$ and $rs++$) have disadvantages. Over the population as a whole, it can be presumed that the complementary advantages and disadvantages of the three genotypes are compensated, as for other genetic polymorphisms (Section 1.2).

The evidence that left-handers have persisted in human populations at about the current level for at least several thousand years (Chapter 3) suggests that there must be advantages associated with sinistrality (given the assumption that handedness has some genetic basis and not all left-handed-ness is pathological). The genotype frequencies deduced in Chapter 15 strongly suggested a balanced polymorphism for the $rs+$ gene, with heterozygote advantage. The basic laws of combination of genes on paired chromosomes imply that the largest possible proportion of $rs+ -$ is .50. This occurs when the alternate alleles at each locus are equally frequent in the population $(.5 + .5 = 1)$. Inspection of the genotype frequencies deduced for the $rs+$ locus suggests that the frequency of the $rs+$ gene has risen above .5 to a small extent (.57), but *without significantly diminishing the proportion of heterozygotes* (.49).

What could be the disadvantages of the $rs- -$ and $rs+ +$ genotypes be? From first formulating the RS theory (Annett, 1972) it was expected that the right shift induced speech development in the left hemisphere, and that those who lacked the right shift might be at some disadvantage for speech and language development. This was argued by Annett and Turner (1974) and is argued further in Chapter 18. What could be the disadvantages of the $rs+ +$ genotype? There seemed to be no way of investigating this problem. It was suggested (Annett, 1978b) that the $rs+ +$ might risk an over-commitment to language skills, at the expense of those other skills on which human evolution depended, the manufacture and use of tools: "The heterozygote and neutral homozygote have advantages in skilled performance (as in famous left handers such as Michaelangelo, Leonardo Da Vinci, Charlie Chaplin and Jimmy Connors) which far outweigh the advantages of ready speech in the dominant homozygote" (Annett, 1978b).

The idea that the $rs+$ gene leads to disadvantages in skilled performance is strongly supported by the findings for hand speeds, as described in Section 17.1. The idea that that the $rs+ +$ might be overcommitted to language skills turned out to be not quite correct, since dyslexics (Chapter 18) give reason to believe that some $rs+ +$ have problems in learning to read. To understand how this could be, further clues are needed as to the possible mechanisms through which the $rs+$ gene induces left-hemisphere speech. These clues are to be found in the following analysis of the actual hand speeds of children and adults in normal samples.

17.1. HAND SKILL FOR PEG MOVING

17.1.1. The Development of Hand Skill With Age and Sex

The peg-moving task (Fig. 11.1), devised to assess the manual impairment of children with hemiplegia, was given to a sample of normal school-children in order to establish standards of movement time for the right and left hands in children between 3.5 and 15 years (Annett, 1970b; norms in Appendix III). The normal children were examined for changes in hand preference and for changes of L–R skill with age, and no changes were found. A graph of left-

and right-hand times (smoothed means in Figure 1 of Annett, 1970b) suggested the parallel development of right- and left-hand speed with age. Absolute differences in favour of the right hand were *larger* in younger than in older children, but this effect was thought to be due to the negative exponential shape of the curves (see Fig. 17.1). These analyses convinced me that the distributions of hand preference and L–R skill are fairly constant with age and that the greater skill of the right hand is not due to practice (Section 4.2).

When all available samples were being re-examined and combined to give the large Ns needed for the analyses of the L–R distributions in Section 16.2, the opportunity was taken to look again at the effects of age and sex in this larger set of data (Kilshaw & Annett, 1983). Table 17.1 gives the findings for hand preference in age groups, ranging from nursery school to 40+ years. There were no statistically significant differences within any of the four sex × age groups. There were no signs of increasing incidences of right-

TABLE 17.1

Hand Preference With Age and Sex in Birthday and Main Samples

A. Birthday samples

Age (yrs)	N	Males Left drawing	Males Right mixed	Males Right consistent	N	Females Left drawing	Females Right mixed	Females Right consistent
3½–5	36	13.9	16.7	69.4	32	15.6	9.4	75.0
6–7	35	11.4	28.6	60.0	38	7.9	21.0	71.1
8–9	27	22.2	14.8	63.0	35	14.3	14.3	71.4
10–11	26	23.1	19.2	57.7	46	17.4	21.7	60.0
12–13	17	17.6	17.6	64.8	20	0.0	15.0	85.0
14–15	17	35.3	17.6	47.1	17	11.8	17.6	70.6
Total	158	19.0	19.6	61.4	188	12.2	17.0	70.7

Preference × age: $\chi^2 = 8.42$, $df = 10$, NS (Males) $\chi^2 = 7.99$, $df = 10$, NS (Females)

B. Main samples

Age	N	Males Left writing	Males Right mixed	Males Right consistent	N	Females Left writing	Females Right mixed	Females Right consistent
LS 12	79	6.3	30.4	63.3	86	7.0	29.1	63.9
DA 16–18	158				158	8.9	34.2	56.9
HL 18–20	140	13.6	28.6	57.8	213	10.3	23.5	66.2
OU 22–29	81	8.6	30.9	60.5	103	12.6	31.1	56.3
OU 30–39	153	6.5	29.4	64.1	168	10.7	27.4	61.9
OU 40–63	149	6.0	20.8	73.2	115	8.7	30.4	60.9
Total	602	8.3	27.4	64.3	843	9.8	28.7	61.4

Preference × age: $\chi^2 = 12.18$, $df = 8$, NS (Males) $\chi^2 = 8.67$, $df = 10$, NS (Females)

Note: Kilshaw and Annett (1983).

LRHB–L

handedness or of decreasing incidences of left-handedness with age. (The differences between the birthday samples and the combined main samples for incidences of mixed-handedness are due to differing methods of ascertainment. See Appendix II.A.1.)

Table 17.2 gives the findings for differences between the hands for peg-moving time, examined in three ways. First, the mean L–R differences are given (in 1/10 s). Within the main samples there were no trends with age. The female groups were highly consistent, and the male groups were consistent except for HL, which had a smaller L–R mean (Section 19.2). Within the birthday samples, there were trends to *decreasing* L–R differences with age, significant for females but not quite significant for males. The second method of presentation gives the L–R means as a proportion of left-hand time [10(L–R)/L]. This analysis shows that the changes of L–R means as a function of the greater slowness of younger children, as argued above. The third analysis of L–R differences with age (L–R<0) gives the proportions of subjects in each age group biased towards the left hand for skill. These proportions also show no consistent trends with age. There are some fluctuations between age groups in the birthday samples, where Ns are

TABLE 17.2

Three Measures of L–R Hand Peg-Moving Time with Age and Sex in Birthday and Main Samples: (a) Mean Difference (in 1/10 s), (b) as a Percentage of Left-Hand Time, and (c) Percentage of Subjects Having a Difference Favouring the Left Hand

| | Age (yrs) | Males | | | | | Females | | | | |
		N	L–R Mean	L–R SD	10(L–R)/L	L–R<0 (%)	N	L–R Mean	L–R SD	10(L–R)/L	L–R<0 (%)
A. Birthday samples											
	3½–5	36	11.6	19.9	5.6	16.7	32	20.2	23.7	9.5	21.9
	6–7	35	10.2	15.7	6.7	17.1	38	14.3	14.5	9.4	13.2
	8–9	27	9.8	13.0	7.3	18.5	35	14.9	11.6	11.0	14.3
	10–11	26	1.9	11.3	1.7	38.5	46	8.0	14.3	6.7	21.7
	12–13	17	3.7	11.4	3.6	29.4	20	12.3	6.1	11.3	0.0
	14–15	17	7.6	8.8	7.3	17.6	17	11.2	9.6	10.5	11.8
B. Main samples											
LS HL+	12	79	6.8	10.7	6.6	15.2	86	7.8	9.3	7.0	15.1
DA	16–20	140	4.0	7.1	4.3	29.6	371	8.1	8.6	8.2	13.2
OU	22–29	81	7.7	9.6	7.9	12.3	103	8.1	7.8	8.0	9.7
OU	30–39	153	6.3	6.9	6.5	13.1	168	7.7	9.0	7.6	16.1
OU	40+	149	7.5	10.8	7.4	13.4	115	7.5	9.3	7.4	13.9

Note: Kilshaw and Annett (1983).

relatively small, but there is no evidence of a systematic shift to dextrality with increasing age.

It is worth noting that the percentages of subjects with a left-hand advantage for skill (L–R <O) are greater than the percentages of those who are left-handed for writing (in Table 17.1) in all but one case in the combined main samples. This observation offers a strong argument against the view that differences in skill between the hands are *caused* by the use of one hand for writing. It accords well with the location of the threshold for left-handedness, as drawn in Fig. 14.1, on the sinistral side of L=R. These analyses of hand preference and L–R skill in age groups spanning most of the life-cycle (when all measures are by observation and not self-report) should lay to rest the behaviourist ghost that variations in hand preference and skill are due to practice. As discussed in Section 4.2, natural variations in skill can be partly compensated by practice, but continued practice is necessary to maintain the compensation; extra scales and exercises for the weaker hand may be needed over decades of piano playing, in my own experience as a right-hander and in that of a left-handed pianist I questioned on this point.

TABLE 17.3

Actual Peg-Moving Time for the Right and Left Hands With Age and Sex in Birthday and Main Samples

	Males					Females				
		Right Hand		Left Hand			Right Hand		Left Hand	
Age (yrs)	N	Mean	SD	Mean	SD	N	Mean	SD	Mean	SD
A. Birthday samples										
3½	8	23.2	3.9	23.8	2.9	7	21.4	3.5	23.2	4.2
4	14	20.4	3.5	21.5	4.3	13	19.5	3.1	21.7	4.1
5	14	16.7	1.6	18.3	2.7	12	17.9	2.4	19.9	2.2
6–7	35	14.3	1.5	15.3	1.8	38	13.7	1.5	15.1	1.8
8–9	27	12.4	1.2	13.4	1.2	35	12.1	1.2	13.6	1.7
10–11	26	11.4	1.3	11.6	1.0	46	11.0	1.1	11.9	1.3
12–13	17	9.8	1.0	10.2	0.8	20	9.7	0.9	10.9	1.1
14–15	17	9.6	0.7	10.4	0.9	17	9.6	0.9	10.7	1.0
B. Main samples										
LS 12	79	9.6	1.0	10.3	1.0	86	10.3	1.0	11.1	1.1
HL+										
DA 16–20	140	8.9	0.9	9.3	0.9	371	9.1	0.8	9.9	0.9
OU 22–29	81	9.0	0.9	9.8	1.1	103	9.3	0.9	10.1	1.0
OU 30–39	153	9.1	1.0	9.7	1.0	168	9.4	0.8	10.1	1.0
OU 40–49	105	9.2	0.9	9.9	1.0	92	9.3	1.0	10.0	1.2
OU 50+	44	9.7	1.2	10.5	1.1	23	9.7	1.1	10.6	1.5

Note: Kilshaw and Annett (1983).

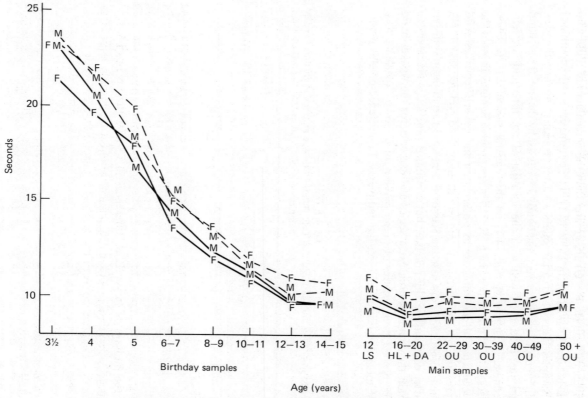

FIG. 17.1.   Times taken by the right hand (———) and the left hand (– – –) for peg moving in age groups for males (M) and females (F). Kilshaw & Annett, 1983.

Interesting features of the analysis emerged when the absolute times taken by each hand were examined for the sexes separately. Table 17.3 gives the means (raw means, not smoothed as in Appendix III), and Figure 17.1 represents them in age groups between 3.5 and 50+ years. (The standard errors could not be shown clearly on the graph as they would be so large for the younger groups as to obscure the means and so small for the older groups as to be within the span of the symbols representing the means; the standard errors can be calculated from the data in Table 17.3.) There are several features of the peg-moving times worth noting. First, hand speeds increase with age—but at a negatively accelerated rate—until late adolescence; the trend is fairly linear in the pre-adolescent years. Second, the means are consistent where the birthday samples and main samples overlap (12 to 15 years in the birthday samples and the LS main sample). Third, the left-hand mean was slower than the right-hand mean in all groups, as expected. Fourth, and this was not expected, the female left-hand mean in all but two groups was slower than the male left-hand mean in all but two groups. Fifth, also not expected, the female right-hand times were faster than the male right-hand times in most age groups up to about 11 years of age, but thereafter males were faster than females with the right hand.

The sex differences were statistically significant in the combined main samples but short of significance in the birthday samples. (The trend in the birthday samples for males to be faster than females with the left hand gave $t = 1.37$, $df = 7$, and the trend for females to be faster than males with the right hand gave $t = 1.21$, $df = 7$, when the means were treated as matched pairs.) More powerful tests of statistical significance were not appropriate, as the absolute times varied strongly with age and the age groups were not matched for N. One way to deal with this problem is to transform all the times for children into standardised scores (using the norms of Appendix III). The birthday samples are re-examined in this way for comparison with the dyslexic sample (Figure 18.2). Normal females tend to be slower than normal males with the left hand, but this is clearly true only for females who are strongly biased to the right hand and are likely to be of $rs + +$ genotype.

Do the findings of larger L–R differences in females than males imply differences in correlation between the hands? Might it be possible to argue that the co-ordination between the cerebral hemispheres differs with sex or age? Table 17.4 gives correlations between the times taken by each hand in sex and age groups in the birthday sample. Most of the correlations are statistically significant. There is no evidence that the hands and hemispheres are more independent in younger than older children or in one sex than the other.

Speculating about differences in the relative efficiency of the two hemispheres with age and sex, it may be said that the evidence suggests that the *right* hemisphere of females tends to be less efficient than the right hemis-

TABLE 17.4

Correlations Between the Hands for Peg-Moving Time in Age Groups in the Birthday Samples

Age	Males		Females	
	N	Pearson's r	N	Pearson's r
3½– 5	36	.878*	32	.761*
6 – 7	35	.567*	38	.614*
8 – 9	27	.413*	35	.737*
10 –11	26	.537*	46	.270
12 –13	17	.242	20	.852*
14 –15	17	.381	17	.540*

Note: Kilshaw and Annett (1983).
* $p = .05$ or less.

phere of males at all ages. The *left* hemisphere of females has an initial advantage in comparison with that of males, but this relative advantage is lost around the time of adolescence.

17.1.2. An Advantage
For Left-Handers in Skill

When the actual peg-moving times for each hand were being assembled for the analyses by age and sex, Mrs. Kilshaw noticed that the means of left-handers were often smaller (faster) than those of right-handers. To examine this difference, right- and left-handers were compared for their preferred hands and nonpreferred hands (taking writing hand as the criterion of preference). There were 22 age and sex groups in which the comparison could be made. For the nonpreferred hand, the right hand of the left-handers was faster than the left hand of the right-handers in 17 comparisons (on the binomial test, $p < .05$). For the preferred hand, the trends differed between the sexes. In males, the left hand of left-handers was faster than the right hand of right-handers in 8 out of 11 comparisons; in females this was true for only 3 out of 10 comparisons (1 equal). Further analyses of these differences were made in the combined main samples and the birthday samples separately.

Figure 17.2 shows the mean times taken by the preferred and nonpreferred hands of all subjects in the combined main samples, classified for sex and hand preference. Table 17.5 gives the statistical analyses. There were highly significant differences between hand preference groups in three of the four analyses, and in each of these three hand speed was linearly related to degree of left-hand preference. That is, the left-handed writers were faster than the mixed-right-handers, who in turned were faster than the right-handers. The

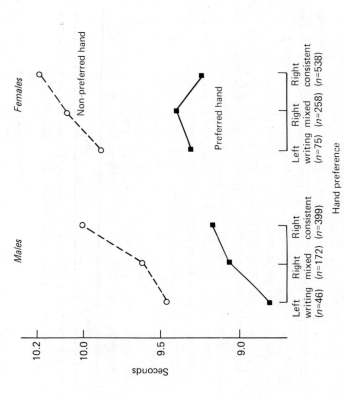

FIG. 17.2. Mean actual peg-moving times by the preferred hand (■——■) and the non-preferred hand (○- - -○) in the combined main samples. Kilshaw & Annett, 1983.

TABLE 17.5

The Significance of Differences Between Preference Groups for Actual Hand Speeds: F Ratios for Between-Groups Comparisons and for Tests of Linear Trend (for the Means Represented in Fig. 17.2)

	F	df	p
Males:			
Preferred hand			
Between groups	3.61	2:614	.05
Linear trend	6.20	1:614	.025
Nonpreferred hand			
Between groups	12.82	2:614	.001
Linear trend	11.66	1:614	.001
Females:			
Preferred hand			
Between groups	2.44	2:860	NS
Linear trend	0.42	1:860	NS
Nonpreferred hand			
Between groups	5.18	2:860	.01
Linear trend	8.23	1:860	.01

Note: Kilshaw and Annett (1983).

exception occurred for females using the preferred hand, where consistent right-handers tended to be faster than mixed- and left-handers, but not significantly. The advantages for left-handers were small in absolute terms (of the order of .5 s between the means of left- and right-handers). The differences were consistent, however, since the linear relationship between peg-moving time and hand preference was highly significant statistically in the three groups in which the relationship was found.

The possibility that left-handers might have an advantage over right-handers in actual peg-moving times was not envisaged at the time the data were collected. The birthday samples were examined to check the reliability of the observations. The children of the birthday samples could not be combined to give large Ns of each sex because of the differing numbers between groups mentioned previously. The means were calculated for each hand preference group within age and sex groups and combined to find the over-all means, as shown in Fig. 17.3. For the nonpreferred hand, the pattern

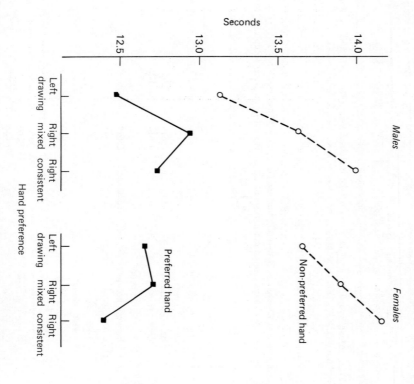

FIG. 17.3.   Mean actual peg-moving times by the preferred hand (■——■) and the non-preferred hand (O—-O) in the birthday samples. Kilshaw & Annett, 1983.

in both sexes was as found for the main samples. Left-handers showed a clear advantage over right-handers (matched pairs $t = 2.30$, $df = 11$, $p < .05$), and mixed-handers were intermediate. For the preferred hands the differences were not significant statistically, but male left-handers and female consistent right-handers tended to be faster than other groups.

The consistency of findings for the nonpreferred hand in both sexes and in both sets of samples suggests that right-handedness is associated with slowness of the nonpreferred (left) hand. There is no evidence that right-handers are faster with the right hand than left-handers with the left (although there are trends in this direction in females only). The outstanding impression given by Figs. 17.2 and 17.3 is of the slowness of the left hand in right-handers, and especially in right-handed females. These observations suggest that the notion of right-hand and left-hemisphere advantage should be reconsidered. Perhaps the right shift of the L–R distribution is induced not by some factor that gives a boost to the left hemisphere but rather by some factor that *handicaps the right hemisphere*. This gives a completely new perspective on questions about the lateralisation of cerebral function. Perhaps language lateralisation for the left hemisphere is induced by some factor that slows down or otherwise impairs the growth of the right hemisphere. We now have a clue as to why the $rs++$ genotype might be disadvantageous, and why the expression of the $rs+$ gene might be limited in males, in comparison with females.

On the RS theory, most left-handed writers are $rs--$, and the differences between their hands in skill can be interpreted as the "natural" asymmetry due to chance variation (perhaps as in other primates). Right-mixed- and right-consistent-handers differ from left-handers mainly in having a slower nonpreferred (left) hand. The impairment is greater in consistent than mixed right-handers. It is greater in females than in males. These trends are just as expected for an effect due to the $rs+$ gene, as the gene should be present more often in consistent than mixed right-handers and it is expressed more strongly in females than in males. Whether or not the $rs+$ gene leads to some impairment of the right hand also is less certain. There seem to be trends in this direction for males. In females, the right hand is no better than the right hand of males (in the combined main samples, although it is better in the birthday samples, where we saw that young females tend to have faster right-hand speeds than young males). It is rather as though the trend to slowness in right-handers is counteracted in females for the right hand; if the trends in Fig. 17.2 had continued for the female preferred hand, the mean right-hand time of females would have been very poor. Only further independent studies can show whether these observations for the preferred hand of female right-handers are reliable.

The most unexpected and dramatic outcome of this analysis is the finding that left-handers have an absolute advantage in hand skill and that the mechanism of action of the $rs+$ gene might be to *impair* the function of the right hemisphere. This is a very important contribution to the hypothesis of a balanced polymorphism and to an understanding of the findings for mathematicians described in Section 17.2.

17.2. MATHEMATICAL ABILITY

When the hypothesis of a balanced polymorphism was suggested by the genotype frequencies, mathematical ability seemed a strong candidate for $rs--$ advantage. Groups of students and school-children studying mathematics had been collected incidentally as part of larger samples, and incidences of sinistrality in both sets of mathematics students were about twice those of the general samples. It was decided to check these findings by collecting new data by questionnaire from students and their families, and also by making personal observations of the lateral preferences and L–R preg-moving times of teachers of mathematics (Annett & Kilshaw, 1982). Members of mathematics departments in several universities and polytechnics in the Midlands took the examination, as well as three female and two male teachers of A-level mathematics in schools. (Additional visits were made in search of female mathematicians; the sex ratio cannot be taken as representative of mathematics teachers in English higher education.)

Table 17.6 describes the hand preference data for male students and their relatives and Table 17.7 the corresponding data for female students. The students were classified for left-handed writing and also for any left-hand preference. Among males there were significantly more left-handers on both criteria over-all. Among females, there were trends in the predicted direction in all samples, but none were significant statistically. There were no significant effects for relatives of students of either sex.

The findings for L–R times in mathematics teachers are given in Table 17.8. Two control samples are listed at the top of the table. The first were the combined main samples (Appendix I.B.10). The second control sample included lecturers in several departments of Coventry (Lanchester) Polytechnic and the University of Warwick in the faculties of social science and arts. This sample did not differ significantly from the combined sample controls, confirming that the latter can be used with its large N.

The mathematicians in Table 17.8 are classified according to their self-description as pure, applied, or general mathematicians, computer scientists, or statisticians and operational researchers. Numbers are small in some groups, especially for female mathematicians, but the analysis is given in this way to show the consistency of findings for most groups. For 9 out of 10 comparisons, the L–R means of the mathematicians were smaller than those of controls. The reduction of L–R mean was statistically significant for male

TABLE 17.6
Male Students: Hand Preferences in Mathematics Students, Controls, and Relatives

| | Students | | | | | | Relatives | | | |
| | Mathematics | | | Non-mathematics | | | Mathematics | | Non-mathematics | |
Sample	N	Any Left	Left Writing	N	Any Left	Left Writing	N	Left or Mixed	N	Left or Mixed
Hull	28	429*	28.6***	435	23.2	11.0	94	10.6	1429	11.2
Coventry and Warwick	41	58.5*	21.9	40	32.5	10.0	135	9.6	122	6.6
Miscell.	17	11.76	5.9				59	8.5		
Total	86	44.2***	20.9**	475	24.0	10.9	288	9.7	1551	10.8

Note: Annett and Kilshaw (1982). In percentages.
Chi square comparisons between mathematics and non-mathematics students. See Appendix I.B.8 for notes on samples.
*** p < .001
** p < .01
* p < .025

TABLE 17.7
Female Students: Hand Preferences in Mathematics Students, Controls, and Relatives

| | | Students | | | | | Relatives | | | |
| | | Mathematics | | | Non-mathematics | | Mathematics | | Non-mathematics | |
Sample	N	Any Left	Left Writing	N	Any Left	Left Writing	N	Left or Mixed	N	Left or Mixed
Hull	8	50.0	12.5	239	34.7	10.5	27	0.0	80	10.4
Schoolgirls	24	37.5	16.7	134	44.0	7.5	95	9.5	510	10.0
Coventry and Warwick	31	25.8	6.4	106	30.2	4.7	113	7.1	335	9.8
Miscell.	31	41.9	12.9				114	13.2		
Total	94	36.2	11.7*	479	36.3	8.3	349	9.2	1614	10.2

Notes: Annett and Kilshaw (1982). In percentages.
Chi square comparisons between mathematics and non-mathematics students. See Appendix I.B.8 for notes on samples.
*1.09 NS.

TABLE 17.8
Mathematics Teachers L–R Time for Peg-Moving (1/10 s)

	Males			Females		
	N	Mean	SD	N	Mean	SD
Controls						
General	617	6.4	8.4	863	8.0	8.8
Academic	50	6.2	8.3	20	10.6	4.7
Mathematicians						
Computer scientists	17	6.5	7.6	4	3.5	
Statisticians and operational researchers	16	4.2	9.5	3	6.0	
Applied	24	5.4	8.5	5	7.2	
Pure	33	3.6**	8.8	12	5.4	8.8
General	7	3.6		3	3.7	
Total Mathematicians	97	4.6**	8.3	27	5.3*	6.5

Note: Annett and Kilshaw (1982).
t test comparisons with general controls.
** p <.05 (1 tail)
* p <.10 (1 tail).

pure mathematicians and for total male mathematicians. The L–R means of the female mathematicians differed from that of the combined main sample controls at a level just short of the 5% criterion, but it was significantly lower than that of the academic controls ($t = 3.06$, $df = 45$, $p < .005$). Whereas the L–R means of female controls were considerably to the right of the corresponding male means (as considered in Chapter 16), the means of female mathematicians were only slightly to the right of the means of male mathematicians. When the mathematics teachers and controls were compared for hand, eye, and foot preferences, more sinistrals were found among mathematicians for each of these measures, but the comparisons were significant only for male pure mathematicians.

Two main impressions are given by these data: first, the consistency of the trends towards a reduction in dextral bias in mathematicians, as predicted, and, second, the relative paucity of statistically significant effects. The lack of statistical significance is due in many cases to the small Ns available for test, but clearly the reductions in L–R time are not as dramatic as would be expected if the majority of professional mathematicians were $rs - -$. Once again, the RS theory led to findings that were clearly in the direction expected, but not confirming the original hunch that outstanding mathematical ability might be linked with the $rs--$ genotype.

Reconsidering the evidence in the light of the balanced polymorphism hypothesis, it is possible to reformulate the possible link between mathematical ability and laterality. Perhaps it is not that mathematicians must be $rs--$ so much as that they must not be $rs++$. The initial premise of the balanced polymorphism hypothesis was that the most advantageous genotype is the heterozygote. Are the present data compatible with the idea that the sample of mathematicians includes $rs--$ and $rs+-$ but not $rs++$ genotypes? It is not possible to *prove* such a hypothesis, on present evidence, but it is possible to test whether the distribution of L–R scores is consistent with expectations for a total distribution that is the sum of the $rs--$ and $rs+-$ distributions as deduced for the control samples in Table 16.5.

Figure 17.4 shows the distribution expected for the sum of these two genotypes. It also shows that for the *same thresholds* that cut off 10% and 35% of the sample in Fig. 16.1, the distributions in Fig. 17.4 would cut off 15% and 49%, respectively. In other words, left-handed writing and "any left" preference would be expected to occur with these frequencies in a sample that consisted only of $rs--$ and $rs+-$ genotypes.

The L–R scores of the male mathematicians were tested using the Kolmogorov–Smirnov computer program (Section 16.2.1) for consistency with expectations for a distribution that is the sum of three genotypes (as in Fig. 16.1 and Table 16.5) or for the sum of two genotypes (as in Fig. 17.4). The first test gave a D value of .137, which is close to the 5% rejection value of .14. The second prediction gave a D value of .049. This demonstrates that the distribution for mathematicians could resemble that for Fig. 17.4. In other words, mathematicians could resemble the rest of the population for L–R times, except that $rs++$ genotypes are absent.

There were too few female mathematicians to make the K–S test of the L–R distributions. The reduction of L–R mean in female mathematicians is consistent with the possibility that female mathematicians also include no $rs++$ genotypes. If the reader will imagine the $rs+-$ and $rs++$ distributions of Fig. 16.1 shifted further to the right by $.2z$ and $.4z$, respectively, as deduced for females in the genetic calculations in Section 16.2, then the thresholds for left-handed writing and for "any left" preference would give about 9% and 31% of the general population of females in these groups. If a similar shift of $.2z$ is made for the $rs+-$ distribution in Fig. 17.4, the corresponding incidences for females would be 13% and 43%. This analysis shows that although exactly the same mechanisms may be at work in female as in male mathematicians, the more effective expression of the $rs+$ gene in females than males would make the increased incidences of left- and mixed-handedness more difficult to demonstrate in females. As far as the reduction of L–R mean is concerned, the difference between mathematicians and

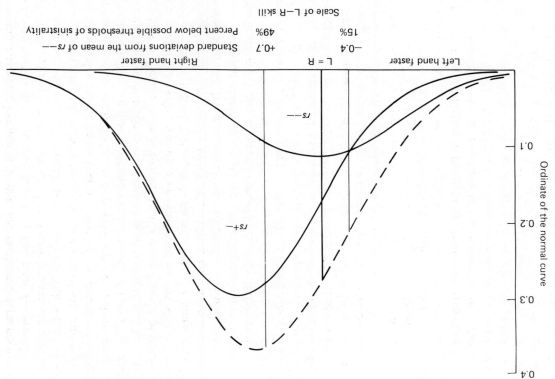

Ordinate of the normal curve

0.4 — 0.3 — 0.2 — 0.1 —

rs+—

rs——

Left hand faster   L = R   Right hand faster

Standard deviations from the mean of *rs* ——	−0.4	+0.7
Percent below possible thresholds of sinistrality	15%	49%

Scale of L—R skill

FIG. 17.4.   Distribution of L–R times hypothesised for mathematicians. (Annett & Kilshaw, 1982.)

controls was greater for females (2.6) than males (1.8). Hence, although the statistical significance of effects was less often demonstrated for female than male mathematicians, there is reason to believe that similar mechanisms are at work in both sexes.

An aspect of the findings worth checking in future research is the smaller standard deviation of female mathematicians than controls. This would be expected if mathematical ability is impaired by strong biases to dextrality associated with the $rs+$ genotype and perhaps also by stronger expression of the $rs+$ gene in the heterozygote in females than males. The stronger expression in females would be consistent, of course, with the greater resistance or greater difficulty experienced by most females in comparison with most males in learning mathematics.

This analysis of relations between mathematical ability and laterality strongly support the idea that genotypes of the $rs+$ locus differ in potential for certain intellectual skills. The study was expected to demonstrate an advantage for the $rs+-$, but it led to a demonstration of a disadvantage for the $rs++$. The evidence is in accord with the possibility that strong biases to the left hemisphere and right hand associated with the $rs++$ genotype are detrimental to mathematical thinking. The stronger expression of the $rs+$ gene in females than males is also consistent with the universal observation that females are less likely to show mathematical ability than males.

When the balanced polymorphism hypothesis for the $rs+$ gene was first formulated, there seemed to be no way of directly investigating the character-istics associated with the $rs+$ genotype. The data for hand skill and for mathematical ability have both clearly pointed to the conclusion that the bias to the left hemisphere and right hand has costs for hand speed and for mathematical thinking. It seems probable that the $rs+$ risk impairments of these aspects of skill and that the risks are greater in females than males.

17.3.   SUMMARY

The persistence of left-handers in the population, in a proportion that has probably remained stable for thousands of years, implies that some advan-tages must be associated with sinistrality. The genotype frequencies deduced in Section 15.2 suggested that the heterozygote must have advantages in comparison with both the $rs--$ and the $rs+-$ genotypes and that there could be a balanced polymorphism for the $rs+$ gene in the population. Analyses of actual hand speed for peg moving in normal samples and measures of preference and skill of mathematicians suggested ways in which the $rs+$ gene might be disadvantageous.

Peg-moving skill was analysed for the actual times taken by each hand in control groups classified for age and sex. This detailed analysis was made to check that although both hands become faster with growth, there are no significant changes with age in the *relative* skill of each hand. Differences between the hands were roughly constant, when considered as a proportion of time taken. There was no support for the idea that the right hand becomes relatively faster than the left as a result of practice. Females were slower than males with the left hand in all age groups. They were faster than males with the right hand in most preadolescent groups but slower thereafter. Correlations between the hands were similar between the sexes.

A surprising discovery in the analysis of actual hand times was that left-handers tended to be *faster* than right-handers. This was found for the preferred and nonpreferred hands of males and for the nonpreferred hands of females. The greater slowness for the nonpreferred hand in right-handers than left-handers of both sexes was confirmed in the birthday samples. In five sets of data, mixed right-handers were intermediate between left- or right-handers. These observations support the possibility that the bias to the right hand in right-handers depends on a *handicap to the left hand.*

Mathematics students and mathematics teachers showed a slight but consistent reduction of L–R bias to the right hand. The data were consistent with the possibility that mathematicians as a group are unlikely to include people of $rs+ +$ genotype. These observations suggest a hypothesis as to the costs and benefits of a balanced polymorphism for the $rs+$ gene. The advantages of developing speech and language functions on the left side are obtained at the cost of some handicap to right-hemisphere function. In the heterozygote $rs+ -$ the handicap is probably very slight, especially in males in whom gene expression is limited. In the $rs+ +$ there is a risk of significant limitation of right-hemisphere function, especially in $rs+ +$ females. Excess-ive bias to the left hemisphere is associated with motor slowness of the left hand, and possibly of the right hand also in males. It is also detrimental to mathematical thinking.

18

More About the Balanced Polymorphism: Reading Difficulties

The long-standing controversies about (a) the existence of dyslexia and (b) the relevance of laterality to problems of learning to read are reviewed in Section 5.1.2. The population surveys of Rutter and colleagues (Rutter, Tizard & Whitmore, 1970; Rutter & Yule, 1975) established that there is a statistically significant excess of children of poor reading ability when level of intelligence is taken into account. Rutter and colleagues distinguished two groups of poor readers, *backward readers* (poor in relation to age but not in relation to intelligence) and *specific reading retardates* (poor in relation to age and intelligence). Follow-up studies of children in these two groups confirmed that the distinction has diagnostic and prognostic implications. The term "dyslexic" will be used as a convenient short term to refer to specific reading retardates, as distinct from backward readers, while acknowledging at the outset that the distinction cannot always be easily made (as will become more evident).

Tests of the hypothesis that dyslexics are more likely to show sinistral preferences than nondyslexics have been complicated by failures to distinguish between the two types of poor readers and also by failures to distinguish between general school samples and clinic samples. It was shown (Section 5.1.2) that when samples of the *general population* are classified for hand and other lateral preferences and the preference groups compared for reading skills or verbal intelligence, significant differences are typically absent. But in *clinic samples* identified as having specific problems in learning to read despite good intelligence, an excess of left- or mixed-handers is often found. Incidences of atypical laterality in such special groups tend to be about twice as high as in control groups, but the excess is not statistically

357

significant unless the number of cases is very large. Slow readers in the general school population, in contrast to slow readers of good intelligence, do not show an excess of left-handers.

18.1.   THE HYPOTHESIS THAT DYSLEXIA IS ASSOCIATED WITH THE $rs--$ GENOTYPE

The RS theory suggests that a substantial minority of the population lacks some boost to the development of language skills enjoyed by the majority. In the 18% of the population hypothesised to be $rs--$, patterns of cerebral specialisation are expected to depend on chance. Many of the chance outcomes are probably satisfactory for language learning, but a small proportion may lead to special difficulties. For example, the perception of speech sounds may be poor, or the auditory and visual analyses needed to match speech sounds with written letters could depend on opposite sides of the brain, so that the co-ordination depends on an immature corpus callosum. If children having these special difficulties are $rs--$, we would expect the proportion of left- and mixed-handers to be higher than in the general population, but the majority to be right-handers (as in Fig. 14.1). On the RS theory, left- or mixed-handedness is not the cause of the language difficulty but a function of the lack of shift to the right hand (left hemisphere) in the $rs--$. The majority of mixed-handers and some left-handers in the general population carry the $rs+$ gene. Hence, language skills are not expected to differ *within samples* (normal or mentally handicapped) as a function of handedness. But handedness is expected to differ *between samples* classified for language skills.

The predictions that there would be (1) no differences for developmental language skills between children in the general school population classified for laterality and (2) an excess of left-handers among children identified as having specific delays in learning to read were supported by the findings of Annett and Turner (1974; Section 5.1.2). If those with specific delays in learning to read include an excess of $rs--$ genotypes, the mean L–R time should be smaller than that of controls. To test this prediction for the Annett and Turner sample, the children selected for birth date only must be used (Appendix I.B.9.b). The sample has been re-analysed using a new criterion of reading delay, a minimum of 20 points' difference between vocabulary IQ (Dunn, 1959) and reading quotient. Table 18.1 gives the mean IQ, RQ, and L–R time of the 13 boys and 3 girls meeting the criterion in the birthday subgroup (sex ratio, 4.3:1). The L–R mean of the males happens to be .0, as predicted for a group of $rs--$ genotypes; for the females, the L–R mean is

TABLE 18.1

L–R Peg Moving of Children with Reading Quotients 20 or More Points Lower than IQ Estimated on a Vocabulary Test

	Males (N = 13)		Females (N = 3)	
	Mean	SD	Mean	SD
IQ	120	13	109	4
RQ	88	16	78	14
L–R time for peg moving (1/10 s)	0.0	13.4	19.7	6.7

Note: Further analysis of data of Annett and Turner (1974).

very much *further to the right* than for birthday sample controls (see Table 16.4).

Pupils attending a dyslexia clinic for remedial teaching were examined to assess the lateral preferences and L–R peg-moving times of a larger sample (Appendix I.A.3). The hypothesis was that the L–R distribution of dyslexics would be less shifted to the right than that of controls. As all pupils had been thoroughly tested previously for intelligence, reading, and spelling attainment, these tests were not repeated, but scores were taken from the case records, which also gave information on neurological or other special investigations.

The assessment procedures for peg-moving time and lateral preference were as used in the several control samples (Appendix II). Information was also sought on the pupil's birth history, early motor and speech development, and on the handedness and the speech development of relatives. Pupils were asked for an opinion on how well they did in mathematics and whether they like making things. This last question aimed to discover whether the pupil regarded him/herself as clumsy or as normally skilful in using the hands.

A preliminary description of the sample (Annett, 1981) reported several findings consistent with the hypothesis of a lesser shift to the right in dyslexics. The main report of the sample (Annett & Kilshaw, 1984) included 109 males and 20 females (sex ratio 5.4:1), whose mean age, verbal and nonverbal IQ, reading and spelling delay, and peg-moving scores are given in Table 18.2. The sexes were similar for all main characteristics, except that females tended to be a little slow with the nonpreferred hand (considered further in the next section). All IQ means were in the good average range. Mean reading delays were in the range between 3 and 4 years, and spelling delays between 2 and 3 years. (The small number of mature pupils were

TABLE 18.2

The Dyslexic Sample: Age, Verbal and Nonverbal IQ, Extent of Reading or Spelling Delay, and Standardised Peg-Moving Scores by Each Hand

	Males			Females		
	N	Mean	SD	N	Mean	SD
Age in years	109	12.3	2.8	20	12.9	4.1
Verbal IQ	84	107.7	14.2	13	106.8	11.7
Nonverbal IQ	83	110.8	13.0	13	110.0	11.1
Reading problems						
C.A.–R.A. in months	70*	45.1	16.9	16	37.8	19.5
Spelling problems only						
C.A.–Sp.A in months	37*	31.0	11.7	4	23.8	12.2
Preferred hand	109	98.8	14.5	20	97.8	11.6
Nonpreferred hand	109	100.6	12.0	20	94.7	14.8

Note: Annett and Kilshaw (1984).
* Assessment details not suitable for inclusion here for 1 pupil in each category.

counted as having standard 36 months' delays for both measures, so as not to inflate the means.)

Incidences of hand, eye, and foot preference are given in Table 18.3. In comparison with controls, dyslexics were significantly more sinistral for hand and foot preferences but not for eye preferences. Table 18.4 represents the incidences for hand and foot preferences in terms of the thresholds of the normal distribution (as illustrated in Fig. 16.1). The several measures of non-right preference are remarkably consistent for the differences in threshold between dyslexics and controls. That is, the incidences in dyslexics are as expected if the distribution were shifted less far to the right than that of controls. (If the incidence of left-handed writing for controls had been about 10%, all differences between thresholds would have been about .35z.) The thresholds for consistent versus any left preference are about 1.5z apart, for controls and dyslexics (comparable to the human and nonhuman samples in Table 13.2); this confirms that the proportions of mixed-handers in all groups are about as expected under the normal curve as it moves to the right for varying distances. Similarly, the proportions of consistent left-handers are as expected under the normal curve in each sample. These observations reinforce the fundamental assumption of the RS

TABLE 18.3
Hand, Eye, and Foot Preferences in Dyslexics and Controls

		Dyslexics			Controls			χ^2 (sexes combined)
		Males	Females	Total	Males	Females	Total	
Hand preference								
	N	109	20	129	617	863	1480	
Right consistent (class 1)		49.5	45.0	48.8	64.7	61.4	62.8	12.16, $df=2$, $p<.005$
Mixed (classes 2–7)		44.0	45.0	44.2	32.7	35.0	34.0	
Left consistent (class 8)		6.4	10.0	7.0	2.6	3.6	3.2	
Left-hand writing		19.3	15.0	18.6	7.5	8.7	8.2	15.74, $df=1$, $p<.001$
Eye preference								
	N	109	20	129	383	405	788	
Mixed or left		43.1	40.0	42.6	36.3	46.9	41.7	NS
Foot preference								
	N	109	20	129	388	404	792	
Left or either		25.7	30.0	26.4	16.5	16.8	16.7	7.05, $df=1$, $p<.01$

Note: Annett and Kilshaw (1984).

TABLE 18.4

The Differences Between Dyslexics and Controls in the Thresholds of the Normal Distribution Required to Represent Incidences of Hand and Foot Preference

Criterion	Dyslexics		Controls		
	Percentage Incidence	Location of Threshold*	Percentage Incidence	Location of Threshold*	Difference Between Thresholds
Not consistent right handedness	51.2	+0.030	37.2	−0.326	0.356
Consistent left handedness	7.0	−1.475	3.2	−1.852	0.377
Left-hand writing	18.6	−0.893	8.2	−1.392	0.499
Left or either footedness	26.4	−0.631	16.7	−0.966	0.355

Note: Based on Annett and Kilshaw, 1984.
* Distances from the mean in standard deviation units.

theory that hand preferences depend on an underlying distribution of differences between the hands in skill that can be shifted more or less to the right.

Foot preferences are also strongly influenced by the factors giving a shift to the right, but eye preferences seem to be influenced by these factors only weakly. If eye preferences depended on chance alone, 50% of the population would be right-eyed. The observation that about 66% of student samples are right-eyed (Section 12.1) suggests that the right shift has weaker influence on eye than hand preference; hence, it would be more difficult to detect a reduction in shift of eye than of hand preference.

The relationship between hand preference and L–R skill in dyslexics is examined in Fig. 11.8, which shows that degrees of left-hand preference are associated with degrees of L–R skill in dyslexics in the same way as in controls. If dyslexics include an excess of sinistrals, due to a simple reduction in right shift of the laterality distribution, it should be possible to demonstrate that the L–R means of dyslexics and controls differ significantly. Surprises began in the analysis of the dyslexic sample when this expectation was *not* fulfilled.

Table 18.5 gives the L–R means of the two control samples, the means for dyslexics of both sexes, and for dyslexics distinguished for the presence or absence of relatives with a history of developmental language problems. The trend in most comparisons is in the direction expected, but the only statistically significant finding in the table is that female dyslexics without affected relatives are *more* dextral than controls (as found for the school-girls in Table 18.1). Table 18.6 gives the L–R means of dyslexics classified for

TABLE 18.5

L–R Hand Peg-Moving Time (1/10 s): The Total Sample and Dyslexics With and Without a History of Developmental Language Problems in Relatives

	Males				Females			
	N	Mean	SD	t with controls 1	N	Mean	SD	t with controls 1
Controls								
1. Combined main samples	617	6.4	8.4		863	8.0	8.8	
2. Birthday samples	122	7.1	13.1		156	12.0	12.7	
Dyslexics								
Total sample	109	5.5	10.2	1.05	20	8.8	13.2	NS
Affected relatives								
Absent or unknown	38	4.9	10.1	1.09	8	14.6	9.8	2.14*
Present	71	5.8	10.2	NS	12	4.9	14.1	1.18

Note: Annett and Kilshaw (1984).
*p < 0.05.

hand preference. For mixed- and left-handers, dyslexics resemble controls (as expected from Fig. 11.8). For consistent right-handers, the L–R differences were *larger* in dyslexics than controls. This was true of both sexes, but statistically significant for males only, due to the small female *N*. The discovery that right-handed dyslexics are more strongly dextral than controls led to a careful analysis of the distribution of L–R times in dyslexics and controls.

18.2. ARE DEVELOPMENTAL READING DIFFICULTIES ASSOCIATED WITH *rs––* AND WITH *rs++* GENOTYPES?

Figure 18.1A and **B** show the percentages of males and females, respectively, in the combined main samples and the dyslexic sample having L–R differences in each 1-s interval. Looking first at the left side of the distributions, for all intervals having negative differences (in favour of the left hand), there were more dyslexics than controls in both sexes. This was expected in view of the increased incidences of sinistrality in Table 18.3. If the excess of dyslexics were due simply to a reduction of right shift of the distribution as a whole (the original hypothesis), there should be fewer dyslexics than controls at the dextral side of the distribution. However, there were *more* dyslexics than

364

TABLE 18.6
L–R Peg-Moving Time (1/10 s) in Hand Preference Groups for Dyslexic and Control Males and Females

| | Males | | | | | | | Females | | | | | | |
| | Dyslexics | | | Controls | | | | Dyslexics | | | Controls | | | |
	N	Mean	SD	N	Mean	SD	t	N	Mean	SD	N	Mean	SD	t
Consistent right (Class 1*)	54	12.1	8.1	399	8.3	7.0	3.686*	9	13.8	9.9	530	10.4	7.4	1.373
Right mixed (2–5)	34	2.9	5.1	172	5.5	8.24	1.74	8	9.9	13.9	258	7.1	7.8	<1
Left (6–8)	21	−7.5	6.4	46	−6.4	7.9	<1	3	−9.0	2.6	75	−6.05	7.3	<1

Note: Annett and Kilshaw (1984).
*Hand preference classes (Annett, 1970a).

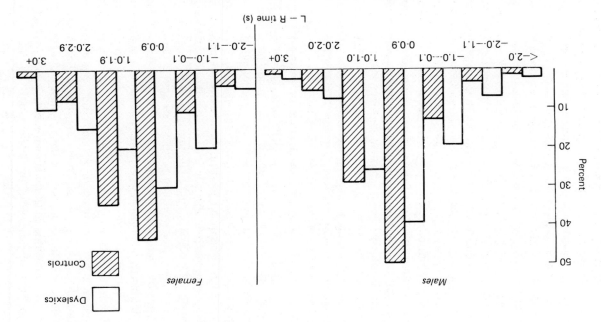

FIG. 18.1. The distribution of L–R times in dyslexics and main sample controls. Annett &
Kilshaw, 1984.

controls at intervals from 2.0+ in both sexes. Among controls (Fig. 11.3), there were more females than males at the dextral side of the distribution. In dyslexics there are also more females than males at the dextral extreme. The most surprising feature of Fig. 18.1A is the excess of male dyslexics at the right, in comparison with control males. In the central intervals of the distribution there are fewer dyslexics than controls of both sexes.

This pattern of findings was not anticipated on the initial hypothesis that developmental language problems are associated with the $rs--$ genotype, but it is in accord with the more general hypothesis that the most advantageous genotype is the heterozygote and that *both* homozygotes are at risk. The main clues found in Chapter 17 as to the risks associated with the $rs++$ genotype were that the strongly dextral have slow left-hand speeds and are likely to be absent among mathematicians. Do dyslexics show poor left-hand speeds, either as a group or only among the strongly dextral? Can dyslexics at the left and the right sides of the distribution be differentiated for hand skills, or for any other characteristic such as clumsiness or mathematical ability?

In examining the actual peg-moving times of the dyslexic sample, considerable attention was paid to the question whether some hand speeds should be considered "abnormal". At some stages of the analysis all pupils with standardised hand speed scores below certain limits were excluded. However, re-examination of the actual hand times of children in the birthday control samples (converted to standardised scores using the norms in Appendix III) showed that some control children also obtained very low scores. It is important to notice that the hand speeds of all the dyslexics included here are normal in the sense that they fall within the range found in birthday sample controls.

In order to avoid ambiguities about which hand was "preferred" and which was "better", the standardised hand scores were re-calculated for the dyslexic and the birthday control samples using right-hand norms for both hands. The means obtained are given in Table 18.7. On this analysis, the means of dyslexics are lower than those of controls, but to about the same extent for each hand and in each sex; three of the four comparisons are statistically significant. However, the main question of interest is whether poor hand speeds are characteristic of all dyslexics, or only those who might be $rs++$.

Figure 18.2 gives the standardised peg-moving means for each hand (on right-hand norms) in dyslexics and birthday sample controls of both sexes. Subjects are grouped for L–R intervals, as represented in Fig. 18.1, but combining the extreme groups. Right-hand times increase and left-hand times decrease from left to right, as expected, as subjects are classified for L–R time. The control data confirm what was shown earlier (Figs. 17.2 and 17.3) that the nonpreferred (left) hand of strong right-handers is very much poorer than the nonpreferred (right) hand of those with biases to the left

TABLE 18.7

Comparison of Dyslexics and Birthday Sample Controls for Standardized Peg-Moving Scores of Each Hand (Standardized Mean = 100, SD = 15: Right Hand Norms Applied for Both Hands)

	Dyslexics			Controls			
	N	Mean	SD	N	Mean	SD	t
Right hand							
Males	109	96.4	16.3	122	101.4	16.4	2.31*
Females	20	95.2	15.0	156	103.6	16.0	2.22*
Left hand							
Males	109	87.2	15.0	122	92.4	16.1	2.55*
Females	20	79.8	18.9	156	87.3	20.7	1.52

Note: Annett and Kilshaw (1984).
*p<.05.

(L–R <0). The point to be made about the dyslexic sample is that *these same features are present, but more pronounced than in controls*. In controls, the left-hand means of those with L–R differences of 2.0+ were equivalent to standardised scores of 80 for males and 71 for females; in dyslexics, the corresponding means were 74 and 114. Right-hand means for these groups ranged between 102 and 114. Hence, extreme dextrality in controls and dyslexics is associated with poor left-hand rather than fast right-hand speeds. The strongly right-handed dyslexics show an exaggeration of the trend in controls towards very slow left-hand time. This would be expected if dyslexics include an excess of $rs++$ genotypes but are not otherwise abnormal.

It is of interest to look at the hand speeds of children at the sinistral side of the distribution (L–R <0) in the light of the idea that left-handedness might be due to pathologies of the left hemisphere and right hand (Section 4.3.1). In controls, the right hands of those biased to the left hand for skill are at least as good as the left hands of all other groups. In dyslexics (with L–R <0) the right hand means are a little slower than those of controls, but the slowness of the right hand in sinistral dyslexics is much less marked than the slowness of the left hand in strongly dextral dyslexics. Dyslexics with a slight bias to the right hand (0–.9) do not differ from controls in standardised hand speeds. This detailed comparison of dyslexics and birthday sample controls leads to the conclusion that dyslexics are not abnormal for peg-moving times but that they are more likely to include individuals at both extremes of the normal range, while those in the centre of the range are underrepresented.

For mathematicians, the distribution of L–R times was compatible with the sum of two distributions, $rs--$ and $rs+-$, omitting the $rs++$ from the

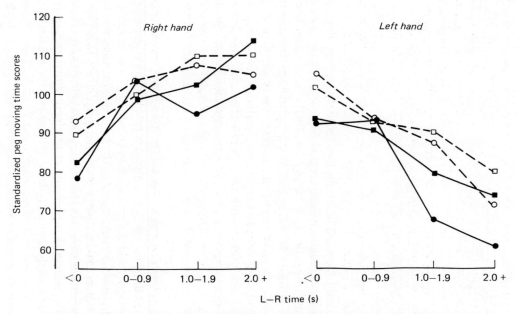

FIG. 18.2. Mean standardised scores for peg-moving time in male and female dyslexics and birthday sample controls, grouped for L–R differences. Right hand norms, mean 100, SD 15, used for both hands. Dyslexic males (■——■), dyslexic females (●– – –●), control males (□– – –□), control females (○– – –○). Annett & Kilshaw, 1984.

general population distribution (Section 17.2). Is it possible that the dyslexic sample includes $rs--$ and $rs++$ genotypes, but that the $rs+-$ (the most favourable heterozygote) is missing? This hypothesis can be tested using the Kolmogorov–Smirnov computer program used in Sections 16.2.1 and 17.2 and taking the means and standard deviations found most appropriate for controls in Table 16.5. In the general population about 18% are expected to be $rs--$ and about 32% $rs++$. The dyslexic sample was not compatible with the sum of these two distributions in the same relative proportions (36:64). It was compatible with the sum of the two homozygote distributions if the proportions were about equal or in favour of the $rs--$. For example, if the proportions of $rs--$ and $rs++$ were taken to be 60:40, the means as in Table 16.5, and the standard deviation of both distributions as 8, the D value obtained was .035. This close fit demonstrates that the dyslexic sample could consist of these two genotypes, but of course it does not prove the hypothesis correct.

Is it possible to show that the sinistral and dextral dyslexics differ in ways expected for the $rs--$ and $rs++$ genotypes on other grounds? If certain characteristics are associated with sinistral or dextral dyslexics, it should be possible to show that groups classified for the presence or absence of these characteristics differ for L–R time. It was shown in Table 18.5 that female dyslexics differed strongly for L–R time between those having relatives with a history of developmental language difficulty (who had a smaller L–R mean) and those without such relatives (with a larger L–R mean). Male dyslexics did not show this trend for presence of any affected relative, but they did show the trend for *any affected female relative*, as shown in Table 18.8. Other comparisons for males showed trends in the expected direction (for those likely to be of $rs--$ genotype), namely that they were less likely to have a history of perinatal problems, more likely to enjoy mathematics at school, and more likely to have a history of speech difficulties. The difference between male dyslexics who enjoyed and did not enjoy making things was statistically significant.

It is especially interesting that for the 93 (85%) of male dyslexics who reported enjoyment in making things there was a significant reduction of L–R time in comparison with controls. This substantial proportion of the male sample fulfils the original expectation of a reduced shift to the right for the total mean. The small number of male dyslexics who described themselves as not enjoying making things showed extremely strong dextral biases. These children were more strongly dextral than controls (as shown in Table 18.8) and also more strongly dextral than male dyslexics who did enjoy making things ($t = 2.56$, $df = 107$, $p < .02$). This difference for practical skills agrees with the expectation of Annett (1978b) for differences between the $rs--$ and $rs++$. It was surprising to find this idea so strongly supported in the dyslexic sample, when the criterion was the pupils' own report of liking or

TABLE 18.8

L–R Hand Peg-Moving Time (1/10 s) in Male Dyslexics Classified for Several Characteristics

		N	Mean	SD	t
Controls		617	6.4	8.4	
Dyslexics					
History of perinatal problems	+	54	6.0	8.8	
	–	55	4.9	11.5	1.22
Mathematics problems	+	31	6.3	10.8	
	–	78	5.1	10.1	1.25
Speech problems	–	53	6.5	10.6	
	+	56	4.5	9.9	1.62
Affected female relatives	–	74	6.2	10.1	
	+	35	3.8	10.4	1.75*
Enjoys making things	–	16	11.4	11.3	
	+	93	4.4	9.7	2.06**

Note: Annett and Kiishaw (1984).

** $p < 0.05$.

* $p < 0.10$.

disliking for making things. If strong dextrality is associated with a limitation of right-hemisphere function, and the right hemisphere has a special role in visuo-spatial skills, certain kinds of clumsiness would be associated with strong right-handedness, as suggested here.

Looking back to the distinction between retarded readers and backward readers (Section 5.1.2), there is an evident parallel with the present observations. Rutter and colleagues (Rutter, Tizard & Whitmore, 1970; Rutter & Yule, 1975) found backward readers to be more likely to have neurological abnormalities, to be clumsy, to have problems with mathematics, and to include a higher proportion of females. The more dextral dyslexics showed trends (Table 18.8) towards a history of perinatal stress, dislike of mathematics and clumsiness. The sex ratio in pupils at the dextral extreme (L – R = 2.0+) was 1.8:1, in contrast to 5.5:1 for the total sample. Of course, all pupils had been accepted for remedial teaching on the assumption that they were retarded rather than backward. Nevertheless, there was within this selected clinic sample a subgroup that resembled the "backward" readers of Rutter and colleagues, except that they happened to have reasonably high IQs. It is possible that if strongly dextral children with problems in learning to read were distinguished from the less dextral, differences would be found in sex ratios and in the type of reading problem experienced (Boder, 1973). No information was available for the present sample as to types of reading difficulty. This is a question for further research.

With regard to sex ratios, the predictions follow from the hypothesis that the $rs+$ gene is expressed more strongly in females than males (Chapter 16). Among $rs-$ genotypes no sex differences are expected; children of both sexes are expected to be at equal risk for developmental language difficulties. Sex differences at the sinistral side of the distribution depend on the $rs+-$, in whom boys are at much greater risk than girls. The deficits associated with the absence or reduced expression of the gene are expected to show themselves in problems of speech acquisition. Perhaps these depend on failure to establish efficient articulatory-phonemic speech production and perception mechanisms (see Section 6.3). No other intellectual deficit is expected in these cases, and the problem would present as a "classic" dyslexia (or specific reading retardation in the context of good intelligence). There would be an excess of left- and mixed-handers and a marked excess of males, as mentioned previously. The risk of dyslexia in association with reduced expression of the $rs+$ gene must also be a little higher in twins than in the singleborn. It would also be increased by any factors that impeded the normal process of cerebral maturation if gene expression depends on relative rates of hemisphere growth in the neonatal period. Aberrations of cerebral anatomy described in post-mortem examinations of the brains of dyslexics (Galaburda, Geschwind, LeMay, & Kemper, 1978; Galaburda, 1983) may have a specific role in the causation of reading problems, or they may indicate pathological influences on development, which impeded the expression of the $rs+$ gene.

Sex ratios at the dextral side of the L–R distribution should be biased in favour of females. The deficits at the dextral extreme are expected to depend on overexpression of the $rs++$ genotype, leading to some impairment of right-hemisphere function. Reading problems in strongly dextral children are expected to be associated with very poor left-hand skill, poor nonverbal IQ, and perhaps some loss of general intellectual power. Most of the children would present as backward rather than retarded readers and, in theory, should include an excess of girls. It was said above that in the present sample the excess of males was greatly reduced in strong right-handers, and in the samples of Rutter and colleagues (Rutter, Tizard, & Whitmore, 1970; Rutter & Yule, 1975) the sexes were about equally represented among backward readers. Lovell, Shapton, and Warren (1964) described two large surveys of reading skills in normal school-children. Among poor readers of low nonverbal IQ (less than 90), the proportions of males to females were fairly similar (1.2:1 and 1.4:1). Among those of average IQ (100 and above) there was a marked excess of males (9.4:1 and 3.3:1). Section 19.1 describes further evidence of intellectual deficits at both extremes of the L–R distribution, and especially among girls at the dextral side.

Other evidence supporting the possibility that there are at least two main types of children with reading difficulty can be found in studies of perceptual asymmetries in poor readers. On the hypothesis that the majority of specific reading retardates are likely to be $rs--$, a reduction of the typical biases in favour of the left hemisphere would be expected. Smaller asymmetries in dyslexics than controls have been reported in several studies (Dalby & Gibson, 1981; Marcel, Katz, & Smith, 1974; Pirozzolo & Rayner, 1979; Olson, 1973; Thompson, 1976; Zurif & Carson, 1970). Other studies have found poor readers as strongly biased as controls but with an unusually large proportion with biases in the atypical direction (Pipe & Beale, 1983; Witelson & Rabinovitch, 1972). Yeni-Komshian, Isenberg, and Goldberg (1975) reported that scores for material presented to the *right* hemisphere were especially poor in their sample of slow readers (as expected if some were suffering right-hemisphere impairments). Keefe and Swinney (1979) found a bimodal distribution of scores in poor readers both for a visual and for an auditory task. Normal controls showed a unimodal distribution with a mean indicating moderate advantages for the right ear and the right visual field. The poor readers showed one mode at 0 (as expected for the $rs++$) and one mode well to the right of the normal mean (as expected for the $rs--$). Thus, there are several indications that poor reading ability may be associated with both extremes of the lateral asymmetry distribution and that in the hypothesised balanced polymorphism for the $rs+$ gene both homozygotes risk problems in learning to read.

18.3.   IS THERE A GENE FOR DYSLEXIA OR A FAMILIAL RISK ASSOCIATED WITH THE $rs--$ GENOTYPE?

The hypothesis of a genetic influence on dyslexia was prompted by the observation that children with specific reading difficulties often have relatives said to be similarly affected (Hallgren, 1950; Owen, 1978). A genetic linkage analysis has suggested that a gene playing a role in reading disability is located on chromosome number 15 (Smith, Kimberling, Pennington, & Lubs, 1983).

When relatives of dyslexics were given tests of reading under stress (such as nonsense passages or text printed backwards, upside down, or in mirror image), 45% were found to have severe difficulties, as would be expected if their reading skills were insecure (Finucci, Guthrie, Childs, Abbey, & Childs, 1976). If there is a gene for dyslexia, its mode of transmission could not be deduced from the pedigrees of the affected families. Finucci et al. concluded that the disorder is genetically heterogeneous and that subgroups of disabled readers should be looked for.

On the assumption of the **RS** theory that specific reading difficulties arise by chance in the $rs-$, a small increase in the proportion of relatives experiencing reading difficulty might be expected but not a large one. The reasons for suggesting that the increase would be small can be seen from inspection of the distribution of genotypes in families (Appendices IV and V). All family types are expected to show a mixture of all genotypes. The majority of $rs-$ in the population are born to two heterozygote parents, who themselves carry the most favourable genotype. For any $rs-$ individual with reading difficulties, there is only a slight increase in the risk for relatives.

The attempt to work out the implications of the **RS** theory for a possible familial association for dyslexia due to the $rs-$ genotype is complicated by the discovery that a subgroup of pupils attending a dyslexia clinic are strongly dextral and possibly of $rs++$ genotype (Section 18.2). Does this group of poor readers also have an increased proportion of affected relatives? Rutter, Tizard, and Whitmore (1970) found similar incidences (about 33%) of positive family history in backward readers and in specific reading retardates. In the present sample there were a number of findings that suggest that familial effects might depend on the sinistral tail more than on the dextral tail of the lateral asymmetry distribution. These included the difference between females with and without affected relatives (Table 18.5), and the difference between males with and without affected female relatives (Table 18.8). Further, the analysis for the Kolmogorov–Smirnov test suggested that in this sample there were more $rs-$ and fewer $rs++$ than if these genotypes were drawn at random from the population. If the risk of reading difficulty is smaller in the $rs++$ than the $rs-$, the association between relatives would also be smaller. Of course, this may not be true of the general population. Further studies are needed to clarify these possibilities.

If the complications introduced by the strongly dextral dyslexics are put aside for the present and it is assumed that familial effects relate to "specific" rather than "backward" readers, it can be asked whether the presence of affected relatives is attributable to risks associated with the $rs-$ genotype. The pedigrees found by Finucci et al. would be consistent with this possibility, but, of course, it would not be possible to deduce a precise mode of transmission, as not all of the $rs-$ are affected, only those with certain patterns of cerebral specialisation that arise by chance. However, by looking at a group in which the rs — — genotype is expected to be especially frequent, the parents and children of L × L families, some assessment can be made of the risk of developmental language difficulties in the rs — —. It can then be asked whether the incidence of affected relatives in dyslexics exceeds this level.

Standard questions about developmental problems of speech, reading, writing, and spelling were asked in several samples. These included the parents of L × L families, mathematics lecturers, their academic controls, and the parents of dyslexics. Table 18.9 gives the percentages of individuals reported to have experienced any developmental language problem. The percentages are surprisingly high for all groups of males. If 18% of male academics in arts and social science faculties report some personal developmental language problem, it seems likely that most families of reasonable size would be able to report at least one affected member. Incidences for other males range from 20 to 29%, and those of the fathers and sons of L × L families dyslexics resemble those of the fathers and brothers of.

Among females, only 1 of 20 female academics in arts and social science reported a developmental language problem. Incidences were higher in all other groups of females in Table 18.9, but not at statistically significant levels, partly attributable to the small N for the academic controls. As for

TABLE 18.9

Reports of Developmental Problems of Speech, Reading, Writing and Spelling

	Males		Females		Sex ratio
	N	%	N	%	
A. Self-report					
Academics in art & social science	50	18.0	20	5.0	3.6:1
Mathematics teachers	97	19.6	27	22.2	1:1.1
B. Report by mother or other informant					
L × L families					
Father	55	21.8	Mother 55	9.1	2.4:1
Son	58	29.3	Daughter 57	15.8	1.9:1
Dyslexics' families					
Father	116	29.3	Mother 117	16.2	1.8:1
Brothers	78	20.5	Sisters 75	13.3	1.5:1

Note: Annett and Kilshaw (1984).

males, incidences were similar in the relatives of dyslexics and the members of L × L families. (The mothers of L × L families had taken the initiative of writing a letter in response to my appeals for such families, so they cannot be regarded as unselected with regard to language skills.) Whether or not there is a true increase of risk of developmental language problems in members of L × L families cannot be decided on this evidence. It suggests, however, that the relatives of dyslexics are at no greater risk than members of families hypothesised, on the RS theory, to include a majority of rs− − genotypes. Hence, it is possible that familial effects for language difficulties could be due to the rs− − genotype rather than to a specific agent for dyslexia.

The sex ratios in Table 18.9 support this interpretation. A marked excess of males is usually found in studies of children with developmental problems of speech and reading (Chapter 5), but in the relatives of dyslexics this excess is much reduced (Hallgren, 1950; Owen, 1978). The ratio of affected male to female academics in the arts and social sciences is comparable to that of general samples, whereas the sex ratio for all other groups shows a reduced excess of males. These findings are as expected on the hypothesis that the rs+ gene is expressed more effectively in females than males but that the frequency of the gene is reduced in female mathematicians, mothers and daughters in L × L families, and in the relatives of dyslexics. It is especially interesting that female lecturers in mathematics reported developmental language problems more often than other academic females; the risk in female mathematicians seems to be comparable to that of males. This is just the reciprocal relationship expected if mathematical ability is associated with the absence or reduced expression of the rs+ gene, as argued earlier (Section 17.2). The reduction of sex difference in liability to language difficulties in the relatives of dyslexics is a problem for theories that hypothesise a gene for dyslexia. It is another piece of the puzzle that falls into place on the RS theory, given the assumption that the rs+ gene is expressed more effectively in females than in males. When the gene is absent, sex differences for dyslexia are absent, in the same way that sex differences for handedness are also absent (Table 15.3).

Does it matter whether the affected relatives are on the mother's or the father's side of the family? Sex differences that are due to sex variation in gene expression (as argued in Chapter 16) should apply to both sides of the family. Table 18.10 shows that there are no effects due to the side of the family reported to have affected relatives. The small number of pupils with affected relatives on both sides of the family had a very small L–R mean. The mean was comparable to that of children in L × L families without pathologically sinistral parents. That is, there was a small, nonsignificant bias to the right hand and no evidence of group bias to the left hand.

TABLE 18.10

L–R Hand Peg-Moving Time (1/10 s) in Dyslexics Classified for Type of Relative with Development Language Problem

	N	Mean	SD	t with controls
Controls	617	6.4	8.4	
Paternal or maternal relatives				
Father and his kin only	37	5.6	10.5	—
Mother and her kin only	36	7.1	10.9	—
Both paternal and maternal kin	10	0.9	10.7	2.07*
Sex of affected relatives				
Male only	43	6.9	10.1	—
Female	40	4.3	11.4	1.49

Note: Annett and Kilshaw (1984).

*$p < .05$.

18.4.   SUMMARY

The hypothesis that children with specific reading difficulties despite good intelligence lack the boost to language growth associated with the $rs+$ gene was tested in children attending a dyslexic clinic. It was predicted that the distribution of L–R skill would be like that of controls but less shifted to the right. Dyslexics were more often left- and mixed-handed and also left-footed than controls, as expected if the distribution were less right shifted but L–R means did *not* differ significantly.

A close look at distributions of L–R times revealed an excess of dyslexics at the *dextral* extreme as well as at the sinistral extreme, and a relative deficit in the proportion with moderate biases to the right hand. Strongly dextral dyslexics were especially likely to have slow left-hand times (although all in the normal range) in keeping with the possibility that they include an excess of $rs++$ genotypes. Strongly dextral dyslexics differed from more sinistral dyslexics in a number of ways that need to be checked in further studies. However, it is possible that the more sinistral pupils resembled the specific reading retardates and the more dextral pupils resembled the backward readers distinguished by Rutter, Tizard, and Whitmore (1970).

A comparison of reports of developmental language problems in the relatives of dyslexics, with reports of such problems in L × L families, found similar incidences. This suggests that it may be unnecessary to postulate a gene for dyslexia, in addition to the risks inherent in the $rs--$ genotype. There are several sex differences that are consistent with the possibility that the $rs+$ gene is expressed more strongly in females than in males and that sex differences in handedness and in the risks of language problem are lacking in those in whom the gene is likely to be absent.

19

Further Implications of the Right Shift Theory

19.1. VOCABULARY SCORE IN NORMAL SCHOOL-CHILDREN

The $rs+$ gene is hypothesised to facilitate left-hemisphere speech. If the mechanism of gene action gave direct advantages to language growth, it would seem to follow that the $rs++$ should have especially well-developed language skills. However, the findings for strongly right-handed dyslexics (Chapter 18) introduced the unexpected possibility that the $rs++$ might have problems in learning to read. This seemed very surprising while the gene was thought to facilitate language development, but no longer surprising if the mechanism of gene action is to impair right-hemisphere function. Many avenues for further research are opened up by these speculations.

The hypothesis of a balanced polymorphism with heterozygote advantage suggests that within the school population, children of $rs+-$ genotype should be especially well equipped for the acquisition of all language skills. These children probably learn in school relatively easily, while children of $rs--$ and $rs++$ genotype are more likely to have learning problems. There is no method available at present of identifying the gentoypes, but there are indications that poor readers at each extreme of the laterality distribution experience different types of problem, as considered in Chapter 18. Inspection of Fig. 16.1 shows that for L–R hand skill, all genotypes are represented over almost all of the range of differences in skill; chance is the major variable in the production of relative hand skill, and the biases introduced by the $rs+$ gene are small. However, the relative proportions of the three genotypes are expected to differ from left to right of the continuum of L–R skill.

The idea that children of heterozygote genotype might be especially well equipped for learning could be examined in data already available for the birthday samples. All children in both samples had been given the Peabody Picture Vocabulary Test (Dunn, 1959), which simply requires the child to point to one of four pictures to show the meaning of a word spoken by the examiner. The children were classified for L–R times (as in Fig. 18.2), and the groups were compared for vocabulary test IQs, as shown in Table 19.1. In both sexes, the highest mean scores were obtained by the group with a moderate bias to the right hand (0–.9) and the means were lower at each extreme. Tests of trend were not significant for males, but for females there was a highly significant quadratic trend. This effect was quite unexpected and unlooked for until this re-analysis of old data was prompted by the balanced polymorphism hypothesis. Both of the birthday samples had been previously examined for associations between handedness and abilities, and no convincing relationships found. This new analysis confirms that right-handers are heterogeneous for L–R skill and supports the possibility that intellectual performance varies between $rs+-$ and $rs++$ genotypes.

Sex differences should not be examined closely in Table 19.1 because there are reasons to believe that left-handers were over-represented among males (Kilshaw & Annett, 1983). However, it may be noted that at the extreme right (L–R = 2.0+) males were less frequent than females (males 15%; females 26%), and also relatively better for vocabulary IQ. Both of these differences are in accord with the assumption that the risks of over-expression of the $rs+$ gene are mitigated in males.

TABLE 19.1
Vocabulary Test IQs in Birthday Sample Controls Classified for L–R Time

	Males			Females		
L–R time	N	Mean	SD	N	Mean	SD
<0	30	112.2	18.0	22	99.0	21.3
0–0.9	41	116.2	18.0	37	109.2	21.1
1.0–1.9	33	111.9	17.3	57	107.7	17.1
2.0+	18	107.9	16.0	40	99.8	21.0
	F	df	p	F	df	p
F ratios for trend						
Linear	1.096	1.118	NS	—	—	—
Quadratic	1.428	1.118	NS	7.283	1.152	<.01

Note: Annett and Kilshaw (1984).

19.2. ARE UNIVERSITY SAMPLES
LESS BIASED TO THE RIGHT HAND
THAN GENERAL SAMPLES?

The hypothesis of heterozygote advantage and the analysis of the last section suggest that university students might include more $rs+-$ genotypes than the general population. In Chapter 14, the $rs+$ gene was treated as dominant in the sense that all gene carriers were expected to have left-hemisphere speech. The suggestion that the $rs+-$ and $rs++$ genotypes differ for intellectual ability implies that the gene has additive effects for hemisphere specialisation. The gene may or may not also have additive effects for handedness. Chapter 16 could find no convincing evidence for or against the additive and dominant versions of the theory; however, it should be noted that the data considered in Chapter 16 depended on incidences of left-handedness (the left side of the L–R distribution), whereas critical evidence for additive effects is more likely to be found at the dextral side of the L–R distribution (as in Fig. 18.1).

To test the hypothesis that students are less biased to the right hand than the general population it would be necessary to collect data using the same procedures for undergraduates and samples of the general population of comparable age. My questionnaire samples included undergraduates and service recruits (Appendix I.B.5). Comparison of the distributions of consistent left-, mixed-, and consistent right-handedness (in Table 1 of Annett, 1970a) found a significant value ($\chi^2 = 6.318$, $df = 2$, $p < .05$); the percentages of consistent left-handers were the same for students and recruits (4.3%), but there were more mixed-handers and fewer consistent right-handers among students than recruits, as expected if students are less strongly biased to the right hand.

The control samples used above (Appendix I.B.9 and 10) included university and polytechnic undergraduates (HL and OU), comprehensive school-children (LS) and selected school-girls (DA) as well as the birthday samples drawn from the general school population. The distributions of hand preferences in these samples are given in Table 16.3 and the distribution of L–R times in Table 16.4. Comparisons of the samples shows that the HL males were significantly less biased to the right hand than other males (Annett & Kilshaw, 1983). The HL females did not differ significantly from other main sample females, but they did have the smallest mean. The birthday sample school-girls were significantly more biased to the right hand than main sample females. These various trends could be due to chance effects and certainly need confirmation. They are consistent with the possibility, however, that undergraduates are less strongly biased to the right hand than the general population.

The possibility that undergraduates are more often of $rs+-$ genotype would imply not only a smaller mean, but also a smaller variance of L–R scores. The greater variability of the birthday samples than the main samples is probably attributable mainly to age differences, but it would be consistent with greater genotype uniformity in undergraduates.

Psychological research has relied heavily on student subjects. The possibility that undergraduates are more often heterozygote for the $rs+$ gene implies that student samples cannot be assumed to be representative of the general population, for laterality and for other characteristics suggested above to vary with $rs+$ genotypes. It is possible that the combined main samples above *underestimate* the right shift of the general population, and perhaps also underestimate the variance of the laterality distribution, as the majority of these subjects were undergraduates. This would imply that when the combined main samples were used as controls, they offered *conservative* tests of differences for mathematicians and dyslexics. It would also imply that the distributions of handedness in families of students are influenced by selection biases that may have contributed to the lack of fit of some predictions in Table 16.7.

19.3. SPECIAL SKILLS: TENNIS PLAYERS AND VETERINARY SURGEONS

The possibility that the $rs+$ gene might be associated with risks to capacities for skilled performance was suggested when the single-allele hypothesis was first formulated (Annett, 1978b), and it was later discovered that left-handers have absolute advantages in hand speed over right-handers (Section 17.1.2). This was clear for the nonpreferred hand of both sexes in both groups of samples; male left-handers in the combined main samples also showed faster preferred hand times than mixed- and right-handers (Figs. 17.2 and 17.3). These observations, and the analyses for mathematicians and dyslexics, led to the idea that the gene promotes left-hemisphere specialisation for language through right-hemisphere impairment.

Skilled performance might be handicapped by right-hemisphere impairment in several ways. There could be defects in capacities for visuo-spatial thinking, for the fine control of both hands, or for fast reactions to stimuli on both sides. Footballers need to kick well with either foot, boxers must see the punch coming from the left or the right, athletes must have good whole-body coordination (Section 5.2.1). The observation that outstanding players of several sports include a high proportion of left-handers supports the assumption that skilled performance must be part of the costs and benefits of the balanced polymorphism of the $rs+$ gene.

Table 19.2A gives the proportions of left-handed tennis players of both sexes in the 1978 Wimbledon tournament and the handedness of champions between 1946 and 1978, counting by years, not individual players (Jones—personal communication). The proportions of left-handed male players and champions were almost twice as high as the 8.1% reporting left-handed use of a tennis racquet in my questionnaire samples (Table 10.3). There is no effect evident for females. The percentages for champions were not higher than for players, which seems to imply that within the professional group handedness is irrelevant to success.

Table 19.2B shows the percentages of left-handers among male tennis professionals as ranked in the final rankings for 1982 (Volvo Grand Prix Media Guide, 1983). Here, the proportion of left-handers is greater in those of higher rank. If the cohort of players is divided between the top 185 and bottom 184, there is a statistically significant excess of left-handers in the former ($\chi^2 = 12.60$, $df = 1$, $p < .001$). The reliability of this observation must be checked in future years.

What would these observations imply for the balanced polymorphism of the $rs+$ gene? An incidence of about 16% found for the majority of tennis professionals is about as expected if tennis players include $rs--$ and $rs+-$ but not $rs++$ genotypes, as hypothesised for mathematicians (Fig. 17.4). As argued for female mathematicians, the same mechanisms may be at work in

TABLE 19.2

Incidences of Left-Handedness in Tennis Players

A. The Wimbledon Programme for 1978

	Males		Females	
	N	Left-handed players (%)	N	Left-handed players (%)
Singles players	128	15.6	96	9.4
Champions 1947–78, inclusive	33	15.1	33	6.1

B. Computer Rankings of the Association of Tennis Professionals 1982

Male Ranks	Left-handed Players (%)
1–10	30
11–100	14
101–360	6

female tennis players as male ones, but they would be more difficult to demonstrate in view of the stronger expression of the $rs+$ gene in females. If it should be confirmed that in outstanding (star) tennis professionals, the incidence of left-handedness is about 30%, it would suggest that these players are more likely to be of $rs--$ genotype (see Table 15.2). This would imply that *any* impairment of the right hemisphere, even in male heterozygotes, is associated with some loss of potential for skilled sensorimotor performance.

These analyses have been based on the hand used for playing tennis, as this is the only information available. More detailed assessments of hand preference and skill would probably reveal that most players are not strongly biased to either side, and that many show mixed hand preferences, as found for other sports (Section 5.2.1). The fact that many outstanding players are right-handed is no problem for the RS theory, of course, as the majority of $rs--$ are expected to be right-handed (Fig. 16.1). As for mathematical ability and for dyslexia, the increased incidence of left-handedness in tennis players is a by-product of the genotype distribution. The special ability or disability is not caused by the atypical sinistrality.

With regard to the incidence of left-handedness in surgeons, data was collected through a handedness questionnaire distributed to members of an association for small-animal veterinarians. The questionnaire (Fig. 10.1) included an additional question, asking whether or not surgery was a main interest. The data relied, of course, on voluntary returns, but a comparison could be made within the sample between those who reported that surgery was, or was not, a main interest. Only 23 vets said that surgery was not a main interest, and of these, 8.7% were left-handed writers, and 26.1% showed some sinistral preference. Among 87 vets for whom surgery was a main interest, 13.8% were left-handed writers, and 41.4% reported some left-handed preference. The difference between groups was not statistically significant for this small sample, but it was in the direction expected. The percentages of left- and mixed-hand preference found among veterinary surgeons are compatible with a reduction of the right shift found in the general population. As for mathematicians and tennis players, the percentages are consistent with the possibility that surgeons include $rs--$ and $rs+-$ but not $rs++$ genotypes.

The Old Testament description of the 700 slingers in the army of the Children of Benjamin who could sling stones at a hair breadth and not miss was cited in Section 3.1. This ancient witness to the special skill of some left-handers now has a possible explanation in the greater visuo-motor skill in those lacking the $rs+$ genotype. Contrary to the speculations of Carlyle (Section 4.2), primitive warfare must have ensured the preservation of $rs-$ genes and hence *left-handers* in the population through the advantages they would have in direct combat fighting. Of course, left-handed sportsmen and fighters might enjoy some advantages over right-handers because they can strike from the less frequent direction, but the findings for visuo-motor skill in peg moving suggest that they have absolute advantages also.

Another ancient idea, that some people might be "ambilevous" (having two left hands) as opposed to "ambidextrous", needs some qualification. If ambilevous means being clumsy with both hands, it is highly inappropriate to natural left-handers. Clumsy left hands are most likely to be found in strong right-handers.

19.4. SOME PUZZLES ABOUT SCHIZOPHRENIA AND ABOUT PATHOLOGICAL SINISTRALITY

The review (in Section 5.3) of questions about handedness in relation to personality and mental illness found no consistent effects for schizophrenia. There was no evidence that schizophrenics have increased tendencies to mixed- or to left-handedness. There were suggestions that schizophrenics could include an excess of strong right-handers. If this evidence depends on a greater reluctance of some patients to give "either" responses to question-naires (Section 10.1), the apparent handedness difference may be verbal rather than actual. If schizophrenics should be found to be more strongly dextral on objective tests of L–R skill than general control samples (*not* students, for reasons discussed in Section 19.2), then it would be worth asking whether liability to schizophrenia is associated with greater risk in the $rs++$ genotype. Recent evidence of poor inter-hemispheric communication in schizophrenics (Section 8.4) could be associated with the right-hemisphere impairment through which the $rs+$ gene has been hypothesised to work, as much as to the poor commissural connections so far suggested.

One of the curious findings about schizophrenia mentioned in Section 5.3 is the observation of Slater (1953) and of Gottesman and Shields (1972) that MZ twins who were discordant for handedness were more often discordant for schizophrenia than MZ twins who were concordant for handedness. If this relationship between discordance for handedness and discordance for schizophrenia should be confirmed, what contribution could the RS theory make to its explanation? On the calculations in Table 16.11B, for example, MZ male RR pairs would include $rs++$, $rs+-$, and $rs--$ genotypes in the proportions .40:.49:.11, respectively, while in RL pairs the corresponding proportions would be .11:.52:.37. All genotypes are represented in both types of twin pair, but comparison of the proportions suggests that discordance for schizophrenia in RL pairs might be function of the smaller proportion of $rs++$ and larger proportion of $rs--$ genotypes. Perhaps the chance factors determining cerebral lateralisation in the latter lead to arrangements that are more favourable for one twin than the other. Another possibility is that the

$rs+ -$ genotype, as the most favourable heterozygote, offers some protection from the disorder.

Another puzzling observation about laterality and schizophrenia was Taylor's (1975) report of patients who had been treated by temporal lobectomy for the relief of epilepsy and later developed a schizophrenia-like psychosis. Of 13 patients who became psychotic, 7 were left-handed. Neither lesion side nor handedness were specifically related to the risk of breakdown. The resected temporal lobes of these patients frequently showed lesions that were probably congenital. On the RS theory, pathological left-handedness may be induced by any factors that interfere with the usual processes of cerebral maturation. If the gene mechanism depends on processes governing the relative rates of growth of the right and left hemispheres, small distortions of these processes may be sufficient to interfere with the expression of the $rs+$ gene. That is, pathology of either hemisphere could lead to a loss of the normal bias to the right hand, and in groups of such cases up to 50% could be left-handed, as observed in the highly selected group of temporal lobectomy psychotics.

Similarly, an examination of the handedness and lateralisation of EEG abnormalities in mental retardates (Section 4.3.1) found an increased incidence of left-handedness in those with bilateral EEG anomalies, as well as those with left-hemisphere pathology (Silva & Satz, 1979). Geschwind and Behan (1982) reported raised incidences of left-handedness in patients with a variety of immune disorders, as well as increased frequencies of immune disorders in left-handers. They suggested a mechanism to account for these relationships, which involved slowing of the neuronal development of the left hemisphere. The RS theory would suggest that *any* slowing of neural development would lead to an increased proportion of left-handers, whether or not the left hemisphere were specifically affected.

19.5. GENOTYPES IN FAMILIES AND EXPECTATIONS FOR FAMILIAL EFFECTS

If the genetic assumptions in Chapters 15 and 16 are correct and if the distributions of genotypes in families are approximately as calculated in Appendices IV and V, some interesting points can be made about genotypes in families. The first is that most families must include most genotypes. The most advantageous genotype, the $rs+ -$, predominates in the families of R × R and L × R parents, as well as in the population as a whole. A second point to notice is that in matings of the most advantageous genotype $(rs+ - \times rs+ -)$, the children will, on average, include 50% $rs+ -$, 25%

$rs--$, and 25% $rs++$; that is, one half of the children will be of the less favoured genotypes. All of the nine possible matings (Table 1.1 and Appendices IV and V) are expected to occur, and there are no grounds for suggesting assortive mating for the $rs+$ gene locus. However, it is tempting to speculate that there might be an attraction of opposites between the two different homozygotes, because when parents of the less favoured genotypes marry ($rs++ \times rs--$), all the children will be of the most favoured genotype ($rs+-$).

If the balanced polymorphism hypothesis is correct and the genotypes have implications for intellectual and physical skills, they would also have implications for educational and socio-economic status. Leiber and Axelrod (1981b) found that in parents of undergraduates there were significantly more sinistrals among those of higher rather than lower educational and occupational status. The higher proportion of left-handers, and also of mixed-handers, was observed for fathers and mothers, but statistically significant for the former only. The handedness of the student respondents did not differ with parental educational or occupational status. This is as expected on the RS theory, as the student respondents were selected for abilities probably associated with the $rs+-$ genotype. Further, genotypes are *not* transmitted directly to the next generation. The $rs+$ system may be involved in upward and downward mobility in socioeconomic status, but it cannot be involved in the perpetuation of such status.

In studies of lateral asymmetries of normal subjects (Sections 6.1.3 and 7.2), it has become customary to classify subjects for the presence of left-handedness in relatives, as well as for personal handedness. Would the RS theory expect the handedness of relatives to be a relevant variable in studying cerebral asymmetries? If the significant variable for atypical cerebral speech is possession of the $rs--$ genotype, the presence of one left-handed relative will add little to the probability that this genotype is present. The possession of two left-handed relatives, even when these are the parents, does not guarantee that the individual will be $rs--$. Inspection of the proportions of genotypes in families, in Appendices IV and V, confirms that the presence of sinistral relatives adds very little to the information gained from knowledge of personal handedness. No noticeable effects were found associated with the presence of familial sinistrality in the study of visual asymmetries (Table 7.9). No differences were found in incidences of left-handedness in the relatives of mathematicians or dyslexics in comparison with controls. This negative evidence supports the argument that the presence of sinistral relatives should not have strong implications for individual laterality.

However, if the variables under study are related to the *dextral* side of the laterality distribution, the presence of sinistral relatives might be more predictive of the *absence* of $rs++$ genotypes. It is evident that simple statements cannot be made, in our current state of ignorance, about the implications of the presence of left-handed relatives for lateral asymmetries.

19.6. SUMMARY

The surprising implication in Chapter 18 is that strong shifts to the left hemisphere and right hand (presumably in those of the $rs++$ genotype) are associated with *handicaps* to *language development* was checked in a re-examination of data for vocabulary IQs in birthday sample school-children. Higher IQs were found in children with moderate bias to the right hand than in children at *both* extremes of the L–R distribution. These trends were especially clear in females.

The hypothesis of heterozygote advantage suggests that undergraduates may include relatively more $rs+-$ genotypes than the general population. There is little evidence on this question, but the data available is in accord with the possibility.

The balanced polymorphism hypothesis offers an explanation of the slightly higher proportion of left-handers among skilled performers in several fields. Evidence is examined for professional tennis players and for veterinary surgeons. The popular idea that the left hand is "cack"-handed may apply to the left hand of right-handers and perhaps to the left hand of "pathological" left-handers, but certainly not to the left hand of natural left-handers.

Reports on the laterality of schizophrenics give no reason to believe that the $rs+$ gene is directly relevant to this disorder. However, the report of discordance for schizophrenia in MZ twins who are discordant for handed-ness suggests the possibility that the chance factors influencing the cerebral organisation of $rs+-$ genotypes may be more favourable for one twin than the other and give some protection from breakdown. The excess of left-handers in cases of temporal lobectomy who later became schizophrenic is probably due to early cerebral pathology, which prevented the expression of the $rs+$ gene and led to chance determination of handedness.

Although a genetic foundation is postulated for the right shift of the human laterality distribution, and although the genotypes are expected to differ in advantages and disadvantages for certain physical and intellectual skills, familial effects are expected to be limited. This is because the most advan-tageous genotype is the most frequent genotype in the population and also in $R \times R$ and $L \times R$ families. Children can be expected to differ from parents about as often as they resemble them, over the population as a whole. The practice of classifying subjects in psychological studies of laterality for the handedness of relatives probably has little value (especially if the subjects are undergraduates of $rs+-$ genotype).

20

A Cross-Cultural Test of Findings for Hand Preference and Skill on Children in Guatemala

The question whether findings for handedness in English school-children are replicable in children of other races and cultures has been examined by Demarest (1982) for children of two racial groups in Guatemala. The majority of the population of Guatemala are Spanish-speaking, of mixed Spanish and Indian ancestry, and known as Ladinos. The native Indian population are Maya who speak some 20 Mayan languages but must learn Spanish if they are to be educated in school. Demarest set out in 1976 to check on findings reported for English school-children (Annett, 1970b; Annett & Turner, 1974).

These were as follows:

1. The distributions of hand preference and of relative manual skill are unchanged during growth in the school years.
2. Females are more asymmetrical to the right than males.
3. Right-, mixed-, and left-handers (defined as fully consistent right or left, and inconsistent) are in binomial proportions.
4. Degrees of hand preference and degrees of L–R skill are systematically related.
5. Children of poorer language skills include an excess of non–right-handers.

A sixth test was added to check the observation of Kilshaw and Annett (1983):

6. Left-handers are faster than right-handers in hand speed.

389

Four samples of children were examined, three Ladino and one Indian. The first Ladino sample (LI) was of preschool children tested in their homes in North Guatemala city. The second Ladino sample (LII) was of pupils attending an elementary school in South Guatemala city. The third Ladino sample (LIII) was of school-children in San Pedro Soloma, a township in the mountains north of Guatemala city. The Maya sample (M) was of children attending schools in and around Soloma.

The procedures used included the peg-moving task, which was given to all children. The apparatus and method were based on the description of Annett (1970b). Demarest devised a Bean test to check the generality and consistency of findings for the peg task. The bean test required children to pick up seven dried beans and place them in a narrow-necked aspirin bottle. Five trials were given for each hand, timed by stopwatch. The bean test was given to all but the first Guatemalan sample.

Observations of lateral preference were introduced during the testing of LII and continued for other samples. These were to wave goodbye, throw a ball, kick a soccer ball, insert beans in a bottle, screw on the lid of a jar, sight through a tube, eat with a spoon, and use a pencil. As the findings for hand preference are not reported separately from those for foot and eye preference, and as the hand tests include a gesture (waving), which requires no skill, the findings for preference cannot be compared closely with those for hand preference in other samples.

Demarest's findings are of particular interest from two main viewpoints. The first is their bearing on questions of the relevance of age, sex, and race for differences between the hands in skill. The second is the check he was able to make on aspects of the balanced polymorphism hypothesis. In a group of slow language learners, would biases to the right for L–R skill be reduced (as considered in Chapter 18)? Among left-handed children, are absolute hand speeds faster than among right-handed children (Section 17.1.2)? This surprising discovery was made in the analysis of English samples, long after the data were gathered. Would Demarest also find this absolute hand speed advantage in left-handers, also long after making the measurements?

20.1. SEX, AGE AND RACE

The question whether there are *sex* differences in extent of right shift can be answered as unequivocally for Demarest's Guatemalan samples as for my English ones. In all four Guatemalan samples the girls gave larger L–R differences and larger z scores than males on the peg-board task. On the bean test, girls showed larger differences than males in the Ladino samples, but the Maya did not differ for mean L–R time. Demarest points out that the sex difference is not due to differing numbers of left-handers. If the left-handers are excluded and L–R differences are examined for right-handers only, the relatively greater bias of females to the right is still evident. On the RS theory, of course, the sex difference is due to stronger expression of the $rs+$ gene in females, so that sex differences are expected among right-handers and not among left-handers.

The findings for L–R differences on the peg-moving and bean tests are summarised in Table 20.1 for the four Guatemalan samples and for the English birthday samples. The latter are as in Table 17.2 but combined for sex. Table 20.1 gives the peg-moving test findings for the actual difference between the hands (L–R mean and SD in 1/10 s), the mean difference as a percentage of absolute time for the left hand (percent–left) and the mean difference as a z score. The z score indicates the distance of the mean difference from 0, or the extent of right shift, as illustrated in Fig. 14.1. The z score for the bean test is also given where this is available.

There are several important points to be made about these data. With regard to age, there is an obvious trend in almost all samples for the L–R difference to *fall* with increasing age. This implies that the hands become more similar in time taken with age. The hands certainly do not become more differentiated, as would be expected if the greater skill of the right hand were a product of extra practice in the use of that hand. However, this apparent change in the difference between the hands is a function of the greater slowness and greater variability of younger than older children. If the mean difference is examined as a proportion of time taken (percent–left) or as a proportion of the SD (z score), no systematic changes with age are apparent. The L–R differences are remarkably stable across age groups from the pre-school to mid-teen years. These observations fully support the conclusion of Annett (1970b) that the distribution of relative manual speed is unchanged during growth.

There are certain fluctuations between the measurements of groups, as expected on account of accidental differences between samples and measure-ments. The LIII children in grades 4 to 6 obtained an especially large L–R difference on the peg task, which gave them a larger percent–left and a larger z score than found in any other age group in any sample. However, the bean test scores of this group were not exceptional, which suggests that there was some peculiarity of the peg-task measurements for this group, rather than a true excessive dextrality. The English 10- to 11-year-olds obtained a smaller L–R mean than any other age group and a correspondingly smaller percent–left and z score. This group included an unusually high proportion of left-handers, which was almost certainly due to sampling factors. These excep-tional groups give no ground for doubting the general conclusion that the distribution of differences between the hands in skill, which is presumed by the RS theory to underlie observed preferences, is stable throughout growth.

With regard to *race*, the Maya appear to be less biased to the right hand for

TABLE 20.1

L–R Hand Time in Age Groups in Four Samples of Guatemalan Children and in English Children: Peg-Moving Test for All Samples (Time in 1/10 s) and z Scores for the Bean Test in Three Samples

	N	L–R mean	SD	Percent Left**	z***	Bean Test z
			Peg-Moving Task			
Ladinos I						
Age*						
3.8–5.5	44	29.6	31.8	10.5	0.9	
5.6–6.8	51	25.7	26.5	10.8	1.0	
6.9–9.7	51	19.0	16.7	9.7	1.1	
Ladinos II						
Grade						
K	35	25.4	19.6	10.8	1.3	1.6
1	86	19.1	16.6	10.2	1.2	1.4
2	72	14.1	11.5	9.2	1.2	1.6
3	85	14.0	11.2	9.5	1.3	2.0
4	85	11.9	10.0	8.6	1.2	1.7
5	68	11.6	11.1	8.8	1.2	1.5
6	54	10.8	11.4	8.3	0.9	1.3
Ladinos III						
Grade						
K–1	59	16.1	16.8	8.7	1.0	0.9
2–3	57	13.5	18.6	8.4	0.7	0.9
4–6	56	17.8	12.2	12.4	1.5	1.1
Maya						
Age						
5.0–8.4	76	11.1	15.6	6.1	0.7	0.7
8.5–10.10	78	8.6	13.4	5.3	0.6	0.6
10.11–16.7	79	7.9	13.4	5.5	0.6	0.7
English						
Age						
3.6–5.3	68	15.6	22.0	7.4	0.7	
5.10–7.3	73	12.3	15.1	8.1	0.8	
7.10–9.2	62	12.7	12.4	9.4	1.0	
9.10–11.2	72	5.8	13.5	4.9	0.4	
11.11–13.1	37	8.2	9.8	7.9	0.8	
13.11–15.1	34	9.4	9.3	8.9	1.0	

Note: Guatemalan data from Demarest (1982), and English data adapted from Annett and Kilshaw (1983).

* Age = years. months.
** Percent Left = 100 (L–R)/L.
*** z Score = $\dfrac{\text{MEAN L–R}}{\text{(SD L–R)}}$.

L–R skill than the Ladinos. This difference is apparent for the bean test and the peg-moving test. Table 20.2 gives the mean percent–left scores and the mean z scores for the groups of children of each race. Tests of differences between races were made by analysis of variance and the Tukey test for honestly significant differences. For the percent–left score, the over-all test of differences between the races was highly significant ($F = 14.38$, $df = 2.19$, $p < .001$); on the Tukey test, the Maya differed from the English at the 5% level and from the Ladinos at the 1% level of confidence. For z scores ($F = 9.08$, $df = 2.19$, $p < .01$), the Maya differed significantly from the Ladinos at the 1% level of confidence but did not differ significantly from the English; the English and Ladinos differed at almost the 5% level of confidence.

Both of these analyses of L–R differences found the Maya considerably less biased to the right hand than the Ladinos, and in both cases the English bias is intermediate. In comparison with my English samples, the Ladinos show a stronger right shift, and the Maya a slightly lesser right shift. These differences concern the L–R differences between the hands in skill, which are presumed to underlie observed preferences. So far in this book, it has been assumed that differences between racial groups in hand preferences for writing and other skilled actions are due to cultural pressures that affect the *threshold* at which sinistrality is manifested. If the present observations for differing z scores on measures of skill are confirmed in further research, the possibility must be considered that there are racial differences in right shift.

Racial differences could occur either because there were differences in the frequency of the $rs+$ gene or because there were differences in the expressivity of the gene. Differences in expressivity have been postulated between the sexes and between twins and the singleborn, and these have been tentatively attributed to differences in relative growth and/or maturity at birth. Cross-cultural studies of neonatal maturity and development in infancy have reported several differences between racial groups, but the evidence is insufficient to reach any firm conclusions about the relative rates of maturation of Ladinos and Mayan children (Super, 1981). Assuming a lesser right

TABLE 20.2

Comparisons of Ladinos, Maya and English Groups for L–R Differences in Peg Moving

	No. Groups	Percent Left		z Score	
		Mean	SD	Mean	SD
Ladino	13	9.9	1.2	1.1	.2
English	6	7.8	1.6	0.8	.2
Maya	3	5.6	0.4	0.6	.1

Note: Data from Table 20.1.

shift is associated with lesser maturity at birth (as postulated for males and twins), the Maya would be expected to be slightly less mature than Ladinos. Studies of Maya Indians in Mexico (Brazelton, Robey, & Collier, 1969) and of Hopi Indians in the United States (Dennis, 1940) both concluded that development in infancy paralleled that of Caucasian children but was approximately 1 month delayed; this delay was found in the latter sample in infants who had been tied to the cradleboard and also in those for whom this traditional practice had been abandoned. Brazelton, Robey and Collier (1969) described several other characteristics of their sample that could be relevant to the expression of the $rs+$ gene. The newborn observed were very small (about 5 lbs), though not premature. On tests of development, items concerning quality of vocalisation could not be scored because of the *paucity of social babbling*. The main aim of the mothers seemed to be to keep the infants quiet, but it seems remarkable that the voice play that is so evident in Caucasian children in the second half of the first year should be so reduced.

With regard to possible differences in gene frequency between Ladinos and Maya, it may be tentatively pointed out that the acceptance of Indians into the majority Ladinos culture depends on a facility for learning the Spanish language. If the $rs+$ gene facilitates language skills, it is possible that there may have been selective transfer of Indians carrying the $rs+$ gene into the Ladinos population for several generations. This might have augmented the frequency of the $rs+$ gene and given a greater bias to dextrality in Ladinos. Whether the differences between Ladinos and Maya are due to gene frequency or expressivity, the typical bias to left-hemisphere speech should be smaller in the Maya than Ladinos. Present measures of hemisphere speech laterality (Sections 6.1.3 and 7.2.1) are probably not sensitive enough to give a reliable test of this possibility. A surprising left-ear dichotic listening superiority was reported for a group of native Navajo college students (Scott, Hynd, Hunt, & Weed, 1979).

The tests of lateral preference used by Demarest included measures of foot and eye preference, as well as the unskilled action of waving good-bye, as mentioned above. The findings for 179 children in the LII sample were in general accord with those of English school-children (Annett, 1970b); the proportions of consistent right-, mixed-, and consistent left-handers showed slightly greater bias to the right than in English samples (as expected given the larger z scores in Table 20.1); they are also in binomial proportion. In the LIII and M samples very large proportions of mixed-handers were recorded (44–55% and 76% for M girls). Many of these children were tested at the beginning of their school career in Soloma and when retested 8 months later the proportions were said to have changed dramatically. This suggests that the initially high mixed-hand usage was due to unfamiliarity with the material used in the preference tests and perhaps also with the experience of being tested by strange adults (see Section 4.2). Apart from this change for the younger children, the data for preference support the conclusions drawn for L–R hand times; first, that there are no systematic increases in dextrality with age and, second, that the Maya are less biased to the right hand than are Ladinos.

20.2. THE DISADVANTAGE FOR LANGUAGE LEARNING AND THE ADVANTAGE FOR HAND SPEED ASSOCIATED WITH REDUCED RIGHT SHIFT

Demarest was guided by the analysis of Annett and Turner (1974) in examining the relations between laterality and language skills. The right-shift theory predicts an absence of significant differences in language ability between children classified for lateral preference in general samples of the population, but in those identified as having a specific difficulty in language learning, an excess of mixed- and left-handers is expected if these children include more of the $rs--$ genotype (Chapter 18).

As mentioned above, education in Guatemala depends on mastery of Spanish. A vocabulary test was given to 123 Indian children in their first year in school. They were asked to name 48 familiar items in their native language, Kanjobal, and for all items correctly named they were asked to give the name in Spanish. Children were asked whether members of their families knew some Spanish, and there were no differences in handedness between children with and without Spanish-speaking relatives. There were no significant differences between hand preference groups for numbers of errors. The critical test for the RS theory depended on a comparison of the 99 children who did well on the Spanish vocabulary test and the remaining 24 who did not. The prediction that the latter would show a lesser right shift was confirmed. The L–R means of high scorers (9.5) and low scorers (3.8) differed significantly in the predicted direction ($t = 1.69$, $df = 121$, $p = .047$).

Comparisons of left- and right-handers for actual times taken by the preferred and nonpreferred hands on the pegboard and bean tests were made after Demarest received a prepublication copy of the paper reporting the advantages found for left-handers (Kilshaw & Annett, 1983; Section 17.1.2). For the Guatemalan samples, as for the English ones, these analyses were made long after the original data had been collected. Even if it might be argued that the differences found for the English samples were "post hoc" and perhaps depended on some improbable conjunction of accidents, the chances that such accidents would be repeated in an independent test of children of other cultures is so unlikely as to merit no serious consideration. Demarest compared left- and right-handers on the pegboard task in four samples and on the bean test in three samples, giving 7 comparisons for the preferred hand and 7 for the nonpreferred hand. In 13 out of 14 comparisons the absolute mean times favoured the left-handers, and in the 14th case there was no difference between the handedness groups. As for English samples, the differences tended to be clearer for the nonpreferred hand than for the preferred hand. The differences in favour of left-handers were statistically significant for 3 out of 7 comparisons for the nonpreferred hand and only 1 in 7 times for the preferred hand. The advantage to left-handers was as clear in the Maya as in the Ladinos. Thus, faster hand speed in left- than right-handers, evident for both hands but more marked for the nonpreferred hand, has been found in three racial groups.

20.3.   SUMMARY

An independent replication of aspects of the birthday sample studies was made on Guatemalan children of Ladinos and Maya races by William Demarest (1982). Females were more strongly biased to the right hand than males on *two* tests of L-R skill, the peg-moving task and a bean-placing test. No systematic changes were found for L-R skill with age.

It had been assumed (Section 4.2) that differences between races in incidences of left-handedness are mainly due to the relatively superficial effects of threshold changes (see Fig. 14.1) that are expected to vary with changing social pressures against sinistrality. Demarest found evidence of racial differences in L-R skill, the foundation on which preferences are expected to depend. The L-R means of Maya children were significantly smaller than those of Ladinos; the means of my English samples were intermediate. If these differences are confirmed, they will suggest that there may be differences between races, either in the frequency of the $rs+$ gene, or in its expressivity.

It is especially interesting that two important findings in English children for relationships between laterality and ability were confirmed in Guatemalan children. First, the report of Annett and Turner (1974) that there is no difference for language ability between right- and left-handed children in general samples but a reduced right shift in children identified as having special language difficulties was supported in a study of Mayan children's progress in learning Spanish. Second, when the actual hand speeds of right- and left-handed children were compared for peg moving and for bean placing, the left-handers were faster than the right-handers in 13 out of 14 comparisons. Faster times for left-handers were found in Maya and in Ladinos children, as in English children. Thus the assumptions basic to the balanced polymorphism hypothesis, that the bias to the right hand gives advantages to language learning but at the cost of actual hand speed, is supported by this independent cross-cultural study.

VI

CONCLUSIONS

21 Reconstruction

When a detective reconstructs a crime or a palaeontologist reconstructs an extinct creature from a few fragments, there is an obligation to use all the evidence available but a need to go beyond the evidence. This is inevitable if attempts are to be made to see how the pieces fit together and to discover where new evidence should be sought. This chapter attempts to reconstruct the development of human lateral asymmetry in order to put together the pieces discovered in previous chapters and to see where new research might be usefully directed.

When genetic instructions for the growth of a complex organism guide the development of the anatomy and physiology of an individual, there is considerable scope for error. In building a bilaterally symmetrical structure, the same blueprint may be used for both sides, but small differences in the actual construction lead to asymmetries of the finished product, just as a building or other artefact designed to be symmetrical may not be so if small differences arise in the making of each side. For an animal possessing such a slightly asymmetrical body, it will be discovered that one paw or other limb does what is wanted more quickly than the other, and the animal will come to prefer to use that paw when a choice is available. The asymmetry is accidental and physical but discovered in the course of use. The greater skill of one side implies no fundamental difference but merely that one side is found, through experience, to be more efficient for a specific activity. In so far as various activities depend on different parts of the body or on different levels of the nervous system, different sides may be preferred. Thus, one side may be better for striking movements as in hammering and the other side for throwing movements. One side may have better control of eye movements and the other of foot movements.

These differences between the sides are discovered (not necessarily consciously) through the experience of the individual in trying to perform particular actions. In this sense the preference is a product of experience and also of constraints of the physical and social environment. The preference is based, however, on a physical superiority of one side. In some cases the superiority will be so marked as to give the individual little choice as to the side to use, even if this requires resistance to external pressures. In the majority, the superiority will be so slight as to allow the individual to use either side, and conformity to the world bias (whether physical or social) will present no problem. Asymmetries of lateral skill arise as accidents in the growth of each individual in all complex animals with scope for choice in the use of limbs or sense organs.

In primates, the development of strong hand preferences in some individuals is expected because of the complexity of the nervous system and because of the capacity to use the hands for finely controlled movements. Strong individual preferences for the left or the right hand have been found in all primates studied, but none except man has been shown so far to differ from a racemic mixture of left and right, about 50% animals preferring each side. In the course of human evolution some small change occurred in the genome that gave a slight weighting in favour of right-handedness. A change in a single allele at one locus would be sufficient to account for this human bias. In humans carrying the right-shift gene ($rs+-$ or $rs++$), hand, foot, and eye preferences depend on a combination of accidental variation *and* the effect of a small bias to the right side. The latter may not be sufficient to outweigh a strong accidental bias to the left. In humans not carrying this gene ($rs--$), lateral asymmetries depend on accidental variation alone, as in all primates.

The main function of the $rs+$ gene is to ensure that the production and perception of speech sounds depends on the left cerebral hemisphere. Before the human child can say words and understand their meanings, it must learn to recognise and reproduce some very fine distinctions between the speech noises made by adults. A useful aid in this process is the voice play in which the infant practises making sounds, listens to the noises produced, and tries to repeat particular effects. To be able to "do that again" is an essential part of the acquisition of control. Following a period of practice with attention to feedback, action schemas probably become part of an automatic repertoire, which can then be used in learning at the next level of complexity (Pew, 1974; Shaffer, 1984). This is not to say that language learning is impossible for a child who cannot talk, as will be discussed further, but that normal language learning is facilitated if the child can hear and reproduce in its own babble the fine differences between sounds that carry meaning in human speech.

The important point with regard to speech sounds is that learning is likely to be more efficient if feedback from the vocal tract and from the ear *are on the same side of the brain*. Sensorimotor feedback from the mouth and from the ear presumably must be co-ordinated if speech production and perception are to be efficient. Studies of left-hemisphere language through electrical stimulation mapping have found that phoneme discrimination and the control of mouth movements tend to depend on the same cortical areas (Ojemann & Mateer, 1979; see Section 2.4). If sensory information from the mouth and from the ear were received on opposite sides of the brain, co-ordination would depend on connections via the corpus callosum, and the use of this longer route might hinder the infant's discovery of some of the subtleties of speech timing.

There is considerable variation between infants in the quantity of voice play during the first year; some, but not necessarily all, of this variability may be associated with effects of the *rs+* gene. Ramsay (1980) found that infants who used left-hand reaching strategies were delayed in comparison with infants using right-hand strategies in producing combinations of phonemes in speech. When the co-ordination of information from mouth and ear is less than optimal, for whatever reason, the infant may be less interested in voice play. The exact nature of the difficulty experienced may differ according to accidental variations in cerebral organisation. There may be delay in learning to speak, or poor production of some speech sounds, or an inability to analyse the sound structure of some words as required in learning how to read and write.

Children with gross defects of the speech apparatus may still learn to understand speech (Lennenberg, 1962). The human capacity for speech is a species universal that is more fundamental than the bias to the left hemisphere. The *rs+* gene is a late and relatively trivial modification of the human genome that assists the development of speech by promoting speech production and analysis on the left side of the brain. The fact that speech can be understood by children whose developmental pathways are grossly abnormal does not prove that speech production is irrelevant to the language learning of the normal child, nor can it cast serious doubt on the argument that the optimal developmental path involves a close co-ordination of information from the mouth and the ear. When the optimal developmental path cannot be followed, as in children with early lesions of the left hemisphere (Section 6.2), alternative routes to speech development can be found in most cases. No differences were detected in the psychological test performance of hemiplegic children with lesions on the two sides, provided they were matched for physical disability, except for a *history of delay in speech acquisition*, more frequent for those with left-brain lesions.

It seems that the main role of the *rs+* gene is to facilitate the development of a speech output-input system on the left side of the brain. The concept of an "articulatory rehearsal loop" has become an important feature of theories of adult memory. Baddeley (1976), in reviewing this literature, suggests that the "Articulatory or verbal loop may function as a limited-capacity 'slave' system, which can be used to supplement the central processor" (p. 176). Evidence for a "privileged loop", free from the interference that typically prevents humans from trying to do more than one cognitive task at once, has been found for shadowing speech (McLeod & Posner, 1984). A relatively automatic input–output system of this kind is perhaps at work in those mentally handicapped children who produce echolalic speech, or who learn to read easily but mechanically, without understanding. For most normal children, the automatic loop serves to assist the further growth of language skills. Jorm (1983) has argued that retarded readers may have deficits in ability to use the articulatory loop. In learning how to control the mouth so as to produce better speech-like sounds, there must be an intimate coordination of inputs to somatosensory mouth cortex and auditory receiving cortex.

The anatomical basis of the speech output–input loop must include the primary motor and sensory areas for the mouth, the auditory receiving cortex, Broca's and Wernicke's areas (Figure 2.2). During speech development, external feedback is required and in normal development this is provided by the sound of the speaker's voice. In learning how to control the mouth so as to produce better speech-like sounds, there must be an intimate coordination of inputs to somatosensory mouth cortex and auditory receiving cortex.

Why the left side should be especially fitted, in most people, to serve the speech output–input loop is not certain, but it seems likely that it depends on the enlargement of the planum temporale in the last quarter of fetal life, in about two out of three brains. Evidence has been found for bias towards a larger motor speech area on the left also (see Section 6.3). Somatosensory mouth areas have not been compared on the two sides, to my knowledge. The main point for the RS theory is that the close proximity of the mouth and hand areas in the sensorimotor cortical strip suggests that any advantage to the left-hemisphere mouth area would be likely to give an *incidental advantage to the right hand*. Alternatively, if the gene works by inhibiting the growth of right-hemisphere mouth cortex, there would be an incidental inhibition of the growth of the sensorimotor cortex for the left hand.

Comparisons of the cerebral hemispheres of fetal brains were made by Cunningham (1902) for evidence of superior growth of the left motor cortex in the arm area; the findings were the opposite of those expected in that there was a slight advantage to the *right* motor cortex, which Cunningham believed was detectable in ape as well as human brains, though less marked in the former. Chi, Dooling, and Gilles (1977) also found that fetal brain development was slightly faster on the right than the left side. Cunningham noted, however, that in four out of five brains belonging to the eighth month of fetal development there was an excess of growth on the *left* side. This asymmetry of fetal development has not been remarked upon, to my knowledge, by any more recent observer.

Whether the gene works by accelerating or decelerating growth on the right or the left, some inequality is introduced, which biases the random chances of superiority on either side in favour of left-hemisphere speech and preference for the right hand. Regional cerebral blood flow studies have shown that the right sensorimotor strip is active during speech, although there is greater activation on the left side. Split-brain studies have found the right hemisphere to have a considerable vocabulary for word recognition. These observations lead to the speculation that the chief difference between the hemispheres in most people could lie in the absence of a connecting loop between output and input on the right.

When the gene is absent, the speech output–input loop involves either or both hemispheres, by chance. The inherent advantages of control from one side probably lead to the development of an efficient system on one side or the other, which may be left or right with equal frequency. In some proportion of *rs*– genotypes, both hemispheres may be involved in speech production. There are no grounds for suggesting that this would necessarily lead to problems of speech control, but there must be an increased *risk* of such problems. It is interesting to recall (Section 14.2) that Penfield and Roberts (1959) noted disturbances of *articulation only* after brain operations to either hemisphere, but none of these were counted as aphasic in their series. It was seen (Table 14.7B) that rapid recoveries from speech disorder following war head injuries occurred for wounds on each side of the brain, but formed a higher proportion of right-lesion than left-lesion cases. These observations suggest that both hemispheres may be involved in the speech production of some *rs*– genotypes, and that in the event of a unilateral brain lesion it is a relatively simple matter for the other hemisphere to take control. Recovery in these cases probably occurs so rapidly that they are rarely seen by clinical neurologists, whose patients usually present with more massive or more chronic speech difficulties. In recognising the possibility that both hemispheres become involved in speech production in some *rs*– genotypes, it must not be forgotten that 40% of aphasics with right-hemisphere lesions remained aphasic for years. In these cases, the right hemisphere served speech as fully as the left hemisphere in the majority of the population. Cerebral organisation in the *rs*– probably varies in both the direction and the strength of dependence on each hemisphere for speech.

The mechanisms through which the *rs*+ gene promotes left-hemisphere specialisation for speech seem likely to depend on differential growth rates of the two sides of the brain, even though it cannot be decided on present evidence just what these mechanisms are. Asymmetries of development have been found for several organs in many species (Sections 3.2 and 9.1). The differentiation of primitive gonads into testes and ovaries seems to be influenced by asymmetrical rates of growth on each side of the body, and these differ between birds and mammals (Mittwoch, 1977; Mittwoch & Mahadevaiah, 1980). Differential growth rates of the two sides of the brain appear to be significant for the anatomical and physiological bases of imprinting in birds (Section 9.3) and for the effects of sex hormones on brain development in mammals (Nordeen & Yahr, 1982). The chances that humans will develop epilepsy following early cerebral lesions to either side vary with age at the time of insult (Taylor, 1969).

The $rs+$ gene probably introduces some slight modification of the primate pattern of cerebral maturation. The modification increases the chances that the left mouth–ear association cortex will be at an optimal stage for learning during the first year of life when most babies establish their speech sound repertoire. How this is achieved is not known, but it seems to involve some cost to right-hemisphere function. The danger is that the right hemisphere might suffer a serious loss of learning capacity. The risk is sufficient to have prevented the $rs+$ gene from becoming universal in humans, and also to have limited the expression of the gene in males. The $rs-$ allele(s) could have persisted since the divergence of hominids from apes, and it is unlikely that they have been entirely replaced by $rs+$ alleles in any large human population.

The regulation of the growth processes through which these relative advantages and disadvantages are produced in those carrying the $rs+$ gene varies with any factor that influences growth. The maximum asymmetry in favour of the left hemisphere is expected to occur in females who carry a double dose of the gene ($rs++$) and who are early maturers. Lesser asymmetries are expected in those of $rs+-$ genotype, in males, twins, and any whose developmental progress is delayed or distorted by extraneous factors. Thus, the incidence of right-handedness should be highest in early-maturing girls and lowest in late-maturing boys. It should be relatively easy to test this prediction. Evidence for an advantage in verbal compared with spatial test scores in early developers and the reverse pattern in late developers has been reported by Waber (1976).

A review of the development of verbal and nonverbal abilities of children with sex chromosome anomalies (XO, XXY, and XXX sex chromosome complements) has led to the view that the critical variable may be maturation rate. Netley and Rovet (1983) tentatively suggested that the pattern of findings would be consistent with the possibility that rapid development gives relative advantages to verbal skills and deficits of spatial skills, while late development gives the reverse pattern. This is almost, but not quite, the suggestion made by the RS theory. Early maturers are expected to show stronger expression of the $rs+$ gene than late maturers; this implies a stronger bias to the left hemisphere for speech but at the cost of some weakening of the right hemisphere. Early maturers should show rapid speech acquisition but poorer visuo-spatial skills. Late maturers risk poorer development of the speech control mechanisms but avoid the risks of right-hemisphere impairment of early maturers. In normal development, these relative advantages and disadvantages are probably so slight as to be of little practical significance.

The implications of the gene for psychological processes can be regarded as trivial from several points of view, but in so far as the gene modulates the development of certain capacities, it may be relevant at each extreme of the normal range. Most children learn to speak, to read, to count, and to play games and perhaps musical instruments with varying levels of skill. Levels of achievement depend on a multitude of factors that are independent of the $rs+$ gene. However, the gene assists the development of language skills at the risk of some imbalance of cerebral function due to loss of right-hemisphere capacity. In those who carry a single dose of the gene's effects ($rs+-$) there is optimal opportunity for early speech acquisition, without serious risk to the right hemisphere. Outstanding achievement in any area that requires maximum efficiency on *both* sides of the brain, for skilled control of the hands (as in surgery or in playing musical instruments), for sports (as in tennis, football, and gymnastics) and for the application of spatial and mathematical concepts is unlikely in those who carry a double dose of the gene ($rs++$).

It is important to recognise that the increased incidence of left-handedness in some groups is not a cause of the language problem or the special skill. It would be clearly ridiculous to say, "This child is left-handed so s/he will be a late reader but an outstanding surgeon/musician/tennis player/mathematician." These outcomes depend on many special capacities and opportunities. It is possible, however, that some people who have strong talents in various directions are prevented from attaining the highest levels of achievement because the left side of the body (and the right hemisphere) cannot be controlled as efficiently as its owner could wish. For others, it is possible that the speech production mechanisms cannot be controlled as efficiently as desired. As discussed for language skills in Sections 5.1 and 18.1, classifying normal samples for handedness gives no clues as to levels of attainment. Neither would such a classification give any clues as to potential for football. But among children with serious delays in learning to read despite good intelligence and among children with outstanding gifts for football, mathematics, or music there will often be a slight excess of left-handers.

The sexes differ slightly for effects associated with the $rs+$ gene because the gene is expressed more strongly in early maturers and because females tend to mature earlier than males. It would be as ridiculous to suppose that the $rs+$ gene is the *only* factor involved in sex differences in ability as it would be to suppose it is the only factor involved in musical or sports ability. However, that portion of the difference between the sexes that is attributable to the $rs+$ gene should be reduced or absent in female left-handers, in twins, and in any in whom the expression of the gene is absent or reduced. It will be difficult to test this aspect of the theory because there is no gene marker; some left-handers are expected to carry the gene, and when criteria of sinistrality are generous, the majority will be gene carriers. In both males and females of $rs++$ genotype, there is a risk of serious deficit of right-hemisphere function, which could lead to over-reliance on the left hemisphere, as postulated by Inglis and his colleagues (see Section 8.5) for females in general. On the RS theory, this would be a risk that was not due to sex as such but rather to the $rs+$ gene, whose effects are more evident in females.

How would the RS theory be disproved? The main innovation of the theory is to suggest that there is a subgroup of the population in which lateral asymmetries arise at random. This can be regarded as a "null" hypothesis waiting to be rejected. It could be rejected if groups were found that reliably showed several asymmetries in the atypical direction. Alternatively, it might be shown that all groups with atypical asymmetries are pathological. Claims to disprove the theory must be based on substantial numbers of cases; the groups of 10 to 12 subjects used in most "laterality" experiments are insufficient to demonstrate real effects when the major influence on laterality is chance. Until evidence of atypical biases in substantial groups is found, the RS theory offers the simplest possible explanation of human lateral asymmetries.

With regard to further research, independent replication is necessary for the secure foundation of all theories. Most of the assumptions on which the RS theory was based (as outlined in Chapter 13) depend on personally replicated findings. The chief exception is the assumption that the $rs+$ gene induces left-hemisphere speech. A wealth of circumstantial evidence (in Chapter 14) and the power of the heuristic of deriving parameters of the genetic model from data for dysphasics (in Chapters 15 and 16) make this assumption very strong. It should be possible to test the assumptions for cerebral speech and for genetic transmission when a marker for the gene and a safe, reliable method for diagnosing cerebral speech asymmetry in large samples of the general population are found.

The exploration of the implications of the theory in Chapters 16 to 19 depended on relatively recent analyses of findings, which were not all replicated. The confirmation of aspects of the balanced polymorphism hypothesis in the independent study of children in Guatemala (Chapter 20) gives strong support to the basic assumption of advantages and disadvantages associated with the shift to the right. Further work is needed on the distinction between the more sinistral and more dextral poor readers. If it is possible to analyse the nature of the special difficulties experienced by children with problems at each extreme of the asymmetry distribution, it might be possible to devise methods of remedial teaching appropriate to their presumably different handicaps.

This book began with questions about the human behavioural difference evident in right- and left-hand preference. It is ending with the conclusion that differences in hand preference are of little direct significance, as they depend mainly on chance. They are indirectly related, however, to more fundamental behavioural differences concerned with the development of speech. There are few benefits without costs in nature. The price of rapid acquisition of clear and fluent speech is a potential impairment of left-hand skill and of right-hemisphere brain power. About 50% of humans maximise the benefits and minimise the costs by being genetically heterozygote ($rs+-$ genotype). This advantageous genotype for so large a proportion of the population cannot be achieved unless the remaining 50% risk the disadvantages of either slow language development ($rs--$) or poor motor and visuospatial skills ($rs++$). This state of affairs has arisen because of its advantages for humans as a species.

The idea that human physical and intellectual development is influenced by such genetic variation is bound to be resisted in many quarters. My hope is that the recognition that there are biologically based differences in children's approaches to similar learning situations and that these are part of *normal* variation will lead to useful analyses of the different ways in which children actually learn. Most children learn to read and to do basic arithmetic relatively easily. Some children may need to be taught fundamental skills, perhaps in phonological analysis or in spatial thinking, which come naturally to other children. If the bases of these special problems can be discovered, it should be possible to devise teaching methods to circumvent them. To close our minds to the possibility of such special needs would be to neglect opportunities to compensate for them.

APPENDICES

Appendix I:
Notes on the Samples

A.   CLINIC SAMPLES

1.   *Children with lateralized EEG foci* (Annett, Lee, & Ounsted, 1961)
The sample was selected from a continuous series of children attending an acute neuropsychiatric unit. It included all children seen between certain dates who fulfilled criteria of satisfactory EEG recording, intelligence assessment, and questionnaire information on handedness. The 109 children in the total sample included 40 with evidence of EEG foci.

2.   *Childhood hemiplegics* (Annett, 1973b)
All children recorded as hemiplegic at four paediatric centres—Hull, Pontefract, York, and Leeds—were included in the initial sample; those whose hemiplegias were associated with other severe disorders (such as hydrocephaly or recent head injury) were then excluded. The main sample consisted of 106 children, 5 to 18 years old at examination, whose main handicap was a hemiplegia of several years' duration and predominantly spastic in type.

3.   *Dyslexics* (Annett & Kilshaw, 1984)
Pupils attending the dyslexia clinic at St. Bartholomew's Hospital, London, for remedial teaching in reading or spelling were included in the sample if they were 8 years old or over, scored not less than 80 on any assessment of intelligence, showed clear evidence of delay in learning to read or spell when age and IQ were taken into account, and had no record of neurological handicap. Letters requesting permission to test were sent to the homes of those fulfilling these criteria, and pupils attending during the author's visits

to the clinic were invited to take part. The sample was collected during the summers of 1979 and 1980.

B. NORMAL SAMPLES ASSESSED FOR HAND PREFERENCE

4. *Demonstration of binomial proportions* (Annett, 1967)

Seven samples (listed in Table 13.1) were tested for incidences of right-, mixed-, and left-handedness against predictions for binomial proportions (on the single locus model of two alternate alleles, r or l). These included three samples assessed by questionnaire 1 (the first 8 items of Fig. 10.1), two samples assessed by questionnaire 2 (as in Fig. 10.1), and two samples assessed by observation of hand usage. The samples were drawn from students at the Universities of Aberdeen and Hull, enlisted men and school-children. The last four samples (of Table 13.1) were complete in that all questionnaires were distributed and collected in the *same class* or obser-vations were made on all members of the random sample or class group.

5. *Association analysis* (Annett, 1970a)

The total sample was made up of three subgroups, psychology students attending the University of Hull over a three-year period, nonpsychology students (who received questionnaires sent to their homes before the start of their first term), and new recruits to one of the armed services. For the first and third groups, questionnaires were distributed and collected in the same class, ensuring that the samples were as complete as possible. In the second group, questionnaires were collected as the students registered for university admission. This procedure was intended to ensure as high a response rate as possible; this was estimated to be about 65%.

6. *Family samples by questionnaire*

a. *Hull sample* (Annett, 1973a). Samples as in 4 and 5, excluding all families where the respondent or a parent was a twin and where members were known to be non-British (Table 16.7B7).

b. *Hull sample: self report* (Annett, 1978a). The subset of the Hull sample for which questionnaires had been sent to students' homes before the start of their first term, with copies of the questionnaire for personal completion by each parent and the student. This sample could be analysed for left-handed writing in both generations (Table 16.7A-6) or any left preference in both generations (Table 16.7A5).

c. *OU sample* (Annett, 1979). Students attending summer schools of the course Introduction to Psychology, DS261, observed each other performing the actions in Fig. 10.1 and answered questions about the hand preferences of their parents, siblings, spouses, and children. The OU sample could be examined for

i. the students and their siblings as the filial generation for left-handed writing (Table 16.7B4),

ii. the students as the filial generation for the generous criterion of "any left" preference (Table 16.7B3),

iii. the students as the parental generation (Table 16.7B2).

d. *Lanchester Polytechnic samples* (previously unpublished). Question-naires were sent to the homes of new entrants before the start of the first term, with copies for personal completion by parents, students and siblings. The questionnaires were collected in departments at the beginning of the session.

The questionnaires asked parents for information about their parents and siblings. The samples can be analysed for

i. Self-report by parents, students, and siblings for left-handed writing (Table 16.7A4).

ii. Self-report by parents, students, and siblings for the generous criterion of "any left" preference (Table 16.7A3).

iii. Mixed report: Parents and their siblings as the filial generation (Table 16.7B6).

e. *Families of left-handed parents by questionnaire* (Annett, 1972). Appeals for information about handedness in families of left-handed parents were made through press and radio, and information was also sought through students who were given sets of questionnaires to take home during vacations. Families were classified in both gene-rations for consistent right-, mixed-, and consistent left-handedness, as required to test the strong form of the hypothesis that heterozygotes are mixed-handed (Table 3.5C2).

7. *Family samples: Personal observation*

a. *Left- × left-handed parents*

i. *Families in Hull* (Annett, 1974) and its environs who responded to appeals through the media. All families with children of school age were asked to permit a family visit by myself and one assistant. Observations were made of hand preference, eye and foot preference, and measurements were made of peg-moving time by each hand. Parents were questioned about the birth history and developmental language problems of themselves and their children and about the hand preference of relatives.

ii. *Second sample* (Annett, 1983) included all families seen from the closing of the first sample, mainly in Coventry and the Midlands.

b. *R×R, L×R, and R×L families* (Annett, 1978a). Appeals for R×R families were made through a talk to a women's group in Bedfordshire and for L×R and R×L families through the media in Coventry. These samples depended on volunteers, and it is not possible to assess how far families with left-handed children were more likely to offer help. The data were analysed for correlations between relatives for L–R peg-moving time (Table 3.7).

8. *Mathematicians* (Annett & Kilshaw, 1982)

a. *Subgroups of other samples*

i. *Hull University undergraduates.* One of the questionnaires distributed to nonpsychology students included a question about faculty and main subject. Respondents included 28 mathematics students.

ii. *School-girls age 16–18 years.* The D.A. sample (10b) included 24 taking Advanced Level courses in mathematics.

b. *Questionnaires to mathematics students.* These were distributed at Coventry (Lanchester) Polytechnic (as part of 6d above) and also at the Mathematics Department of the University of Warwick (Coventry).

c. *Teachers of mathematics.* Observations of hand, eye, and foot preferences and measures of peg-moving time were made for teachers in the mathematics and statistics departments of Universities (Aston, Loughborough, and Warwick) and Polytechnics (Birmingham, Coventry, and Leicester). Additional visits to see female teachers of mathematics were made to the Universities of Oxford, Birmingham, Leicester, and the Open University. Additionally, three female and two male teachers of A-level mathematics in school were included in the sample.

9. *The birthday samples: Observed preferences and peg-moving times*

a. *Hull normative sample* (Annett, 1970b). Children in eight schools in different districts of Hull were selected for testing according to birth date. All children were within one month of their birthday, and all or a random proportion of children of appropriate birthdays were seen in each school. In most cases there was no ambiguity about which children the teacher should send for testing; the high proportion of left-handed males in some age groups leads to the question whether some selection bias towards left-handers did occur in some groups (Kilshaw & Annett, 1983).

The main purpose of this sample was to establish norms for actual hand speed against which to assess the impairments of hemiplegic children (norms in Appendix III). Children from $3\frac{1}{2}$ to 5 years were tested at 6-month age intervals and from 6 to 15 years in 1-year age groups. Observations of hand preference were made for 5 items in primary and 7 items in nursery school children.

b. *Laterality and ability sample* (Annett & Turner, 1974). Children in five schools in a large village near Hull were assessed for lateral preferences, peg-moving times, and scores on vocabulary and non-verbal tests. To ensure sufficient numbers of left-handers for the comparisons to be made for ability, children were selected in two subgroups.

　i. *Birthday sample.*   Children were selected for birth date as in 9a, at ages 5, 6, 8, and 10 years. These children were a *random* sample.

　ii. *Left-handers.*   All left-handers in the classes visited who were not selected in the random sample were also tested to give a *complete sample* of left-handers.

These two subsets were fully distinguishable and combined only for specific purposes when extra left-handers were required. Where the birthday samples are used for normative purposes, only the birthday subset was used, in combinations with the Hull sample (above). For analyses of actual hand speeds with age and sex (Kilshaw & Annett, 1983) children from $3\frac{1}{2}$ to 15 were included (158 boys and 188 girls). For subsequent analyses of the L-R distribution (Annett & Kilshaw, 1983), children from 6 to 15 years were included, of which 122 were males and 156 females.

10. *The combined main samples* (Annett & Kilshaw, 1983; Kilshaw & Annett, 1983).

These are all samples available where hand preference had been assessed by observation and hand skill assessed by peg moving.

　a. **LS:** 12-year-old school-children.   Observations of hand use and tests of peg-moving speed were made with the help of a small team of assistants on a year group of children in a large comprehensive school, the children being about 12 years old. The sample included 79 males and 86 females.

　b. **DA:** Sixth-form school-girls.   A small group of girls examined their colleagues in the sixth form of a large girls' school, as part of a statistics project. There were 158 subjects, 16 to 18 years.

　c. **HL:** Undergraduates at the University of Hull and at the Coventry (Lanchester) Polytechnic.   Students observed and tested each other for hand preferences and skill, acting as experimenter and subject in turn, as part of laboratory practical classes. Instructions as to procedures were given in a handout at the start of the class, and performance was monitored by lecturers and demonstrators. Copies of the findings for these and other tasks were handed in so that group data could be reported back to the class.

This procedure was followed for several year groups of psychology undergraduates at Hull University and for one year group of under-graduates taking a psychology course at Coventry (Lanchester) Poly-technic. As the Hull and Coventry students were similar in age and in measures for performance, they were combined for the main sample analyses. These subjects were 18 to 20 years of age, except for occasional mature students. There were 140 males and 213 females.

d. OU: Undergraduates attending Open University summer schools. The procedures developed for the HL sample were adapted for inclusion in a laboratory exercise at the first of the summer schools for the course Introduction to Psychology, DS261. Students made copies of their findings, which were collected and sent to me for analysis.

Any student reporting physical problems of the hands or arms, such as a history of trauma or arthritis, was excluded. Usable forms were received from 398 males and 406 females. For the 383 males and 386 females who recorded their ages, the mean ages were 36.7, SD = 11.4 years, and 35.8, SD = 7.7 years, respectively: ages ranged from 22 to 63 years. As far as could be ascertained, about two-thirds of all students who had initially registered for the psychology summer schools sent in usable forms. This group is not strictly complete in the sense of the other main samples, but there was no excess of left-handers in the OU sample, rather a shortage of male left-handers.

Appendix II:
Notes on Methods of
Assessment of Laterality

A. OBSERVATIONS ON LATERAL PREFERENCES

1. Hand preferences

Materials such as matches, playing cards, needle and thread, scissors, jar with a screw-top lid, a nail partially driven into a piece of wood and a toy hammer, and table tennis bat and ball were provided for subjects to perform physically the actions enquired about; the long-handled broom and spade could not be provided when materials had to be transported, but subjects were asked to mime the use of these items.

Performance of the 12 items of Fig. 10.1 was observed for the combined main samples. Fewer items were observed in the birthday samples. (These were pointing to pictures, drawing, cutting with scissors, throwing, and screwing up a screw-top jar, with two additional items for nursery-school children, using a long-handled child's sand spade and picking up small buttons and placing them in a small-necked bottle for the Annett, 1970a sample; drawing, throwing, cutting with scissors, hammering, and placing buttons in a narrow-necked bottle for the Annett and Turner, 1974 sample.)

2. Eye preference

Four tasks were used in the majority of samples where eye preferences were tested.

   a. Sighting through a hollow tube.

   b. Sighting a distant line through a small hole in the centre of a cardboard held at arm's length by both hands.

c. Sighting a near object, such as a pencil held at arm's length through the hole in cardboard held at half-arm's length.

d. Sighting a distant line through a hole in cardboard and bringing the board slowly towards the nose, keeping the line in view.

The eye can be observed directly in (a) and (d) and by covering each eye in turn with a small card in (b) and (c).

3. *Foot preferences*

Subjects were asked to kick a ball, or to mime kicking to score a goal in soccer.

B. THE PEG-MOVING TASK

The task was to move 10 dowelling pegs ($3/8 \times 2$ in. from a row of 10 holes (1/2 in. diameter, 7/8 in. deep, and 1 in. apart) to another similar row, parallel and 8 in. from the first row. The apparatus was placed on a table of convenient height for the *standing* subject. For small children it was placed on a firm chair. The pegs were always moved from right to left by the right hand and from left to right by the left hand. They were picked up and placed one by one (subjects were not permitted to grasp two at once).

A trial consisted of moving the 10 pegs, timed from touching the first peg to releasing the last. If a peg was dropped, the trial was restarted. Trials were made by the hands alternately, subjects being randomly assigned to R–L or L–R orders. In most samples five trials were made by each hand. Timing was by stop watch and recorded in 1/10 s. The time taken was always announced so that subjects had a standard to try to beat on the next trial. The measures used were the mean of left-hand trials, mean of right-hand trials, and the difference between the hands (L–R).

For children of nursery school age, three trials were given, to avoid risk of boredom. Young or handicapped children were asked to put the hand not being used behind the back or into a pocket.

Appendix III:
Peg-Moving Task Norms

TABLE AIII.1
Peg-Moving Task Norms

Age (yr)	Right hand		Left hand	
	Mean (sec)	SD	Mean (sec)	SD
3½	26.96	6.95	29.53	11.97
4	21.83	2.80	24.19	6.54
4½	19.32	2.42	20.90	4.23
5	17.40	2.07	18.67	2.71
5½	16.35	1.96	17.56	2.53
6	15.58	1.75	16.67	2.29
6½	14.88	1.66	15.98	2.15
7	14.01	1.47	15.13	1.97
7½	13.48	1.39	14.53	1.86
8	12.65	1.28	13.69	1.65
8½	12.24	1.21	13.28	1.59
9	11.78	1.15	12.84	1.53
9½	11.34	1.06	12.35	1.43
10	10.98	0.97	11.95	1.34
10½	10.71	0.94	11.64	1.27
11	10.39	0.89	11.31	1.21
11½	10.20	0.89	11.11	1.16
12	9.95	0.86	10.83	1.07
12½	9.88	0.85	10.78	1.05
13	9.76	0.87	10.66	1.01
13½	9.71	0.85	10.62	0.99
14	9.65	0.84	10.61	0.98
14½	9.63	0.79	10.60	0.95
15	9.61	0.77	10.58	0.93

The actual mean times of children tested were smoothed by combining adjacent groups to derive norms for peg moving times by each hand, at 6-month intervals. As the children were drawn at random (according to birthday) the norms should be representative of the general population of school-children in Hull, England in the late 1960s (Annett, 1970b).

Note that the data in Table 17.3A combines the two birthday samples (Annett, 1970b; Annett & Turner, 1974) and is unsmoothed.

Appendix IV:
An Example of the Genetic Calculations in Section 15.2

Data of Chamberlain (1928) as analysed by Annett (1978b).
Main Assumptions (1) The $rs+$ gene is fully dominant (2) the $rs+$ gene frequency = .57, (3) the extent of right shift induced by the $rs+$ gene is $1.937z$, (4) sex differences can be ignored (see Appendix V for an example not ignoring sex differences).

A. *Calculate the proportions of right and left handers having each genotype in the total population of parents*
Parental incidence = .0356

Population Genotypes	Population Frequency	Distance of threshold from the mean of each genotype	Dextral proportions under normal curves	Proportions of genotypes in the total population	
				Dextral	Sinistral
$rs++$	.3242	−2.844	.9978	.3235	.0007 *
$rs+−$	.4904	−2.844	.9978	.4893	.0011
$rs−−$	.1854	−0.907	.1878	.1516	.0338
					.0356

B. *Calculate the genotype of offspring of R × R, L × R and L × L matings*

Parental genotypes	Filial genotypes		
	+ +	+ −	− −
Right × Right			
+ + × + +	.104637		
+ + × + −	.079140	.079140	
+ + × − −		.049046	
+ − × + +	.079140	.079140	
+ − × + −	.059855	.119710	.059855
+ − × − −		.037094	.037094
− − × + +		.049046	
− − × + −		.037094	.037094
− − × − −			.022989
	.322772	.450270	.157032 Total = .930074
Genotype as prop. within R × R families	.347039	.484123	.168838
Left × Right			
+ + × + +	.000234		
+ + × + −	.000177	.000177	
+ + × − −		.000110	
+ − × + +	.000177	.000177	
+ − × + −	.000134	.000268	.000134
+ − × − −		.000083	.000083
− − × + +		.010927	
− − × + −		.008264	.008264
− − × − −			.005122
	.000721	.020005	.013603 Total = .034329 (×2 for the total population which includes R × L matings)
Genotype as a prop. within L × R families	.0210137	.582745	.396243
Left × Left			
+ + × + +	.0000052		
+ + × + −	.0000039	.0000039	
+ + × − −		.0002442	
+ − × + +	.0000039	.0000039	
+ − × + −	.0000030	.0000060	.0000030
+ − × − −		.0001847	.0001847
− − × + +		.0002442	
− − × + −		.0001847	.0001847
− − × − −			.00114108
	.00000160	.0008716	.0017862 Total = .00126738
Genotypes as a prop. within L × L families	.001262	.068772	.929966

C. *Calculate the proportions of right- and left-handers having each genotype in the filial generation*

Filial incidence = .0477

Calculations as in (a) when the threshold of left handedness is at $-2.6455z$ for the $rs++$ and $rs+-$ distributions and at $-0.7085z$ for the $rs--$ distribution. The proportions called sinistral are 0.00408 of $rs++$ and $rs+-$ and 0.2394 of $rs--$. The genotype frequencies deduced for each family type in (b) are multiplied by these proportions. For example, the proportion of left-handers in $R \times R$ families is calculated as follows:

$$++ .347039 \times .00408 = .001416$$
$$+- .484123 \times .00408 = .001975$$
$$-- .168838 \times .2394 = .040420$$

$$\overline{.043811}$$

D. *Compare the numbers of left-handed children expected in each family type with the observed numbers*

	Total N children in each family type	Expected Proportion Sinistral	Expected Number Sinistral	Observed Number Sinistral	x^2
Right × Right	7225	.0438	316.5	308	.2302
Left × Right	464	.0973	45.2	53	1.3617
Left × Left	25	.2229	5.6	7	.3655
					$\overline{1.9574}$

(NS for 1 or 2*df*.)**

*All calculations were made using more decimals than shown: ideally the dextral and sinistral proportions calculated in (A) are entered immediately into the memories of the calculator and recalled for each multiplication.

**I have sought advice on the appropriate degrees of freedom but remain uncertain of the correct value: it is usual to deduct one degree of freedom in tests of significance if the gene frequencies were estimated from the data. Here, the gene frequencies were estimated from independent data.

Appendix V: An Example of the Genetic Calculations in Section 16.3

Data of Ashton (1982) for left-handers plus ambidexters. *Main assumptions* (1) The $rs+$ gene is fully additive, (2) the $rs+$ gene frequency $= .57$, (3) the sexes differ for extent of right shift, (4) the extents of shift for the $rs+-$ and $rs++$ genotypes are $1.0z$ and $2.0z$ in males and $1.2z$ and $2.4z$ in females, respectively.

A. *The proportions of right and left handers having each genotype in the total populations of fathers and mothers*

Population Genotypes	Population Frequency	Distance of Threshold From the Mean of Each Genotype	Proportions Under the Normal Curves		Proportions of Genotypes in the Total Population	
			Dextral	Sinistral	Dextral	Sinistral
Fathers (sinistral incidence = 0.0897)						
$rs+ +$	.3242	-2.52	.9942	.0058	.3223	.0019
$rs+ -$	.4904	-1.52	.9351	.0649	.4585	.0318
$rs- -$	.1854	-0.52	.6980	.3120	.1294	.0560
						.0896
Mothers (sinistral incidence = 0.0764)						
$rs+ +$	.3242	-2.93	.9985	.0015	.3237	.0006
$rs+ -$	.4904	-1.73	.9576	.0424	.4696	.0207
$rs- -$	.1854	-0.53	.7017	.2983	.1301	.0553
						.0766

B. *Calculate the genotypes of children in R × R, L × R, R × L and L × L matings*

Genotypes of Father × Mother	Filial genotypes		
	+ +	+ -	- -
Right × Right			
+ + × + +	.104324		
+ + × + -	.075684	.075684	
+ + × - -		.041916	
+ - × + +	.074212	.074212	
+ - × + -	.053838	.107677	.053838
+ - × - -		.029818	.029818
- - × + +		.041886	
- - × + -		.030387	.030387
- - × - -			.016823
	.308058	.401580	.130872
			Total = .840510
Left × Right			
+ + × + +	.000625	.000453	
+ + × + -	.000453	.000251	
+ + × - -			
+ - × + +	.005148	.005148	
+ - × + -	.003735	.007470	.003735
+ - × - -		.002068	.002068
- - × + +		.018124	
- - × + -		.013149	.013149
- - × - -			.007282
	.009961	.046663	.026234
			Total = .082858
Right × Left			
+ + × + +	.000180	.003340	
+ + × + -	.003340	.017839	
+ + × - -			
+ - × + +	.000128	.000128	
+ - × + -	.002376	.004751	.002376
+ - × - -		.012690	.012690
- - × + +		.000072	
- - × + -		.001341	.001341
- - × - -			.007162
	.006024	.040161	.023569
			Total = .069754

B. *Calculate the genotypes of children in R × R, L × R, R × L and L × L matings (continued)*

Genotypes of Father × Mother	Filial genotypes		
	+ +	+ −	− −
Left × Left			
+ + × + +	.000001		
+ + × + −	.000020		
+ + × − −		.000009	
+ − × + +	.000009		
+ − × + −	.000165	.000330	.000165
+ − × − −		.000880	.000880
− − × + +		.000031	
− − × + −		.000580	.000580
− − × − −			.003100
	.000195	.001957	.004725 Total = .006877

C. *The proportion of right and left handers having each genotype in sons and in daughters*

Population Genotypes	Population Frequency	Sons: sinistral incidence = .1665		Daughters: sinistral incidence = .1435	
		Threshold distances (sons)	Sinistral proportion	Threshold distances (daughters)	Sinistral proportion
rs + +	.3242	−2.045	.0204	−2.445	.0072
rs + −	.4904	−1.045	.1480	−1.245	.1066
rs − −	.1854	−0.045	.4808	−0.045	.4808

D. *Compare the numbers of left-handed children expected in each family type with the numbers observed*

(Predictions are based on the sums in (B) directly, not transformed to proportions within family types, so that expectations are for the total sample; that is, how many sons, or daughters will be left handed and belong to each family type)

	Expected Proportion	Sons: N = 1435			Daughters: N = 1491			
		Expected Number	Observed Number	χ^2	Expected Proportion	Expected Number	Observed Number	χ^2
Right × Right	.1287	184.6	191	.2196	.1080	161.0	161	.0000
Left × Right	.0197	28.3	27	.0602	.0177	26.3	21	1.0794
Right × Left	.0174	25.0	17	2.5439	.0157	23.3	29	1.3700
Left × Left	.0026	3.7	4	.0276	.0025	3.7	3	.1326
				2.8513				2.5820

*Calculations based on more decimals than shown.

References

Alcock, J. (1984) *Animal behavior: An evolutionary approach* (3rd ed.). Sunderland, Mass.: Sinauer.

Allard, F., & Scott, B. L. (1975) Burst cues, transitive cues and hemispheric specialization with real speech sounds. *Quarterly Journal of Experimental Psychology*, **27**, 487–497.

Anderson, J. R. (1980). *Cognitive psychology and its implications.* San Francisco: W. H. Freeman.

Andrews, G., Quinn, P. T., & Sorby, W. A. (1972) Stuttering: An investigation into cerebral dominance for speech. *Journal of Neurology, Neurosurgery and Psychology*, **35**, 414–418.

Annett, J., Annett, M., Hudson, P. T. W., & Turner, A. (1979) The control of movement in the preferred and non-preferred hands. *Quarterly Journal of Experimental Psychology*, **31**, 641–652.

Annett, J., Golby, C. W., & Kay, H. (1958) The measurement of elements in an assembly task— The information output of the human motor system. *Quarterly Journal of Experimental Psychology*, **10**, 1–11.

Annett, J., & Sheridan, M. R. (1973) Effects of S–R and R–R compatibility on bimanual movement time. *Quarterly Journal of Experimental Psychology*, **25**, 247–252.

Annett, M. (1959) The classification of instances of four common class concepts by children and adults. *British Journal of Educational Psychology*, **29**, 223–236.

Annett, M. (1964) A model of the inheritance of handedness and cerebral dominance. *Nature, Lond.*, **204**, 59–60.

Annett, M. (1967) The binomial distribution of right, mixed and left handedness. *Quarterly Journal of Experimental Psychology*, **29**, 327–333.

Annett, M. (1970a) A classification of hand preference by association analysis. *British Journal of Psychology*, **61**, 303–321.

Annett, M. (1970b) The growth of manual preference and speed. *British Journal of Psychology*, **61**, 545–558.

Annett, M. (1972) The distribution of manual asymmetry. *British Journal of Psychology*, **63**, 343–358.

Annett, M. (1973a) Handedness in families. *Annals of Human Genetics*, **37**, 93–105.

Annett, M. (1973b) Laterality of childhood hemiplegia and the growth of speech and intelligence. *Cortex*, **9**, 4–33.

428 REFERENCES

Annett, M. (1974) Handedness in the children of two left handed parents. *British Journal of Psychology*, **65**, 129–131.

Annett, M. (1975) Hand preference and the laterality of cerebral speech. *Cortex*, **11**, 305–328.

Annett, M. (1976a) A coordination of hand preference and skill replicated. *British Journal of Psychology*, **67**, 587–592.

Annett, M. (1976b) Handedness and the cerebral representation of speech. *Annals of Human Biology*, **3**, 317–328.

Annett, M. (1978a) Genetic and nongenetic influences on handedness. *Behavior Genetics*, **8**, 227–249.

Annett, M. (1978b) *A Single gene explanation of right and left handedness and brainedness*. Coventry: Lanchester Polytechnic.

Annett, M. (1979) Family handedness in three generations predicted by the right shift theory. *Annals of Human Genetics*, **42**, 479–491.

Annett, M. (1980) Sex differences in laterality—Meaningfulness versus reliability. *The Behavioral and Brain Sciences*, **3**, 227–228.

Annett, M. (1981) The right shift theory of handedness and developmental language problems. *Bulletin of the Orton Society*, **31**, 103–121.

Annett, M. (1982) Handedness. In Beaumont, J. G. (Ed.), *Divided visual field studies of cerebral organisation*. London: Academic Press.

Annett, M. (1983a) Hand preference and skill in 115 children of two left handed parents. *British Journal of Psychology*, **74**, 17–32.

Annett, M. (1983b) Individual variation in directional bias in visual perception. *Perception*, **12**, 71–84.

Annett, M. (1985) Which theory fails? A reply to McManus. *British Journal of Psychology*, in press.

Annett, M., & Annett, J. (1979) Individual differences in right and left reaction time. *British Journal of Psychology*, **70**, 393–404.

Annett, M., Hudson, P. T. W., & Turner, A. (1974) The reliability of differences between the hands in motor skill. *Neuropsychologia*, **12**, 527–531.

Annett, M., & Kilshaw, D. (1982) Mathematical ability and lateral asymmetry. *Cortex*, **18**, 547–568.

Annett, M., & Kilshaw, D. (1983) Right and left hand skill II: Estimating the parameters of the distribution of L–R differences in males and females. *British Journal of Psychology*, **74**, 269–283.

Annett, M., Lee, D., & Ounsted, C. O. (1961) Intellectual disabilities in relation to lateralized features of the EEG. In *Hemiplegic cerebral palsy in children and adults. Little Club Clinics in Developmental Medicine*, No. 4. London: Heinemann.

Annett, M., & Ockwell, A. (1980) Birth order, birth stress and handedness. *Cortex*, **16**, 181–188.

Annett, M., & Turner, A. (1974) Laterality and the growth of intellectual abilities. *British Journal of Educational Psychology*, **44**, 37–46.

Ardrey, R. (1976) *The hunting hypothesis*. London: Collins.

Arndt, S., & Berger, D. E. (1978) Cognitive mode and asymmetry in cerebral functioning. *Cortex*, **14**, 78–86.

Ashton, G. C. (1982) Handedness: An alternative hypothesis. *Behavior Genetics*, **12**, 125–147.

Baddeley, A. D. (1976) *The psychology of memory*. New York: Harper & Row.

Bakan, P. (1971) Handedness and birth order. *Nature. Lond.*, **229**, 195.

Bakan, P. (1973) Left-handedness and alcoholism. *Perceptual and Motor Skills*, **36**, 514.

Bakan, P. (1977) Left-handedness and birth order revisited. *Neuropsychologia*, **15**, 837–839.

Bakan, P., Dibb, G., & Reed, P. (1973) Handedness and birth stress. *Neuropsychologia, 11*, 363–366.

Barnes, F. (1975) Temperament, adaptability and left-handers. *New Scientist,* 24 July, *67*, 202–203.

Barnsley, R. H., & Rabinovitch, M. S. (1970) Handedness: Proficiency versus stated preference. *Perceptual & Motor Skills, 30*, 343–362.

Barsley, M. (1966) *The left-handed book.* London: Souvenir Press.

Basser, L. S. (1962) Hemiplegia of early onset and the faculty of speech with special reference to the effects of hemispherectomy. *Brain 85*, 427–460.

Beaton, A. (1979) Hemisphere function and dual task performance. *Neuropsychologia, 17*, 629–635.

Beaumont, J. G. (1974) Handedness and hemisphere function. In S. J. Dimond & J. G. Beaumont (Eds.), *Hemisphere function in the human brain.* London: Elek Science.

Beaumont, J. G. (1982) *Divided visual field studies of cerebral organisation.* London: Academic Press.

Beaumont, J. G. (1983) Methods for studying cerebral hemisphere function. In A. W. Young (Ed.), *Functions of the right cerebral hemisphere.* London: Academic Press.

Beaumont, J. G., & Dimond, S. J. (1975) Interhemispheric transfer of figural information in right- and non-right-handed subjects. *Acta Psychologia, 39*, 97–104.

Beaumont, J. G., & McCarthy, R. (1981) Dichotic ear asymmetry and writing posture. *Neuropsychologia, 19*, 469–472.

Bee, H. (1981) *The developing child* (3rd ed.). New York: Harper International.

Beech, H. R., & Fransella, F. (1968) *Research and experiment in stuttering.* Oxford: Pergamon.

Belmont, L., & Birch, H. G. (1965) Lateral dominance, lateral awareness and reading disability. *Child Development, 36*, 57–71.

Benton, A. L. (1962) Clinical symptomatology in right and left hemisphere lesions. In V. B. Mountcastle (Ed.), *Interhemispheric relations and cerebral dominance.* Baltimore: John Hopkins Press.

Benton, A. L. (1979) Visuoperceptive, visuospatial and visuoconstructive disorders. In K. M. Heilman & E. Valenstein (Eds.), *Clinical neuropsychology.* New York: Oxford University Press.

Berg, M. R., & Harris, L. J. (1980) The effect of experimenter location and subject anxiety on cerebral activation as measured by lateral eye movements. *Neuropsychologia, 18*, 89–93.

Beukelaar, L. J., & Kroonenberg, P. M. (1983) Towards a conceptualization of hand preference. *British Journal of Psychology, 74*, 33–45.

Bever, T. G., & Chiarello, R. J. (1974) Cerebral dominance in musicians and nonmusicians. *Science, 185*, 137–139.

Bingley, T. (1958) Mental symptoms in temporal lobe epilepsy and temporal lobe gliomas. *Acta Psychiatrica et Neurologica, Scandinavica* Supplementum 120, *33*.

Bisiach, E., Capitani, E., Luzzatti, C., & Perani, D. (1981) Brain and conscious representation of outside reality. *Neuropsychologia, 19*, 543–551.

Blau, A. (1946) The Master Hand. *American Orthopsychiatric Association.* Research monograph. no. 5.

Blau, T. H. (1977) Torque and schizophrenic vulnerability. *American Psychologist, 32*, 997–1005.

Boder, E. (1973) Developmental dyslexia: A diagnostic approach based on three atypical reading-spelling patterns. *Developmental Medicine and Child Neurology, 15*, 663–687.

Bodmer, W. F., & Cavalli-Sforza, L. L. (1976) *Genetics, evolution and man.* San Francisco: W. H. Freeman.

Bogen, J. E. (1969) The other side of the brain II: An appositional mind. *Bulletin of the Los Angeles Neurological Societies,* **34,** 135–162.

Bogen, J. E., DeZure, R., Tenhouten, W. D., & Marsh, S. F. (1972) The other side of the brain IV: The A/P ratio. *Bulletin of the Los Angeles Neurological Society,* **37,** 49–61.

Boklage, C. E. (1981). On the distribution of nonright-handedness among twins and their families. *Acta Geneticae Medicae et Gemellologiae,* **30,** 167–187.

Borod, J. C., Caron, H. S., & Koff, E. (1981) Asymmetry in positive and negative facial expressions: sex differences. *Neuropsychologia,* **19,** 819–824.

Boucher, J. (1977) Hand preference in autistic children. *Journal of Autism and Childhood Schizophrenia,* **7,** 177–187.

Boycott, A. E., Diver, C., Garstang, G. S. L., & Turner, F. M. (1930) The inheritance of sinistrality in limnaea peregra. *Philosophical transactions of the Royal Society of London,* **B219,** 51–131.

Brackenbridge, C. J. (1981) Secular variation in handedness over 90 years. *Neuropsychologia,* **19,** 459–462.

Bradley, J. V. (1957) Direction of knob-turn stereotypes. *United States Air Force, Wright Air Development Center.* Technical report.

Bradley, P., & Horn, G. (1981) Imprinting: A study of cholinergic receptor sites in parts of the chick brain. *Experimental Brain Research,* **41,** 121–123.

Bradley, P., Horn, G., & Bateson, P. (1981) Imprinting: An electron microscopic study of chick hyperstriatum ventrale. *Experimental Brain Research,* **41,** 115–120.

Bradshaw, J. L., & Gates, E. A. (1978) Visual field differences in verbal tasks: Effects of task familiarity and sex of subject. *Brain and Language,* **5,** 166–187.

Bradshaw, J. L., Gates, E. A., & Nettleton, N. C. (1977) Bihemispheric involvement in lexical decisions: Handedness and a possible sex difference. *Neuropsychologia,* **15,** 277–286.

Bradshaw, J. L., & Nettleton, N. C. (1983) *Human cerebral asymmetry.* Englewood Cliffs, New Jersey: Prentice-Hall.

Bradshaw, J. L., Nettleton, N. C., & Taylor, M. J. (1981) Right hemisphere language and cognitive deficit in sinistrals? *Neuropsychologia,* **19,** 113–132.

Bradshaw, J. L., & Taylor, M. J. (1979) A word naming deficit in nonfamilial sinistrals? Laterality effects of vocal responses to tachistoscopically presented letter strings. *Neuropsychologia,* **17,** 21–32.

Brain, W. R. (1941) Visual disorientation with special reference to lesions of the right cerebral hemisphere. *Brain,* **64,** 244–272.

Brain, W. R. (1945) Speech and handedness. *Lancet* **249,** 837–841.

Branch, C., Milner, B., & Rasmussen, T. (1964) Intracarotid sodium amytal for the lateralization of cerebral dominance. *Journal of Neurosurgery,* **21,** 399–405.

Brazelton, T. B., Robey, J. S., & Collier, G. A. (1969) Infant development in the Zincanteco Indians of Southern Mexico. *Pediatrics,* **44,** 274–290.

Brenner, M. W., & Gillman, S. (1966) Visuomotor ability in school children—A survey. *Developmental Medicine and Child Neurology,* **8,** 686–703.

Bresson, F., Maury, L., Pieraut-Le Bonniec, G., & Schonen, S. de. (1977) Organization and lateralization of reaching in infants: An instance of asymmetric functions in hands collaboration. *Neuropsychologia,* **15,** 311–320.

Briggs, G. G., & Nebes, R. D. (1975) Patterns of hand preference in a student population. *Cortex,* **11,** 230–238.

Briggs, G. G., & Nebes, R. D. (1976) the effects of handedness family history and sex on the performance of a dichotic listening task. *Neuropsychologia,* **14,** 129–134.

Briggs, G. G., Nebes, R. D., & Kinsbourne, M. (1976) Intellectual differences in relation to personal and family handedness. *Quarterly Journal of Experimental Psychology,* **28,** 591–601.

Brinkman, J., & Kuypers, H. G. J. M. (1973) Cerebral control of contralateral and ipsilateral arm, hand and finger movements in the split-brain rhesus monkey. *Brain,* **96,** 653–674.

Broadbent, D. E. (1956) Successive responses to simultaneous stimuli. *Quarterly Journal of Experimental Psychology,* **8,** 145–152.

Broadbent, D. E. (1974) Division of function and integration of behavior. In F. O. Schmitt & F. G. Worden (Eds.), *The neurosciences: Third study program.* Cambridge, Mass.: M.I.T. Press.

Broadbent, D. E., & Weiskrantz, L. (1982) The neuropsychology of cognitive function. *Philosophical Transactions of the Royal Society of London,* **B298,** 1–226.

Brooker, R. J., Lehman, R. A. W., Heimbuch, R. C., & Kidd, K. K. (1981) Hand usage in a colony of Bonnett monkeys (*Macaca radiata*). *Behavior Genetics,* **11,** 49–56.

Brown, J. A. C. (1961) *Freud and the post Freudians.* Harmondsworth, Middlesex: Penguin Books.

Brown, J. L. (1962) Differential hand usage in three year old children. *Journal of Genetic Psychology,* **100,** 167–175.

Browne, T. (1981) *Pseudoxia epidemica* (R. Robbins, Ed.). Oxford: Oxford University Press (originally published 1646).

Brust, J. C., Plank, C., Burke, A., Guobadia, M. M., & Healton, E. B. (1982) Language disorder in a right hander after occlusion of the right anterior cerebral artery. *Neurology,* **32,** 492–497.

Bryden, M. P. (1964) Tachistoscopic recognition and cerebral dominance. *Perceptual and Motor Skills,* **19,** 686.

Bryden, M. P. (1965) Tachistoscopic recognition, handedness and cerebral dominance. *Neuropsychologia,* **3,** 1–8.

Bryden, M. P. (1973) Perceptual asymmetry in vision: relation to handedness, eyedness and speech lateralization. *Cortex,* **9,** 419–435.

Bryden, M. P. (1975) Speech lateralization in families: A preliminary study using dichotic listening. *Brain and Language,* **2,** 201–211.

Bryden, M. P. (1977) Measuring handedness with questionnaires. *Neuropsychologia,* **15,** 617–624.

Bryden, M. P. (1978) Strategy effects in the assessment of hemisphere activity. In G. Underwood (Ed.), *Strategies in information processing.* London: Academic Press.

Bryden, M. P. (1979) Evidence for sex-related differences in cerebral organization. In M. Wittig & A. C. Petersen (Eds.), *Sex-related differences in cognitive functioning: Developmental issues.* New York: Academic Press.

Bryden, M. P. (1982) *Laterality: Functional asymmetry in the intact brain.* New York: Academic Press.

Buffery, A. W. H., & Gray, J. A. (1972) Sex differences in the development of spatial and linguistic skills. In C. Ounsted & D. C. Taylor (Eds.), *Gender differences: Their ontogeny and significance.* Edinburgh: Churchill Livingstone.

Burt, C. (1937) *The backward child.* London: University of London Press.

Butler, H. J. (1968) *Human intelligence: Its nature and assessment.* London: Methuen.

Butler, C. R., & Francis, A. C. (1973) Specialization of the left hemisphere in the baboon—Evidence from directional preferences. *Neuropsychologia,* **11,** 351–354.

Butler, S. R., & Glass, A. (1974) Asymmetries in the electroencephalogram associated with cerebral dominance. *Electroencephalography and Clinical Neurophysiology,* **36,** 481–491.

Byrne, B. (1974) Handedness and musical ability. *British Journal of Psychology,* **65,** 279–281.

Campbell, R. (1978) Asymmetries in interpreting and expressing a posed facial expression. *Cortex,* **14,** 327–342.

Caplan, B., & Kinsbourne, M. (1982) Cognitive style and dichotic asymmetries in disabled readers. *Cortex,* **18,** 357–366.

Capobianco, R. J. (1966) Ocular-manual laterality and reading in adolescent mental retardates. *American Journal of Mental Deficiency,* **70,** 781–785.

Carter, C. O. (1961) Inheritance of congenital pyloric stenosis. *British Medical Bulletin,* **17,** 251–253.

Carter, C. O. (1962) *Human Heredity.* Harmondsworth, Middlesex: Penguin.

432 REFERENCES

Carter, D. B. (1953) A further demonstration of phi movement cerebral dominance. *Journal of Psychology*, **36**, 299–309.

Carter, R. L., Hohenegger, M., & Satz, P. (1980) Handedness and aphasia: An inferential method for determining the mode of cerebral speech specialization. *Neuropsychologia*, **18**, 569–574.

Carter-Saltzman, L. (1979) Patterns of cognitive functioning in relation to handedness and sex related differences. In M. A. Wittig & A. C. Petersen (Eds.), *Sex-related differences in cognitive functioning*. New York: Academic Press.

Carter-Saltzman, L. (1980). Biological and sociocultural effects on handedness. Comparison between biological and adoptive families. *Science*, **209**, 1263–1265.

Chamberlain, H. D. (1928) The inheritance of left handedness. *Journal of Heredity*, **19**, 557–559.

Chapanis, A., & Gropper, B. A. (1968) The effect of the operator's handedness on some directional stereotypes in control-display relationships. *Human Factors*, **10**, 303–320.

Cherfas, J. (1983) Trees have made man upright. *New Scientist*, 20 January, 172–178.

Cherry, E. C. (1953) Some experiments on the recognition of speech, with one and with two ears. *Journal of the Acoustical Society of America*, **25**, 975–979.

Chesher, E. C. (1936) Some observations concerning the relation of handedness to the language mechanism. *Bulletin of the Neurological Institute of New York*, **4**, 556–562.

Chi, J. G., Dooling, E. C., & Gilles, F. H. (1977) Gyral development of the human brain. *Annals of Neurology*, **1**, 86–93.

Chivers, D. J. (1974) *The siamang in Malaya: A field study of a primate in tropical rain forest* (Contributions of Primatology 4). Basel: Karger.

Chui, H. C., & Damasio, A. R. (1980) Human cerebral asymmetries evaluated by computed tomography. *Journal of Neurology, Neurosurgery and Psychiatry*, **43**, 873–878.

Churchill, J. A. (1966) On the origin of focal motor epilepsy. *Neurology, Minneapolis*, **16**, 49–58.

Churchill, J. A. (1968) A study of hemiplegic cerebral palsy. *Developmental Medicine and Child Neurology*, **10**, 453–459.

Churchill, J. A., Igna, E., & Senf, R. (1962) The association of position at birth and handedness. *Pediatrics*, **29**, 307–309.

Cipollo-Neto, J., Horn, G., & McCabe, B. J. (1982) Hemispheric asymmetry and imprinting: The effect of sequential lesions to the hyperstriatum ventrale. *Experimental Brain Research*, **48**, 22–27.

Clark, H. H., & Clark, E. V. (1977) *Psychology and language: An introduction to psycholinguistics*. New York: Harcourt, Brace Jovanovitch.

Clark, M. M. (1957) *Left-handedness*. London: University of London Press.

Clark, M. M. (1970) *Reading difficulties in schools*. Harmondsworth, Middlesex: Penguin.

Clark, W. E. Le Gros. (1934) The asymmetry of the occipital region of the brain and skull. *Man*, **55**, 35–37.

Cohen, G. (1972) Hemisphere differences in a letter classification task. *Perception and Psychophysics*, **11**, 139–142.

Colby, K. M., & Parkinson, C. (1977) Handedness in autistic children. *Journal of Autism and Childhood Schizophrenia*, **7**, 3–9.

Cole, J. (1955) Paw preference in cats related to hand preference in animals and men. *Journal of Comparative and Physiological Psychology*, **48**, 137–140.

Collins, R. L. (1969) On the inheritance of handedness: II. Selection for sinistrality in mice. *Journal of Heredity*, **60**, 117–119.

Collins, R. L. (1970) The sound of one paw clapping: An inquiry into the origin of left handedness. In G. Lindzey & D. D. Thiessen (Eds.), *Contribution to behavior-genetic analysis—The mouse as a prototype*. New York: Appleton-Century-Crofts.

Collins, R. L. (1975) When left handed mice live in right handed worlds. *Science*, **187**, 181–184.

Collins, R. L. (1977) Toward an admissable genetic model for the inheritance of degree and direction of asymmetry. In S. Harnad, R. W. Doty, L. Goldstein, J. Jaynes, G. Krauthamer (Eds.), *Lateralization in the nervous system*. New York: Academic Press.

Connolly, K., & Elliott, J. (1972) The evolution and ontogeny of hand function. In N. G. Blurton-Jones (Ed.), *Ethological studies of child behaviour*. Cambridge: Cambridge University Press.

Conrad, K. (1949) Über aphäsische Sprachstörungen bei Hirnverletzten Linkshänder. *Nervenarzt*, **20**, 148–154.

Corballis, M. C. (1983) *Human Laterality*. New York: Academic Press.

Corballis, M. C., Anuza, T., & Blake, L. (1978) Tachistoscopic perception under head tilt. *Perception and Psychophysics*, **24**, 274–284.

Corballis, M. C., & Morgan, M. J. (1978) On the biological basis of human laterality: I. Evidence for maturational left–right gradient. *The Behavioral and Brain Sciences*, **1**, 261–269.

Coren, S., & Porac, C. (1977) Fifty centuries of right handedness: The historical record. *Science*, **198**, 631–632.

Coren, S., & Porac, C. (1978) The validity and reliability of self report items for the measurement of lateral preference. *British Journal of Psychology*, **69**, 207–211.

Coren, S., & Porac, C. (1979) Normative data on hand position during writing. *Cortex*, **15**, 679–682.

Coren, S., & Porac, C. (1982) Lateral preference and cognitive skills: An indirect test. *Perceptual and Motor Skills*, **54**, 787–792.

Crabtree, T. (1976) Dyslexia goodbye. *New Society*, 1 January, 10–11.

Craig, J. D. (1980) A dichotic rhythm task: Advantage for the left handed. *Cortex*, **16**, 613–620.

Critchley, M. (1970a) *Aphasiology and other aspects of language*. London: Edward Arnold.

Critchley, M. (1970b) *The dyslexic child*. London: William Heineman.

Crovitz, H. F. (1961) Differential acuity of two eyes and the problem of ocular dominance. *Science*, **134**, 614.

Crovitz, H. F., & Zener, K. A. (1962) A group test for assessing hand and eye dominance. *American Journal of Psychology*, **75**, 271–276.

Cruikshank, W. M., & Raus, G. M. (1955) *Cerebral palsy: Its individual and community problems*. Syracuse: Syracuse University Press.

Cunningham, D. J. (1902) Right handedness and left brainedness. *Journal of the Royal Anthropological Institute of Great Britain and Ireland*, **32**, 273–296.

Curry, F. K., & Rutherford, D. R. (1967) Recognition and recall of dichotically presented verbal stimuli by right and left handed persons. *Neuropsychologia*, **5**, 119–126.

Dalby, J. T., & Gibson, D. (1981) Functional cerebral lateralization in subtypes of disabled readers. *Brain and Language*, **14**, 34–48.

Dalby, J. T., Gibson, D., Grossi, V., & Schneider, R. D. (1980) Lateralized hand gesture during speech. *Journal of Motor Behavior*, **12**, 292–297.

Dart, R. A. (1925) *Australopithecus africanus*: The man-ape of South Africa. *Nature, Lond.*, **115**, 195–199.

Dart, R. A. (1949) The predatory implemental technique of Australopithecus. *American Journal of Physical Anthropology*, **7**, 1–38.

Darwin, C. (1859) *The origin of species*. London: John Murray.

Darwin, C. J. (1971) Ear differences in the recall of fricatives and vowels. *Quarterly Journal of Experimental Psychology*, **23**, 46–62.

Davidoff, J. B. (1975) Hemispheric differences in the perception of lightness. *Neuropsychologia*, **13**, 121–124.

Davis, R., Wehrkamp, R., & Smith, K. U. (1951) Dimensional analysis of motion: I. Effects of laterality and movement direction. *Journal of Applied Psychology*, **35**, 363–366.

Dawkins, R. (1982) *The extended phenotype: The gene as the unit of selection*. Oxford: W. H. Freeman.

Dee, H. L. (1971) Auditory asymmetry and strength of manual preference. *Cortex*, **7**, 236–245.

Delis, D. C., Knight, R. T., & Simpson, G. (1983) Reversed hemispheric organization in a left hander. *Neuropsychologia*, **21**, 13–24.

Demarest, W. J. (1982) *Manual asymmetry in Guatemalan populations: A cross-cultural test of Annett's right shift theory.* Unpublished doctoral dissertation, University of Stanford.

Denneberg, V. H. (1981) Hemispheric laterality in animals and the effects of early experience. *The Behavioral and Brain Sciences*, **4**, 1–49.

Dennis, M., & Whitaker, H. A. (1977) Hemisphere equipotentiality and language acquisition. In S. J. Segalowitz & F. A. Gruber (Eds.), *Language development and neurological theory.* New York: Academic Press.

Dennis, W. (1940) *The Hopi child.* New York: Wiley.

Dennis, W. (1958) Early graphic evidence of dextrality in man. *Perceptual and Motor Skills*, **8**, 147–149.

De Renzi, E. (1978) Hemispheric asymmetry as evidenced by spatial disorders. In M. Kinsbourne (Ed.), *Asymmetrical function of the brain.* Cambridge: Cambridge University Press.

De Renzi, E. (1982) *Disorders of space exploration and cognition.* Chichester, Sussex: John Wiley.

De Renzi, E., Faglioni, P., & Ferrari, P. (1980) The influence of sex and age on the incidence and type of aphasia. *Cortex*, **16**, 627–630.

De Renzi, E., & Spinnler, H. (1966a) Facial recognition in brain-damaged patients. *Neurology*, **16**, 145–152.

De Renzi, E., & Spinnler, H. (1966b) Visual recognition in patients with unilateral cerebral disease. *Journal of Nervous and Mental Disease*, **142**, 515–525.

Deutsch, D. (1978) Pitch memory: An advantage for the left handed. *Science*, **199**, 559–560.

Deutsch, D. (1980) Handedness and memory for tonal pitch. In J. Herron (Ed.), *Neuropsychology of left handedness.* New York: Academic Press.

Dewson, J. H. (1977) Preliminary evidence of hemispheric asymmetry of auditory function in monkeys. In S. Harnad, R. W. Doty, L. Goldstein, J. Jaynes, & G. Krauthamer (Eds.), *Lateralization in the nervous system.* New York: Academic Press.

Dimond, S. J. (1976) Depletion of attentional capacity after total commissurotomy in man. *Brain*, **99**, 347–356.

Dimond, S. J. (1979) Disconnection and psychopathology. In J. Gruzelier & P. Flor-Henry (Eds.), *Hemispheric asymmetries of function in psychopathology.* Amsterdam: Elsevier/North Holland Biomedical Press.

Dimond, S. J., & Beaumont, J. G. (1974) Hemispheric function and paired associate learning. *British Journal of Psychology*, **65**, 275–278.

Divenyi, P. L., & Efron, R. (1979) Spectral versus temporal features in dichotic listening. *Brain and Language*, **7**, 375–386.

Donchin, E., Kutas, M., & McCarthy, G. (1977) Electrocortical indices of hemispheric utilization. In S. Harnad, R. W. Doty, L. Goldstein, J. Jaynes, & G. Krauthamer (Eds.), *Lateralization in the nervous system.* New York: Academic Press.

Dunn, L. M. (1959) *The Peabody Picture Vocabulary Test.* Minnesota: American Guidance Service Inc.

Dusek, C. D., & Hicks, R. A. (1980) Multiple birth risk factors and handedness in elementary school children. *Cortex*, **16**, 471–478.

Ehrlichman, H., & Weinberger, A. (1978) Lateral eye movements and hemispheric asymmetry: A critical review. *Psychological Bulletin*, **85**, 1080–1101.

Ehrlichman, H., Weiner, S. L., & Baker, A. H. (1974) Effects of verbal and spatial questions on initial gaze shifts. *Neuropsychologia*, **12**, 265–277.

Ellenberg, L., & Sperry, R. W. (1979) Capacity for holding sustained attention following commissurotomy. *Cortex*, **15**, 421–438.

Ettlinger, G. (1961) Lateral preferences in monkeys. *Behavior*, **17**, 275–287.

Ettlinger, G., Blakemore, C. B., & Milner, A. D. (1968) Opposite hand preferences in two sense modalities. *Nature, London*, **218**, 1276.

Ettlinger, G., Jackson, C. V., & Zangwill, O. L. (1956) Cerebral dominance in sinistrals. *Brain*, **79**, 569–588.

Ettlinger, G., & Moffett, A. (1964) Lateral preferences in the monkey. *Nature, London*, **204**, 606.

Eysenck, H. J., & Eysenck, S. B. G. (1963) *Eysenck Personality Inventory*. London: Hodder and Stoughton.

Fagan-Dubin, L. (1974) Lateral dominance and development of cerebral specialization. *Cortex*, **10**, 69–74.

Fairweather, H. (1976) Sex differences in cognition. *Cognition*, **4**, 231–280.

Falconer, D. S. (1965) The inheritance of liability to certain diseases, estimated from the incidence among relatives. *Annals of Human Genetics, London*, **29**, 51–76.

Falek, A. (1959) Handedness: A family study. *American Journal of Human Genetics*, **11**, 52–62.

Falzi, G., Perrone, P., & Vignolo, L. A. (1982) Right–left asymmetry in anterior speech region. *Archives of Neurology*, **39**, 239–240.

Fennell, E. B., Bowers, D., & Satz, P. (1977a). Within-modal and cross-modal reliabilities of two laterality tests. *Brain and Language*, **4**, 63–69.

Fennell, E., Bowers, D., & Satz, P. (1977b) Within-modal and cross-modal reliabilities of two laterality tests among left handers. *Perceptual and Motor Skills*, **45**, 451–456.

Fennell, E., Satz, P., & Wise, R. (1967) Laterality differences in the perception of pressure. *Journal of Neurology, Neurosurgery and Psychiatry*, **30**, 337–340.

Finch, G. (1941) Chimpanzee handedness. *Science*, **94**, 117–118.

Finucci, J. M., Guthrie, J. T., Childs, A. L., Abbey, H., & Childs, B. (1976) The genetics of specific reading disability. *Annals of Human Genetics*, **40**, 1–23.

Fitts, P. M. (1954) The information capacity of the human motor system in controlling the amplitude of movement. *Journal of Experimental Psychology*, **47**, 381–402.

Fitzhugh, K. B. (1973) Some neuropsychological features of delinquent subjects. *Perceptual and Motor Skills*, **36**, 494.

Fleishman, E. A. (1958) Dimensional analysis of movement reactions. *Journal of Experimental Psychology*, **55**, 438–453.

Fleishman, E. A., & Ellison, G. D. (1962) A factor analysis of fine manipulative tests. *Journal of Applied Psychology*, **46**, 96–105.

Fleishman, E. A., & Hempel, W. E. Jr. (1954) A factor analysis of dexterity tests. *Personnel Psychology*, **7**, 15–32.

Fleminger, J. J., Dalton, R., & Standage, K. F. (1977) Age as a factor in the handedness of adults. *Neuropsychologia*, **15**, 471–473.

Flowers, K. (1975) Handedness and controlled movement. *British Journal of Psychology*, **66**, 39–52.

Franco, L., & Sperry, R. W. (1977) Hemisphere lateralization for cognitive processing of geometry. *Neuropsychologia*, **15**, 107–114.

Fried, I., Mateer, C., Ojemann, G., Wohns, R., & Fedio, P. (1982) Organization of visuospatial functions in human cortex: Evidence from electrical stimulation. *Brain*, **105**, 349–371.

Friedman, A., & Polson, M. C. (1981) Hemispheres as independent resource systems: Limited capacity processing and cerebral specialization. *Journal of Experimental Psychology: Human Perception and Performance*, **7**, 1031–1058.

Frith, C. D. (1979) Consciousness, information processing and schizophrenia. *British Journal of Psychiatry*, **134**, 225–235.

Fry, D. B. (1975) Ear advantage for speech in groups of right and left handed subjects. *Language and Speech*, **18**, 264–269.

Gaede, S. E., Parsons, O. A., & Bertera, J. H. (1978) Hemispheric differences in music perception: Aptitude vs. experience. *Neuropsychologia*, **16**, 369–373.

Galaburda, A. (1983) Anatomy of developmental dyslexia: Biological perspective. Paper presented to The Dyslexia Institute Conference, Stratford-upon-Avon, 14–16 October, 1983.

Galaburda, A. M., Geschwind, N., LeMay, M., Kemper, T. L. (1978) Right–left asymmetries in the brain. *Science*, **199**, 852–856.

Galin, D., Johnstone, J., & Herron, J. (1978) Effects of task difficulty on EEG measures of cerebral engagement. *Neuropsychologia*, **16**, 461–472.

Galin, D., Ornstein, R., Herron, J., & Johnstone, J. (1982) Sex and handedness differences in EEG measures of hemispheric specialization. *Brain and Language*, **16**, 19–55.

Gardner, E. B., English, A. G., Flannery, B. M., Hartnett, M. B., McCormick, J. K., & Wilhelmy, B. B. (1977) Shape-recognition accuracy and response latency in a bilateral tactile task. *Neuropsychologia*, **15**, 607–616.

Gardner, E. J., & Snustad, D. P. (1981) *Principles of genetics* (6th ed.), New York: Wiley.

Gardner, M. (1967) *The ambidextrous universe.* London: Allen Lane.

Gardner, R. A., & Gardner, B. T. (1969) Teaching sign language to a chimpanzee. *Science*, **165**, 664–672.

Gautrin, D., & Ettinger, G. (1970) Lateral preferences in the monkey. *Cortex*, **6**, 287–292.

Gazzaniga, M. S. (1967) The split brain in man. *Scientific American*, **217**(2), 24–29.

Gazzaniga, M. S. (1983) Right hemisphere language following brain bisection: A 20-year perspective. *American Psychologist*, **5**, 525–537.

Gazzaniga, M. S., & LeDoux, J E. (1978) *The integrated mind.* New York: Plenum Press.

Gazzaniga, M. S., & Sperry, R. W. (1967) Language after section of the cerebral commissures. *Brain*, **90**, 131–148.

Gazzaniga, M. S., Volpe, B. T., Smylie, C. S., Wilson, D. H., & LeDoux, J. E. (1979) Plasticity in speech organization following commissurotomy. *Brain*, **102**, 805–815.

Gedye, J. L. (1964) Hand preference in aircrew: A study of the consistency and strength of lateral preference for simple unimanual tasks. *Aerospace Medicine*, **35**, 757–763.

Geffen, G., Bradshaw, J. C., & Nettleton, N. C. (1972) Hemispheric asymmetry: Verbal and spatial encoding of visual stimuli. *Journal of Experimental Psychology*, **95**, 25–31.

Geffen, G., & Traub, E. (1980) The effects of duration of stimulation, preferred hand and familial sinistrality in dichotic monitoring. *Cortex*, **16**, 83–94.

Geffen, G., Traub, E., & Stierman, I. (1978) Language laterality assessed by unilateral ECT and dichotic monitoring. *Journal of Neurology, Neurosurgery and Psychiatry*, **41**, 354–360.

Geschwind, N. (1975) The apraxias: Neural mechanism of disorders of learned movement. *American Scientist*, **63**, 188–195.

Geschwind, N. (1979) Specializations of the human brain. *Scientific American*, **241**(3), 158–168.

Geschwind, N., & Behan, P. (1982) Left handedness: Association with immune disease, migraine, and developmental learning disorder. *Proceedings of the National Academy of Sciences, USA*, **79**, 5097–5100.

Geschwind, N., & Levitsky, W. (1968) Human brain: Left right asymmetries in temporal speech region. *Science*, **161**, 186–187.

Gesell, A. (1940) *The first five years of life.* New York: Harper & Row.

Gesell, A., & Ames, L. B. (1947) The development of handedness. *Journal of Genetic Psychology*, **70**, 155–176.

Ghent, L. (1961) Developmental changes in tactual thresholds on dominant and nondominant sides. *Journal of comparative and physiological psychology*, **54**, 670–673.

Gibson, J. B. (1973) Intelligence and handedness. *Nature, London*, **243**, 482.

Gilbert, C. (1977) Non verbal perceptual abilities in relation to left handedness and cerebral lateralization. *Neuropsychologia*, **15**, 779–791.

Gilbert, C., & Bakan, P. (1973) Visual asymmetry in perception of faces. *Neuropsychologia*, **11**, 355–362.

Gillies, S. M., MacSweeney, D. A., & Zangwill, O. L. (1960) A note on some unusual handedness patterns. *Quarterly Journal of Experimental Psychology*, **12**, 113–116.

Glees, P., & Cole, J. (1952) Ipsilateral representation in the cerebral cortex. *Lancet*, 1952 14 June, 1191.

Glick, S. D., Jerussi, T. P., & Zimmerberg, B. (1977) Behavioral and neuropharmacological correlates of nigrostriatal asymmetry in rats. In S. Harnad, R. W. Doty, L. Goldstein, J. Jaynes, & G. Krauthamer (Eds.), *Lateralization in the nervous system*. New York: Academic Press.

Gloning, I., Gloning, K., Haub, G., & Quatember, R. (1969) Comparison of verbal behavior in right-handed and non-right-handed patients with anatomically verified lesion of one hemisphere. *Cortex*, **5**, 41–52.

Gloning, K., & Quatember, R. (1966) Statistical evidence of neuropsychological syndromes in left-handed and ambidextrous patients. *Cortex*, **2**, 484–488.

Good News Bible: Today's English Version. London: Collins/Fontana, 1976.

Goodall, J. (1983) Population dynamics during a 15 yr. period in one community of free-living chimpanzees in the Zambia National Park, Tanzania. *Zeitschrift Fur Tierpsychologie*, **61**, 1–60.

Goodglass, H., & Quadfasel, F. A. (1954) Language laterality in left handed aphasics. *Brain*, **77**, 521–548.

Gordon, H. (1921) Left handedness, and mirror writing, especially among defective children. *Brain*, **43**, 313–368.

Gordon, H. W. (1980) Degree of ear asymmetries for perception of dichotic chords and for illusory chord localization in musicians of different levels of competence. *Journal of Experimental Psychology: Human Perception and Performance*, **6**, 516–527.

Gordon, H. W. (1983) Music and the right hemisphere. In A. W. Young (Ed.), *Functions of the right cerebral hemisphere*. London: Academic Press.

Gottesman, I. I., & Shields, J. (1972) *Schizophrenia and genetics: A twin study vantage point*. New York: Academic Press.

Granjon-Galifret, N., & Ajuriaguerra, J. (1951) Troubles de l'apprentissage de la lecture et dominance laterale. *Encephale*, **40**, 385–398.

Grant, D. A., & Kaestner, N. F. (1955) Constant velocity tracking as a function of subjects' handedness and the rate and direction of the target course. *Journal of Experimental Psychology*, **49**, 203–208.

Grapin, P., & Perpère, C. (1968) Symétrie et lateralisation du nourrisson. In R. Kourlisky & P. Grapin (Ed.), *Main droite et main gauche*. Paris: Presses Universitaires de France.

Graves, R., Goodglass, H., & Landis, T. (1982) Mouth asymmetry during spontaneous speech. *Neuropsychologia*, **20**, 371–381.

Gray, R., Hentschke, R., Isaac, S., Mead, R., Ozturk, A., Rieley, P., Smale, K., & Stern, R. (1971) Sampling variation of reported results. *Nature, London*, **234**, 230–231.

Green, P., Glass, A., & O'Callaghan, M. A. (1979) Some implications of abnormal hemisphere interaction in schizophrenia. In J. Gruzelier & P. Flor-Henry (Eds.), *Hemisphere asymmetries of function in psychopathology*. Amsterdam: Elsevier/North Holland Biomedical Press.

Griffith, H., & Davidson, M. (1966) Long term changes in intellect and behaviour after hemispherectomy. *Journal of Neurology, Neurosurgery and Psychiatry*, **29**, 571–576.

Groves, C. P., & Humphrey, N. K. (1973) Asymmetry in gorilla skulls: Evidence of lateralized brain function. *Nature, London*, **244**, 53–54.

Gur, R. C., Gur, R. E., Obrist, W. D., Hungerbuhler, J. P., Younkin, D., Rosen, A. D., Skolnick, B. E., & Reivich, M. (1982) Sex and handedness differences in cerebral blood flow during rest and cognitive activity. *Science*, **217**, 659–661.

Gur, R. C., & Reivich, M. (1980) Cognitive task effects on hemispheric blood flow in humans: Evidence for individual differences in hemisphere activation. *Brain and Language*, **9**, 78–92.

Gur, R. E., Gur, R. C., & Harris, L. J. (1975) Cerebral activation as measured by subjects' lateral eye movements is influenced by experimenter location. *Neuropsychologia*, **13**, 35–44.

Hallgren, B. (1950) Specific dyslexia: A clinical and genetic study. *Acta Psychiatrica et Neurologica Scandinavia*, Suppl. 65, 1–287.

Hamilton, C. R. (1977) An assessment of hemispheric specialization in monkeys. *Annals of the New York Academy of Sciences*, **299**, 222–232.

Hammil, D., & Irwin, O. C. (1966) IQ differences of right and left spastic hemiplegic children. *Perceptual and Motor Skills*, **22**, 193–194.

Hammond, G. R., & Kaplan, R. J. (1982) Language lateralization and handedness: Estimates based on clinical data. *Brain and Language*, **16**, 348–351.

Harding, D. W. (1953) *Social psychology and individual values*. London: Hutchinson.

Hardyck, C. (1977a) Handedness and part-whole relationships: A replication. *Cortex*, **13**, 177–183.

Hardyck, C. (1977b) Laterality and intellectual ability: A just not noticeable difference. *British Journal of Educational Psychology*, **47**, 305–311.

Hardyck, C. (1977c) A model of individual differences in hemispheric functioning. In H. Whitaker & H. A. Whitaker (Eds.), *Studies in neurolinguistics* (Vol. 3). New York: Academic Press.

Hardyck, C., Goldman, R., & Petrinovich, L. (1975) Handedness and sex, race and age. *Human Biology*, **47**, 369–375.

Hardyck, C., Petrinovich, L. F., & Goldman, R. D. (1976) Left handedness and cognitive deficit. *Cortex*, **12**, 266–279.

Harris, A. J. (1957) Lateral dominance, directional confusion and reading disability. *Journal of Psychology*, **44**, 283–294.

Harris, A. J. (1958) *Harris Tests of Lateral Dominance: Manual of directions for administration and interpretation* (3rd ed.). New York: Psychological Corporation.

Harris, H. (1980) *The principles of human biochemical genetics* (3rd ed.). Amsterdam: Elsevier/North Holland Biomedical Press.

Harris, L. J. (1978) Sex differences in spatial ability: Possible environmental, genetic and neurological factors. In M. Kinsbourne (Ed.), *Asymmetrical function of the brain*. Cambridge: Cambridge University Press.

Harris, L. J. (1980a) Left handedness: Early theories, facts and fancies. In J. Herron (Ed.), *Neuropsychology of left handedness*. New York: Academic Press.

Harris, L. J. (1980b) Which hand is the "eye" of the blind? A new look at an old question. In J. Herron (Ed.), *Neuropsychology of left handedness*. New York: Academic Press.

Hathaway, S. R. & McKinley, J. C. (1948) *Minnesota Multiphasic Personality Inventory*. New York: Psychological Corporation.

Haun, F. (1978) Functional dissociation of the hemispheres using foveal visual input. *Neuropsychologia*, **16**, 725–733.

Hécaen, H. (1983) Acquired aphasia in children: Revisited. *Neuropsychologia*, **21**, 581–587.

Hécaen, H., & Ajuriaguerra, J. (1964) *Left handedness: Manual superiority and cerebral dominance*. New York: Grune and Stratton.

Hécaen, H., De Agostini, M., & Monzon-Montes, A. (1981) Cerebral organization in left handers. *Brain and Language*, **12**, 261–284.

Hécaen, H., Mazars, G., Ramier, A. M., Goldblum, M. C., & Merienne, L. (1971) Aphasie croisée chez un sujet droitier bilingue (vietnamien–français). *Revue Neurologique, Paris*, **124**, 319–323.

Hécaen, H. & Piercy, M. (1956) Paroxysmal dysphasia and the problem of cerebral dominance. *Journal of Neurology, Neurosurgery and Psychiatry*, **18**, 194–201.

Hécaen, H., & Sauguet, J. (1971) Cerebral dominance in left-handed subjects. *Cortex*, **7**, 19–48.

Heilman, K. M. (1979) The neuropsychological basis of skilled movement in man. In M. S. Gazzaniga (Ed.), *Handbook of behavioral neurobiology* (Vol. 2): *Neuropsychology*. New York: Plenum.

Heilman, K. M., Coyle, J. M., Gonyea, E. F., & Geschwind, N. (1973) Apraxia and agraphia in a left hander. *Brain*, **96**, 21–28.

Heilman, K. M., Gonyea, E. F., & Geshwind, N. (1974) Apraxia and agraphia in a right hander. *Cortex*, **10**, 284–288.

Heim, A. W. & Watts, K. P. (1976) Handedness and cognitive bias. *Quarterly Journal of Experimental Psychology*, **28**, 355–360.

Heller, W., & Levy, J. (1981) Perception and expression of emotion in right handers and left handers. *Neuropsychologia*, **19**, 263–272.

Hellige, J. B. (1983) *Cerebral hemisphere asymmetry: Method, theory and application*. New York: Praeger.

Herrmann, D. J., & Van Dyke, K. (1978) Handedness and the mental rotation of perceived patterns. *Cortex*, **14**, 521–529.

Herron, J. (1980) Two hands, two brains, two sexes. In J. Herron (Ed.), *Neuropsychology of left handedness*. New York: Academic Press.

Herron, J., Galin, D., Johnstone, J., & Ornstein, R. E. (1979) Cerebral specialization, writing posture and motor control of writing in left handers. *Science*, **205**, 1285–1289.

Hicks, R. A., & Pellegrini, R. J. (1978a) Handedness and anxiety. *Cortex*, **14**, 119–121.

Hicks, R. A., & Pellegrini, R. J. (1978b) Handedness and locus of control. *Perceptual and Motor Skills*, **46**, 369–370.

Hicks, R. A., Pellegrini, R. J., & Evans, E. A. (1978) Handedness and birth risk. *Neuropsychologia*, **16**, 243–245.

Hicks, R. E., & Kinsbourne, M. (1976) Human handedness: A partial cross fostering study. *Science*, **192**, 908–910.

Hier, D. B., Le May, M., & Rosenberger, P. B. (1979) Autism and unfavourable left–right asymmetries of the brain. *Journal of Autism and Developmental Disorders*, **9**, 153–159.

Higenbottam, J. A. (1973) Relationships between sets of lateral and perceptual preference measures. *Cortex*, **9**, 403–410.

Hinde, R. A. (1982) *Ethology*. Oxford: Oxford University Press.

Hines, D., & Satz, P. (1974) Cross-modal asymmetries in perception related to asymmetry in cerebral function. *Neuropsychologia*, **12**, 239–247.

Hitch, G. J. (1980) Developing the concept of working memory. In G. Claxton (Ed.), *Cognitive psychology: New directions*. London: Routledge and Kegan Paul.

Hoadley, M. F., & Pearson, K. (1929) On measurement of the internal diameter of the skull in relation: I. To the prediction of its capacity, II. To the "pre-eminence" of the left hemisphere. *Biometrika*, **21**, 85–123.

Hochberg, F. H., & LeMay, M. (1975) Arteriographic correlates of handedness. *Neurology*, **25**, 218–222.

Holloway, R. L. (1974) The casts of fossil *hominid* brains. *Scientific American*, **231**(1), 106–115.

Holloway, R. L. (1981) Exploring the dorsal surface of *hominoid* brain endocasts by stereoplotter and discriminant analysis. *Philosophical Transactions of the Royal Society of London*, **B292**, 155–166.

Holloway, R. L., & LaCoste-Lareymondie, M. C. de. (1982) Brain endocast asymmetry in pongids and hominids: Some preliminary findings on the paleontology of cerebral dominance. *American Journal of Physical Anthropology*, **58**, 101–110.

Holmes, J. M., & Marshall, J. C. (1974) Handedness and lateralized word perception: Reading habits versus hemispheric specialization. *IRCS*, **2**, 1462.

Honda, H. (1982) Rightward superiority of eye movements in a bimanual aiming task. *Quarterly Journal of Experimental Psychology*, **34A**, 499–513.

Howarth, C. I., & Beggs, W. D. A. (1981) Discrete movements. In D. Holding (Ed.), *Human skills*. Chichester: John Wiley & Sons.

Hubbard, J. I. (1971) Handedness not a function of birth order. *Nature*, **232**, 276–277.

440 REFERENCES

Hubel, D. H., & Wiesel, T. M. (1979) Brain mechanisms of vision. *Scientific American*, **241**(3), 130–144.

Hudson, P. T. W. (1975) The genetics of handedness—A reply to Levy and Nagylaki. *Neuropsychologia*, **13**, 331–339.

Hummel, K. P., & Chapman, D. B. (1959) Visceral inversion and associated anomalies in the mouse. *Journal of Heredity*, **50**, 9–13.

Humphrey, M. E. (1951) Consistency of hand usage. *British Journal of Educational Psychology*, **21**, 214–225.

Humphrey, M. E., & Zangwill, O. L. (1952) Dysphasia in left handed patients with unilateral brain lesions. *Journal of Neurology, Neurosurgery and Psychiatry*, **15**, 184–193.

Hutt, C. (1972) *Males and females*. Harmondsworth, Middlesex: Penguin.

Inglis, J., & Lawson, J. S. (1981) Sex differences in the effects of unilateral brain damage on intelligence. *Science*, **212**, 693–695.

Inglis, J., & Lawson, J. S. (1982) A meta-analysis of sex differences in the effects of unilateral brain damage on intelligence test results. *Canadian Journal of Psychology*, **36**, 670–683.

Inglis, J., Ruckman, M. S., Lawson, J. S., MacLean, A. W., & Monga, T. N. (1982) Sex differences in the cognitive effects of unilateral brain damage. *Cortex*, **18**, 257–276.

Ingram, D. (1975) Motor asymmetries in young children. *Neuropsychologia*, **13**, 95–102.

Ingram, T. T. S. (1959a) Specific developmental disorders of speech in childhood. *Brain*, **82**, 450–467.

Ingram, T. T. S. (1959b) A description and classification of the common disorders of speech in children. *Archives of Disease in Childhood*, **34**, 444–455.

Jackson, J. H. (1876) Case of large cerebral tumour without optic neuritis and with left hemiplegia and imperception. *Royal London Ophthalmic Hospital Reports*, **8**, 434–444.

Jackson, J. H. (1915) On the nature of the duality of the brain. *Brain*, **30**, 80–86 (originally published, 1874).

Jantz, R. L., Fohl, F. H., & Zahler, J. W. (1979) Finger ridge-counts and handedness. *Human Biology*, **51**, 91–99.

Jasper, H. H. (1932) A laboratory study of diagnostic indices of bilateral neuro-muscular organization in stutterers and normal speakers. *Psychological Monographs*, **43**, 72–174.

Jasper, H. H., & Raney, E. T. (1937) The physiology of lateral cerebral dominance. *Psychological Bulletin*, **34**, 151–165.

Jeeves, M. A. (1972) Hemisphere differences in response rates to visual stimuli in children. *Psychonomic Science*, **27**, 201–203.

Jeeves, M. A., & Dixon, N. F. (1970) Hemisphere differences in response rates to visual stimuli. *Psychonomic Science*, **20**, 249–250.

Johanson, D. C., & Edey, M. A. (1981) *Lucy: The beginnings of humankind*. London: Granada.

Johnstone, J., Galin, D., & Herron, J. (1979) Choice of handedness measures in studies of hemisphere specialization. *International Journal of Neuroscience*, **9**, 71–80.

Jones, R. K. (1966) Observations of stammering after localized cerebral injury. *Journal of Neurology, Neurosurgery and Psychiatry*, **29**, 192–195.

Jordan, H. E. (1911) The inheritance of left-handedness. *American Breeders Magazine*, **2**, 19–29 & 113–124.

Jordan, H. E. (1914) Hereditary left-handedness, with a note on twinning (Study III). *Journal of Genetics*, **4**, 67–81.

Jorm, A. F. (1983) Specific reading retardation and working memory: A review. *British Journal of Psychology*, **74**, 311–342.

Karpinos, B. D., & Grossman, H. A. (1953) Prevalence of left-handedness among selective service registrants. *Human Biology*, **25**, 36–49.

Kasinov, V. B. (1973) Handedness in Lemnaceae: On the determination of left and right types of development in *Lemna* clones and on its alteration by means of external influences. *Beiträge zur Biologie der Pflanzen*, **49**, 321–337.

Keefe, B., & Swinney, D. (1979) On the relationship of hemispheric specialization and developmental dyslexia. *Cortex*, **15**, 471–481.

Keeley, L. H. (1977) The functions of paleolithic flint tools. *Scientific American*, **237**(5), 108–126.

Keogh, B. K. (1972) Preschool children's performance on measures of spatial organization, lateral preference and lateral usage. *Perceptual and Motor Skills*, **34**, 299–302.

Kertesz, A., & Geschwind, N. (1971) Patterns of pyramidal decussation and their relationship to handedness. *Archives of Neurology*, **4**, 326–332.

Kertesz, A., & Sheppard, A. (1981) The epidemiology of aphasic and cognitive impairment in stroke. Age, sex, aphasia type and laterality differences. *Brain*, **104**, 117–128.

Kilshaw, D., & Annett, M. (1983) Right and left hand skill I: Effects of age, sex and hand preference showing superior skill in left handers. *British Journal of Psychology*, **74**, 253–268.

Kimura, D. (1961) Cerebral dominance and the perception of verbal stimuli. *Canadian Journal of Psychology*, **15**, 166–171.

Kimura, D. (1964) Left–right differences in the perception of melodies. *Quarterly Journal of Experimental Psychology*, **16**, 355–358.

Kimura, D. (1973a) Manual activity during speaking. I. Right handers. *Neuropsychologia*, **11**, 45–50.

Kimura, D. (1973b) Manual activity during speaking. II. Left handers. *Neuropsychologia*, **11**, 51–55.

Kimura, D. (1983a) Sex differences in cerebral organization for speech and praxic function. *Canadian Journal of Psychology*, **37**, 19–35.

Kimura, D. (1983b) Speech representation in an unbiased sample of left-handers. *Human Neurobiology*, **2**, 147–154.

Kimura, D., & Vanderwolf, C. H. (1970) The relation between hand preference and the performance of individual finger movements by left and right hands. *Brain*, **93**, 769–774.

Kinsbourne, M. (1970) The cerebral basis of lateral asymmetries in attention. *Acta Psychologica*, **33**, 193–201.

Kinsbourne, M. (1971) The minor cerebral hemisphere. *Archives of Neurology*, **25**, 302–306.

Kinsbourne, M. (1974) Direction of gaze and distribution of cerebral thought processes. *Neurolopsychologia*, **12**, 279–281.

Knox, A. W., & Boone, D. R. (1970) Auditory laterality and tested handedness. *Cortex*, **6**, 164–173.

Knox, C., & Kimura, D. (1970) Cerebral processing of nonverbal sounds in boys and girls. *Neuropsychologia*, **8**, 227–237.

Kocel, K. M. (1980) Age-related changes in cognitive abilities and hemispheric specialization. In J. Herron (Ed.), *Neuropsychology of left handedness*. New York: Academic Press.

Koff, E., Borod, J. C., & White, B. (1981) Asymmetries for hemiface size and mobility. *Neuropsychologia*, **19**, 825–830.

Kohn, B., & Dennis, M. (1974) Selective impairments of visuo-spatial abilities in infantile hemiplegics after right cerebral hemidecortication. *Neuropsychologia*, **12**, 505–512.

Kolata, G. (1983) Math genius may have hormonal basis. *Science*, **222**, 1312.

Kolb, B., & Whishaw, I. Q. (1980) *Fundamentals of human neuropsychology*. San Francisco: Freeman.

Komai, T., & Fukuoka, G. (1934) A study of the frequency of left handedness and left footedness among Japanese school children. *Human Biology*, **6**, 33–42.

Kortlandt, A. (1972) *New perspectives on ape and human evolution*. Preliminary edition. Stichting voor Psychobiologie. Amsterdam (cited by Passingham, 1982).

Kruper, D. C., Patton, R. A., & Koskoff, Y. D. (1971) Hand and eye preference in unilaterally brain ablated monkeys. *Physiology and Behavior*, **7**, 181–185.

Lackner, J. R., & Teuber, H. L. (1973) Alterations in auditory fusion thresholds after cerebral injury in man. *Neuropsychologia*, **11**, 409–415.

442   REFERENCES

Lake, D. A., & Bryden, M. P. (1976) Handedness and sex differences in hemispheric asymmetry. *Brain and Language*, **3**, 266–282.

Lassen, N. A., Ingvar, D. H., & Skinhøj, E. (1978) Brain function and blood flow. *Scientific American*, **239**(4), 50–59.

Lawick-Goodall, J. van (1971) *In the shadow of man*. London: Collins.

Lawson, N. C. (1978) Inverted writing in right- and left-handers in relation to lateralization of face recognition. *Cortex*, **14**, 207–211.

Layton, W. M. Jr. (1976) Random determination of a developmental process. *Journal of Heredity*, **67**, 336–338.

Leakey, R. E. (1981) *The making of mankind*. London: Michael Joseph.

LeDoux, J. E., Wilson, D. H., & Gazzaniga, M. S. (1977) Manipulo-spatial aspects of cerebral lateralization: Clues to the origin of lateralization. *Neuropsychologia*, **15**, 743–750.

Lehman, R. A. W. (1972) Constancy of hand preference following forebrain bisection in monkeys. *Neurology*, **22**, 763–768.

Lehman, R. A. W. (1978) The handedness of rhesus monkeys. I, Distribution. *Neuropsychologia*, **16**, 33–42.

Leiber, L., & Axelrod, S. (1981a) Intra-familial learning is only a minor factor in manifest handedness. *Neuropsychologia*, **19**, 273–288.

Leiber, L., & Axelrod, S. (1981b) Not all sinistrality is pathological. *Cortex*, **17**, 259–272.

LeMay, M. (1976) Morphological cerebral asymmetries of modern man, fossil man and nonhuman primate. *Annals of the New York Academy of Sciences*, **280**, 349–366.

LeMay, M. (1977) Asymmetries of the skull and handedness: Phrenology revisited. *Journal of the Neurological Sciences*, **32**, 243–253.

LeMay, M., Billig, M. S., & Geschwind, N. (1982) Asymmetries of the brains and skulls of nonhuman primates. In E. Armstrong & D. Falk (Eds.), *Primate brain evolution: Methods and concepts*. New York: Academic Press.

LeMay, M., & Culebras, A. (1972) Human brain morphologic differences in the hemispheres demonstrable by caroitd angiography. *New England Journal of Medicine*, **287**, 168–170.

Lenneberg, E. H. (1962) Understanding language without the ability to speak. *Journal of Abnormal and Social Psychology*, **65**, 419–425.

Lenneberg, E. H. (1967) *Biological foundations of language*. New York: Wiley.

Leviton, A., & Kilty, T. (1976) Birth order and left handedness. *Archives of Neurology*, **33**, 664.

Levy, J. (1969) Possible basis for the evolution of lateral specialization of the human brain. *Nature, London*, **224**, 614–615.

Levy, J. (1973) Lateral specialization of the human brain: Behavioral manifestations and possible evolutionary basis. In J. Kiger (Ed.), *The biology of behavior*. Corvallis: Oregon State University Press.

Levy, J. (1974) Psychobiological implications of bilateral asymmetry. In S. J. Dimond & J. G. Beaumont (Eds.), *Hemisphere function in the human brain*. London: Elek Science.

Levy, J. (1976) A review of evidence for a genetic component in the determination of handedness. *Behavior Genetics*, **6**, 429–453.

Levy, J. (1977) A reply to Hudson regarding the Levy–Nagylaki model for the genetics of handedness. *Neuropsychologia*, **15**, 187–190.

Levy, J. (1982) Handwriting posture and cerebral organization: How are they related? *Psychological Bulletin*, **91**, 589–608.

Levy, J., & Gur, R. C. (1980) Individual differences in psychoneurological organization. In J. Herron (Ed.), *Neuropsychology of left-handedness*. New York: Academic Press.

Levy, J., & Nagylaki, T. (1972) A model for the genetics of handedness. *Genetics*, **72**, 117–128.

Levy, J., & Reid, M. (1976) Variations in writing posture and cerebral organization. *Science*, **194**, 337–339.

Levy, J., & Reid, M. (1978) Variations in cerebral organization as a function of handedness, hand posture in writing, and sex. *Journal of Experimental Psychology: General*, **107**, 119–144.

Levy, J., & Trevarthen, C. (1977) Perceptual, semantic and phonetic aspects of elementary language processes in split-brain patients. *Brain*, **100**, 105–118.

Levy, J., Trevarthen, C., & Sperry, R. W. (1972) Perception of bilateral chimeric figures following hemispheric deconnexion. *Brain*, **95**, 61–78.

Liberman, A. M. (1974) The specialization of the language hemisphere. In F. O. Schmitt, & F. G. Worden (Eds.), *The neurosciences: Third study program.* Cambridge, Mass.: The MIT Press.

Lieberman, P. (1979) Hominid evolution, supralaryngeal vocal tract physiology, and the fossil evidence for reconstruction. *Brain and Language*, **7**, 101–126.

Liederman, J., & Kinsbourne, M. (1980) Rightward motor bias in newborns depends upon parental right handedness. *Neuropsychologia*, **18**, 579–584.

Lishman, W. A., & McMeekan, E. R. L. (1976) Hand preference patterns in psychiatric patients. *British Journal of Psychiatry*, **129**, 158–166.

Lishman, W. A., & McMeekan, E. R. L. (1977) Handedness in relation to direction and degree of cerebral dominance for language. *Cortex*, **13**, 30–43.

Loehlin, J. C., & Nichols, R. C. (1976) *Heredity, environment and personality.* Austin, Texas: University of Texas Press.

Loiseau, L. (1974) Experimental study of H. Jasper's method for determining visual dominance. *Année Psychologique*, **74**, 35–42.

Lombroso, C. (1903) Left-handedness and left-sidedness. *North American Review*, **177**, 440–444.

Longstreth, L. E. (1980) Human handedness: More evidence for genetic involvement. *Journal of Genetic Psychology*, **137**, 275–283.

Lorenz, K. (1970) *Studies in animal and human behavior, Vols. 1 & 2.* Cambridge, Mass.: Harvard University Press.

Lovell, K., Shapton, D., & Warren, N. S. (1964) A study of some cognitive and other disabilities in backward readers of average intelligence as assessed by a non-verbal test. *British Journal of Educational Psychology*, **34**, 58–64.

Luchins, D. J. (1983) Psychopathology and cerebral asymmetries detected by computed tomography. In P. Flor-Henry and J. Gruzelier (Eds.), *Laterality and psychopathology.* Amsterdam: Elsevier Science.

Luchins, D., Pollin, W., & Wyatt, R. J. (1980) Laterality in monozygotic schizophrenic twins: An alternative hypothesis. *Biological Psychiatry*, **15**, 87–93.

Luchins, D. J., Weinberger, D. R., & Wyatt, R. J. (1979) Schizophrenia: Evidence of a subgroup with reversed cerebral asymmetry. *Archives of General Psychiatry*, **36**, 1309–1311.

Luria, A. R. (1966) *Higher cortical functions in man.* London: Tavistock Publications.

Luria, A. R. (1970) *Traumatic aphasia.* The Hague: Mouton (originally published 1947).

Lyle, J. G., & Johnson, E. G. (1976) Development of lateral consistency and its relation to reading and reversals. *Perceptual and Motor Skills*, **43**, 695–698.

Lyon, M. F. (1962) Sex chromatin and gene action in the mammalian X-chromosome. *American Journal of Human Genetics*, **14**, 135.

Malcolm, J. E., & Pound, D. P. B. (1971) Direction of spiral of the umbilical cord. *Journal of the Royal College of General Practitioners*, **21**, 746–747.

Maple, T. L. (1980) *Orang-utan behavior.* New York: Van Nostrand Reinhold.

Marcel, T., Katz, L., & Smith, M. (1974) Laterality and reading proficiency. *Neuropsychologia*, **12**, 131–139.

Marshall, J. C. & Holmes, J. M. (1974) Sex, handedness and differential hemispheric specialization for components of word perception. *IRCS*, **2**, 1344.

Mascie-Taylor, C. G. N. (1981) Hand preference and personality traits. *Cortex*, **17**, 319–322.

Mason, S. (1984) The left hand of nature. *New Scientist*, 19 January, 10–14.

Masure, M. C., & Benton, A. L. (1983) Visuospatial performance in left handed patients with unilateral brain lesions. *Neuropsychologia*, **21**, 179–181.

Mayr, E. (1970) *Populations, species and evolution.* Cambridge, Mass.: Belknap Press of Harvard University Press.

Mateer, C. A. (1983) Motor and perceptual functions of the left hemisphere and their interaction. In S. J. Segalowitz (Ed.), *Language functions and brain organization.* New York: Academic Press.

McFie, J. (1952) Cerebral dominance in cases of reading disability. *Journal of Neurology, Neurosurgery and Psychiatry,* **15**, 194–199.

McGee, M. G. (1979) Human spatial abilities: Psychometric studies and environmental, genetic, hormonal and neurological influences. *Psychological Bulletin,* **86**, 889–918.

McGee, M. G., & Cozad, T. (1980) Population genetic analysis of human hand preference: Evidence for generation differences, familial resemblance and maternal effects. *Behavior Genetics,* **10**, 263–275.

McGlone, J. (1977) Sex differences in cerebral organization of cerebral functions in patients with unilateral brain lesions. *Brain,* **100**, 775–793.

McGlone, J. (1978) Sex differences in functional brain asymmetry. *Cortex,* **14**, 122–128.

McGlone, J. (1980) Sex differences in human brain asymmetry: A critical survey. *The Brain and Behavioral Science,* **3**, 215–227.

McGlone, J., & Davidson, W. (1973) The relationship between cerebral speech laterality and spatial ability with special reference to sex and hand preference. *Neuropsychologia,* **11**, 105–113.

McGuire, W. J., & McGuire, C. V. (1980) Salience of handedness in the spontaneous self-concept. *Perceptual and Motor Skills,* **50**, 3–7.

McKeever, W. F. (1979) Handwriting posture in left-handers: Sex, familial sinistrality and language laterality correlates. *Neuropsychologia,* **17**, 429–444.

McKeever, W. F., & Gill, K. M. (1972) Visual half-field differences in masking effects for sequential letter stimuli in the right and left handed. *Neuropsychologia,* **10**, 111–117.

McKeever, W. F., Gill, K. M., & Van Deventer, A. D. (1975) Letter versus dot stimuli as tools for splitting the normal brain with reaction time. *Quarterly Journal of Experimental Psychology,* **27**, 363–373.

McKeever, W. F., & Hoff, A. L. (1979) Evidence of a possible isolation of left hemisphere visual and motor areas in sinistrals employing an inverted handwriting posture. *Neuropsychologia,* **17**, 445–455.

McKeever, W. F., & Jackson, T. L. (1979) Cerebral dominance assessed by object and color naming latencies: Sex and familial sinistrality effects. *Brain and Language,* **7**, 175–190.

McKeever, W. F., Seitz, K. S., Hoff, A. L., Marino, M. F., & Diehl, J. A. (1983) Interacting sex and familial sinistrality characteristics influence both language lateralization and spatial ability in right handers. *Neuropsychologia,* **21**, 661–668.

McKeever, W. F., & Van Deventer, A. D. (1977a) Failure to confirm a spatial ability impairment. *Cortex,* **13**, 321–326.

McKeever, W. F., & Van Deventer, A. D. (1977b) Familial sinistrality and degree of left handedness. *British Journal of Psychology,* **68**, 469–471.

McKeever, W. F., & Van Deventer, A. D. (1977c) Visual and auditory language processing asymmetries: Influences of handedness, familial sinistrality and sex. *Cortex,* **13**, 225–241.

McKeever, W. F., & Van Deventer, A. D. (1980) Inverted handwriting position, language laterality and the Levy-Nagylaki genetic model of handedness and cerebral organization. *Neuropsychologia,* **18**, 99–102.

McKeever, W. F., Van Deventer, A. D., & Suberi, M. (1973) Avowed, assessed and familial handedness and differential hemispheric processing of brief sequential and non-sequential visual stimuli. *Neuropsychologia,* **11**, 235–238.

McLeod, P., & Posner, M. I. (1984) Privileged loops from percept to act. In H. Bouma & D. G. Bouwhuis (Eds.), *Attention and performance X: Control of language processes.* London: Lawrence Erlbaum.

McManus, I. C. (1980a) Handedness in twins: A critical review. *Neuropsychologia,* **18**, 347–355.

McManus, I. C. (1980b) Left handedness and epilepsy. *Cortex,* **16**, 487–491.

McManus, I. C. (1981) Handedness and birth stress. *Psychological Medicine*, **11**, 485–496.

McManus, I. C. (1985) Right- and left-hand skill. Failure of the right shift model. *British Journal of Psychology*, in press.

McMeekan, E. R. L., & Lishman, W. A. (1975) Retest reliabilities and interrelationship of the Annett Hand Preference Questionnaire and the Edinburgh Handedness Inventory. *British Journal of Psychology*, **66**, 53–60.

McRae, D. L., Branch, C. L., & Milner, B. (1968) The occipital horns and cerebral dominance. *Neurology*, **18**, 95–98.

Mebert, C. J., & Michel, G. F. (1980) Handedness in artists. In J. Herron (Ed.), *Neuropsychology of left handedness*. New York: Academic Press.

Medawar, P. B. (1957) *The uniqueness of the individual*. London: Methuen.

Merrell, D. J. (1957) Dominance of eye and hand. *Human Biology*, **29**, 314–328.

Merrill-Palmer (1931) *Scale of mental tests*. New York: Harcourt Brace and World Inc.

Meyer, V., & Yates, A. J. (1955) Intellectual changes following temporal lobectomy for psychomotor epilepsy. *Journal of Neurology, Neurosurgery and Psychiatry*, **18**, 44–52.

Michel, G. F. (1981) Right handedness: A consequence of infant supine head orientation preference. *Science*, **212**, 685–687.

Michel, G. F., & Goodwin, R. (1979) Intra-uterine birth position predicts newborn supine head position preference. *Infant Behavior and Development*, **2**, 29.

Miller, E. (1971) Handedness and the pattern of human ability. *British Journal of Psychology*, **62**, 111–112.

Milner, A. D. (1969) Distribution of hand preferences in monkeys. *Neuropsychologia*, **7**, 375–377.

Milner, B. (1954) Intellectual function of the temporal lobes. *Psychological Bulletin*, **51**, 42–62.

Milner, B. (1962) Laterality effects in audition. In V. B. Mountcastle (Ed.), *Interhemispheric relations and cerebral dominance*. Baltimore: Johns Hopkins.

Milner, B. (1964) Some effects of frontal lobectomy in man. In J. M. Warren & K. Akert (Eds.), *The frontal granular cortex and behavior*. New York: McGraw-Hill.

Milner, B. (1974) Hemispheric specialization: Scope and limits. In F. O. Schmitt & F. G. Worden (Eds.), *The neurosciences: Third study program*. Cambridge, Mass.: MIT Press.

Milner, B. (1982) Some cognitive effects of frontal lobe lesions in man. *Philosophical Transactions of the Royal Society of London*, **B298**, 211–226.

Milner, B., Branch, C., & Rasmussen, T. (1964) Observations on cerebral dominance. In A. V. S. De Reuck & M. O'Connor (Eds.), *Disorders of language* (CIBA Foundation Symposium). London: Churchill.

Mitler, B., & Taylor, L. (1972) Right hemisphere superiority in tactile pattern-recognition after cerebral commissurotomy: Evidence of non-verbal memory. *Neuropsychologia*, **10**, 1–17.

Mittler, P. (1971) *The study of twins*. Harmondsworth, Middlesex: Penguin.

Mittwoch, U. (1973) *Genetics of sex differentiation*. New York: Academic Press.

Mittwoch, U. (1977) To be right is to be born male. *New Scientist*, 13 January, 74–76.

Mittwoch, U., & Mahadevaiah, S. (1980) Additional growth—A link between mammalian testes, avian ovaries, gonadal asymmetry in hermaphrodites and the expression of the H-Y antigen. *Growth*, **44**, 287–300.

Mizuno, N., Nakamura, Y., & Okamoto, M. (1968) The frequency of occurrence of Barnes' ventrolateral pyramidal tract. *Journal of Comparative Neurology*, **134**, 1–8.

Money, J. (1972) Studies of the function of sighting dominance. *Quarterly Journal of Experimental Psychology*, **24**, 454–464.

Morais, J., & Bertelson, P. (1973) Laterality effects in diotic listening. *Perception*, **2**, 107–111.

Morais, J., Peretz, I., Gudanski, M., & Guiard, Y. (1982) Ear asymmetry for chord recognition in musicians and nonmusicians. *Neuropsychologia*, **20**, 351–354.

Moray House Intelligence tests. (1952) Department of Education, University of Edinburgh. London: University of London Press.

Morgan, M. J. (1977) Embryology and inheritance of asymmetry. In S. Harnad, R. W. Doty, L. Goldstein, J. Jaynes, & G. Krauthamer (Eds.), *Lateralization in the nervous system*. New York: Academic Press.

Morgan, M. J., & Corballis, M. C. (1978) On the biological basis of human laterality. II. The Mechanism of Inheritance. *The Behavioral and Brain Sciences*, **1**, 270–277.

Morley, M. E. (1957) *The development and disorders of speech in childhood*. Edinburgh: E. & S. Livingstone.

Morrisby, J. R. (1955) *Differential test battery*. London: National Foundation for Educational Research.

Moscovitch, M., & Olds, J. (1982) Asymmetries in spontaneous facial expressions and their possible relation to hemispheric specialisation. *Neuropsychologia*, **20**, 71–81.

Mountcastle, V. B., Lynch, J. C., Georgopolous, A., Sakata, H., & Acuna, C. (1975) Posterior parietal association cortex of the monkey: Common functions for operations within extrapersonal space. *Journal of Neurophysiology*, **38**, 871–908.

Myles, M. F. (1972) *A textbook for midwives*. Edinburgh: Churchill-Livingstone.

Nagylaki, T., & Levy, J. (1973) "The sound of one paw clapping" isn't sound. *Behavior Genetics*, **3**, 279–292.

Naidoo, S. (1972) *Specific dyslexia*. London: Pitman.

Napier, J. (1971) *The roots of mankind*. London: George Allen & Unwin.

Napier, J. (1980) *Hands*. London: George Allen & Unwin.

Nebes, R. D. (1971a) Handedness and the perception of part-whole relationships. *Cortex*, **7**, 350–356.

Nebes, R. D. (1971b) Superiority of the minor hemisphere in commissurotomized man for perception of whole-part relations. *Cortex*, **7**, 333–349.

Nebes, R. D. (1972) Dominance of the minor hemisphere in commissurotomized man on a test of figural unification. *Brain*, **95**, 633–638.

Nebes, R. D. (1973) Perception of spatial relationships by the right and left hemispheres in commissurotomized man. *Neuropsychologia*, **11**, 285–289.

Nebes, R. D., & Briggs, G. G. (1974) Handedness and the retention of visual material. *Cortex*, **10**, 209–214.

Ness, A. R. (1967) A measure of asymmetry of the skulls of odontocete whales. *Journal of Zoology*, **153**, 209–221.

Netley, C., & Rovet, J. (1983) Relationships among brain organization, maturation rate and the development of verbal and nonverbal ability. In S. J. Segalowitz (Ed.), *Language functions and brain organization*. New York: Academic Press.

Newcombe, F., & Ratcliff, G. G. (1973) Handedness, speech lateralization and ability. *Neuropsychologia*, **11**, 399–407.

Newcombe, F. G., Ratcliff, G. G., Carrivick, P. J., Hiorns, R. W., Harrison, G. A., & Gibson, J. B. (1975) Hand preference and IQ in a group of Oxfordshire villages. *Annals of Human Biology*, **2**, 235–242.

Newcombe, F., & Russell, W. R. (1969) Dissociated visual perceptual and spatial deficits in focal lesions of the right hemisphere. *Journal of Neurology, Neurosurgery and Psychiatry*, **32**, 73–81.

Nicoletti, R., Anzola, G. P., Luppino, G., Rizzolatti, G., & Umiltà, C. (1982) Spatial compatibility effects on the same side of the body midline. *Journal of Experimental Psychology: Human Perception and Performance*, **8**, 664–673.

Nilsson, J., Glencross, D., & Geffen, G. (1980) The effects of familial sinistrality and preferred hand on dichaptic and dichotic tasks. *Brain and Language*, **10**, 390–404.

Norden, E. J., & Yahr, P. (1982) Hemispheric asymmetries in the behavioral and hormonal effects of sexually differentiating mammalian brain. *Science*, **218**, 391–393.

Nottebohm, F. (1970) Ontogeny of bird song. *Science*, **167**, 950–956.

Nottebohm, F. (1977) Asymmetries in neural control of vocalization in the canary. In S. Harnad, R. W. Doty, L. Goldstein, J. Jaynes, & G. Krauthamer (Eds.), *Lateralization in the nervous system*. New York: Academic Press.

Nottebohm, F. (1981) Laterality, seasons and space govern the learning of a motor skill. *Trends in Neurosciences*, **4**, 104–106.

Oddy, H. L., & Lobstein, T. J. (1972) Hand and eye dominance in schizophrenia. *British Journal of Psychiatry*, **120**, 331–333.

Ojemann, G. A. (1983a) Brain organization for language from the perspective of electrical stimulation mapping. *The Behavioral and Brain Sciences*, **6**, 189–206.

Ojemann, G. A. (1983b) The intrahemispheric organization of human language, derived with electrical stimulation techniques. *Trends in Neurosciences*, **6**, 184–189.

Ojemann, G., & Mateer, C. (1979) Human language cortex: Localization of memory, syntax and sequential motor-phoneme identification systems. *Science*, **205**, 1401–1403.

Oldfield, R. C. (1969) Handedness in musicians. *British Journal of Psychology*, **60**, 91–99.

Oldfield, R. C. (1971) The assessment and analysis of handedness: The Edinburgh Inventory. *Neuropsychologia*, **9**, 97–114.

Olson, M. E. (1973) Laterality differences in tachistoscopic word recognition in normal and delayed readers in elementary school. *Neuropsychologia*, **11**, 343–350.

Oppenheimer, J. M. (1974) Asymmetry revisited. *American Zoologist*, **14**, 867–879.

Orlando, C. P. (1972) Measures of handedness as indicators of language lateralization. *Bulletin of the Orton Society*, **22**, 14–26.

Orme, J. E. (1970) Left handedness, ability and emotional instability. *British Journal of Social and Clinical Psychology*, **9**, 87–88.

Ornstein, S. T. (1972) *The psychology of consciousness*. San Francisco: W. H. Freeman.

Orton, S. T. (1937) *Reading, writing and speech problems in children*. London: Chapman & Hall.

Owen, F. W. (1978) Dyslexia: Genetic aspects. In A. L. Benton & D. Pearl (Eds.), *Dyslexia: An appraisal of current knowledge*. New York: Oxford University Press.

Paillard, J. (1982) Apraxia and the neurophysiology of motor control. *Philosophical Transactions of the Royal Society of London*, **B298**, 111–134.

Paivio, A., & Begg, I. (1981) *Psychology of language*. London: Prentice-Hall.

Palmer, R. D. (1963) Hand differentiation and psychological functioning. *Journal of Personality*, **31**, 445–461.

Palmer, R. D. (1964) Development of a differentiated handedness. *Psychological Bulletin*, **62**, 257–272.

Papçun, G., Krashen, S., Terbeek, D., Remington, R., & Harshman, R. (1974) Is the left hemisphere specialized for speech, language and/or something else? *Journal of the Acoustic Society of America*, **55**, 319–327.

Parlow, S. (1978) Differential finger movements and hand preference. *Cortex*, **14**, 608–611.

Pasamanick, B., & Knobloch, A. (1960) Brain damage and reproductive casualty. *American Journal of Orthopsychiatry*, **30**, 298–305.

Passingham, R. E. (1982) *The human primate*. Oxford & San Francisco: Freeman.

Penfield, W., & Jasper, H. H. (1954) *Epilepsy and the functional anatomy of the human brain*. Boston: Little, Brown.

Penfield, W., & Roberts, L. (1959) *Speech and brain mechanisms*. Princeton, N.J.: Princeton University Press.

Perlstein, M. A., & Hood, P. N. (1957) Infantile spastic hemiplegia: Intelligence and age of walking and talking. *American Journal of Mental Deficiency*, **61**, 534–542.

Peters, M. (1976) Prolonged practice of a simple motor task by preferred and nonpreferred hands. *Perceptual and Motor Skills*, **43**, 447–450.

Peters, M. (1980) Why the preferred hand taps more quickly than the nonpreferred hand: Three experiments on handedness. *Canadian Journal of Psychology*, **34**, 62–71.

448 REFERENCES

Peters, M. (1981) Handedness: Effects of prolonged practice on between hand performance differences. *Neuropsychologia*, **19**, 587–590.

Peters, M., & Durding, B. (1978) Handedness measured by finger tapping: A continuous variable. *Canadian Journal of Psychology*, **32**, 257–261.

Peters, M., & Durding, B. (1979) Left handers and right handers compared on a motor task. *Journal of Motor Behavior*, **11**, 103–111.

Peters, M., & Pedersen, K. (1978) Incidences of left handers with inverted writing position in a population of 5910 elementary school children. *Neuropsychologia*, **16**, 743–746.

Petersen, M. R., Beecher, M. D., Zoloth, S. R., Moody, D. B., & Stebbins, W. C. (1978) Neural lateralization of species specific vocalization by Japanese macaques (Macaca fuscata). *Science*, **202**, 324–327.

Peterson, G. M. (1934) Mechanisms of handedness in the rat. *Comparative Psychology Monographs*, No. 46.

Peterson, G. M., & Chaplin, J. P. (1942) Extrapyramidal mechanisms of handedness in the rat. *Journal of Comparative Psychology*, **33**, 343–361.

Peterson, J., & Lansky, L. (1974) Left handedness among architects: Some facts and speculation. *Perceptual and Motor Skills*, **38**, 547–550.

Pettit, J. M., & Noll, J. D. (1979) Cerebral dominance in aphasia recovery. *Brain and Language*, **7**, 191–200.

Pew, R. W. (1974) Human perceptual-motor performance. In B. H. Kantowitz (Ed.), *Human information processing: Tutorials in performance and cognition.* Hillsdale, N.J.: Lawrence Erlbaum Associates.

Piaget, J. (1950) *The psychology of intelligence.* London: Routledge and Kegan Paul.

Piaget, J. (1951) *Play, dreams and imitation in childhood.* London: Routledge and Kegan Paul.

Piaget, J. (1952) *The child's conception of number.* London: Routledge and Kegan Paul.

Piazza, D. M. (1980) The influence of sex and handedness in the hemispheric specialization of verbal and nonverbal tasks. *Neuropsychologia*, **18**, 163–176.

Pierson, J. M., Bradshaw, J. L., & Nettleton, N. C. (1983) Head and body space to left and right, front and rear—I. Unidirectional comparative auditory stimulation. *Neuropsychologia*, **21**, 463–473.

Pilbeam, D. (1984) The descent of hominoids and hominids. *Scientific American*, **250**(3), 60–69.

Pipe, M. E., & Beale, I. L. (1983) Hemispheric specialization for speech in retarded children. *Neuropsychologia*, **21**, 91–98.

Pirozzolo, F. J., & Rayner, K. (1979) Cerebral organization and reading disability. *Neuropsychologia*, **17**, 485–491.

Pirsig, R. M. (1974) *Zen and the art of motorcycle maintenance: An enquiry into values.* London: Bodley Head.

Pizzamiglio, L., Pascalis, C. de, & Vignati, A. (1974) Stability of dichotic listening test. *Cortex*, **10**, 203–205.

Poeck, K., & Lehmkuhl, G. (1980) Ideatory apraxia in a left handed patient with right sided brain lesion. *Cortex*, **16**, 273–284.

Poffenberger, A. T. (1912) Reaction time to retinal stimulation with special reference to the time lost in conduction through nerve centres. *Archives of Psychology*, **23**, 1–73.

Policansky, D. (1982a) The asymmetry of flounders. *Scientific American*, **246**(5), 96–102.

Policansky, D. (1982b) Flatfishes and the inheritance of asymmetries. *The Behavioral and Brain Sciences*, **5**, 262–265.

Popper, K. R. (1963) Conjectures and refutations: The growth of scientific knowledge. London: Routledge and Kegan Paul.

Popper, K. R., & Eccles, J. C. (1977) *The self and its brain.* Berlin: Springer International.

Porac, C., & Coren, S. (1976) The dominant eye. *Psychological Bulletin*, **33**, 880–897.

Porac, C., & Coren, S. (1979) A test of the validity of offsprings report of parental handedness. *Perceptual and Motor Skills*, **49**, 227–231.

Porac, C., & Coren, S. (1981) *Lateral preferences and human behavior*. New York: Springer Verlag.

Porac, C., Coren, S., & Duncan, P. (1980) Life-span age trends in laterality. *Journal of Gerontology*, **35**, 715–721.

Porac, C., Coren, S., Steiger, J. H., & Duncan, P. (1980) Human laterality: A multidimensional approach. *Canadian Journal of Psychology*, **34**, 91–96.

Preilowski, B. F. B. (1972) Possible contribution of the anterior forebrain commissures to bilateral motor coordination. *Neuropsychologia*, **10**, 267–277.

Premack, A. J., & Premack, D. (1972) Teaching language to an ape. *Scientific American*, **227**(4), 92–99.

Pringle, M. L. K. (1961) The incidence of some supposedly adverse family conditions and of left handedness in schools for maladjusted children. *British Journal of Educational Psychology*, **31**, 183–193.

Prior, M. R., & Bradshaw, J. L. (1979) Hemisphere functioning in autistic children. *Cortex*, **15**, 73–81.

Provins, K. A., & Cunliffe, P. (1972) The reliability of some motor performance tests of handedness. *Neuropsychologia*, **10**, 199–206.

Provins, K. A., & Glencross, D. J. (1968) Handwriting, typewriting and handedness. *Quarterly Journal of Experimental Psychology*, **20**, 282–289.

Provins, K. A., Milner, A. D., & Kerr, P. (1982) Asymmetry of manual preference and performance. *Perceptual and Motor Skills*, **54**, 179–194.

Pucetti, R. (1981) The case for mental duality: Evidence from split-brain data and other considerations. *The Brain and Behavioral Sciences*, **4**, 93–99.

Pykett, I. L. (1982) NMR imaging in medicine. *Scientific American*, **246**(5), 54–64.

Raczkowski, D., Kalat, J. W., & Nebes, R. (1974) Reliability and validity of some handedness questionnaire items. *Neuropsychologia*, **12**, 43–47.

Ramaley, F. (1913) Inheritance of left-handedness. *The American Naturalist*, **47**, 730–738.

Ramsay, D. S. (1979) Manual preference for tapping in infants. *Developmental Psychology*, **15**, 437–442.

Ramsay, D. S. (1980) Beginnings of bimanual handedness and speech in infants. *Infant Behavior and Development*, **3**, 67–77.

Raney, E. T. (1935) A Phi-test for the determination of lateral dominance involving the visual perception of movement. *Psychological Bulletin*, **32**, 740.

Rasmussen, T., & Milner, B. (1975) Clinical and surgical studies of the cerebral speech areas in man. In K. J. Zulch, O. Creutzfeldt, & G. C. Galbraith (Eds.), *Otfrid Foerster Symposium on Cerebral Localization*. Heidelberg: Springer.

Rasmussen, T., & Milner, B. (1977) The role of early left-brain injury in determining lateralization of cerebral speech functions. *Annals of the New York Academy of Sciences*, **299**, 355–369.

Ratcliff, G., Dila, C., Taylor, L., & Milner, B. (1980) The morphological asymmetry of the hemispheres and cerebral dominance for speech: A possible relationship. *Brain and Language*, **11**, 87–98.

Raven, J. C. (1958a) *Mill Hill vocabulary scale* (2nd ed.). London: H. K. Lewis.

Raven, J. C. (1958b) *Standard progressive matrices* (2nd ed.). London: H. K. Lewis.

Reed, G. F., & Smith, A. C. (1961) Laterality and directional preferences in a simple perceptual-motor task. *Quarterly Journal of Experimental Psychology*, **13**, 122–124.

Reed, G. F., & Smith, A. C. (1962) A further experimental investigation of the relative speeds of left- and right-handed writers. *Journal of Genetic Psychology*, **100**, 275–288.

Reed, J. C., & Reitan, R. M. (1969) Verbal and performance differences among brain-injured children with lateralized motor deficits. *Perceptual & Motor Skills*, **29**, 747–752.

Repp, B. H. (1977) Measuring laterality effects in dichotic listening. *Journal of the Acoustical Society of America*, **62**, 720–737.

Rhodes, D. L., & Schwartz, G. E. (1981) Lateralized sensitivity to vibrotactile stimulation: Individual differences revealed by interaction of threshold and signal detection tasks. *Neuropsychologia*, **19**, 831–835.

Richardson, J. T. E., & Firlej, M. D. E. (1979) Laterality and reading attainment. *Cortex*, **15**, 581–595.

Rife, D. C. (1940) Handedness with special reference to twins. *Genetics*, **25**, 178–186.

Rife, D. C. (1950) An application of gene frequency analysis to the interpretation of data for twins. *Human Biology*, **22**, 136–145.

Rife, D. C. (1955) Hand prints and handedness. *American Journal of Human Genetics*, **7**, 170–179.

Rife, D. C. (1978) Genes and melting pots. In R. T. Osborne, C. E. Noble, & N. Weyl (Eds.), *Human variation: The biopsychology of age, race and sex*. New York: Academic Press.

Roberts, J. A. F. (1959) *An introduction to medical genetics*. London: Oxford University Press.

Roberts, L. (1969) Aphasia, apraxia and agnosia in abnormal states of cerebral dominance. In P. J. Vinken and G. W. Bruyn (Eds.), *Handbook of clinical psychology* (Vol. 4). Amsterdam: North-Holland.

Roberts, L. D. (1974) Intelligence and handedness. *Nature*, **252**, 180.

Roszkowski, M. J., Snelbecker, G. E., & Sacks, R. (1980) Is age correlated with right-handedness? *Perceptual and Motor Skills*, **51**, 862.

Rubens, A. B. (1977) Anatomical asymmetries of human cerebral cortex. In S. Harnad, R. W. Doty, L. Goldstein, J. Jaynes, & G. Krauthamer (Eds.), *Lateralization in the nervous system*. New York: Academic Press.

Rumbaugh, D. M. (1977) *Language learning by a chimpanzee: The Lana project*. New York: Academic Press.

Russell, W. R., & Espir, M. L. E. (1961) *Traumatic aphasia*. Oxford: Oxford University Press.

Rutter, M. (1978) Prevalence and types of dyslexia. In A. L. Benton & D. Pearl (Eds.), *Dyslexia: An appraisal of current knowledge*. New York: Oxford University Press.

Rutter, M., Tizard, J., & Whitmore, K. (1970) *Education, health and behaviour*. London: Longman.

Rutter, M., & Yule, W. (1975) The concept of specific reading retardation. *Journal of Child Psychology and Psychiatry*, **16**, 181–197.

Sanders, B., Wilson, J. R., & Vandenberg, S. G. (1982) Handedness and spatial ability. *Cortex*, **18**, 79–90.

Satz, P. (1972) Pathological left-handedness: An explanatory model. *Cortex*, **8**, 121–135.

Satz, P. (1973) Left-handedness and early brain insult: An explanation. *Neuropsychologia*, **11**, 115–117.

Satz, P. (1977) Laterality tests: An inferential problem. *Cortex*, **13**, 203–212.

Satz, P., Achenbach, K., & Fennell, E. (1967) Correlations between assessed manual laterality and predicted speech laterality in a normal population. *Neuropsychologia*, **5**, 295–310.

Satz, P., & Sparrow, S. S. (1970) Specific developmental dyslexia: A theoretical formulation. In D. J. Bakker & P. Satz (Eds.), *Specific reading disability: Advances in theory and method*. Rotterdam: Rotterdam University Press.

Satz, P., Taylor, G., Friel, J., & Fletcher, J. (1978) Some developmental and predictive precursors of reading disabilities: A six year follow up. In A. L. Benton & D. Pearl (Eds.), *Dyslexia: An appraisal of current knowledge*. New York: Oxford University Press.

Schaller, G. B. (1963) *The mountain gorilla: Ecology and behavior*. Chicago: Chicago University Press.

Schouten, M. E. (1980) The case against a speech mode of perception. *Acta Psychologica*, **44**, 71–98.

Schultz, A. H. (1956) Postembryonic age changes. *Primatologia*, **1**, 887–964.

Schwartz, J., & Tallal, P. (1980) Rate of acoustic change may underlie hemispheric specialization for speech perception. *Science*, **207**, 1380–1381.

Schwartz, M. (1977) Left-handedness and high-risk pregnancy. *Neuropsychologia*, **15**, 341–344.

Scott, A. (1984) A new twist to the DNA story. *New Scientist*, 22 March, 42–44.

Scott, S., Hynd, G. W., Hunt, L. & Weed, W. (1979) Cerebral speech lateralization in the native American Navajo. *Neuropsychologia*, **17**, 89–92.

Searleman, A. (1980) Subject variables and cerebral organization for language. *Cortex*, **16**, 239–254.

Searleman, A., Tsao, W. C., & Balzer, W. (1980) A reexamination of the relationship between birth stress and handedness. *Clinical Neuropsychology*, **2**, 124–128.

Sekuler, R., Tynan, P., & Levinson, E. (1973) Visual temporal order: A new illusion. *Science*, **180**, 210–212.

Semmes, J. (1968) Hemispheric specialization: A possible clue to mechanism. *Neuropsychologia*, **6**, 11–26.

Sergent, J. (1982) The cerebral balance of power: Confrontation or cooperation. *Journal of Experimental Psychology: Human Perception and Performance*, **8**, 253–272.

Shaffer, L. H. (1984) Motor programming in language production. In H. Bouma & D. G. Bouwhuis (Eds.), *Attention and performance X: Control of language processes*. London: Lawrence Erlbaum.

Shankweiler, D., & Studdert-Kennedy, M. (1967) Identification of consonants and vowels presented to left and right ears. *Journal of Experimental Psychology*, **19**, 59–63.

Shankweiler, D., & Studdert-Kennedy, M. (1975) A continuum of lateralization for speech perception? *Brain and Language*, **2**, 212–225.

Shaw, J. C., Colter, N., & Resek, G. (1983) EEG coherence, lateral preference and schizophrenia. *Psychological Medicine*, **13**, 299–306.

Shaw, J. C., O'Connor, K., & Ongley, C. (1978) EEG coherence as a measure of cerebral functional organization. In M. A. B. Brazier & H. Petsche (Eds.), *Architectonics of the cerebral cortex*. New York: Raven Press.

Sherman, J. A. (1978) *Sex-related cognitive differences: An essay on theory and evidence*. Springfield, Illinois: Charles C. Thomas.

Silva, D. A., & Satz, P. (1979) Pathological left-handedness: Evaluation of a model. *Brain and Language*, **7**, 8–16.

Simon, J. R. (1964) Steadiness, handedness and hand preference. *Perceptual and Motor Skills*, **18**, 203–206.

Simon, J. R., De Crow, T. W., Lincoln, R. S., & Smith, K. U. (1952) Effects of handedness on tracking accuracy. *Perceptual and Motor Skills Research Exchange*, **4**, 53–57.

Simon, J. R., Hinrichs, J. V., & Craft, J. L. (1970) Auditory S–R compatibility: Reaction time as a function of ear-hand correspondence and ear–response–location correspondence. *Journal of Experimental Psychology*, **86**, 97–102.

Slater, E. (with the assistance of J. Shields). (1953) *Psychotic and neurotic illness in twins*. Medical Research Council Special Report Series. No. 278. London: Her Majesty's Stationery Office.

Smart, J. L., Jeffery, C., & Richards, B. (1980) A retrospective study of the relationship between birth history and handedness at six years. *Early Human Development*, **4**, 79–88.

Smith, A. (1966) Intellectual functions in patients with lateralized frontal tumor. *Journal of Neurology, Neurosurgery and Psychiatry*, **29**, 52–59.

Smith, A. C., & Reed, G. F. (1959) An experimental investigation of the relative speeds of left and right handed writers. *Journal of Genetic Psychology*, **94**, 67–76.

Smith, L. C., & Moscovitch, M. (1979) Writing posture, hemispheric control of movement and cerebral dominance in individuals with inverted and noninverted hand postures during writing. *Neuropsychologia*, **17**, 637–644.

Smith, S. D., Kimberling, W. J., Pennington, B. F., & Lubs, H. A. (1983) Specific reading disability: Identification of an inherited form through linkage analysis. *Science*, **219**, 1345–1357.

Sperry, R. W. (1974) Lateral specialization in the surgically separated hemispheres. In F. O.

Schmidt and F. G. Worden (Eds.), *The neurosciences: Third study program.* Cambridge, Mass.: MIT Press.

Spiegler, B. J., & Yeni-Komshian, G. H. (1983) Incidences of left handed writing in a college population with reference to family patterns of hand preference. *Neuropsychologia,* 21, 651–659.

Spreen, O., Miller, C. G., & Benton, A. L. (1966) The phi-test and measures of laterality in children and adults. *Cortex,* 2, 308–321.

Springer, S., & Searleman, A. (1978) Laterality in twins: The relationship between handedness and hemispheric asymmetry for speech. *Behavior Genetics,* 8, 349–357.

Stephens, W. E., Cunningham, W. E., & Stigler, B. J. (1967) Reading readiness and eye hand preference patterns in first grade children. *Exceptional Children,* 33, 481–488.

Studdert-Kennedy, M., & Shankweiler, D. (1970) Hemispheric specialization for speech perception. *Journal of the Acoustical Society of America,* 48, 579–594.

Subirana, A. (1958) The prognosis in aphasia in relation to cerebral dominance and handedness. *Brain,* 81, 415–425.

Subirana, A. (1969) Handedness and cerebral dominance. In P. J. Vinken, & G. W. Bruyn (Eds.), *Handbook of clinical neurology,* Vol. 4. Amsterdam: North Holland.

Super, C. M. (1981) Cross-cultural research on infancy. In H. C. Triandis & A. Heron (Eds.), *Handbook of cross-cultural psychology: Developmental psychology:* Vol. 4. Boston: Allyn & Bacon.

Sutton, P. R. N. (1963) Handedness and facial asymmetry: Lateral position of the nose in two racial groups. *Nature, London,* 198, 909.

Tan, L. E., & Nettleton, N. C. (1980) Left handedness, birth order, and birth stress. *Cortex,* 16, 363–373.

Tanner, J. M. (1978) *Foetus into man.* London: Open Books.

Taylor, D. C. (1969) Differential rates of cerebral maturation between sexes and between hemispheres. *Lancet,* 19 July, 140–142.

Taylor, D. C. (1975) Factors influencing the occurrence of schizophrenic-like psychosis in patients with temporal lobe epilepsy. *Psychological Medicine,* 5, 249–254.

Taylor, P. J., Brown, R., & Gunn, J. (1983) Violence, psychosis and handedness. In P. Flor-Henry & J. Gruzelier (Eds.), *Laterality and psychopathology.* Amsterdam: Elsevier Science Publishers B.V.

Taylor, P. J., Dalton, R., & Fleminger, J. J. (1980) Handedness in schizophrenia. *British Journal of Psychiatry,* 136, 375–383.

Taylor, P. J., Dalton, R., Fleminger, J. J., & Lishman, W. A. (1982) Differences between two studies of hand preference in psychiatric patients. *British Journal of Psychiatry,* 140, 166–173.

Teng, E. L. (1980) Dichotic pairing of digits with tones: High performance level and lack of ear effect. *Quarterly Journal of Experimental Psychology,* 32, 287–293.

Teng, E. L. (1981) Dichotic ear difference is a poor index for the functional asymmetry between the cerebral hemispheres. *Neuropsychologia,* 19, 235–240.

Teng, E. L., Lee, P-H, Yang, K-S, Chang, P. C. (1976) Handedness in a Chinese population: Biological, social and pathological factors. *Science,* 193, 1148–1150.

Terrace, H. S., Petitto, L. A., Sanders, R. J., & Bever, T. G. (1979) Can an ape create a sentence? *Science,* 206, 891–902.

Teuber, H. L. (1974) Why two brains? In F. O. Schmitt, & F. G. Worden, (Eds.), *The neurosciences: Third study program.* Cambridge, Mass.: MIT Press.

Thomas, D. G., Campos, J. J. (1978) The relationship of handedness to a "lateralized" task. *Neuropsychologia,* 16, 511–515.

Thompson, M. E. (1976) A comparison of laterality effects in dyslexics and controls using verbal dichotic listening tasks. *Neuropsychologia,* 14, 243–246.

Tinbergen, N. (1951) *The study of instinct.* Oxford: Oxford University Press.

Torgerson, J. (1950) Situs inversus, asymmetry and twinning. *American Journal of Human Genetics,* **2,** 361–370.

Trankell, A. (1955) Aspects of genetics in psychology. *American Journal of Human Genetics,* **7,** 264–276.

Travis, L. E. (1959) *Handbook of speech pathology.* London: Peter Owen.

Trevarthen, C. (1970) Experimental evidence of a brain-stem contribution to visual perception in man. *Brain, Behavior and Evolution,* **3,** 338–352.

Trevarthen, C. (1974) Cerebral embryology and the split brain. In M. Kinsbourne, & W. L. Smith (Eds.), *Hemisphere disconnection and cerebral function.* Springfield, Ill.: Charles C. Thomas.

Trevarthen, C. (1978) Manipulative strategies of baboons and the origins of cerebral asymmetry. In M. Kinsbourne (Ed.), *Hemispheric asymmetry of function.* London: Tavistock.

Turkewitz, G. (1977) The development of lateral differences in the human infant. In S. Harnad, R. W. Doty, L. Goldstein, J. Jaynes, & G. Krauthamer (Eds.), *Lateralization in the nervous system.* New York: Academic Press.

Uhrbrock, R. S. (1969) Bovine laterality. *Journal of Genetic Psychology,* **115,** 77–79.

Van Riper, C. (1935) The quantitative measurement of laterality. *Journal of Experimental Psychology,* **18,** 372–382.

Vernberg, F. J., & Costlow, J. D. (1966) Handedness in fiddler crabs (Genus *UCA*). *Crustaceama,* **11,** 61–64.

Vernon, M. D. (1957) *Backwardness in reading.* Cambridge: Cambridge University Press.

Volvo Grand Prix Media Guide. (1983) Lynn, Mass.: Zimman.

Von Bonin, G. (1962) Anatomical asymmetries of the cerebral hemispheres. In V. B. Mountcastle (Ed.), *Interhemispheric relations and cerebral dominance.* Baltimore: Johns Hopkins University Press.

Waber, D. P. (1976) Sex differences in cognition: A function of maturation rates. *Science,* **192,** 572–574.

Wada, J. A., Clarke, R., & Hamm, A. (1975) Cerebral hemispheric asymmetry in humans. *Archives of Neurology,* **32,** 239–246.

Waddington, C. H. (1957) *The strategy of the genes.* London: George Allen & Unwin.

Walker, S. F. (1980) Lateralization of functions in the vertebrate brain. *British Journal of Psychology,* **71,** 329–367.

Walls, G. L. (1951) A theory of ocular dominance. *A.M.A. Archives of Ophthalmology,* **45,** 387–412.

Warren, J. M. (1953) Handedness in the rhesus monkey. *Science,* **118,** 622–623.

Warren, J. M. (1977) Handedness and cerebral dominance in monkeys. In S. Harnad, R. W. Doty, L. Goldstein, J. Jaynes, & G. Krauthamer (Eds.), *Lateralization of the nervous system.* New York: Academic Press.

Warren, J. M., Ablanalp, J. M., & Warren, H. B. (1967) The development of handedness in cats and rhesus monkeys. In H. W. Stevenson, E. H. Hess, & H. L. Rheingold (Eds.), *Early behavior: Comparative and developmental approaches.* New York: Wiley.

Warren, J. M., Cornwell, P. R., Webster, W. G., & Pubols, B. H. (1972) Unilateral cortical lesions and paw preferences in cats. *Journal of Comparative and Physiological Psychology,* **81,** 410–422.

Warrington, E. K. (1982) Neuropsychological studies of object recognition. *Philosophical Transactions of the Royal Society of London,* **B298,** 15–33.

Warrington, E. K., & Pratt, R. T. C. (1973) Language laterality in left handers assessed by unilateral ECT. *Neuropsychologia,* **11,** 423–428.

Wason, P. C. (1960) On the failure to eliminate hypotheses in a conceptual task. *Quarterly Journal of Experimental Psychology,* **12,** 129–140.

454   REFERENCES

Way, E. E. (1958) Relationship of lateral dominance to scores of motor ability and selected skill tests. *Research Quarterly*, **29**, 360–369.

Webster, W. G. (1977) Hemispheric asymmetry in cats. In S. Harnad, R. W. Doty, L. Goldstein, J. Jaynes, & G. Krauthamer (Eds.), *Lateralization in the nervous system*. New York: Academic Press.

Wechsler, D. (1941) *The measurement of adult intelligence*. Baltimore, Md.: Williams and Wilkins.

Wechsler, D. (1949) *Wechsler intelligence scale for children*. New York: The Psychological Corporation.

Wehmaker, A. (1969) Right–left asymmetry and situs inversus in *Triturus alpestris*. *Wilhelm Roux Archives*, **163**, 1–32.

Weinstein, S., & Sersen, E. A. (1961) Tactual sensitivity as a function of handedness and laterality. *Journal of Comparative and Physiological Psychology*, **54**, 665–669.

Weiskrantz, L. (1980) Varieties of residual experience. *Quarterly Journal of Experimental Psychology*, **32**, 365–386.

Wexler, B. E., & Halwes, T. (1983) Increasing the power of dichotic methods: The fused rhymed words test. *Neuropsychologia*, **21**, 59–66.

White, K., & Ashton, R. (1976) Handedness assessment inventory. *Neuropsychologia*, **14**, 261–264.

Wienrich, A. M., Wells, P. A., & McManus, C. (1982) Handedness, anxiety and sex differences. *British Journal of Psychology*, **73**, 69–72.

Wile, I. S. (1934) *Handedness: Right and left*. Boston: Lothrop, Lee and Sheppard.

Williams, M. (1972) *Laterality of suckling by foals*. Paper presented at a conference of the Europäischen Vereinung für Tierzucht, Freiburg.

Williams, W. T., & Lambert, J. M. (1959) Multivariate methods in plant ecology I. Association analysis in plant communities. *Journal of Ecology*, **47**, 83–101.

Williams, W. T., & Lambert, J. M. (1960) Multivariate methods of plant ecology II. The use of an electronic digital computer for association analysis. *Journal of Ecology*, **48**, 689–710.

Williams, W. T., & Lambert J. M. (1961) Multivariate methods in plant ecology III. Inverse association analysis. *Journal of Ecology*, **49**, 717–729.

Wilson, D. (1891) *Left handedness*. London: MacMillan.

Wilson, J. R., De Fries, J. C., McClearn, G. E., Vandenberg, S. G., Johnson, R. C., & Rashad, M. D. (1975) Cognitive abilities: Use of family data as a control to assess sex and age differences in two ethnic groups. *International Journal of Aging and Human Development*, **6**, 261–276.

Witelson, S. F. (1976) Sex and the single hemisphere: Specialization of the right hemisphere for spatial processing. *Science*, **193**, 425–427.

Witelson, S. F. 1980 Neuroanatomical asymmetry in left-handers. A review and implications for functional asymmetry. In J. Herron (Ed.) *Neuropsychology of left-handedness*. New York: Academic Press.

Witelson, S. F. (1983) Bumps on the brain: Right–left anatomic asymmetry as a key to functional lateralization. In S. J. Segalowitz (Ed.), *Language functions and brain organization*. New York: Academic Press.

Witelson, S. F., & Pallie, W. (1973) Left hemisphere specialization for language in the newborn: Neuroanatomical evidence of asymmetry. *Brain*, **96**, 641–646.

Witelson, S. F., & Rabinovitch, M. S. (1972) Hemispheric speech lateralization in children with auditory–linguistic deficits. *Cortex*, **8**, 412–426.

Witkin, H. A., Goodenough, D. R., & Oltman, P. K. (1979) Psychological differentiation: Current status. *Journal of Personality and Social Psychology*, **37**, 1127–1145.

Witty, P. A., & Kopel, D. (1936) Sinistral and mixed manual-ocular behavior in reading disability. *Journal of Educational Psychology*, **27**, 119–134.

Woo, T. L., & Pearson, K. (1927) Dextrality and sinistrality of hand and eye. *Biometrika*, **19**, 165–199.

Wood, F., Stump, D., McKeehan, A., Sheldon, S., & Proctor, J. (1980) Patterns of regional cerebral blood flow during attempted reading aloud by stutterers both on and off haloperidol medication: Evidence for inadequate left frontal activation during stuttering. *Brain and Language*, **9**, 141–144.

Woodworth, R. S. (1899) The accuracy of voluntary movement. *Psychological Review, Monograph Supplement No. 2*, **3**.

Yakovlev, P. I., & Lecours, A. R. (1967) The myelogenetic cycles of regional maturation of the brain. In A. Minkowski (Ed.), *Regional development of the brain in early life*. Oxford: Blackwell.

Yakovlev, P. I., & Rakic, P. (1966) Patterns of decussation of bulbar pyramids and distribution of pyramidal tracts on the two sides of the spinal cord. *Transactions of the American Neurological Association*, **91**, 366–367.

Yeni-Komshian, G. H., & Benson, D. A. (1976) Anatomical study of cerebral asymmetry in the temporal lobe of humans, chimpanzees and rhesus monkeys. *Science*, **192**, 387–389.

Yeni-Komshian, G. H., Isenberg, D., & Goldberg, H. (1975) Cerebral dominance and reading disability: Left visual field deficit in poor readers. *Neuropsychologia*, **13**, 83–94.

Yin, R. K. (1970) Face recognition by brain injured patients: A dissociable ability? *Neuropsychology*, **8**, 395–402.

Young, G. (1977) Manual specialization in infancy: Implications for lateralization of brain functions. In S. J. Segalowitz & F. A. Gruber (Eds.), *Language development and neurological theory*. New York: Academic Press.

Zaidel, D., & Sperry, R. W. (1977) Some long-term motor effects of cerebral commissurotomy in man. *Neuropsychologia*, **15**, 193–204.

Zaidel, E. (1976) Auditory vocabulary of the right hemisphere following brain bisection or hemidecortication. *Cortex*, **12**, 191–211.

Zaidel, E. (1977) Unilateral auditory language comprehension on the Token Test following cerebral commissurotomy and hemispherectomy. *Neuropsychologia*, **15**, 1–18.

Zaidel, E. (1978) Auditory language comprehension in the right hemisphere following cerebral commissurotomy and hemispherectomy: A comparison with child language and aphasia. In A. Caramazzo, & E. B. Zurif (Eds.), *Language acquisition and language breakdown*. Baltimore, Md.: Johns Hopkins University Press.

Zangwill, O. L. (1960) *Cerebral dominance and its relation to psychological function*. Edinburgh: Oliver and Boyd.

Zangwill, O. L. (1967) Speech and the minor hemisphere. *Acta Neurologica et Psychiatrica Belgica*, **67**, 1013–1020.

Zangwill, O. L. (1979) Two cases of crossed aphasia in dextrlas. *Neuropsychologia*, **17**, 167–172.

Zazzo, R. (1960) *Les Jumeaux: Le couple et la personne*. Paris: Presses Universitaire de France.

Zeman, S. S. (1967) A summary of research concerning laterality and reading. *Journal of the Reading Specialist*, **6**, 116–123.

Zihl, J. (1980) "Blindsight": Improvement of visually guided eye movements by systematic practice in patients with cerebral blindness. *Neuropsychologia*, **18**, 71–77.

Zurif, E. B., & Bryden, M. P. (1969) Familial handedness and left–right differences in auditory and visual perception. *Neuropsychologia*, **7**, 179–187.

Zurif, E. B., & Carson, G. (1970) Dyslexia in relation to cerebral dominance and temporal analysis. *Neuropsychologia*, **8**, 351–361.

Author Index

Subject Index

ACKNOWLEDGEMENTS

The author and publisher are grateful to the following for their permission to reproduce copyright material:

Table 3.2.   T. Rasmussen, B. Milner, and Springer-Verlag
Table 6.1.   D. Kimura and The Canadian Psychological Association, © 1961
Table 6.3.   T. Rasmussen, B. Milner, and The New York Academy of Sciences
Figure 2.1.   B. Kolb, I. Q. Whishaw and W. H. Freeman and Co.: *Fundamentals of Human Neuropsychology*. © 1980

Figure 2.5.   K. R. Popper, J. Eccles and Springer-Verlag
Figure 2.6.   G. A. Ojemann and Cambridge University Press
Figure 3.4.   M. LeMay and The New York Academy of Sciences
Figure 6.1.   R. W. Sperry and the MIT Press: *The Neurosciences: Third Study Program*, © 1974

Figure 6.2.   J. Levy, C. Trevarthen, R. W. Sperry and Oxford University Press
Figure 8.2.   J. Inglis, J. McGlone and La Tipografica Varese
Figure 9.1.   D. Policansky and Cambridge University Press
Figure 9.3.   G. Finch and the American Association for the Advancement of Science; *Science*, © 1941

Figure 9.5.   R. L. Collins and The American Genetic Association
Figure 9.7.   R. E. Passingham and W. H. Freeman and Co. (© Academic Press Inc., 1979)

Figure 11.9. M. Peters, B. Durding and The Canadian Psychological Association, © 1978
Figure 13.2. P. J. Carter

474